JAMAICA
HANDBOOK
SECOND EDITION

JAMAICA
HANDBOOK
SECOND EDITION

KARL LUNTTA

MOON
PUBLICATIONS INC.

JAMAICA HANDBOOK
SECOND EDITION

Published by
Moon Publications, Inc.
P.O. Box 3040
Chico, California 95927-3040, USA

Printed by
Colorcraft Ltd.

Please send all comments,
corrections, additions,
amendments, and critiques to:

**JAMAICA HANDBOOK
c/o MOON PUBLICATIONS, INC.
P.O. BOX 3040
CHICO, CA 95927-3040, USA**

Library of Congress Cataloging in Publication Data
Luntta, Karl, 1955—
    Jamaica Handbook / Karl Luntta. — 2nd ed.
    p. cm.
    Includes bibliographical references and index.
    ISBN 1-56691-012-9:
    1. Jamaica—Guidebooks.   I. Title.
F1869.L86 1993   93-29905
917.29204'6—dc20   CIP

Printing History
    1st edition—November 1991
    Reprinted — July 1992
    2nd edition—December 1993

Editor: Gina Wilson Birtcil
Copy Editors: Elizabeth Kim, Mark Arends
Production & Design: Aaron Yamaguchi
Cartographers: Bob Race, Brian Bardwell
Index: Mark Arends

Front cover photo courtesy of the Jamaica Tourist Board
All photos by Phyllis Luntta unless otherwise noted.

Printed in Hong Kong

Distributed in the United States by Publishers Group West

For Phyllis
just when you think life
couldn't get much better
And for Kaarlo
it does

ຈ

CONTENTS

CHARTS

MAPS

MAP SYMBOLS

NUMBERED HIGHWAY

MOUNTAIN

WATERFALL

WATER

AIRPORT

TOWNS / VILLAGES

CITIES

ACCOMMODATION

POINT OF INTEREST

COUNTY BORDER

PARISH BORDER

PAVED ROADS

UNPAVED ROADS

MAIN ROAD

BRIDGE

RAILROAD

FOOT PATHS

ALL MAPS ARE ORIENTED WITH NORTH AT TOP UNLESS NOTED

ABBREVIATIONS

a/c—air-conditioned
d—double occupancy
GCT—General Consumption Tax
JATCHA—Jamaica Alternative Tourism,
       Camping, and Hiking Associa-
       tion
JAVA—Jamaica Association of Villas and
       Apartments
J$—Jamaican dollars
JLP—Jamaica Labor Party
JRC—Jamaican Railway Corporation
JTB—Jamaica Tourist Board

mph—miles per hour
OW—one way
PADI—Professional Association of Diving
       Instructors
p/d—per day
PNP—People's National Party
pp—per person
RT—roundtrip
s—single occupancy
t—triple occupancy
US$—U.S. dollars

ACKNOWLEDGEMENTS

A great many people put substantial effort into creating this book. In Jamaica it's my pleasure to thank Jackie Goldson and Heather Martin of the Jamaica Tourist Board, Kingston; and directors and employees of the tourist board throughout the island, including Norma Taylor in Montego Bay, Volney Williams and Marcia Brown in Negril, and Winston Cannicle in Port Antonio. Many thanks to Madge Allen in Mandeville for taking some time, and special thanks to our good and gracious friend Judith Clarke in Ocho Rios. In addition, I'd like to thank Dudley Miller and Joshua Seabourne for numerous insider's tours of Kingston that I'm sure would have been only half as successful without them. Andrea Bernard pointed the way in Montego Bay. The staff of the Institute of Jamaica, including June Vernon of the National Library, and others at the University of the West Indies, were very helpful and gave of their time and effort freely. Jamaicans throughout the country, in all capacities, were most helpful with their time and insights. They include Mike Henry, Johnny Guthrie, Andy Williams, Marcia Smith, Sista P, Brother John, Sister Pat Cassier, Madge Grant, Sister Love, Busta Prendergast, Stafford Haughton, Roy and Barbara Grant, Janet Walker, Helga Stockert, Donna Hayes, Leila Rutty, Hope Campbell, Howard McGowan of the *Daily Gleaner,* and Carmen McKnight—all were congenial and I thank them. Also, thanks to Renee Anne Shirley and Robert Hall for teatime, and to Suzanne Levy and the Levy family for their hospitality. Special gratitude to Joey Issa for his undertakings on my behalf.

Readers who used previous editions of this book and who offered valuable insights are Dave Woodman, Mr. and Mrs. Donald B. Howard, Darryl and Chris Minsky, Mary Butler, and Paul Hepler—many thanks, keep in touch. Many helpful comments were also offered by Anthony Winkler, Parchi Parchment, and Jackie Waite. Many thanks to the Agfa Film Corporation for their graciousness.

Others contributed in ways that are hard to describe. Top among them is my father, Hans K. Luntta, whose inspired travel in his youth served to spark my own; and my mother, Anna Bordonaro Luntta, whose lasagna was always good to come home to. Thanks also to Dominic and Anne Radocchia, Mark Luntta, Naida Arcenas, Steve and Heidi Dwyer, Howard Hyatt, Larry Sombke, Cathy Herman, and Nikki Mannathoko. Hans Jr., keep those cards and letters coming in. Special thanks to Steve Radocchia for being our own personal Photomat, to Jack and Chris Radocchia for rum research, and to Julie and Nicky for special insights.

INTRODUCTION

For my part, I travel not to go anywhere, but to go. I travel for travel's sake. The great affair is to move.

—Robert Louis Stevenson,
Travels With A Donkey

My wife went down to the islands last week.
Jamaica?
No, she wanted to go.

—old joke,
portending the death of vaudeville

I stepped onto a wharf. People gathered around. I was recognized at once. "It's Errol Flynn!"
They were black. They spoke beautiful English. Who were they?
"What is this place?" I asked.
"Jamaica. This is Kingston."
"Jamaica?" So that was it.

—Errol Flynn,
My Wicked, Wicked Ways

Jamaica is the rooster of the Caribbean—a loud and swaggering country, nattily plumed, and relentlessly seductive. From the aboriginal Arawaks to Christopher Columbus to the loud and swaggering Errol Flynn—all of whom were seduced by its dark beauty—the island has been home or bounty or both. The Arawaks suffered and died for it. The Spanish had it, fought for it, and lost it. The British had it, fought for it, and prospered from it. Generations of displaced Africans who hadn't wanted it, at least in the way it came to them, have it now.

Others had it, in their own way. Individuals such as Ian Fleming, who wrote some of his most exotic James Bond tales in Jamaica, lived at Goldeneye, his north coast home. Noel Coward, who spent the last decade of his life at his hilltop mansion overlooking Port Maria, had there his own personal "room with a view."

In many ways, Jamaica is a place that has become the stuff of travel posters. Who among us hasn't had daydreams of rum-driven evenings limboing under a viscous night sky, of loafing on severely pretty sand beaches, of dancing with long, elegant people. Yet Jamaica is really much more than that. It is a living theater of harsh history and stubborn human enterprise. It just happens to be accompanied by a nonpareil musical score, set against one of the most alluring backdrops in the Caribbean.

Jamaica is the place you were always going to get to, but something held you back. Didn't they have *problems* a while ago? Wasn't there *political trouble?* They did and there was. The growing pains of a country that achieved its independence relatively recently (in 1962) made headlines in the '70s. Internal conflicts turned into political turbulence and showed the world that trouble in paradise can be a bad sort of trouble indeed. Some Jamaicans fought and died as opposing parties claimed turf and serfs. Politics went haywire. It drove investors and tourists away, and drove Jamaica deeper into a quagmire of debt, economic shadow, and uneasy relationships with its neighbors. It seemed, then, that Jamaica had begun to flail about in a weird kinesis, like a lopsided ball bearing in a pinball machine.

It would be too easy to say that all that has changed. The truth is, some has and some has not. Political discourse is still energetic, but violence is no longer the resort, so to speak, of choice. Tourism virtually exploded back on the scene in the mid-'80s and hasn't abated since, thanks to the abundance of resources, Jamaica's natural beauty, and to no small effort by the government and private tourism sector. Tourism now earns more foreign exchange than any other industry in the country. Services have improved and literacy is high, yet the large numbers of poor and disenfranchised have not seen the full benefits of monies trickled down from tourism. Jamaica's economy will not, in our lifetime, battle the bulge. Paradise remains paradise, but without the guileless narcissism of, well, paradise.

And still, life goes on. Buses career around corners while horns blare and children scatter;

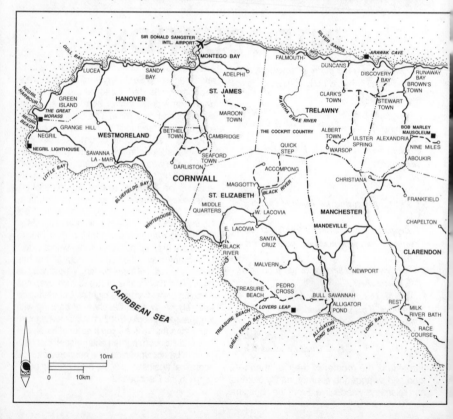

mobile DJs blast bone-thumping, reggae dancehall music through tall-as-a-man speakers and crowds of sweating libertines. Saturdays promise stimulating anarchy at the markets. See for yourself.

THE LAND

Q: Which is farthest west—Barbados, Haiti or Jamaica?
A: Jamaica

—from TRIVIAL PURSUIT®
(owned by and used with permission of
©Horn Abbot Ltd.)

Defining The Caribbean

The islands of the Caribbean form a sweeping arc from Aruba, Bonaire, and Curaçao, commonly know as the ABC Islands, to the east through the Venezuelan islands and Trinidad and Tobago, then north and west on to Cuba, the northwestern tip of which lies between Key West and Mexico's Yucatán Peninsula. The body of water encompassed by these islands is the Caribbean Sea, an area of more than one million square miles. (It is a small point, but some people say Ca-RIB-be-an and some say Ca-rib-BE-an. Both are correct and Jamaicans tend toward Ca-rib-BE-an.)

The West Indies is the name given to the Caribbean islands and their immediate neighbors to the north—the Bahamas and Turks and Caicos Islands. The Antilles archipelago refers

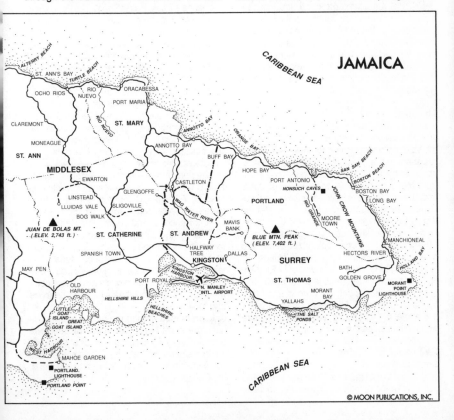

© MOON PUBLICATIONS, INC.

to the West Indies but not the Bahamas. The Greater Antilles consists of (in order of descending size) Cuba, Hispaniola (Haiti and the Dominican Republic), Jamaica, and Puerto Rico, plus their smaller adjacent islands. The three Cayman Islands also lie in the waters of the Greater Antilles. The Lesser Antilles consists of the Leeward Islands group (British Virgin Islands, U.S. Virgin Islands, Anguilla, St. Martin/Sint Maarten, Saba, Sint Eustatius, St. Barthélemy, St. Kitts and Nevis, Antigua and Barbuda, Montserrat, Guadeloupe, and adjacent islands); the Windward Islands (Dominica, Martinique, St. Lucia, St. Vincent and the Grenadines, Grenada, and adjacent islands); and the remaining Caribbean islands of Aruba, Curaçao, Bonaire, Barbados, Trinidad and Tobago (sometimes called TNT), and the Venezuelan islands.

Political affiliations often overlap the geographical grouping of Caribbean islands. For instance, the Netherlands Antilles consists of Bonaire, Curaçao, Saba, Sint Eustatius, Sint Maarten, and Aruba. Many more islands in the Caribbean have political affiliations with the U.S., U.K., France, and South and Central America.

The Facts

Jamaica is 146 miles long and 22-55 miles wide, with an area of 4,411 square miles. It is roughly the size of Connecticut or, for those who prefer it, Lebanon. It is, practically speaking, a one-island country, just 700 miles and under two hours from Miami by plane, 90 miles south of Cuba, and 100 miles west of Haiti. Jamaica is the third-largest island in the Greater Antilles and the largest English-speaking island in the Caribbean. Its nearest English-speaking neighbor in South America is Cartagena, Colombia, some 445 miles south. Its capital, Kingston, at latitude 18° N and longitude 78° W, is the largest English-speaking city in the Americas south of Miami.

Politically, the country is divided into three counties—Cornwall, Middlesex, and Surrey—and a total of 14 parishes, each with an administrative capital (see map on p. 27).

Mountains And Plains

Jamaica is shimmering green and tall, an island thrust out of the sea 30 million years ago during a series of violent, underwater volcanic eruptions. The process, which took place over hundreds of thousands of years or more, has created an island of diverse topography and beauty, half of which is 1,000 feet above sea level. Hills, crags, and deep, lush valleys cut by mountain streams spill onto grassy plains and sand beaches. This diversity is accessible via a series of fairly good roads, hiking trails, and a rather assertive public transport system.

The country is dominated by a spine of mountainous hills that rise from the west and central parts of the country. They culminate in the spectacular Blue Mountain Range in eastern Portland and St. Thomas, home to cocoa (cacao) and coffee growers, hikers, and anxiety-ridden drivers. Here stands Blue Mountain Peak, at 7,402 feet above sea level the highest in the country. Southwest of the cool, misty Blue Mountains lies the Port Royal Range, nestled around St. Catherine's Peak, at 5,069 feet. The John Crow Mountains, in eastern Portland, roll down into the sea from over 3,700 feet. Other, lesser ranges such as Juan de Bolas, Mt. Diablo, and Bull Head Mountains shadow the coastal plains and flatlands of St. Catherine and Clarendon. The mountains are populated, though not densely, with small settlements of farmers growing subsistence crops, coffee, and the inevitable and profitable marijuana, or ganja. Life in the mountains isn't easy; lack of phones and transportation all but isolates the hill people from the rest of the country. Many, including the older, sequestered Rastafarian groups, like it that way.

The north coast—from Port Antonio to Montego Bay—and the coastal areas of Westmoreland, St. Elizabeth, Clarendon, and St. Catherine are characterized by rolling plains. They are ideal for coconut and sugarcane plantations, and for raising cattle. The land is fertile and forms the backbone of the agricultural output of the country. Citrus, tobacco, bananas, plantains, and cassava are among other crops grown in these areas. These regions also account for much of the country's beautiful sand beaches and tourist resorts.

Interspersed among the plains and mountains are elevated, rugged areas of limestone and rock, covering almost two-thirds of the country. In the parish of Trelawny, eroding limestone has formed one of Jamaica's most unique areas, the Cockpit Country.

Rain collects in the surface crevices of lime-stone and gradually dissolves the rock as it seeps. When the water can no longer flow down-ward, it flows sideways, dissolving limestone as it forms channels between rocks. The water even-tually joins other streams to form huge hollows, or cockpits, among the giant, stalagmitelike lime-stone zeniths. Large streams run underground, where they form the many caves you'll find in Jamaica. (The gaping Windsor Caves of Tre-lawny have been penetrated for a distance of over three miles.) The result is a rugged, mazelike terrain of fissures and large limestone bumps that looks much like the enlarged bottom of a crepe-soled shoe. The Cockpit Country itself, once the hideout of the tenacious Maroons (see p. 26), is largely uninhabited today and remains the sanctuary of a melange of indigenous flora and fauna.

Rivers And Coast

Most of Jamaica's 120 rivers flow from the moun-tains. Some move slowly but most are swift and even dangerous in heavy rains. In a heavy rain, water can collect on and flow down small moun-tain roads to join with larger roads, not unlike tributaries into a river, creating pressurized and dangerous torrents. The gushing mess often empties into main arteries at the base of the mountain, or simply goes over the side to cre-ate havoc with traffic and the road.

The rivers of Jamaica are generally not navi-gable, due to their origins in the hills, resulting in treacherous but often beautiful and dramatic plunges over cliffs. The **Black River,** Jamaica's longest at 44 miles, begins in northern Man-chester and flows west into the Cockpit Coun-try. Here it disappears and reappears a number of times, under names like **One Eye River** and **Noisy River,** until it finally becomes the Black River at Mexico, St. Elizabeth. It's navigable from the town of Black River for a distance of 12-17 miles, depending on conditions. An excellent river tour by South Coast Safaris, Ltd., takes you five miles upstream from the coastal town of Black River (see "The Southwest Coast," p. 128).

Other rivers along the coast—the **Rio Grande, Martha Brae,** and **White River** to name a few—are more quiescent and popular for bamboo raft-ing and sightseeing. River tours, complete with rafting guides, are available all along the north coast, as are guided hikes along river gorges.

Rivers such as the **Wag Water, Hope,** and **Milk River** supply towns and farming areas with water for consumption and irrigation.

In Jamaica, the issue of whether the interior mountains are more physically compelling than the coast becomes unimportant—most points on the island can be reached within a day (two days at a leisurely pace). It is easy enough to see it all.

Long the attraction for tourists and Jamaicans on vacation, the country's coast along the north shore from Manchioneal to Montego Bay has dozens of small inlets, natural harbors, offshore is-lands, and white-sand beaches, as well as a reef that is, in places, close enough to snorkel from shore. In particular, the towns of Port Antonio, Ocho Rios, and Montego Bay have become tourist meccas, complete with the questionable high-rise hotels, quaint guesthouses, elaborate restaurants, and tasty roadside food of the fast variety.

The seven-mile beach and the stunning cliffs of Negril are drawing more visitors yearly, turn-ing the once-budget dropout haven into an up-scale dropout haven. The sedate southwest coastal region from Savanna-la-mar to Trea-sure Beach, on to Kingston and beyond, is at-tractive for its wide panoramas, quiet waters, and lack of tourist buzz. Small, proper towns, fishing villages, and beaches dot the coast-line, hugging harbors and inlets.

Along the southern coast, groups of uninhab-ited cays (sometimes pronounced "keys") lie off-shore at Portland Point in Clarendon, Port Royal in Kingston, and Morant Point in St. Thomas. The **Pedro Cays,** four in number and 40-50 miles south of Portland Point, are an important fishing area. They were once the home of the now-en-dangered, tropical Pedro seal. The cays south of Port Royal, including **Rackham's Cay, Maid-en's Cay,** and **Drunken Man's Cay,** are mainly used for fishing and recreation. The four, small **Morant Cays,** 33 miles offshore, used to be an annual June resting place for thousands of seabirds. Their valuable deposits of guano, used for fertilizer, were exploited in the 19th century, and the birds were hunted for food. Today the islands are used as fishing bases. Other parts of the coast have smaller cays visible from shore.

Along the south coast at Milk River, Kingston, and Bath are some of the country's reputedly therapeutic mineral spas (see desti-nation sections).

The south coast's Kingston, the seventh-largest and one of the more efficient natural harbors in the world, has a number of good beaches in the area, plus views and easy access to the towering Blue Mountains.

CLIMATE

Your first physical contact with a country is the air you breathe as you step off the plane. In Jamaica, the air is thick; warm and thick along the coast and plains, cooler and thick in the mountains. It has taste. It seems like it's about to *do* something.

The country's climate is near perfect for living and playing. Jamaica lies just south of the Tropic of Capricorn, putting it in "the tropics," but its distance north from the equator has a relative cooling effect that gives the country a semi-tropical climate with high humidity. The moderating sea breezes and mountainous terrain regulate the country's climate; Jamaica generally experiences no extremes. Temperatures vary mainly with elevation rather than season.

The average year-round temperature is 80° F (27° C), yet 90° F (32° C) days are not uncommon in the lowlands. Temperatures generally decrease by about one Fahrenheit degree for every 300 feet of ascent, so the annual average temperature in the mountains is considerably cooler. Blue Mountain Peak averages a downright chilly 56° F (13° C) and can go as low as 40° F (13° C), while the town of Mandeville, at 2,061 feet, cools off at an average 78° F (26° C). **Beware:** Nights in the mountains are always cool. Bring a sweater.

Jamaica's thick air is due to the country's year-round high humidity, which varies with seasonal rainfall and location on the island. The rainy season, that is to say when it rains more than during the dry season, occurs May-June and Sept.-October. The average rainfall along the coast is 30 inches, and in the mountains up to 200 inches.

The north and northeast regions of the island receive the most rain, brought by prevailing moisture-bearing trade winds from the northeast. As the winds roll over the island, they encounter the central and eastern mountain ranges where they are forced to rise. This creates condensation, resulting in heavy rain on the windward, or northeastern side of the mountains. Portland is Jamaica's wettest parish, with Port Antonio receiving an average of 17 inches of rain every November. The wettest town in Jamaica is Millbank, Portland, with an annual average of over 240 inches. The entire northeast coast is noticeably lush and tropical, with overgrown, ripe rainforests often spilling over and

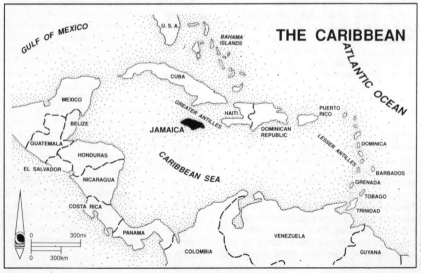

THE CARIBBEAN

GULF OF MEXICO

U.S.A.

BAHAMA ISLANDS

ATLANTIC OCEAN

MEXICO

CUBA

BELIZE

GREATER ANTILLES

HAITI

PUERTO RICO

JAMAICA

DOMINICAN REPUBLIC

GUATEMALA

DOMINICA

HONDURAS

LESSER ANTILLES

EL SALVADOR

CARIBBEAN SEA

NICARAGUA

BARBADOS

GRENADA

COSTA RICA

TOBAGO

TRINIDAD

PANAMA

VENEZUELA

COLOMBIA

GUYANA

0   300mi
0   300km

threatening the coastal road with mud and branches.

By comparison, the country's southeast lies in the rain shadow, and generally receives fewer wet days. The region is grassy, sporting species of acacia thornbush and the indigenous melon cactus, dildo cactus, prickly pear cactus, and tuna cactus, which create a semidesert appearance in some areas.

Hurricanes

A hurricane is a wild, high-pressure storm of intense wind that revolves around a low-pressure center, the placid vortex or "eye" of the storm. The shifting eye varies in diameter but can reach up to 100 miles, and generally moves in a westward direction. As high-pressure winds revolve around and move toward the center, they're whipped into a frenzy by centrifugal force, and can reach speeds of 120 mph or more. Thunder, lightning, and torrential rain usually accompany a hurricane.

Jamaica has had its share of hurricanes. One of the most destructive was Hurricane Gilbert, which struck the island in Sept. 1988. So profound was Gilbert's impact that people today still refer to the island in "before-Gilbert" and "after-Gilbert" terms.

The hurricane left 45 dead and 500,000 homeless, and tore the roofs from almost 80% of the country's homes, mostly small shacks with tenuous supports. Hardest hit was the fragile agricultural sector in which 35% of the nation is employed. Tourism and other businesses were hurt. A great amount of international aid helped put Jamaica back on its feet again. Still, in Portland and St. Thomas, two of the more harshly hit parishes, evidence of Gilbert exists: the facility at Port Antonio's Blue Lagoon is no longer under supervision, with the restaurant and service areas closed indefinitely. The historic Bath Fountain Hotel was shut down for renovations for years and reopened only recently, still smarting from the storm.

Jamaica's hurricane season is July-Oct., though June and November have been visited in the past. A simple ditty is used to explain it: "June, too soon; July, standby; August, prepare you must; September, remember; October, all over."

An informative pamphlet called *Precautions For Hurricanes and Earthquakes* is available from the Office of Disaster Preparedness and Emergency Relief Co-ordination (O.D.P), Box 122, Kingston 5, Jamaica, West Indies.

FLORA AND FAUNA

You could eat a tomato and spit the seeds on the ground.
Tomorrow, you'll see more tomatoes.
—Mr. Busta Prendergast,
Oracabessa resident,
commenting on the fertility of the land

FLORA

Given its warm, wet climate and disparate terrain, Jamaica has great capability for a diversity of plantlife. Much of the country's flora has been imported over the years by various settlers, conquerors, and immigrants, but quite a few indigenous and endemic plants exist—and still more are being discovered. The more famous imports are maize, cassava, sweet potato, cocoa, and tobacco, introduced by the island's original inhabitants, the Arawaks. The

ackee tree, which bears the national fruit of the same name, is thought to have been introduced by African slaves. It has been recorded, however, that *ackee* was definitely imported by the captain of a slave ship in 1778. The Spanish imported bananas, sugarcane (originally from the Far East), coconut, ginger, turmeric, tamarind, oranges, limes, and lemons. Indian laborers brought ganja, and the British contributed garden vegetables and the famous breadfruit, which was the basis for the trip that inspired Fletcher Christian's mutinous brawl with Captain Bligh in the South Pacific. From the same cargo that introduced breadfruit, Bligh brought the brilliant, flowering *otaheite* apple tree from its native Tahiti.

Wild pines and over 200 species of grasses grow, though Jamaica's most famous grasses, sugarcane and bamboo, are not indigenous.

Other edible imports have been the eggplant, or aubergine, and the sesame seed, imported by immigrating Jews in the 17th century. The Jamaican pineapple, featured on the country's coat of arms, was introduced to Jamaica by the Spanish from Central and South America, and from here it is believed to have been exported to Hawaii. Today, Hawaii is the world's largest producer of the sweet, acidic fruit.

Jamaica has virtually no indigenous export plants, save the successful pimento seed from the tree of the same name. Called *pimenta* by the Spanish, the tree's fragrant berry combines the flavors of cinnamon, clove, and nutmeg. Some say there's a bit of pepper in it, too. The seed of the berry is ground and the resulting spice is marketed as allspice in some parts of the world.

The hybrid *ortanique* is a Jamaican creation, a cross between an orange and tangerine. The name implies the uniqueness of the hybrid. The Jamaican ugly or *ugli* fruit is a cross between a grapefruit and a tangerine, and has enjoyed some success on the international market. Yes, it is ugly, a sort of wizened, lonely looking fruit. It tastes, however, nothing like it looks—more like sweet grapefruit.

Ferns

It is estimated that over 550 species of ferns are indigenous to Jamaica. They grow throughout the country in the hills and plains. Ferns are easily seen along Fern Gully, a three-mile scenic drive south of Ocho Rios, where the thick vegetation forms an archway over the road, cooling it and giving it an eerie jungle ambience. Here you can see the imposing tree ferns, some up to 30 feet tall. Silver ferns and gold ferns are named for the silver and gold outlines that remain when the delicate underside of the plant is pressed against an object. Some Jamaican ferns are so small they cannot be seen with the naked eye.

Flowers

The country hosts an estimated 3,000 species of flowering plants, including 200 species of orchids (more than 30 of which are endemic to Jamaica). Bougainvillea, the ostentatious flowering vine of the tropics, is also one of the more prolific flowers in Jamaica. Its delicate white, rich purple, and orange flowers snake along trees, fences, and other bushes. Added to the scenery are the multicolored hibiscus, allamanda, and oleander bushes.

Trees

Before the arrival of humans, Jamaica was almost completely forested, except for the coastal mangrove and swamp regions (called morasses) north of Negril and Black River and west of Morant Point. Today, large amounts of forest have given way to settlements, farms, and bauxite mines. Only about one-fourth of the country is forested now, and Jamaica currently imports much of its timber from Canada and Belize. Deforestation has caused the usual round of attendant problems, including severe erosion of topsoil in some hill and farm areas. Jamaica's Forestry Department now maintains some 20,000 acres of forest plantations, notably in the Cockpit Country, Blue Mountains, John Crow Mountains, and Hellshire Hills of St. Catherine. They hope to stem the erosion tide through supervised planting.

Cultivation of local timber for export has been difficult because of rugged terrain, but the world still pays for Jamaican mahogany, cedar, and blue mahoe, the national tree. The lignum vitae (tree of life) is said to have medicinal properties in its bark and leaves. It produces the bright blue national flower of the same name.

Other common trees include the logwood, which produces a black or dark dye. The cotton tree, thought to be the largest species in Jamaica, was a favorite of the Arawaks for building canoes (see p. 16). The cotton tree, it is believed, is also a favored residence of *duppies* (ghosts). The soursop, sweetsop, mango, almond, and pawpaw (or papaya) are all fruit-bearing trees. The tall royal palm, satinwood, and poinsettia trees are found in gardens and throughout the forest.

Despite deforestation, some areas of Jamaica are thought to be relatively untouched by humans. The very highest peaks of the Blue Mountains and John Crow Mountains, as well as areas in the heart of the Cockpit Country and the morasses of Negril, Black River, and Morant Point, have the same vegetation today that they did when Columbus arrived.

Throughout the country, a number of private and public botanical gardens are not only pretty to walk through, but display a vivid, succinct picture of Jamaican flora.

A FEW OF JAMAICA'S COMMON HERBS AND PLANTS

aloe—Also known as "sinkle bible" in Jamaica. A bitter, viscous liquid drips from its rubbery leaves and is applied externally for burns, sunburn, warts, and eyewash when diluted; also used as a laxative. It originates in southern Africa, and legend has it that Adam and Eve filched it from the Garden of Eden.

arrowroot—Starchy flour made from the root of the plant of the same name. It's used to make cookies and is said to be helpful in curing diarrhea.

breadfruit—Not only did Captain Bligh's famous fruit help feed a slave population, the leaves are said to help headaches when applied directly to the forehead or taken as tea.

cerasee—A wild vine which produces an orange fruit. Tea made from the leaves is used for colds, for general stomach pains, and as a laxative. The tea's purgative effect is strong, so it should be used in moderation. The leaf is also used to treat acne.

chainy root—When boiled and mixed with other roots for a somewhat bittersweet tonic, it's said to be high in minerals. Some local root tonics utilize literally hundreds of roots per mixture.

coconut water—Water from the green nut is best. It's cheaper than a soft drink, naturally clean. The water is excellent as electrolyte replacement for dehydration caused by diarrhea or vomiting—the Gatorade of the tropics.

dogblood—Taken internally for bruising and hemorrhaging. It tastes better than it sounds.

fever grass—Also known as lemon grass or lemon oil grass, it's used as spice in some curried foods, in perfume, and as medicinal tea for fevers and colds.

ganja—Marijuana. Many Jamaicans believe in the curative powers of this notorious herb. Aside from smoking it, many boil it to make tea, sprinkle it on food, or eat it straight, so to speak. Eye problems, stomach problems, fevers, and a host of other complaints are said to be waylaid by the drug.

ginger—The crushed root, boiled with sugar to make a tea, is good for stomachaches and indigestion.

guava—The small tree produces a rich fruit that can be eaten raw or made into jelly. The root and leaves are used for stomach ailments.

khus khus—A fragrant grass used to make perfume.

leaf of life—Not to be confused with the national flower, this prolific herb is used for hypertension, colds, and external skin problems.

pawpaw—The tree produces a soft, sweet fruit (called papaya in some parts of the world) high in vitamin C. Meat wrapped in the leaves becomes tender.

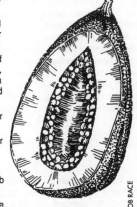

pawpaw

BOB RACE

pepper elder—Tea made from the leaves relieves gastric problems, indigestion, and flatulence.

shame lady—Fernlike plant also called the sensitive plant, *shama, shy mi lady,* and other names for its unique property of closing its leaves. At the slightest touch, the plant will squeeze shut and reopen minutes later. Used for colds, bronchial problems, and reportedly against gonorrhea.

Botanic Gardens

Bath Botanic Garden in St. Thomas is one of the oldest botanical gardens in the Western Hemisphere, established in 1779. Many of the trees introduced to Jamaica were planted here first. The descendants of the original mango, jackfruit, jacaranda, and cinnamon trees, as well as Captain Bligh's breadfruit, can be seen here.

The **Royal Botanic Gardens** in Hope, Kingston (commonly known as the **Hope Gardens),** is pretty, free, and big on indigenous flowers and the tall sago palm. It is attached to the Hope

Zoo, a wonderful place to see a few of Jamaica's animals as well as animals common to the Caribbean.

Other gardens, including the **Castleton Botanic Gardens, Shaw Park Gardens,** and **The Botanic Gardens,** Liguanea, as well as numerous plantation tours and private gardens, give a full account of plant growth in Jamaica.

Herbs

A great many Jamaicans are believers in the curative powers of Western medicine, as well as those of religion, spirits, folk medicine, mineral baths, magic, and herbs. True to the syncretic nature of lifestyles that have their roots in Africa, the Caribbean, and the West, many people believe that the expanded choices merely up the odds for success, especially when combined.

On the other hand, medicinal and nutritive herbs have their roots grounded, so to speak, in reality. From African days and from the days when doctors were not available to slaves, herbs have been tested, tried, and, it appears, true. Rural and urban Jamaicans, young and old, those who can afford a doctor and those who can't or have no access, know of the herbs and other folk medicines. They generally consult the proper sources for their treatment. Proper sources may be revivalist leaders, obeah men (practitioners of magic) or herbalists. (See p. 47.)

FAUNA

Early Spanish settlers brought with them an assortment of domestic animals, including dogs, cattle, horses, donkeys, fowl, and pigs. The pigs soon reproduced at a rate that outpaced their owners' capacities, and eventually ran wild in the mountains. Rats stowed away on Spanish ships. By and large, however, Jamaica is not a land brimming with mammalia. Birds, reptiles, and insects inhabit the land, and they do so with a colorful flamboyance.

Birds

At least 252 species of birds exist in the country, and over 20 are endemic. The most well known is the doctor bird, or swallowtail hummingbird, the national bird of Jamaica. The bird is characterized by shimmering green and blue feathers and, on the male bird, two long, sweeping tails. The doctor bird, which feeds on mango blossoms, is said to get its name from the needlelike appearance of its long, thin beak, which it uses to extract nectar. The bee hummingbird, one of the smallest in the world, resembles a large butterfly, and is another of the four species of hummingbird found in Jamaica. Most of Jamaica's endemic birds are protected by law.

Seagoing booby birds, or terns, wait out most of the year at sea and return to outlying cays to lay eggs. The ubiquitous John crow is not a crow, but a buzzard—a bird with a face only a mother buzzard could love. Resembling the turkey buzzard of North America, it is graceful in flight and can be seen almost everywhere, soaring and circling high in the mountains or close to the shore. The bird was originally called the carrion crow and it is possible that its current name is a local corruption of the word "carrion." Another legend attributes the name to a Rev. John Crow, whose black gown spread like the wings of the bird as he leaned against his pulpit.

The kling-kling is a noisy, mynahlike scavenger that frequents outdoor cafes and restaurants, at the ready to pounce on patrons' plates should they go off to the restroom. Another endemic bird, the *tody,* digs a two-foot tunnel in which to make a nest and lay eggs. The white owl and screech owl are both called *patoos,* after the West African word *patu,* and are steeped in mysticism. The cry of a *patoo* is often regarded as a sign of approaching bad luck.

Other resident birds include several species of egret (snowy and cattle), starling, and house sparrow. Nonresidents, the axiomatic North American birds that go south for the winter, include thrushes, warblers, and orioles.

Amphibians And Reptiles

The snakes, lizards, and frogs of Jamaica are harmless. Reportedly, five species of snake exist, all land dwellers, all rarely seen. The largest is the nocturnal yellow snake, sometimes reaching lengths of up to 10 feet. Another, the two-headed snake, is so named because its tail is bigger than its head. Insect-eating grass snakes dwell under woodpiles and tall grass.

Lizards are much more abundant. One of the most common is the croaking lizard, a member of the gecko family. Croaking lizards tend to

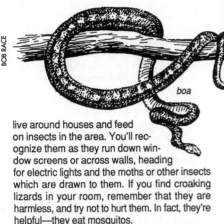

BOB RACE

boa

live around houses and feed on insects in the area. You'll recognize them as they run down window screens or across walls, heading for electric lights and the moths or other insects which are drawn to them. If you find croaking lizards in your room, remember that they are harmless, and try not to hurt them. In fact, they're helpful—they eat mosquitos.

A fairly common Jamaican lizard has the generic name *anolid*. A characteristic of all species is the male's ability to dramatically puff out its throat when threatened or threatening, giving it the appearance of having just swallowed a small Ping-Pong ball.

The indigenous iguana is probably now extinct, having fallen victim to the miscreant mongoose, an unfortunate introduction to Jamaica (see "Mammals"). The ground lizard has also been pursued by the mongoose, and its numbers greatly reduced. Folklore has it that the *galliwasp* lizard is dangerous and that, at its bite, you must race it to the water: Whoever arrives first lives. Actually, the *galliwasp* is harmless.

The misnamed alligator is really an American crocodile and is said to be harmless, "shy, and inoffensive" unless threatened, according to Capt. Charles Swaby of South Coast Safaris. Even then it is said to merely snap at an intruder, with no intention of dragging him or her underwater. (It's just something about the word "snap" that doesn't sound harmless.) Crocs, which are featured on the Jamaican coat of arms, used to be great sport for hunters but are now protected by law. About 300 crocodiles remain in the swamps of the Black River, and not many more in the 16,000 acres of wetlands along Jamaica's south coast.

Tree frogs, whistling frogs, and large frogs that actually snore contribute to the cacophony that is Jamaica at night. Thirteen species of southern frog inhabit different elevations in the hills and mountains. In some places frogs are called "spring chicks," "chickens," or variations thereof. The large bullfrog is in fact not a frog but a toad, the only toad in the country. It was introduced from Barbados in the 1840s in an ill-fated attempt to help control cane rats, which were then destroying great quantities of sugarcane. The bullfrog reproduced prolifically, and now can be seen throughout the country.

Insects

Jamaica has a lively array of insects, some of which seem to look at you as one big meal. Mosquitoes, of course, and some blackflies and sand fleas make sleeping nets and repellent a necessity when hiking or spending time outdoors. Jamaica's most notable insects are its butterflies, of which there are over 20 recorded endemic species. Striking among them is the yellow and black swallowtail butterfly, which can have a wingspan of up to six inches. This butterfly is endemic to Jamaica, and can be seen most frequently in the Blue Mountains.

Mammals

The most notorious Jamaican mammal is the mongoose, an animal introduced by sugarcane farmers to help control the destructive eating habits of the cane rat. In 1872, a Jamaican farmer named William Espeut imported the long, furry rodents from India. By the turn of the century the mongoose was under the skin of Jamaicans—it was blamed for hunting chickens, fish, crabs, insects, and other harmless creatures, and also for threatening the Jamaican iguana and one of the few native mammals, the coney.

The small, brown coney is now an endangered species. This nocturnal, plant-eating rodent is believed to dwell in the eastern parts of the country: Portland, St. Thomas, and the Hellshire Hills southwest of Kingston. While the mongoose can be blamed for hunting the coney, its numbers have actually been decreasing since Arawak times, when it was hunted by humans as a delicacy.

Twenty-five species of harmless bats, locally called "rat bats," live in caves and the cool shade of mangrove swamps, feeding on fruit, fish, and insects.

Marinelife

Ocean life begins in and around coral reefs with the smaller, microscopic inhabitants that rank low on the food chain. Coral reefs are actually colonies of living creatures called polyps, along with the corallite or skeletal remains of past polyps. The structure accommodates a life-and-death cycle that uses past skeletal remains as building blocks, giving the coral the appearance of growth. When snorkeling or diving a reef, the often brilliant colors seen on coral are provided by zooxanthellae, tiny plant cells that live within the coral structure itself. The polyps also provide color, but their skeletons are usually white. (The topsoil of coral atolls in the South Pacific is formed, in part, from broken corallite remains.) The organism itself is generally hollow and tubular, with an anterior mouth surrounded by tentacles for gathering tiny food particles. Polyps range in size from microscopic to inches across. The coral polyp life-form has been in existence for over 100 million years.

Always popular with snorkelers and divers, a coral reef is one of nature's most sublime and quietly beautiful structures. The abundance of life in the reef is astonishing, if not always evident. It accommodates scores of life-forms, including algae, some forms of sea sponge, and sea fans. Small and exotic fish, shrimp, and the spiny lobster make their homes in and among certain coral limbs, taking advantage of the rich fare that passes their way.

Coral grows in warm, clear salt water, generally no deeper than 100 feet below the surface. But it often grows in shallow water, closer to shore, aided by the sun. Much of Jamaica's reef is within sight or a 5-10-minute boat ride from shore. Divers can take advantage of up to 100-foot dives less than one mile from shore where the ocean walls drop off drastically, in some areas for a depth of five miles.

In some places, coral brushes the water's surface at low tide. As such, coral is easily threatened by changes in ocean current and weather, particularly hurricanes, and by careless divers. Today, the biggest threat to Jamaica's reefs is from fishermen and divers (both local and tourist).

Coral life found in Jamaican waters includes staghorn and elkhorn corals, so named for their resemblance to the horns of those animals.

Cathedral (also called majestic) coral generally thrives as isolated colonies, away from the main reef. Finger coral, small finger coral, and club finger coral are all common, as is brain coral, named for its resemblance to the outer membrane of the human organ.

Soft corals (those with flexible skeletal remains) are mesmerizing as they undulate back and forth with the ocean. Gorgonian coral,

---

FIRST AID ON THE REEF

While many reef dwellers are beautiful to look at, one touch could ruin your day. The following suggestions may help ease the pain, but a doctor is really the best bet when in doubt.

Sea Urchins: If the barbs break off in your skin, remove the fragments as soon as possible. Expect painful swelling. Soak the affected area in vinegar or diluted ammonia. Urine will suffice if it is the only option. See a doctor.

Bristle Worms: If those white whiskers become imbedded in your skin, follow the treatment for sea urchins and try to remove the bristles—lightly applied sticky tape is effective. See a doctor.

Jellyfish: Splash the affected area with alcohol but avoid rubbing it or you might activate detached stingers. Talcum powder and other drying agents

such as sand are useful for relieving the pain of a jellyfish sting. See a doctor.

Live Coral: Treat the sting with vinegar or diluted ammonia and get to a doctor.

Red Fire Sponge: Most important, do not touch! Treat the affected area with vinegar or diluted ammonia. The itchy, burning sensation may last for several days. In serious cases, see a doctor.

The most important first-aid method is prevention. When diving, be aware of your buoyancy control, and touch only coral rock, not live coral. Walking or standing on the ocean floor invites encounters with urchins, bristle worms, and the like. The less you touch, the less chance you have of being stung, and the less chance you have of destroying a living sea organism.

named for the snake-hair sisters in Greek mythology, includes sea whips and sea feathers. Gorgonian coral is among the prettiest, commonly in shades of green, purple, and orange.

Black coral is also abundant, as anyone who has walked down streets in Montego Bay will know. The men who carve and offer it for sale as jewelry are skilled and persistent. And some of it is very tempting. But you can be fairly certain that it wasn't found, already broken, on the ocean floor. And even if it was, black coral, as well as white coral, is protected by law—its sale is illegal.

More types of coral exist than can be mentioned here, and the best way to satisfy your curiosity is to just jump in and see it for yourself.

Fish And Other Ocean Dwellers

The fish along Jamaica's reef are plentiful and every bit as colorful as their host coral and sponge colonies. About 700 or so species are associated with the coral reef, and while you may not see every one, it'll seem like you have.

Many types of groupers, snappers, and the red squirrel fish (all good eating) feed on the reef. Flounders, including the common peacock flounder, are plentiful. The multicolored parrot fishes, tiny butterfly fish, hamlets, and wrasses fill in the spectrum. Angelfish, including the tasty doctor fish (usually tossed in a nice fish stew), are among the more recognizable reef fish. In addition, a variety of nocturnal fish, including the cardinal fish, is visible.

Game fish and larger fish found in deeper Jamaican waters include the blue marlin, a favorite of deep-sea fishers for its fighting prowess and value as a food source. The annual weeklong **Port Antonio International Marlin Tournament** attracts hundreds of anglers from Jamaica and around the world each October. Other major tournaments are held in Montego Bay and Ocho Rios in autumn. The largest recorded marlin caught in Jamaican waters was a 726-pound blue caught by a commercial fisherman, while the largest caught on a rod and reel was 680 pounds.

Other large fish, many protected by fishing regulations, include the white marlin, wahoo, tuna, barracuda, and blunt-nosed dolphin fish (not the mammal).

Tarpons live at the mouths of rivers and often travel upstream for feeding. Bonito and kingfish run in the deep waters, the latter often found along the rich south coast fishing banks.

Eels, rays, and turtles also are common among Jamaica's ocean fauna. The most common eel is the spotted moray, a creature that seems to be all mouth and teeth. It is generally harmless and tends to feed at night. Stay an arm's length away. Morays should not be eaten—they're known to carry toxins that cause food poisoning. The snake eel resembles a snake and may be handled—but gently. The giant manta ray, also known as the devilfish, have been known to give divers a hitch. The manta is a slow-motion ocean fish, its pectoral

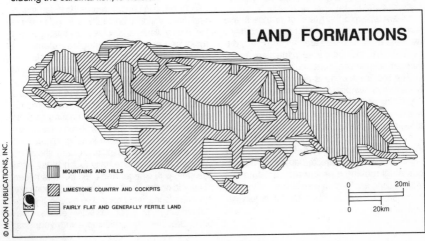

LAND FORMATIONS

MOUNTAINS AND HILLS

LIMESTONE COUNTRY AND COCKPITS

FAIRLY FLAT AND GENERALLY FERTILE LAND

0   20mi

0   20km

fins propelling it with elegant, wavy swells. The most common sea turtle is the green turtle, which is actually brown. This turtle, once considered a delicacy, is now protected by law.

Sharks are not common on the Jamaican reef, but occasionally a nurse shark, as long as 14 feet, can be observed lying motionless on the ocean floor. It is not aggressive but it is, after all, a shark. If agitated, it will strike. Keep a safe distance.

One of life's largest and simplest creatures is the manatee, or sea cow. The manatee is a beautifully homely vegetarian mammal that lives in the ocean. It can grow to 12 feet in length and weigh up to a ton, feasting on 100 pounds of seaweed per day. Once hunted for its meat, the manatee is now endangered and protected by law. An estimated 100 manatees live in Jamaican waters. The worldwide total is about 1,500.

Other reef dwellers are a variety of starfish, sea worms, snails, and shellfish. The conch is prized for its meat and shell, which can be seen by the hundreds at roadside stands along the north and west coast. Avoid the porcupinelike sea urchins, especially the black, long-spined urchin. The strong barbs will pierce your skin and break off, resulting in painful swelling. Remove the fragments as soon as possible and soak the affected area in straight vinegar or a strong ammonia solution (urine will do in a pinch). Treat with antiseptic as soon as possible. Then see a doctor. Urchin meat is a table delicacy for some.

Likewise, avoid the green or orange bristle worm, which can also make for a very bad day if its brittle white whiskers are touched. They detach and become imbedded in the skin. Again, vinegar and medical treatment should follow.

The red fire sponge is also nice to look at, but will cause swelling and discomfort if touched. Try to stay clear of all forms of jellyfish, which are not fish at all, but primordial globs of membrane and primitive intelligence—again, nice to look at but not to touch. Their tentacles have small, stinging organisms that detach if brushed against. Splash the affected area with alcohol but avoid rubbing it or you may activate detached stingers. Talcum powder and other drying agents such as sand are useful for jellyfish encounters.

Jumping In And Seeing It
Most diving in Jamaica is done along the north, windward coast, where the waters are clearer. Fewer rivers run along this coast, and the result is a clean reef less modified by the island's inland weather. As well, the north side has a relatively narrow ocean shelf, about one mile out compared to up to 15 miles out along the south coast.

Excellent facilities are available along the coast and in hotels for divers, diving instruction, and snorkelers. Certified divers should bring their certification cards. Noncertified divers can receive PADI (Professional Association of Diving Instructors) beginner's training, which will allow a supervised 30-foot dive, a sort of introduction to the world below. If you're interested and have the time and money, certification is available from various dive centers for an average US$350, which generally includes daily dive fees, manuals, dive tables, a log book, and certification processing fees.

If diving isn't your cup of sea, then snorkeling will do nicely. All hotels and dive centers rent equipment, and it's cheap enough to do as often as you like. Snorkeling is generally safe, but keep in mind: test the equipment first. Get used to your mask and snorkel by practicing in a pool or shallow water, and don't snorkel or swim alone. The Jamaican water is a comfortable 80° F (27° C) year-round, so wetsuits or lycra covering are not necessary. Some people like to wear a T-shirt for protection against the sun and accidental brushes with coral.

Snorkeling in choppy seas is both dangerous and futile. Visibility is greatly reduced in sloshing, murky water, and waves can push you into rocks and coral. Even though the Jamaican coast has minor tides and gentle currents, you should ask and be aware of where currents are if you are snorkeling or diving.

Never touch live coral, for the organism's safety and for your own. All corals can be harmful; they can give you a slow-healing gash or release toxins on touch. Avoid even the smooth-looking coral. Fire corals and stinging corals do what their names suggest, and clearly should be avoided. If you accidentally touch them, treat the sting with vinegar and seek treatment (see "First Aid on the Reef"). If you want to touch underwater fauna, wear protective gloves. If you're not wearing fins, wear protective shoes. Likewise, breaking coral, kicking it with your fins, brushing it with your underwater camera, or other injurious behavior can traumatize the delicate ecological balance of the reef.

Snorkeling with a local who can point out reef life is both rewarding and safe. Many hotels offer guides for snorkelers as well as for divers.

Wildlife Conservation

The Jamaican government has realized the need for protecting marinelife through legislation. This became evident after years of unchecked land and sea development seriously threatened some species of flora and fauna, and eliminated others. It is now common knowledge that inland development affects the coast and sea, and vice versa. In 1991, two important regulatory bodies were established to help ensure continuing efforts to modulate development and promote conservation activities.

The **Protected Areas Resource Conservation Project (PARC)** is responsible for the development of Jamaica's national parks. PARC has established a marine park at Montego Bay, a 15-square-mile park where marine environments are studied and a limited amount of snorkeling, scuba diving, and sailing is permitted.

PARC has also established a 193,300-acre **Blue Mountain National Park,** which is the largest conservation area in Jamaica and contains half the acreage of all Jamaica's current and proposed national parks. Blue Mountain National Park will help protect hundreds of Jamaica's endemic plant and animal species that live in the Blue Mountains, including the Jamaican **tody** and the swallowtailed butterfly.

The **National Resources Conservation Authority (NRCA)** was established to help identify and address environmental problems, as well as to promote public awareness of the country's ecosystems.

The University of the West Indies, headquartered in Kingston, operates two marine laboratories in Jamaica. The labs, at Port Royal in Kingston and the north coast's Discovery Bay, are researching the growing problem of overfishing. This will help Jamaica's commercial fishermen address the issue of conserving depleted species while concurrently making a living.

The Wildlife Protection Act (1945) and the Beach Protection Act (1978) are both aimed at environmental protection. Under the wildlife laws, the crocodile, manatee, yellow snake, and freshwater terrapin are protected. The sea turtle is also protected. Black coral and white coral fall under the same act. Birds are protected by seasonal hunting laws (something relatively recent in Jamaica), and some, such as the doctor bird, are not hunted at all. A recent development protects the spiny lobster from hunting during its reproduction season, 1 April-30 June every year. Help by not eating or buying lobster during these months.

The Jamaica Association of Dive Operators (JADO) is charged with ensuring safe, ecologically responsible dives by its member dive shops. This means, they say, "take photos; leave bubbles." JADO-approved dive operations are probably the safest and best maintained on the island.

A number of beaches throughout the country are run by the government's Urban Development Corporation (UDC). The UDC beaches charge nominal admission, as do some privately owned beaches, and the money goes toward beach and area maintenance. The government also plans to establish more marine parks and fish sanctuaries. One is soon to open in Ocho Rios, and more are planned for the hopefully not-too-distant future.

Eco-tourism

One of the fastest-growing trends in the tourism arena—and this applies worldwide as well as in Jamaica—is the establishment of tours and attractions that promise "eco-tourism." What exactly does this mean?

For some tour companies, it is a buzzword that is meant to attract nature lovers, and that's that—you simply get people outside, and you claim to have an eco-tour. This type of promotional gimmick is widespread in Jamaica. For others, it means some sort of breathless, quasi-religious relationship with nature that borders on mysticism. The answer, most likely, lies somewhere in between and involves no small amount of subjective judgment on the part of the visitor. A general definition might be this: Eco-tourism is a type of activity that emphasizes the ecological and human cultural aspects of an environment, where the ecology and culture are not altered by the presence or acts of visitors to that environment.

Sound weighty? Not really. Quite a bit of it is common sense. Swimming in a mountain stream seems fine. Buzzing the beach at 30 mph in a jet-ski is most probably not eco-tourism. Riding a motorcycle on the beach, which compacts sand and accelerates the erosion of the beach, is not, either. The list goes on. While eco-tourism is perhaps just a bit more than remembering to pick up your candy wrappers from the ground, it is not always much more that. With a bit of forethought, we can all help stem the tide of destruction of some of the world's cultures and natural wonders.

For information about local tour companies that provide nature-oriented eco-tours, see p. 90.

HISTORY

"I think I know vhat is wrong with this island," she said softly.

"Vhat's wrong?"

"Too many lies. Not enough hate."

"Vhat dat?"

"There is reason for hate. Poor people everywhere you look. A few rich people. There should be hate. But there is no hate. That is vhat wrong with this place. It needs more hate."

"Hate?"

"In Europe, ve have lots of hate. This is why Europe is strong and rich. This is vhy Jamaica is poor."

"Bumbo," whispered the tree. "Listen dis now."

—Anthony C. Winkler, The Lunatic

THE ARAWAKS

Before intrepid European adventurers sailed toward ports unknown to discover the New World, a more localized migration had been going on for some time. The first known inhabitants of Jamaica were Amerindian Arawaks, a dauntless group of seafarers who crossed the Caribbean Sea in two waves, so to speak—the first about A.D. 500 and the second between A.D. 850 and 900—from their traditional areas in the Amazon River Valley and Orinoco regions of northern Brazil and Venezuela. They settled the Antilles in groups from Trinidad to Cuba, where Christopher Columbus would first encounter them in his late-15th-century voyages.

The Arawaks appear to have led peaceful lives, though it's doubtful they were the outright "happy natives" from the famous cliche. They were a fishing and farming culture, fond of ceremony and organized games, and had little history of attacking others. In fact, upon the arrival of the Spanish they offered little real resistance and were routed all too easily by the newcomers' crossbows and armor.

They settled in large villages of up to 1,000 huts and 3,000 people, generally by the sea or near rivers. The entrances to their octagonal huts always faced eastward. They were skilled in shaping and milling *canoes,* originally an Arawak word which made its way to English via Spanish. That the Arawaks were expert sailors there isn't much doubt, and their canoes seemed to vary in size and purpose. Some fishing canoes held only one person; traveling vessels held up to 60.

Despite their seagoing nature, evidence shows that some Arawak groups inhabited parts of Jamaica's interior. Skilled Arawak artists left paintings on cave walls that indicate they lived in the central and upland areas of the island.

The Arawaks were a diminutive people (averaging five feet), dark, with Asiatic features. In Jamaica they grew cotton with great success, supplying neighboring islands with cotton cloth. From their cotton we have adopted an important (and fortunate) Arawak invention and word: *hammock.* (Today, drive along the north shore and you'll see hundreds of hammocks for sale in small roadside huts.) The Arawaks also crafted jewelry and working implements from stone and shell.

The Arawaks were fond of and grew tobacco —the word derived from the name of their pipe— and used it both socially and ritually. They grew fruit and vegetables, including the two main staples, maize and cassava (*yuca*), the starchy staple of many tropical areas. The Arawaks grew two types of cassava, what are commonly known as the sweet and bitter varieties. Sweet cassava is harmless and can be cooked and eaten directly as a staple starch. The bitter variety contains high levels of toxins, and must go through a washing and grating process before it is safe to consume. It is this type of cassava that is the staple of the popular *bammy* of today. During the Spanish occupation of Jamaica, when the Arawaks were enslaved under harsh conditions, many committed suicide by drinking bitter cassava extract.

The now-famous pepperpot stew is also Arawak in origins. Guava, a fruit that has taken its name from the Arawak language, was utilized as well.

Gender roles were clear: men worked at building and fishing, while women cared for children, worked the gardens, and spent time spinning and weaving cotton.

Some anthropologists believe that the Arawaks held a concept of an earth mother and sky father, not unlike other American indigenous groups. Their deities were male and female, and were involved in all aspects of Arawak life, from creation (of life, not of the earth; the Arawaks seemed to believe that the earth had always been in existence), to the interplay of elements, to death. In one creation myth, the god Iocauna created man, who emerged from caves and the earth. Later he created the sun, the moon, and the fish in the sea. Some linguists believe that the Arawak word for the staple crop cassava, *yuca,* is related to the name of the god Iocauna. The female god Attabeira performed other functions, including Mother of Tides and Springs.

In death, the spirits of departed Arawaks, called *opias,* were said to wander around in the bush at night, indistinguishable from the living save for the lack of a navel. The Arawaks buried their dead in caves, sometimes placing the head and other body parts in large pottery bowls. These bowls and preserved skulls are on display today in museums around the country.

Jamaica's first inhabitants were also responsible for the introduction of the words "barbecue," "hurricane," and "manatee" into various languages, and, importantly, the word "Xaymaca" which, though its meaning is disputed ("Land of Wood and Water," "Island of Springs"), gives us the beautiful and poetic name of the island.

For centuries the Arawak existed unperturbed in Jamaica until the arrival of the bellicose and cannibalistic Caribs, another seagoing indigenous group from the Guiana region of South America.

The marauding Caribs, possibly distant relatives of Arawak groups, had over the years made their way from South America to the Lesser Antilles, and on to Cuba and Haiti, leaving murder, depredation, and conquered islands in the wakes of their war canoes. According to some evidence, they captured women, killed and reportedly ate men, and sometimes destroyed entire villages. The Caribs were a fierce group, and their aim was to vanquish—they were feared with good reason. The Caribs were closing in on Jamaica during the latter part of the 15th century at about the time Christopher Columbus was doing the same.

COLUMBUS

In fourteen hundred and ninety-two,
Columbus sailed the ocean blue.
*   —children's ditty*

The First Voyage

In his relentless, some say ego-driven, quest for riches and a route to the New World, the Italian explorer Christopher Columbus (Cristoforo Colombo, in his native language) sailed into both fame and a bit of infamy on his four voyages to the Americas.

The premise of the daring trips, which inspired the Spanish sovereigns Ferdinand and Isabella to supply sponsorship, was that the ever-growing European demand for Asian luxuries necessitated a simpler and more efficient route to obtain them. The current overland routes were rough, time-consuming, and costly. It was part of Columbus's grand plan, the "Enterprise of the Indies," to find an ocean route west from Spain to Asia, and to secure any discovered land for Spain's empire. No one knew, of course, that the Americas lay uncharted between Europe and Asia. It took many years and no small amount of effort for Columbus to convince his patrons that he could find this shorter route, and thus enrich the Spanish empire and its sovereigns. They were finally convinced, and Columbus set sail with the added incentive that his success would ensure political and property rights for himself and his descendants. He also sailed with a guarantee of 10% of all goods and gold traded or discovered during the voyage.

Columbus, with the title "Admiral of the Ocean Sea, Viceroy and Governor," sailed from Palos, Spain, on 3 Aug. 1492, with a his crew of 90 and fleet of three caravels, the *Niña,* the *Pinta,* and his flagship *Santa Maria.* Columbus was optimistic that the New World was less than 2,800 miles to the west. Due to a gross miscalculation of the earth's size and an overestimation of Asia's easternmost point, his calculations fell drastically short. The actual (airline) distance between Spain and easternmost Asia is about 10,000 miles.

On 12 Oct. 1492, Columbus and his crew sighted land. It was an island the native inhabitants called Guanahani, renamed San Salvador or "Holy Savior" by Columbus, and was most likely today's Watling Island of the Bahamas. Later during this first voyage, Columbus went on to explore Cuba and Española, or "Little Spain" (today's Hispaniola).

Of the native Arawaks Columbus encountered in Hispaniola, he wrote, "They love their neighbors as themselves and their speech is the sweetest and gentlest in the world; and they always speak with a smile." This did not, of course, prevent him from kidnapping six of these apparently sweet and smiling people to serve as guides and to tout as proof of his visit to the New World. His ultimate plan was to both convert and enslave the remainder of the Arawaks for Spain. The enslavement of the Arawaks in Hispaniola began almost immediately, while Columbus established a garrison there to protect Spain's interests in the island.

It is actually a small part of Columbus's eventually heroic legacy that when he landed he erroneously believed he was in the Indies, somewhere close to Japan and China. It would be his lifelong belief that he'd discovered islands off the coast of Asia, gateway to the lands traveled by Marco Polo more than two centuries earlier. His lifelong quest was to make contact with the emperor of China, the Great Khan. He would, of course, never succeed. Nevertheless, he collectively named the islands he discover "West Indies" and the people who inhabited them "Indians." The momentum of history carries those names today.

Columbus In Jamaica

It was on his second voyage, now bearing the lofty title "Viceroy of the Indies," that Columbus discovered Jamaica.

Columbus set sail from Spain on 5 Sept. 1493 with 17 ships, 1,500 men, and the livestock, seeds, and tools needed to settle the New World.

He intended to return to Cuba, believing it to be part of the Asiatic mainland, where he would continue his search for the elusive Great Khan. It was on this trip that he discovered Puerto Rico and first encountered the man-eating Caribs, already settled in the Lesser Antilles. In his journals the great explorer wrote: "As for monsters I have found no trace of them except at one point on the second island on the way to the Indies; it is inhabited by a people considered throughout the island to be most ferocious."

In fact, the word *cannibal* seems to come from the Spanish word for the Caribs, Caribal.

It was also on this trip that Columbus discovered that his small garrison on Hispaniola, established during the first voyage, had been destroyed by sweet and smiling native people apparently driven to retaliation by the now-legendary harsh Spanish treatment.

Columbus had heard of the island of Jamaica, or Xaymaca, from Indians in Cuba and Hispaniola. It was reported to be a lush land, rich in gold, and while lush is certainly one of Jamaica's qualities, rich in gold it is not. Nevertheless, Columbus set sail for Jamaica with exploration and gold in mind.

When Columbus landed at St. Ann's Bay, which he called Santa Gloria, on 5 May 1494, he found the local Arawaks far from receptive. Their hostility may have stemmed from wariness because of recent frequent attacks by Carib groups in nearby Puerto Rico. It may have stemmed from the Spanish themselves who, being bearded, armored, and heavily armed, presented a rather harrowing picture. Whatever the case, Columbus and his ships were met by Arawaks in canoes, and Columbus spent his first night in Jamaica anchored offshore, plotting his next move. He resolved to land somewhere on the island, as his crew needed water and supplies and his ships were in need of repair. The next day he made his way down the coast and, encountering another group of hostile Arawaks, chose this time to engage them. A number were killed by the Spanish crossbows, their blow darts useless against the Spanish armor. The Spanish unleashed dogs; the Arawaks, having never seen such beasts, fled. Columbus claimed Jamaica for Spain, calling it Santiago in honor of St. Jago, the patron saint of Spain.

Days later, after peace offerings of fruit and fish had been brought by the apparently subdued Arawaks, Columbus and his crew sailed along the north coast to a bay he called El Golfo de Buen Tiempo ("Fair Weather Gulf"), the site of today's Montego Bay. The expedition then continued its voyage of discovery, and Columbus would not return to Jamaica until nine years later.

Columbus Returns

When Columbus returned to Jamaica in 1503, on his fourth and final voyage to the Americas, things would not go well for him. His mission was to find a strait leading to the "Indian Ocean," between Cuba and the lands he had discovered in previous voyages. There was, then, no strait. No substantial gold had been found in the New World, and Columbus's Spanish patrons were toe-tapping impatient, threatening to withdraw their support. His caravels, on the tail end of their better years, were rotted and weakened by *teredos*, or shipworms. He was forced to abandon one ship, the *Gallega*, on the coast of Panama. Another was abandoned at Porto Bello, Hispaniola; only constant pumping kept the last two afloat to Jamaica. Finally, with water almost reaching the decks, the ships ran aground at St. Ann's Bay, the site of Columbus's original discovery.

Here Columbus and his crew were marooned for more than a year. The arduous living conditions, despair, and even mutiny attempts would spell the beginning of the end of Columbus's good health. Finally, with the help of Arawak paddlers and canoes, two of his crewmen made the 108-mile journey to Hispaniola, where they were able to charter a ship from the colony. By the time the small rescue vessel arrived to carry Columbus and his remaining crew back to Spain, he was a broken man—spiritually shaken. Less than two years after his return and after constant bickering with his former patron Ferdinand over just payment for his efforts, the famous explorer died.

SPANISH SETTLEMENT

The first group of Spanish colonists arrived in Jamaica in 1510 under the direction of Diego Columbus, Christopher's son. They established the settlement of Sevilla la Nueva, "New Seville," in the area of the first landing near St. Ann's Bay on Jamaica's north coast. It soon became clear that the marsh areas abutting the settlement were unhealthy, and the colonists began the search for a new site. They eventually abandoned Sevilla la Nueva for a site to the south, a place they called Villa de la Vega, or today's Spanish Town.

Colonization

The Spanish colonists energetically set about Christianizing and enslaving the 100,000 Arawaks who lived in Jamaica. Such was the vigor of their proselytizing and harshness of their treatment that the Arawaks were all but eliminated within a few decades of Spanish settlement. Many died from diseases, for which they had little immunity, introduced by the Spaniards. The 16th-century Spanish Bishop Bartolome de Las Casas, witness to the last days of the Arawaks, wrote:

> *In the year 1509, the Islands of St. John and Jamaica that look'd like fruitful gardens, were possessed by the Spaniards, with the same bloudy intentions, as the others were; for there they also exercised their accustomed cruelties, killing, burning, roasting men, and throwing them to the dogs, as also by oppressing them with sundry and various torments in the Gold Mines as if they had come to rid the earth of these innocent and harmlesse creatures, of whom above six hundred thousand were murthered in these two Islands, so lavish were the Spanish swords of the bloud of these poor souls, scarce two hundred more remaining; the rest perished without the least knowledge of God.*

Their local source of slave labor literally exhausted, the Spanish found it necessary to turn elsewhere for strong backs. As did many countries at the time and throughout history, the Spanish used the power of the Catholic church and divine law to justify slavery, including the perplexing and ironic belief that a Christian slave's lot was better than that of a free heathen.

That minor problem of ethics dispensed with, the Spanish turned to Africa, a traditional source of slaves for centuries. In 1517, the first Africans, ancestors of the country's current majority race, were imported to Jamaica. It is interesting to note that some of these first slaves escaped immediately upon arrival, and fled to the hills of Jamaica. With regularity, other slaves escaped, and soon a sub-society of free Africans began to form, more or less independent of Spanish domination (see "The Maroons," p. 26).

The colonization of Jamaica by the Spanish amounted to little more than maintenance of existing resources. Technically ruled by Spain, the island was allowed a certain amount of self-government, much to the relief of the colonists, and not to the island's governors. A Spanish governor, answerable to the monarchy, would consult (and often fight) with the *cabildo,* a local advisory council.

The Spanish monarchy, however, regarded Jamaica as little more than a supply base at which passing ships could lay over and re-provision. Minor trade in lard and animal hides kept the populace in touch with the rest of the world, but by and large the Spanish colonists remained farmers and decidedly unimportant in the eyes of Spain. They did succeed in introducing horses, cattle, swine, and some citrus fruits to the island.

The existing remnants of Jamaica's Spanish culture are no more numerous than those of the Arawaks they converted and eventually eliminated. We see the Spanish influence only in a few words and place-names such as Ocho Rios, Negril, and Savanna-la-mar. Even remnants of the original settlement, New Seville, are sparse. Those that do exist, such as pieces of buildings, tiles, and embellishments, are continually being excavated and archived by the Institute of Jamaica. No Spanish buildings still stand.

By the mid-1600s, Jamaica was a largely forgotten, ill-managed, and often-corrupt Spanish colony. Internal strife and arguments with the Church had weakened its already fragile infrastructure. Governors had been imprisoned, murdered, or rendered politically impotent. The entire Caribbean was experiencing an increase in the frequency of covertly sponsored pirate raids as part of efforts by England and other European countries to force Spain to relinquish territorial and trade rights. The Spanish colonists, with little support from the mother country, repelled attacks by French, Dutch, English, Italian, and Portuguese war frigates with some success—for a while.

THE BRITISH IN JAMAICA

Perhaps it was appropriate to Spain's somewhat vapid interest in Jamaica that the island would ultimately be captured as an afterthought.

It was part of the expansive "Western Design," a plan devised by Oliver Cromwell, lord protector and de facto ruler of Great Britain, to strike at Spanish overseas possessions, thereby weakening their dominance on the seas and in world commerce. In 1654 he assembled an army and fleet under Gen. Robert Venables and Adm. William Penn, with the mission to take Santo Domingo, capital city of Hispaniola. If successful, England would have gained one of Spain's most prized colonies, the second largest island in the Greater Antilles.

As it turned out, the operation was a stunning failure. The fleet under Penn and Venables, with 8,000 men aboard, sailed into the Santo Domingo of a forewarned and well-prepared Spanish defense force. They encountered rain, heat, dysentery, and thirst, for the Spanish had blocked all wells in their landing area. Reports surfaced of near-mutiny, rank cowardice, and quibbling among the commanders. They suffered raids by marauding bands of escaped slaves. Men in armor collapsed from heat exhaustion, others deserted, and provisions ran short. Because of a distance miscalculation made during the landing, the walls of the city were over 37 miles away rather than the expected 10 miles, and were never reached. When the exhausted expedition finally retreated to their ships, it was estimated that 1,000 British troops had perished onshore, most without having ever encountered the enemy.

The situation was not good for Penn and Venables. Cromwell was an ambitious, mercurial, and severe ruler. Venables suggested to Penn that they move quickly and take Jamaica instead, as a somewhat diminished prize to offer upon their return. Penn saw merit in offering appeasement to Cromwell, and on 10 May 1655, the fleet made the landing at Caguaya, soon to be known as Passage Fort, at the western side of today's Kingston Harbor. The Spanish resistance was ineffectual, almost nonexistent. The British fired a few cannons, marched into Spanish Town, and effectively ended more than a century of Spanish rule without a man lost on either side.

Yet the Spanish on Jamaica would remain a thorn in the British side, both directly and indirectly, for some time. During the course of surrender and agreement to terms, the Spanish governor was able to buy time and evacuate Spanish colonists to the north side of the island, where they held out for five years. During that flight, they freed and armed their black slaves in the hope that when Spain eventually returned to reclaim the island, the slaves would join the fight—clearly, the thinking of a desperate people. Spain was never able to fully return and the slaves remained free. They roamed and joined smaller bands of escaped slaves. These freed slaves would later gain fame as the courageous Maroons, whose descendants still exist in Jamaica today.

Spain Out, Britain In

It's interesting to note that Oliver Cromwell showed his appreciation of Penn and Venables's "second prize" offering of Jamaica by tossing them both in London's dreaded Tower for six weeks. After their release they never again received an appointment under a British ruler. Yet Jamaica ultimately became a better investment than the seven-times-larger Hispaniola that Penn and Venables lost, chiefly because of its manageable size and accessibility. Almost at once, the pragmatic Cromwell began Jamaica's settlement by offering favorable terms to those wishing to establish a colony.

The Spanish, their resolve weakened and international power sapped, resisted British occupation of Jamaica sporadically and fruitlessly. Their most noble effort came in 1658 when a large force, commanded by Gov. Cristobal Arnado de Ysassi, landed at Rio Nuevo on the north side of the island. The British forces, commanded by single-minded Col. Edward D'Oyley, met the Spaniards on land and fought one of the most important battles of Jamaican history.

In all, the Spanish lost nearly 300 men for the 28 British killed. Ysassi and his forces were routed, and they fled to the hills to continue the resistance for two years, always with the hope that reinforcements and supplies would be delivered. They were crucially mistaken, as the Spanish monarch was preoccupied with waging war worldwide and could ill afford troops in Jamaica. Finally, on 9 May 1660, the last of the surviving Spanish sailed off to Cuba from a spot near today's Runaway Bay. In 1670, the Spanish officially ceded Jamaica to the British crown under the Treaty of Madrid. The capital was established at Spanish Town.

Growing Pains

Edward D'Oyley, who had sailed with Penn and Venables on their ill-fated mission, was to become Jamaica's first British governor, but not before the colony experienced the earliest of its troubles. (D'Oyley had descended from a long line of crown administrators. His ancestor, Robert D'Oilli, came to England with William the Conqueror. As levy on one of his manors, D'Oilli was required to compensate the king with two linen tablecloths per year. Over centuries, as the women of the manor became skilled at producing the linen embroidery, their fame and name spread, and today lace doilies are their legacy.)

In 1660, soon after the Spanish fled, internal dissent threatened the colony. Colonels Raymond and Tyson, commanders of local regiments, led insurgent troops at Guayanoba Vale, outside Spanish Town. Though the reasons for the rebellion are obscure, they seem to have been related to a desire to end military rule and settle down as colonists, and to D'Oyley's brusque military tactics.

D'Oyley tried unsuccessfully to persuade the mutinous troops to surrender, then brought in reinforcements and rattled them with a show of force. The troops handed in their leaders with a promise of full pardon, and watched as Raymond and Tyson were executed on the spot.

As slaves continued to be imported and Jamaica showed signs of becoming prosperous, the colonists learned how to fight tropical diseases, grow local produce, and trade with nearby British colonies. The British began to see merit in their newest possession.

BUCCANEERS AND PIRATES

During the early British years in Jamaica, one of the colonists' greatest problems was defense. The colony's location understandably rendered it vulnerable; it was situated relatively close to the major Spanish possessions of Cuba, Hispaniola, and Puerto Rico. Yet location also enhanced the colony's value as a base for harassment of the Spaniards, for even after the war with Spain ended (within a decade of British occupation of Jamaica) it was expected, reasonably, that Spain would eventually try to reclaim Jamaica for its strategic value. For that reason and others, hostilities never entirely ceased in the West Indies. The British and Spanish managed to wage war in the most creative ways.

Enter the buccaneers.

A hodgepodge of disparate and desperate scalawags, the buccaneers of the late 17th century were a loose confederation of traders, hunters, and mercenaries bound by communal law and a seething distrust for Spain. Variously called pirates and privateers, (depending upon whose employ they enjoyed), the buccaneers allegiance was only to themselves, though many were French, British, Dutch, or Caribbean-born, and of varied racial background.

The buccaneers began their infamous trek through history as a small group of escaped criminals and malcontents who had drifted, in time, to the small (25 miles in length), barren island of Tortuga, a few miles northwest of Hispaniola. There they traded and bartered with passing ships and spent a great deal of time hunting wild cattle and swine in the forests of nearby Hispaniola. From the *boucan* (wooden rack) they used to dry hides and meat, they became *les boucanier* or buccaneers.

Spain's decision to eliminate them from the Hispaniolan forests drove the buccaneers to sea warfare as sworn, eternal enemies of Spain. It also drove them to Jamaica where the British, sensing staunch, if not entirely honorable, allies, encouraged and employed them. Thus began the five-year run of some of the more colorful and debauched adventurers to roam Jamaica's soil.

The arrival of the buccaneers gave rise to the town of Port Royal, their gathering place,

built at the western end of the Palisadoes peninsula entrance to Kingston Harbor. The town soon earned the reputation as "the wickedest city in Christendom," as well as the richest in the world. The buccaneers' habit of sacking and looting Spanish settlements throughout the Caribbean paid handsomely and made their British employers happy. Blessed with temperate breezes and boasting no less than six forts, Port Royal became the most sinful town in Jamaica. Its proximity to Spanish Town and defense capability inspired confidence in ·the colony's sensible, if more discreet, residents.

Much of Port Royal and its treasure was to disappear into the deep blue sea on 7 June 1692, under an earthquake and the wash of a great tidal wave. Today, in contrast to the frenetic pace of Port Royal's glory days, a small, sleepy fishing village stands in its place. The Archaeological Museum in the old naval hospital building offers a fascinating glimpse at the Port Royal days of old.

Though nominally allied to England as privateers, the rebellious buccaneers lived by their own rules. While justice to the Spanish was served on the edge of a sword, among themselves they evolved a strict code of honor. The first was the principle "No Prey, No Pay." When booty was taken, it was divided among the captains and crew, with the wounded receiving their share first. A common payment scale for the loss of body parts was used: a right arm earned 600 pieces-of-eight or six slaves; a left arm earned 500 pieces-of-eight or five slaves; a right leg earned 500 pieces-of-eight or five slaves; a left leg earned 400 pieces-of-eight or four slaves; an eye earned 100 pieces-of-eight or one slave; and a finger earned 100 pieces-of-eight or one slave.

Henry Morgan

Perhaps the most famous of all buccaneers to emerge during their Jamaican period was the defiant mountebank Welshman, Henry Morgan. Morgan's origins are obscure, but it is generally believed he left Wales for the Caribbean as an indentured laborer, possibly bound first for Barbados. Morgan's achievements would be many, not least of which would be surviving years of ruthless buccaneering before settling down to become a wealthy landowner and governor of Jamaica.

Westmoreland children bathing at roadside falls (Phyllis Luntta)

top: Negril cliffs at sunset (Phyllis Luntta)
middle: sunrise on the beach (Jamaica Tourist Bureau)
bottom: enjoying twilight at Treasure Beach (Phyllis Luntta)

Morgan was a brilliant tactician and daring sea captain, and he won many a battle for Britain as well as booty for himself and his free-spending Port Royal crews. He often earned the displeasure of his English patrons for going overboard, as it were, in his zeal to eliminate the Spanish (and gather treasure for himself). He often sacked inland towns when his commission was to engage ships only on the ocean. He took Puerto Principe in Cuba, and Maracaibo of Venezuela.

Morgan's greatest achievement, and that which cost him his commission, was the sacking of Panama; Spain's then-unequaled achievement in the New World. In that engagement the Spanish, curiously, unleashed 2,000 bulls on Morgan's army during their defense of the city. Yet Morgan triumphed and the taking of prized Panama caused the Spanish to reconsider their regional position—they were angry. Eventually the Spanish negated the Treaty of Madrid, their delicate peace treaty with the British, though it was already largely ignored in the Caribbean. Morgan's actions rankled the British crown, and signaled the beginning of the end of privateering as a sanctioned activity in Britain's war efforts.

Eventually, Morgan regained the favor of Britain and settled in Jamaica as a member of the landed bourgeoisie, soon becoming governor and, ironically, taking up the fight to suppress privateering. "Privateering," he wrote without apparent sarcasm, "is a temptation to the necessitous and unfortunate. I spare no care to put down this growing evil. These privateers discourage Spaniards from private trade with us." It was evident to Morgan that, as Jamaica prospered, trade would increase (and slavery as well) and trading partners such as his old enemy Spain would become most valuable. The times were changing.

Morgan, however, never lost his taste for Port Royal or his excesses. In the end a visitor to his home found him ". . . lean, sallow coloured, his eyes a little yellowish, and belly a little jutting out or prominent. Not being able to abstain from company, much given to drinking and staying up late." When the then-Sir Henry Morgan died in August 1688, his body was removed to Port Royal where, four years later, he joined his favorite taverns and the rest of the city in a final, clamorous soiree as the earthquake and great wave washed them to the bottom of the sea.

Pirates

By 1713, the Treaty of Utrecht brought another war to an end, the War of the Spanish Succession. Fought mainly in Europe, the war was sparked by the death of Spain's heirless Charles II, and had pitted France and Spain against England and the Netherlands in a familiar battle for land and trade rights. The treaty terms deprived Spain of its European possessions, and England was awarded France's *asiento,* or contract for supplying slaves to Spain's Caribbean possessions. Jamaica's excellent location provided a convenient center for England's slave trade.

All was not well, however, with the erstwhile privateers, now increasingly known as pirates. With their city swallowed by the sea and loss of official encouragement from Britain, many began to carry on their activities against ships of all nations, plundering and ravaging their way to infamy. They attacked slave ships, adding continued abduction and confusion to the already miserable plight of the displaced Africans. They made no friends and many enemies. Out of necessity pirates became more cunning, more ruthless, but no less colorful than their sanctioned predecessors, the buccaneers.

The notorious Edward Teach, or "Blackbeard," stands out among them. Said to have fought with flaming matches tied into his flowing black beard and hair, either for effect or at the ready to light cannons at a moment's notice, he was eventually killed in 1718 in a sea battle off the coast of the present-day U.S. state of North Carolina.

Eccentric Jack Rackham, "Calico Jack," was said to have received his name from his inclination for calico (cotton) underclothes. After plying his pirate's trade in the area for years, he was captured at Negril Bay while indulging in a rum binge. He was tried along with two of his more distinguished and surprising associates, captains Mary Read and Anne Bonney. Calico Jack was executed and his body suspended in an iron cage on a tiny islet near Port Royal, still called Rackham's Cay. The women escaped execution by convenient pregnancies. Read later succumbed to fever while in prison. Bonney seems to have mended her ways, and disappears from history thereafter.

Other pirates continued to ply their trade but suffered continued aggravation at the hands of the British and other authorities. They once had sailed the Caribbean with sanctioned purpose and bravado; now they were hunted like the criminals they had become.

And On

The end of the 17th and early 18th centuries saw wars, skirmishes, and varying alliances between Britain, France, and Spain, with valiant defenses by Jamaica's colonists.

The American War of Independence weakened Jamaica's position by diverting British attention to the northern conflict. With Spain and France in the wings waiting to recoup their valuable Caribbean losses, Jamaica was wary and vulnerable. Even at that, the Jamaica House of Assembly threw its support, at least in principal, to the American rebels via a petition to King George. When the British forces surrendered in 1781, their only remaining colonies in the West Indies were Jamaica, Barbados, and Antigua.

The colony continued to be ravaged by hurricanes, disease, and slave resistance, particularly in the form of the burgeoning and rebellious Maroons. However, agriculture boomed and Jamaica was well on its way to becoming one of Britain's important remaining possessions.

The introduction of hundreds of thousands of enslaved Africans and their West African cultures had and still has a profound effect on Jamaica's history and development. While wars were fought and treaties signed, and pirates had their heyday, the slaves of Jamaica continually served their European masters the plate of discontent. In so doing they shaped their future and the future of their reluctantly adopted country.

PLANTATIONS AND SLAVES

Of the crops grown and exported from Jamaica during its early history, cocoa (in Jamaica, also the name of the tree), sugar, tobacco, and cotton prevailed. As well, Jamaica produced 70% of England's indigo dye. Sugar, introduced in 1640, was by far the most lucrative of Jamaica's early exports.

Having taken its cue from the early successes of the sugar industry in Barbados, Jamaica, some 25 times larger than its Caribbean neighbor, soon surpassed it in output. The process would culminate in the 19th century when Jamaica would become the world's premier producer of raw sugar. To accomplish this output, labor was needed, and the labor was African.

In 1673 the population of Jamaica was 17,272, of whom 10,000 were black. By the end of the century the island's total population was over 47,000 of whom 40,000 were black; virtually all of them were slaves. For those 27 years, the white population had remained unchanged while the slave population increased fourfold, a necessity for increasing the wealth of Jamaica's plantation owners. The ownership of numerous slaves also became a status symbol.

The slave trade itself was abhorrent—rife

Bed-stocks served as punishment for intoxication.

NATIONAL LIBRARY OF JAMAICA

with corruption, theft, death, and savage brutality. Some of the transported Africans were slaves before they ever entered the heat and stench-filled bowels of the cargo ships. Often prisoners of war, they were sold by local chiefs in treacherous deals with Europeans. Slave traders also deceptively fanned the flames of old tribal conflicts in the hope of creating wars to bolster the slave supply. But by far the preferred method was to organize raids on villages with the sole purpose of gathering flesh, much like one would organize an animal hunt.

If the hapless Africans survived the manacled march to the African coast, where they would be stored in forts awaiting the arrival of slave ships, many more would not survive the appalling "middle passage" to the West Indies. Dehydration, starvation, and disease awaited them during the often 12-week trip. And it was only the beginning of their humiliation and loss of dignity. On arrival, they were often stripped naked to exhibit their "stock" to potential buyers, then branded by the new owner.

Slave Society

While sugarcane was the beast that pulled the slave-trade cart, it wasn't long before the presence of slaves dominated every aspect of Jamaican society. By far the greatest number were field workers, a backbreaking and grinding labor. But slaves also built roads and plantation houses, cared for children, learned trades, fished and hunted for their masters, slept with them as well, and, in short, built the Jamaican physical infrastructure.

With the expansion of sugar plantations, the need for accelerated slave importation became clear. It was calculated that it took a slave three years to be "broken in" and become productive, and that some slaves, the old and infirm or the very young, were not productive at all. Planters could expect six deaths to occur for every live birth among slaves, as well as other deaths under the lash or from exposure and severe living conditions. Indeed, mortality was high; from 1700 to 1810, about 600,000 slaves were exported to Jamaica, yet in 1834, the year of the British Emancipation Act, the slave population was 250,000.

Plantations, some as large as small villages, had strict codes and rules. Plantation masters were allowed a great deal of discretion in how they handled their slaves, who were regularly and harshly punished with the hope that severe treatment would nip ideas of rebellion in the bud. With such a disproportionate number of slaves to Europeans, planters were constantly concerned about slave uprisings. Hanging, burning alive, and beheading were commonly practiced in the early slave days. Eventually, revisions in the slave codes regulated the masters' whips and brought punishment under greater control.

Saturday afternoons were reserved for slaves to cultivate maize, yams, and other small provisions on land provided by their masters. They would consume some and sell the rest at Sunday market, saving the small amount they earned with the hope of perhaps someday buying their freedom, which was a master's right to grant. Above all, it became important to Jamaica's future that slaves were allowed to cultivate and sustain themselves on Jamaican soil. The folly of relying on imported food became evident during the American War for Independence when, as food supplies to the West Indies were cut off, 15,000 slaves died of starvation.

Later, with the importation of Captain Bligh's breadfruit from Polynesia as well as the introduction of slave foods to the planter's diets, Jamaica began to divert from its strictly European fare. Today the *yabba* (an earthenware pot), and *calabash* (a gourd used to store food or water), as well as the national dish of saltfish and the fruit *ackee,* owe their origins to slave diets (see "Eating and Drinking," p. 69).

The majority of slaves delivered to Jamaica came from a disparate array of West African cultural and linguistic groups, including the Wolof, Fulani, Yoruba, and Ibo (from today's West Africa). While some food, customs, legends, and even words survived, complete languages did not. English was the only form of efficient communication slaves had with plantation masters, and eventually with each other. English became the medium of communication. However, a few African words and place-names found their way into a language that today has evolved into a melodious and distinctly Jamaican creole (see "Language," p. 43).

Sunday was a free day for slaves, and the spirited Sunday market was the place to be. Converging for the sale or trade of plantains, yams, maize, melons, and other produce, as well as small farm stock such as goats and chickens, thousands would banter, barter, gossip, and live the celebratory moment of freedom. The market custom still exists today in virtually all towns and population centers, though the growth of Christianity has moved market days to Friday and Saturday.

The slaves' lot in early Jamaica was grim by any standards. At the whim of churlish masters, deprived of stable family life and often as close to death as farmyard animals (a common view of blacks then), loss of freedom was only one of their many sufferings. Yet they did not go easily to their kismet, nor were they without supporters. Church missionaries, often Moravian, Methodist, Presbyterian, and Baptist, spent time with slaves as teachers and preachers, and were early allies. They would later be instrumental in advocating the abolition of slavery in England.

As well, slavery had constant resistance from within. Contrary to some stereotypes of the time, slaves were not docile and eager for the attention of white masters. Their resistance began in Africa, hence the chains and shackles, and continued in their new world with farm sabotage (breaking tools), mass suicides and, the most common, desertion. Often anger grew to revolt.

From the moment the Spanish first released their slaves, the Maroons, at the onset of the British invasion, blacks had offered violent redress for the anguish of their lives. The ultimate irony may be that the very slave revolts feared by the planters became reality as a result of the terror they imposed on the slaves to suppress those revolts.

REBELLIONS AND MORE REBELLIONS

The Maroons

The word Maroon had come from the Spanish *cimarron,* meaning "wild" or "savage." These first groups of free Africans fled to the hills and settled there for centuries, developing their own culture and living off the land and plunder from increasingly numerous plantation raids. They were not peaceful, and were as dedicated to outwitting and raising havoc with the British as the British were to enslaving or eliminating them.

Over the years they received runaway slaves into their ranks regularly. The Maroons developed intricate systems of guerilla warfare, striking at night and devising an early-warning system utilizing the *abeng* horn to warn their villages of impending attacks. As their numbers grew, so did their daring, as did the planters' fears.

In 1663, so numerous and persistent were the Maroons that they were offered a deal by the authorities: surrender and receive full freedom and parcels of land. This they refused, and in so doing made it more or less official. The government of Jamaica was at war with the Maroons.

Among slaves and Maroons of the time, ethnic differences were still strong and recognized. The oral tradition carried history; *anancy* (traditional tales) were told, and Africa and its heroes were remembered. The Ashanti group from Africa's Gold Coast were considered to be fierce, cunning, and brave. It was no surprise that from them emerged Cudjoe, leader of the Maroon War of 1729. Cudjoe, sometimes Kojo (an Ashanti name assigned to male children born on Monday), and his followers vowed either freedom from the British enslavement threat, or death.

The Maroon War was bloody and protracted. Cudjoe and his guerilla tactics proved superior in the hills of the Cockpit Country, as did his compatriot Quao of the Blue Hills Maroons. The British fell victim to heat exhaustion, inexperience, and clever ruses by the blacks. Finally the British, in fear of losing more lives and money in the engagement, proposed a peace treaty. After 10 years of fighting, a blood-signed treaty gave the Maroons a measure of freedom and autonomy never before seen by Africans in the New World. The main terms of the treaty allowed the Maroons to govern themselves in their own communities and main settlements of Moore Town, Nanny Town, Charles Town, Scotts Hall, and Accompong Town. Cudjoe would become the leader of Trelawny Town, and the Maroons would continue to hunt, fish, and farm unmolested on Maroon land. In return, the Maroons agreed to cease hostilities against the British, refuse sanctuary to escaped slaves, and assist the government in suppressing local uprisings or foreign invasions.

It was the last provision that caused the government to call upon the Maroons in 1760. In

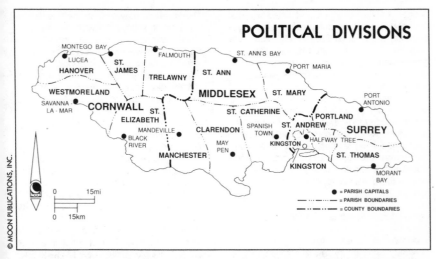

POLITICAL DIVISIONS

MONTEGO BAY
LUCEA
FALMOUTH
ST. ANN'S BAY
HANOVER
ST. JAMES
PORT MARIA
TRELAWNY
ST. ANN
WESTMORELAND
MIDDLESEX
ST. MARY
PORT ANTONIO
SAVANNA LA - MAR
CORNWALL
ST. ELIZABETH
ST. CATHERINE
PORTLAND
MANDEVILLE
CLARENDON
SPANISH TOWN
ST. ANDREW
SURREY
BLACK RIVER
MAY PEN
KINGSTON
HALFWAY TREE
MANCHESTER
KINGSTON
ST. THOMAS
MORANT BAY

0   15mi
0   15km

● = PARISH CAPITALS
—·—·—· = PARISH BOUNDARIES
—··—··— = COUNTY BOUNDARIES

© MOON PUBLICATIONS, INC.

that year the first and most critical of a series of slave rebellions broke out.

It was Tacky's Rebellion, an uprising secretly planned throughout the island among the Coromantees, another Gold Coast group. Tacky, a tribal ruler and the rebellion's chief strategist, gathered a small group near Port Maria, St. Mary, and embarked on a juggernaut of violence that eventually saw over a thousand slaves desert island plantations. They moved across the island, killing planters as they slept, burning homes, and creating the anarchy needed for a full-blown rebellion.

The British militia was called up and they, in turn, called on the Scott's Hall Maroons. After six months of running battles, the Maroons had got the best of Tacky's followers, and the uprising began to fall apart. Many of the discouraged slaves fled the rebellion, returning to their plantations. The tenacious but doomed Tacky was finally killed in battle by a Maroon marksman. Many of Tacky's remaining followers committed suicide rather than submit to slavery again.

In all, 60 whites were killed during the course of the rebellion. With heavy-handed vengeance, the Jamaican authorities demonstrated their increasing paranoia by brutally executing 600 slaves.

Other slave rebellions followed with increasing frequency in Jamaica as well as the rest of the Caribbean, most notably St. Domingue (now called Haiti). A sense of black identity and power was growing throughout the area, and the authority of whites had been eroded during the Haitian Revolution of the late 1700s. It was the only successful slave uprising in Caribbean history, with the black general Toussaint L'Ouverture becoming the first leader of a free black state in the New World. This development, of course, was as inspirational to slaves as it was mightily worrisome for Jamaican planters. They were again experiencing strife at home.

A second Maroon War broke out in 1795. Ostensibly, it was over the flogging of two Trelawny Maroons at Falmouth for stealing pigs. While the sentences, administered under court order, were not particularly severe, the real damage was psychological. The flogging was said to have been carried out and observed by Montego Bay slaves, some of the very people the Maroons had helped recapture as runaways in the first Maroon War. The free and proud Maroons were incensed. Violence broke out in Trelawny Town.

The Maroons, masters of hit-and-run bush warfare, held on for five months in the untamed Cockpit Country before the governor was able to devise a plan. The plan was dogs. A shipload of the lunging beasts was deployed from Cuba, where dogs were commonly used to hunt runaway slaves and criminals. The Maroons, who could outrun militia and outwit the planters, knew they were beaten. The dogs could navigate by scent rather than direction, and would be equal to the twists and convoluted paths of the largely unmapped Cockpit Country. But before the dogs were unleashed, the Maroons capitulated and negotiated a peace settlement that included assurances by the British to let them stay on their land. Later, contrary to terms of the settlement, over 500 Trelawny Maroons were deported to Nova Scotia and then to Sierra Leone, where they became the first group of New World Africans to be relocated to Africa.

The remaining Maroons would never again rise against the Jamaican government. They would quickly become, though still inspirational and symbolic of slave resistance, a legend.

REFORM AND LIBERATION

The Impetus For Change

The early 19th century saw sweeping changes in the world's political systems, changes that signaled the beginning of the end of slavery in the Americas.

The philosophy of the French Revolution had provided the impetus for successful revolution in Haiti. Similar uprisings in Barbados (involving 13,000 slaves), Trinidad, and Antigua rattled the planter establishment and fueled slave confidence. Nascent pressure for abolition of the institution had grown into organized movements, and by 1807 antislavery activists had succeeded in passing laws to make slave trade illegal.

Though it shied away from the question of full freedom, the early antislavery movement in England was successful in publicizing the plight of slaves. Laws were passed revising plantation masters' rights to administer brutal punishments. By the time the movement grew to include abolition in its vocabulary, Jamaican planters were vehemently opposed. The sugar industry, which would peak in 1814 with over 34 million pounds produced, relied on slave labor more than ever.

The year 1831 saw Nat Turner, the slave preacher, lead a group of men throughout the U.S. state of Virginia, freeing other slaves and waging war against whites. That same year, the last and most serious slave revolt in Jamaica's history would predate the abolition of slavery there by just a few years.

Three days after Christmas in 1831, a relaxed time for whites, the signal was given for slaves of Kensington Estate, near Montego Bay, to set fire to plantation work houses. By nightfall on the same day, local rebellion leaders had taken charge of over 20,000 deserted slaves, marching through the countryside, blowing horns to signal freedom, and burning the homes of planters.

Their leader was Sam Sharpe, an articulate, literate Baptist preacher who had organized the rebellion among his four parishes under the guise of nightly prayer meetings. Eventually, his army gained control of all the plantations on the island and the governor was forced to declare a state of martial law.

Manley and Bustamante at the Jamaica Constitutional Conference, 1962

NATIONAL LIBRARY OF JAMAICA

Finally, using the ruse that the British Parliament had just abolished slavery, the governor persuaded the slaves to lay down their weapons. He promised full pardon, but with the slaves in custody, the whites exacted a barbaric vengeance that would shock the mother country. While only 14 whites had been killed in the two-week rebellion, thousands of Jamaican slaves were hanged, shot, and whipped to death. Sam Sharpe, a national hero today, was reported to have said, "I would rather die a slave upon yonder gallows than live in slavery."

He would get his wish, but the accounts of atrocities witnessed in the aftermath of Sharpe's rebellion would be received with revulsion in England, and would help push the abolitionist cause to the forefront. On 1 Aug. 1834, the British Parliament legislated to abolish slavery in all its colonies and protectorates.

Emancipation

The 1834 announcement of emancipation was greeted with whoops and whistles, jubilation, and hope. But the joy was brief when slaves realized that compensation had been paid to their masters, and that they were required to serve four-year apprenticeships before realizing complete freedom.

Thereafter, Jamaica's sugar industry and plantation way of life slowly died. Sugar importers found it cheaper to buy from Cuba and Brazil, where slave labor was still used. Soon, many blacks left the plantations and took to the hills, engaging in farming and agrarian activities. Some learned skills, some migrated to Central America to work on the construction of railroads, yet others remained on the plantations as wage workers. All comprised what was quickly becoming a new peasant class in the country. The mulatto, or mixed race, class began to steadily emerge, an initially displaced group that did not show a great penchant for agricultural work and tended to identify with white culture and values. The merchant Jews, who were quickly buying up land and failed plantations, emerged as another layer in the complicated racial and class structure that exists even today. For a while, the planters imported indentured labor from Asia to replace the vacancies created by free blacks. From 1834 to 1865, over 6,000 East Indians were brought to Jamaica. The infusion may have contributed to the cause of a nationwide cholera epidemic in 1850; 32,000 died.

To bolster the island's faltering economy and keep the new masses in check, tax laws were passed that discriminated against blacks. Land was withheld. In court, "justice" was a only a word for many blacks, especially in disputing land claims against whites. While slaves were free, slave mentality among both groups lingered.

Eventually the new, rather seething society that was Jamaica was bound to lose its temper. It came in the form of the 1865 Morant Bay Rebellion, led by freed slave Paul Bogle evoking the oath, "Cleave to the Black, Colour for Colour," and a call to kill all whites. Because it was a rebellion by freed blacks, it would become a national symbol (and Bogle a national hero) of strength against white oppression. The rebellion was also significant in that it formed part of the basis for a philosophy that would later emerge as black nationalism and the Rastafari movement (see "Ras Tafari," p. 48).

A number of whites were killed, and then-Governor Eyre put the rebellion down with numbing severity, again with the help of local Maroons. Over 1,000 blacks were executed and hundreds more whipped. Bogle himself was hanged aboard a British ship. William Gordon, a leading mixed-race politician and alleged co-conspirator, was also hanged. An outcry in England led to the governor's removal, and the Jamaican Assembly, previously a voice of autonomy on the island, came under fire. Britain exercised its power and Jamaica became a full crown colony under England's rule in 1865.

By 1872, a decision was made to move the expanding capital from Spanish Town to the more convenient and strategic Kingston. The city survived a number of late 19th- and early 20th-century fires and earthquakes, growing rapidly as the tide of urbanism drew poor blacks to the city's promise of work. The colonial governors still wielded considerable power on the island during the early 1900s. During this period the world grew in industrial acumen, and in most countries a working class emerged. The working class was often poor, often a majority and, in Jamaica's case, had no political power.

THE 20TH CENTURY

Toward Independence

The face of the world changed, radically, after

WW I. No longer innocent or isolated, countries like Jamaica saw and experienced worldwide movements that espoused human rights, personal dignity, and the formulation of political parties.

By 1938 the Great Depression had, as well, taken its toll. It was estimated that only 18% of Jamaica's population earned any income at all, and 92% of those earned less than the equivalent of US$6 (in 1938 dollars) per week. Unemployment was almost universal and the population was growing rapidly, continuing the urban flow. The banana crop of that year was wasted by disease. The economic clefts between the whites, blacks, and so-called "browns" (persons of mixed race or other race) were large. The now-famous Marcus Garvey (see p. 49) had been preaching his popular brand of black nationalism for years, and was a source of inspiration to blacks the world over. The country had reached a boiling point, and the desperate conditions sparked islandwide riots and strikes, concentrated in the sugar estates and Kingston docks. The riots were put down, but the message had been delivered: Jamaica's blacks would fight for political power.

The immediate result of the 1938 riots was the British governor's recognition of local leaders and organizers. From these leaders emerged Jamaica's first and strongest political parties.

Alexander Bustamante, the son of an Irish father and a mixed-race mother, formed the Bustamante Industrial Trade Union (BITU), one of the first organized labor unions in Jamaica. Fair-skinned, well-educated, and articulate, Bustamante had earlier changed his surname from Clarke, claiming Spanish ancestry. Not lacking in charisma or confidence, Bustamante appointed himself president-for-life of the union and published a weekly newsletter with his picture on the front of each issue.

The other strong leader to emerge was Norman Washington Manley, a cousin and ally of Bustamante's. A lawyer and proponent of self-government and universal suffrage, his People's National Party (PNP) was an early wing of the BITU.

Differences between the two men, both philosophical and personal, caused a rift when Bustamante was detained by British authorities for over a year for his work with local labor unions. Eventually the PNP, having grown to an estimated 20,000 members, split from the larger BITU. It continued to press for representative government and suffrage under the intellectual Manley. The BITU transformed from a union to a political party, the Jamaica Labour Party (JLP), with the brash Bustamante as head.

By 1944 the British had conceded and Jamaica was given a new constitution that provided for universal adult suffrage and an elected house of representatives. For the first election of those representatives, the PNP and JLP were the two major opponents, with third parties and independents on the fringes. Bustamante's JLP won a resounding house victory with more than 41% of the vote. In 1959, when Britain relinquished complete control of Jamaica's internal affairs and called for full elections, it was Norman Manley of the PNP who emerged as the first prime minister.

The Daily Gleaner

Further assertion of Jamaica's not-yet-granted independence came with its withdrawal from the Federation of the West Indies, an alliance of British Caribbean dependents. The Federation had been formed in 1958. Jamaica was granted only one-third of the federation's representation, yet had more than half the territories' population. Jamaicans believed this to be unfair and, in a 1961 national referendum, voted to withdraw. This signal for independence was stronger than ever and apparently convincing. With the blessing of the British crown, and with much circumstance and a visit by Princess Margaret, Jamaica became an independent nation on 6 Aug. 1962. Elections promptly were called.

Recent History

Emerging as independent Jamaica's first prime minister was now-Sir Alexander Bustamante of the JLP. In 1967, another JLP candidate, Hugh Shearer, became prime minister. It is notable that, then and today, most of Jamaica's political leaders have come from the white and mixed-race (or brown) upper-class socioeconomic stratum. The mixed-race class historically has been associated with white culture and values. It is not unlikely that this similar cultural—and thus political—identity aided Jamaica in gaining its independence with little resistance from the crown. With its eye toward investment, Britain would have been sure to encourage minimal divergence from Western-style democracy and, in so doing, encourage like-thinking individuals in their rise to political power.

During the first years of independence, Jamaica saw its economy grow rapidly with the world's demand for its highly prized and priced bauxite, a mineral used in the production of aluminum. Yet the rich got richer and large amounts of illegal capital found its way out of the country, to the detriment of the economy and the lower classes. With the economy as an election platform staple, the JLP and PNP continued to play political tag until the election of Michael Manley, son of Norman Manley (d. 1969), as party successor and prime minister in 1972.

Manley's PNP was much more radical than his father's, reacting, perhaps, to a different world. He adopted closer ties to Cuba and left-leaning governments. He called his form of government "democratic socialism" and alarmed foreign investors, many of whom withdrew or scaled down investment. Manley encouraged the working class by establishing new minimum wages and job security for pregnant women.

The recession of the mid-'70s hit hard in Jamaica. Professionals and laborers alike began to migrate, particularly to the U.S. and Canada, seeking income security. The middle-class Chinese-Jamaican community emigrated in staggering numbers. The poor became destitute. Yet the PNP won an even larger majority in the turbulent 1976 election. Finally, Manley was forced to go to the International Monetary Fund (IMF) for assistance. When the IMF demanded rigorous restructuring of Jamaica's government spending in 1980, Manley balked and called for new elections.

It was during these elections that Jamaica gained its reputation for often vicious and bilateral campaign violence. Kingston was the worst hit. Hundreds died, with areas of the city sectioned off, marked as PNP or JLP zones. From this election, the JLP emerged victorious with well-known trade unionist Edward Seaga as prime minister. (See "Recent Elections" in the following "Government" section.)

GOVERNMENT

Jamaica's political canvas has always had a British hue, the result of over 300 years of colonial rule. Its traditions and many of its institutions borrow directly from the old country, not the least of which is the recognition of the British monarch as the titular head of state.

Yet Jamaican political discourse is truly Jamaican in both content and conduct. One of the oldest and healthiest democracies in the Caribbean, Jamaica is feisty and singular in its political passion, and capable of drawing worldwide attention. Jamaican politics have been fought on all levels: on political platforms, at rallies of 100,000 or more, in the vigorous free press, on stages with reggae stars, and, in the past, with guns on Kingston streets.

The System

Jamaica is an independent member of the Commonwealth of Nations. Its 1962 constitution decrees that the British monarch is officially head of state, represented in Jamaica by a Jamaican, officially nonpartisan governor general. Commonly referred to as the "GG" by locals, the governor general has a largely ceremonial role, not the least of which is adding a bit of circumstance to political proceedings.

Real power is vested in the winning political party, headed by a prime minister. Unlike U.S. politics, in which candidates, although party-affiliated, are the focal point of an election, Jamaicans vote for and elect a party. After the election, the leader of the winning party is appointed prime minister. While there is no doubt that candidate charisma and personality play an important part in the election process, party ties ultimately decide outcomes.

The Jamaican Parliament is bicameral, comprised of the legislative House of Representatives and Senate chambers. The Senate has 21 members, 13 of whom are recommended by the prime minister and appointed by the governor general. The remaining eight are recommended by the parliament opposition leader. The House of Representatives is made up of as many as 60 members elected for five-year terms. Universal adult suffrage guarantees all Jamaicans age 18 and up the right to vote. Voters come from constituencies in the 14 political divisions—the parishes and corporate areas of Kingston and St. Andrew.

The House of Representatives wields considerable power, even the power to override Senate votes. The prime minister is empowered by his selection of cabinet ministers, as well as his party's majority in the House and Senate. Changes in Jamaica's constitution are made only by a two-thirds majority vote in each house of Parliament.

Jamaica's judicial system also has its roots in British common law. It incorporates a supreme court, a court of appeals, magistrates' courts, and lower courts. Local government is administered by parish councils, one in each of the country's 14 parishes.

Jamaica's multiparty system is guaranteed by the constitution yet the nation has birthed, in effect, just two major political parties: the Jamaica Labour Party (JLP) and the People's National Party (PNP).

The JLP and PNP are not officially class oriented, though their leadership has been dominated by mixed-race members of Jamaica's middle class. (In fact, three of Jamaica's first four prime ministers were from the same family.) Early philosophies championed by the founding party leaders—the blustery Alexander Bustamante of the JLP and quiet, erudite Norman Manley of the PNP—tended to attract certain interest groups. While the JLP advocated grassroots, working-class values, the early PNP was the middle-class, urban, intellectual party; yet it still attracted workers. The JLP has often represented itself as the free-enterprise party while the PNP has in the past endorsed a moderate socialism. Those philosophies have changed and adapted over the years. There have been, of course, variations on each theme and many congruent ideologies and policies by successive governments.

In addition to its membership in the Commonwealth of Nations, Jamaica belongs to the Organization of American States (OAS), the Caribbean Common Market (CARICOM), and the United Nations (UN).

Party Time

Jamaican political parties tend to be fraught

with strong partisan ideology and almost fanatical followings. Some Jamaicans, as evidenced by the troubled 1976 and 1980 elections, take personal and party politics seriously enough to come to violence over them. It is worth noting that tourists have rarely been involved in political turmoil, which has generally been in areas of Kingston's densely populated urban slums.

The 1980 election, in which over 700 people were killed in sectarian violence, and the 1989 election, which saw less potent confrontation, are recent examples of the often turbulent Jamaican political scene.

Recent Elections

The PNP held the government reigns for eight years, beginning in 1972. By 1979, the popular government under Michael Manley found itself over US$148 million in debt. Ongoing JLP and PNP clashes escalated when Manley, beset by a severely crippled economy sparked by increased prices of imported oil and the illegal flow of money from Jamaica, called for parliamentary elections in Oct. 1980, two years before the end of his term.

Both the PNP and JLP took to the streets in their election campaigns. The PNP's open relationship with Cuba was a focal point of the JLP's campaign leaflets—"Communists Capture the PNP" was a typical sentiment. When Manley announced Jamaica's decision to break with the International Monetary Fund (IMF) in March of that year, existing internal PNP divisions were exacerbated, and street violence increased. Graffiti artists of the time suggested that IMF stood for "Is Manley Fault." An extreme right-wing group of the Jamaica Defense Force (JDF), led by Charles Johnson, staged an unsuccessful coup attempt.

While previous elections had earned the JLP a reputation for extreme confrontation, this time both parties managed to stir differences to a boil in the teeming Jamaican slums. From Feb.-Oct. 1980, residents of the poor Kingston neighborhoods of Trench Town, Olympic Gardens, and surrounding areas were exposed to the nightly uproar of weapons fire. The euphemistically dubbed political "muscle" of each party, really just thugs, roamed the streets spray-painting slogans and intimidating residents. PNP areas were besieged; JLP neighborhoods huddled in fear. Accusations of CIA, KGB, Cuban, and communist involvement were leveled against each other by both parties. Ads appeared in local daily newspapers offering rewards for information leading to the conviction of shooters and gun smugglers—Manley and Edward Seaga, the JLP leader, both had shots fired at them. The restructured JDF was often called out to lend support to the overwhelmed police forces, especially during rallies and demonstrations. International attention was riveted on Jamaica.

Yet when elections finally did take place, over 80% of the country's electorate took to the polls, though the streets of ravaged Kingston were understandably deserted. A few polling stations never opened and ballot-stuffing was reported by

*Norman Manley
with demonstrators*

both parties. The JLP and Seaga won a landslide victory, and the PNP retreated for the next round of what would prove to be campaigns without incident.

Seaga

The Boston-born, Harvard-educated Edward Seaga took a much more moderate line than his predecessor and rewarded his conservative allies, many in the U.S., with major reversals of Manley's socialist policies. For this, Jamaica received generous U.S. financial aid. Seaga broke relations with Cuba, and later joined the U.S. in the 1983 invasion of neighboring Grenada.

In 1983 Seaga called for snap elections, a result of his continuing loss of popularity and a declining economy. His support of the Grenada invasion and the dissolution of diplomatic ties with Cuba had inspired many in the area to dub him the "Caribbean Reagan." Seaga called the snap election while opposition leader Michael Manley was out of the country, and was accused of calling elections before the new voter registration had been completed, setting into motion a number of events that led to a boycott of the elections by the PNP. When the election was won by the JLP, the party was without opposition, and Jamaica effectively became a one-party state.

By 1988 the economy was on the rise, yet the Seaga government was losing popularity quickly. Renegotiating the national debt with the IMF had forced strong austerity measures on Jamaica, which affected the country's poor—about 80% of the 2.4 million population. Seaga himself was long on intellect and talent but short on charisma, a vital element in Jamaican politics. And of course Manley's PNP had been agitating.

Elections were called and the populist Manley won an easy landslide victory. Passions were high but violence was sporadic and of little consequence, perhaps because the two parties had moved slightly closer in ideology. More to the point, the PNP had moved closer to the right. In his inaugural address, Manley claimed to have changed his political philosophy during the '80s, and claimed he was now a "mainstream realist." At his 1989 swearing-in Manley said, "We are an island but we are not alone. Therefore, we must explore the world around us, take advantage of what it can offer, and exploit the opportunities which it provides for those with enterprise and initiative."

Promising conciliatory and constructive engagement with the West, the man who had once vowed to demolish capitalism brick by brick again took charge of an energized Jamaica.

By early 1992, ill health had taken its toll on Michael Manley, and he resigned his post as prime minister. Into his shoes stepped longtime PNP party affiliate and former deputy prime minister Percival James Patterson, or P.J. Patterson, as he is known. Patterson was distinguished not only as a 30-year veteran of Jamaica politics but also as the nation's first black prime minister.

ECONOMY

The heyday of Jamaica's sugar industry ended with the dark days of slavery. By the late 20th century, sugar had greatly diminished as the bedrock of the Gross Domestic Product (GDP). Sugar profits had provided great wealth for plantation barons of old, most of whom lived in splendor in England. But exported monies did little for the Jamaican economy, and, at a time when infrastructure and government were being built, private estates had taken much of it away. Continued private and foreign ownership of large Jamaican corporations and industries has increased the flow of money from the country, forcing some government intervention in private industry.

Jamaica was once considered the brightest economic star in the Caribbean. Today Jamaica is a poor country, despite the boomtown surge of its economy from 1960-73, the years immediately prior to and after independence. The 1987 GDP was equivalent to about US$2.9 billion, or US$1160 per person. In 1988, imports totalled US$1.4 billion while export income was reported at US$821 million, a discouraging disparity. Today, roughly one-fourth of Jamaica's work force is unemployed and about one-third of the employed are involved in the agricultural sector. Until independence in 1962, many workers migrated to Great Britain seeking better wages. Since British immigration restrictions were implemented that same year, many Jamaican workers have migrated to the urban sprawls of the U.S. and Canada.

With relentlessly mounting foreign debt and heavy payments for imported services, Jamaica continually faces the discouraging, nearly impossible task of building homegrown industries to meet the pressures of providing services for the poor, especially the urban poor. A liberalization of foreign-exchange regulations and a deregulation of the banking industry in 1990 were aimed at attracting foreign exchange to Jamaica at competitive rates. That worked for a short time, but set off a buying war among banks that saw the Jamaican dollar fluctuate wildly against foreign currencies. The Jamaican-to-U.S.-dollar ratio went from about 7-1 in 1990, to almost 30-1 by 1992. This, of course, was a good turn of events for tourists with access to U.S. dollars, but was devastating for Jamaicans on low incomes. Local businesspeople stepped in and offered to buy large quantities of Jamaican currency at a fixed rate to help stabilize the fluctuation.

Sugar and later bauxite were once mainstays in the Jamaican economy. Today tourism has become the number-one foreign-exchange earner, yet it's unclear whether it can spawn enough industry to provide for Jamaica's people.

Jamaica's infrastructure is equipped to cope with growth in tourism as well as the rest of the economy. There are over 200 miles of railroad track, over 7,800 miles of primary and 2,800 miles of secondary roads, 16 ports (the largest at Kingston), and two major airports (at Montego Bay and Kingston).

BAUXITE

For nearly 30 years Jamaica's rich bauxite deposits were the foundation of the country's economy. Discovered in the late 1800s, bauxite was mined sporadically until WW II when the ore, used in producing alumina and aluminum, was in great demand. During the 1970s bauxite provided half of Jamaica's export income. By 1975, Jamaica accounted for 14% of the world's bauxite production and was the fourth-largest producer in the world. Foreign companies, such as Reynolds and Kaiser Aluminum, owned large percentages of the mining operations. In fact,

when Michael Manley's PNP came to power in 1972, the bauxite industry was totally foreign owned.

True to the socialist policies of his PNP, Manley engineered the nationalization of the bauxite industry by forcing private companies to sell a 51% interest to the government. He also introduced a bauxite levy that fixed the price of the mineral at a percentage of the price of an aluminum ingot, rectifying a long-standing system of lowered price-fixing and tax evasion by the conglomerates. These measures increased bauxite revenues considerably, but could not save the industry from an approaching worldwide slump.

By the late '70s bauxite production by competitors, notably Australia and Brazil, outpaced Jamaica's. Increased production decreased worldwide aluminum prices. By 1980 bauxite production accounted for 9% of Jamaica's GDP; by 1985 Jamaica mined only about 7% of the world's bauxite, even though it has sufficient reserves to last well into the next century. By 1990, however, the world's demand for bauxite took a strong upturn. That year's bauxite industry income of US$600 million ranked as the second-highest foreign-exchange earner in Jamaica. The first was tourism.

An obstacle to the processing of Jamaica's bauxite is the industry's reliance on cheap power. Nearly all the island's power comes from imported oil, a commodity that only seldom has decreased in price in the last 20 years. As well, the high-tech bauxite industry is not labor intensive and employs few Jamaicans. Currently fewer than 10,000 Jamaicans are employed in the industry.

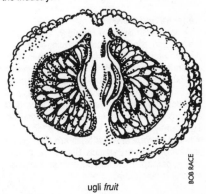

ugli *fruit*

BOB RACE

AGRICULTURE

Over one-third of the employed in Jamaica work in the agricultural sector, the majority in the sugar industry. But Jamaica's long history of subsistence farming by slaves as well as encouragement of plantation-size farms has resulted in a diverse, though not wholly profitable, food-exporting industry.

Historically, Jamaican planters grew crops for export and did little for the production of locally consumed foodstuffs. They let slaves, soon to become free peasantry, fend for themselves with small plots and antiquated farming methods. The tradition continued well into the 20th century. Today Jamaican peasants still farm small plots while large plantations export massive quantities of food, and the country imports food items such as rice and flour for local consumption. Even with efforts by successive governments to check the increase in imports and encourage home-grown foodstuffs, the import bill has risen to over US$600 million.

Sugar
Sugar, once the country's most important cash crop, has been edged from its berth by a fickle world taste for the sweet stuff, as well as by fluctuating economies. The world price of sugar dropped drastically in the early '80s, and Jamaica has not been able to keep up with cost-efficient methods of production, including competing internationally with sugar extracted from sugar beets. Yet the industry remains the single largest employer in Jamaica.

Bananas And More
The Jamaican banana industry, the world's largest until the mid-'30s, has slipped in production recently. Other farm products include coconuts, cocoa, beef, poultry, pork, pimento (allspice), ginger, and premium coffee under the Blue Mountain label. Rum, an offshoot of the sugar industry, is an important local product and export. It flows freely everywhere, it seems, like slightly expensive water with a kick. The hybrid *ortanique* and *ugli* fruits are also grown and exported from Jamaica. But the most celebrated, perhaps most infamous, of all Jamaican exports is marijuana.

Marijuana
The counterculture of America's turbulent '60s engendered a profitable international trade in marijuana. Jamaica was in the forefront, competing with Mexico and Colombia to provide the youthful, beaded iconoclasts with fuel for their dissent. The trade goes on today, continuing Jamaica's 100-year tradition of marijuana cultivation.

Indentured East Indian laborers, brought over to prop up the failing mid-19th-century sugar plantations, carried with them the literal seeds of Jamaica's current marijuana industry. Ganja—Indian hemp, sinsemilla ("ses," the highest grade, in a manner of speaking), pot, cannabis, *calley, bangi,* and other names—was used by the Indians as a medicinal household remedy since ancient times. Use of the easily grown weed caught on among black field workers and the lower economic classes. It soon became an elixir of sorts, company to workers in the harsh labor environments of the fields and mines. Today, though illegal, ganja use is widespread in Jamaican culture, having been incorporated into Rastafarian life and working-class Jamaica. (Rastas and members of the offshoot Ethiopian Zion Coptic Church use it, well, religiously. See "Ras Tafari," p. 48.)

Small-scale farmers grow it, smoke it, drink it as a medicinal tonic, steam it with vegetables, ingest it in cakes, apply it externally, and often sell it. Up to 60% of Jamaica's population uses the soporific herb, with the belief that it can contribute to the cure of colds, stomach disorders, fever, rheumatism, and a host of common ailments.

Large-scale farmers, however, export ganja, though not in the volume they once did. Until the mid-'80s, Jamaica supplied as much as 10% of the U.S. ganga market, an annual trade value of an estimated US$1 billion. The figure is deceptive, however, since much of the profit remains outside Jamaica. Nevertheless, the ganja trade has been big, supported by thousands of large farms and often investments by the island's wealthy upper class. The government's past tacit tolerance of the ganja industry has fostered involvement by doctors, lawyers, and other professionals, even police and some politicians.

Since 1986, however, a government-sponsored marijuana education and eradication program claims to have eliminated up to 70% of Jamaica's ganja production. The U.S. State

Department estimated that ganja smuggling fell to 460 metric tons in 1987, from 1,755 metric tons in 1986. The result was that Jamaica fell to the number-three spot, behind Colombia and Mexico, as a foreign supplier of marijuana to the U.S. A further result has been the economic crunch felt by Jamaica's peasantry, already deprived of income under harsh economic conditions.

The anti-ganja drive has been supported by both of Jamaica's political parties, the PNP and JLP, and is not likely to abate in the near future, despite some intense pro-ganja lobbying. The careers of some smugglers have been diverted to the profit-laden cocaine trade, using Jamaica's ideal location and now often unused illegal airstrips as a stop-off in the South America-to-U.S. drug route. This prompted a call by former prime minister Michael Manley for an international drug-fighting task force, a call that was met with approval, though some questioned the feasibility of such a force.

Nevertheless, a visitor to Jamaica today would be hard-pressed not to see evidence of ganja or, for that matter, other drugs. Small roadside stands that sell beer and soft drinks can be counted on to have the herb available under the counter. It's often sold in conical "spliffs," also called skliffs, not unlike midget ice cream cones of rolled paper and ganja. Patrons of rural bars and beer joints smoke and offer it openly. Young men wave small green baggies at tourists as they drive through the outer districts of towns and cities, particularly tourist-dense Montego Bay.

While ganja is entrenched and certainly available, remember that it is illegal and punishable. Stiff fines and penalties are enforced: three to five years with hard labor for possession; 10 years for cultivation; and more for smuggling. It is a criminal offense to occupy premises used in the preparation, smoking, or selling of the drug, as well as to possess smoking paraphernalia. Police are known to set up road blocks to make spot checks for drugs and other illegal items. Believe this: You do not want to spend time in a Jamaican jail.

TOURISM

Tourism has eclipsed all other industries as Jamaica's number-one foreign-exchange earner.

Approximately 1.4 million tourists visited Jamaica in 1992 (a record year) and the government seems committed to the growth and development of the industry. Tourism numbers appear to be growing at a steady rate of more than 7% per year, including, incredibly, a reported increase of nearly 26% during 1991-92. The Jamaica Tourist Board (JTB) has actively expanded and has six offices throughout the country, as well as numerous overseas agencies.

The natural beauty of Jamaica's coastlines and interior, its proximity to North America, and, let's not kid ourselves, its readily available party substances, have made Jamaica a popular destination for Americans and Canadians searching for an unusual experience. The government has indicated that it will now vigorously court the European market, which former prime minister Michael Manley described as "presenting tremendous opportunities for the future of the tourism industry in Jamaica." For some it seems that tourism *is* the future of Jamaica, the one industry that has succeeded where others have required bolstering by foreign aid and loans.

In 1988 Hurricane Gilbert struck the island, leaving 45 dead and nearly 80% of the country's homes without roofs. Yet it is testimony to Jamaica's appeal that the next year was the best ever in the tourism sector.

Tourism began its indirect ascent to the top of Jamaica's economy via another path, the agricultural sector. An American sea captain, Lorenzo Dow Baker, head of the Boston Fruit Company (later United Fruit), began to bring American visitors to Port Antonio aboard his banana boats around the turn of this century. As world communications and travel improved worldwide, so did tourism industries the world over. By the mid-'60s tourism was a fact of life in Jamaica, and the industry doubled its revenue by the mid-'70s. Some attribute this to the burgeoning "tune in, turn on, drop out" attitude of the times; for others it was the allure of popular music and musicians such as Harry Belafonte, and later Bob Marley and the Wailers; for others still it was the result of a more affluent and mobile world.

If there is a deterrent to Jamaica's tourism at all, it is the reputation of some of the country's more aggressive souvenir higglers (vendors), hustlers, and ganja dealers. As in any place where the poor remain on the outskirts of a money-intensive industry, there will be those who try to cash in on the quick dollar. Young men in tourist centers such as Montego Bay will offer to take you to attractions, become your personal guide, get you anything you want—for a price. A direct and polite "no" works most often, unless, of course, there is in fact something you want. But the aggressiveness has been seen as harassment by enough tourists for the government to recently invest almost US$1 million in tourism-training seminars and programs for managers and workers in all levels of the tourism industry, as well as a public-education program for all Jamaicans. There is even talk of introducing tourism as a subject in grade schools. Billboards peppered about major towns encourage Jamaicans to "Treat Our Tourists Right." In select, tourist-dense areas special "tourist cops"—members of the constabulary—walk the streets, their aim to curtail the hectoring of visitors.

MANUFACTURING

Manufacturing accounted for about one-sixth of Jamaica's GDP in the mid-'80s. Despite the fact that most of Jamaica's goods are still imported, industry has grown over the years. Companies, mostly foreign owned, must import most raw materials, machines, and components to produce the country's manufactured goods. Those goods—processed foods, beverages, textiles, paper products, chemicals, some tools, glass, and assembled clothes and other products—generally remain for domestic consumption or are exported to Jamaica's trade partners in the Caribbean Common Market (CARICOM). Other processed and exported items are sugar, bauxite, cement, petroleum, alumina, gypsum, and silica.

In addition to CARICOM, Jamaica's chief trading partners are the U.S., U.K., Canada, Trinidad and Tobago, and Japan.

FILM

Jamaica's small but increasingly significant film industry centers around the growing number of foreign filmmakers that have been using the country as a location for Jamaican and other generic island environments since the '60s. The film industry has grown over the years, with the production of movies or parts of movies such as *Live and Let Die, Dr. No, 20,000 Leagues Under the Sea,* and *Papillon* all filmed in parts of Jamaica. In the '80s, Port Antonio drew filmmakers in droves. A small cottage industry has developed in that town for locals playing bit parts in movies such as *Clara's Heart, Cocktail, The Mighty Quinn, Treasure Island,* and *Club Paradise,* which starred Robin Williams and Jamaica's Jimmy Cliff. Music videos, including a well-known one featuring Jamaican dancehall artist Shabba Ranks with Eddie Murphy, also have been shot in Jamaica.

Other movies such as *The Harder They Come,* starring Jimmy Cliff as a Kingston rudeboy, and *The Lunatic,* adapted from writer Anthony Winkler's tale of a madman and a German tourist, are set in Jamaica and have Jamaican themes. More recently, *Wide Sargasso Sea,* a steamy tale set in post-emancipation Jamaica, was filmed in Montego Bay and Falmouth.

U.S.-based televison shows, such as the soap *As The World Turns,* have used Jamaica for island scenes that are no doubt fraught with the shows' unerring sense of hackneyed romanticism—but don't hold that against Jamaica. The defunct series *Going to Extremes* was shot entirely at St. Ann's Bay on the north coast, employing about 150 local actors and 5,000 extras.

According to Jamaica Film Office officials, movie and television production brought in revenues totalling US$30 million during 1990-92.

JAMAICA'S PEOPLE

Out Of Many, One People
—Jamaica's national motto

Currently 2.4 million people live in Jamaica. That number will reach 2.6 million by the year 2000 and is expected to approach three million in the year 2020. The country's population growth rate is low and will continue to slow down to about 5% by the turn of the century, primarily due to migration. Migration was particularly high in the '60s and late '80s due to rough economic conditions. (Over a million Jamaicans live overseas, most in the U.S., Canada, and the U.K.) Slightly more women than men are born in Jamaica; population density is 570 persons per square mile. Roughly 700,000 people (and growing), or 28% of the population, crowd the streets of Kingston and St. Andrew. The most populous parish outside of Kingston is St. Catherine, with 359,000 inhabitants; the least populous is tiny Hanover, with a population of 66,000. Urban dwellers account for roughly one-half of Jamaica's people. Currently, over 40 towns are classified as "urban Jamaica," including the Kingston metro area.

AFRICANS

The cultural, political, and economic milieu that is Jamaica today emerged from the culture produced by slavery. The question of whether Jamaica should be called an African-Caribbean culture, simply a Caribbean culture, or even a third-world culture is one that semanticists can and will wrestle with for years. But the observable fact is that today over 95% of the "one people" who have emerged from Jamaica's "many" are of African descent.

Africans In Jamaica

For over a century after the true emancipation of slaves in 1838, the color bar existed in subtle and not-so-subtle ways. Blacks were discriminated against in court, in education, and in job opportunities. Illiteracy among blacks was high. Europeans remained the landowners and ruling class, and a slave mentality lingered.

Plantation masters consorted with slaves and produced offspring. The West Indian whites were often fairly responsible with their mulatto children, sending them to school in England, and allowing them a special place in the household. It was clear that these offspring were between two worlds racially and culturally, but their elevated status among slaves and later freemen became the basis for a bizarre system of color denial and racial classification, not unlike that which prevailed in the U.S. and, until recently, in South Africa. In essence, the whiter the better. A person called a mulatto, a common word today for any degree of mixed race, could be classified as musteefino, octaroon, quadroon, mulatto, or sambo, depending on the imbuement of black heritage (one-sixteenth, one-eighth, one-fourth, one-half, and three-fourths, respectively). A popular water pitcher sold to former slaves after emancipation depicted a dark woman holding a light child, with the inscription "My Fada's hope,

18th-century West Indies newspaper advertisements

My Moda's joy, My Pretty Little Creole Boy."

The emergence of a mixed-race group gave rise to a loyal middle class in post-emancipation Jamaica. Eager to please, browns were considered by whites to be more able in the offices and middle management of industry and trade. Culturally, they often identified with whites and white values. Blacks, ever the "strong backs," remained, most often, just that.

The turn-of-the-century rise of Jamaican black nationalism and its proponent Marcus Garvey, and later the emergence of Rastafarianism (see "Ras Tafari" p. 48), boosted Jamaican blacks' sense of identity. Skin-lightening creams and hair-straightening techniques are largely things of the past. Yet white bias exists in undercurrents, as does racial tension. Social programs and education for the country's poor have steadily improved, often sponsored by church organizations. However, as late as the mid-'70s, none of the 42 companies listed in the Jamaican Stock Exchange were controlled by blacks. Of that year's 219 listed directorships, 125 fell into the hands of 21 white and Chinese families. Until 1992, none of Jamaica's prime ministers had been black.

Culture

African cultures remain strong in Jamaica. Most aspects of Caribbean cultures—religions, family and social structures, verbal and nonverbal communication systems, sense of time, world view—are beliefs and practices formed from old-world systems combined with values acquired in the New World. Only in this cultural hodgepodge could a God-loving Christian consult with an herbalist about both health and magic.

The Africans of Jamaica came from a disparate array of primarily West African ethnic groups. After capture, they were held a number of times in a number of places in both Africa and the Caribbean before being shipped and sold. This jumble resulted in language and cultural confusion, and plantation owners further attempted, unsuccessfully, to suppress remnants of their slaves' former lives by separation and the banishment of language, dance, and folk practices. Yet the music, speech, and dance of Jamaica today reflect strong African heritage.

During the period just after emancipation, 1840-65, some 8,000 Africans were brought to Jamaica as laborers to help bolster the failing sugar plantations. They were indentured but free, and came from the Yoruba and Congo groups. Settling mainly in St. Thomas and Portland, they did much to help revitalize existing African cultural practices.

Anancy, or *anansi,* folktales are among the strongest verbal survivors of Africa. Originating from Africa's west coast, the character Anancy appears as a human at times, but more often as a clever and witty spider in the Jamaican versions. Traditionally told at night, these tales have been used as bedtime stories for children, often made up by parents as they go along. In slave days, Anancy was often the clever and sarcastic antagonist of the plantation master, frustrating his violence and saving slaves from perilous situations. In stories told around the evening camp fire, Anancy represented the triumphs of slaves, even in a small way, over the incredible burden of their lives. Anancy tales have changed over the years, and the tradition is slowly giving way to television and other evening activities. Louise Bennett, "Miss Lou," one of Jamaica's leading authorities on Anancy tales, has numerous books of Anancy tales available at stores throughout the country.

Maroons

After many relocations and dispersals, the fighting Maroons have settled in four principal towns: Scott's Hall, St. Mary; Moore Town and Charles Town, Portland; and Accompong, St. Elizabeth.

Accompong, named after the brother of the great Maroon leader Cudjoe, is the only Maroon town on the west side of the island. The Trelawny Maroons, deported in 1795 after the Second Maroon Rebellion, left behind their settlement, Trelawny Town, which was destroyed by British soldiers. When it was resettled, it was called Maroon Town, but is that in name only. On the east side, Moore Town is the main Maroon town.

The Maroons retain some autonomy in Jamaica, nominally as separate states. They are governed internally, electing a colonel as head of state, and arbitrate most disputes among themselves. Maroons retain certain deep African customs, such as the use of herbs and folk medicines, and communication with the *abeng,* or bull's horn. There is, reportedly, an arcane and mystical African language used only by Maroons.

Accompong and Moore Town are not wholly

open towns. This comes from their long tradition of autonomy. If you wish to visit, you should go with a guide, someone who knows the colonel. Visit the colonel first and allow someone from town, possibly the colonel himself, to show you around. Lately, the trappings of bad tourism have affected the Maroon towns, and tipping for tours might be expected (see "The Southwest Coast," p. 123).

OTHER ETHNIC GROUPS

British
British systems still dominate government, law, education, and, in some instances, culture. The language of institutions is the Queen's English, where schedules are "shedules" and the spare tyre is in the boot of the car, which is driven on the left. The local language, Patois, is many things but not wholly English. The imperial system of measurements is still largely in place even though the British gave it up years ago. Holidays and events such as Boxing Day (the day after Christmas), cricket matches, and numerous visits by the British royal family attest to the British influence. A small percentage of white Jamaicans of British ancestry work in private industry and government, and still own plantations.

Germans
About 1,200 Germans arrived in Jamaica between 1834-38, again as indentured laborers to help bolster the now slave-less plantations. They settled in various parts of the country and worked the plantations, but a small group of 251 moved to the plantation of one Lord Seaford, located in Westmoreland. Seaford didn't give them much in the way of money or their own land, and before long they were living in numbing poverty, with no way to get back home. Their number dwindled to just over 100 within two or three years after their arrival. Yet they stayed.

Today's Seaford Town is still home to about 200 descendants of the original Germans. They are part of the town's heritage and culture, and, in many striking cases, racial homogeny has been maintained. Names like Hacker, Grosskopf, Reimann, and Schleifer are common. The people are farmers and live and work

alongside Jamaicans of African descent. Patois is spoken and most have little recollection of the German language.

Visit the Seaford Town Historical Mini-Museum for an interesting look at this historical anomaly (see "The Southwest Coast," p. 123).

East Indians
East Indians, over 90% Hindus, were also brought to Jamaica as indentured laborers, or "coolies." Indian immigration continued into the 20th century, and today they constitute one of the largest ethnic minorities in the country. The culture is strong and Indians still celebrate ethnic holidays such as October's Deewali (Festival of Lights). A small Moslem community exists here also. Many Indians, however, have been Christian converts for some generations.

Indian influence has spilled over and mingled with Jamaican popular culture. The famous curry dishes, particularly curried goat, are served in most small restaurants. Ganja is an Indian import, as is the word itself. Indian settlements concentrate around old sugar plantation lands and in towns where Indians are often part of the small merchant class. As do many minority groups, large numbers of Indians have settled in Kingston.

Chinese
The Chinese, less than 1% of the population, have contributed significantly to the racial spectrum of the country since the first groups were brought in during the 1840s as part of the British plan to fortify labor forces in post-emancipation Jamaica. A small immigration flow then followed and today the Chinese are prominent in commerce and as restaurateurs.

Lebanese
A small group, again less than 1% of the population, the Lebanese arrived around the turn of the century as small general dealers, many involved in cloth and apparel merchandizing. Today they far outweigh their numbers in economic impact, and many have built literal business dynasties. Jamaicans refer to the group as "Syrians," due to their Middle East origins. (In the 1890s, at the time of their first arrival, the Lebanese district was still ruled by the Ottoman Empire and the area was referred to as Syria.)

Jews

About one-fourth of 1% of the population is Jewish. Again, their influence is felt beyond the numbers. The first Jews in Jamaica were Spanish and Portuguese, and arrived covertly after fleeing the religious persecution of the Spanish Inquisition. They attained full political and religious rights under the British, and have since served in numerous assembly and parliamentary roles.

Jamaican Jews are primarily white, but the obvious similarities between Rastafarianism and Judaism are worth noting. Like Jews, Rastafarians read and interpret the Bible, observe strict dietary rules (often stricter than kosher laws), and look to Zion (Ethiopia) for redemption. They consider themselves (Africans) one of the lost tribes of Israel, and desire an earthly manifestation of the Messiah (see "Ras Tafari," p. 48). Beyond this, of course, they are different and neither group makes much of their similarities.

The United Congregation of Israelites in downtown Kingston is the only synagogue in Jamaica.

JAMAICAN LIFE

Children And Families

Statistically, more girls are born in Jamaica than boys. Therefore, the *average* Jamaican child would be born a poor girl in a rural area. She'd be raised by a woman—her mother or, if the mother has had to take a job elsewhere, an aunt or grandmother. Her mother would have good postnatal care available to her and access to contraceptives. Her father will contribute to her support, visit, and maintain a relationship with her mother, but he may have relationships and children elsewhere. He may, at some point, move in with her mother or even marry her. If, however, her father and mother are married they are more than likely to stay that way and not divorce.

Rural families may have electricity, but would not have a telephone or tap water. Tap water is usually collected at outside taps. Women learn to cook in outdoor kitchens, often over an open fire.

The scenario for boys would be much the same, until they enter school.

Education

School children must take competitive examinations for placement as there are more students than available spaces, at all levels. Schooling is paid for by the government unless a parent chooses to send a child to a private institution. Girls are most likely to complete primary school and quit at that point, though education is compulsory until the age of 14 (Jamaica boasts a literacy rate of 73%). If they don't quit, they are more likely to complete the secondary (high school) level than boys, and less likely to make it to university. Rather than go on to a university, a young woman often attains another type of tertiary education in, for example, nursing, agricultural college, or secretarial school.

Work And Play

Many young men not educated beyond primary school drift from manual job to manual job as drivers, construction workers, and menial hotel staff. An average wage can be as little as US$20 per week. Some will fish or farm and sell to the hotels. Some might sell ganja for decidedly bigger profits. A woman might go to work in a hotel or resort, or as a clerk in a small shop. If she finishes secondary school she might clerk in a bank or hold a middle-management secretarial position, or earn as much as US$2,500 per year as a trained teacher. Women are almost twice as likely as men to be unemployed.

Young adults have an active social life surrounded largely by people of the same sex. Free time is spent listening to reggae and dancehall music, or participating in church activities. Girls are less likely to drink or smoke.

Conduct

Visitors to Jamaica can avoid stepping on cultural toes and everything else by hiding in resorts where the only Jamaicans they'll meet are those safely trained to smile and project the "No Problem" attitude of the posters and T-shirts. That is a vacation. But to get out of the confines of a hotel and experience Jamaicans, their country, and their problems, that is travel.

If your interest in Jamaicans is genuine, it will usually be reciprocated with warmth and open exchange. Of course, the open exchange can be rather pointed, like a verbal probe, but rapport is not hard to establish.

Many higglers (vendors) and hustlers know

that your pockets are lined with a small bit of their future, and will do their best to help you spend it in their direction. Montego Bay is well known for the aggressiveness of its hustlers. Kingston, interestingly, is an aggressive city in other ways, but visitors are relatively free to walk about without a hassle. If you are interested, by all means talk; if you are not, a polite "No, thanks" works. If they persist, here is where you are free to persist and politely decline again. Don't be intimidated; it's a game where you're already the winner before it starts as long as you maintain your dignity and cool and allow the hustlers to do the same. People may try to lead you into their shops. You don't have to go. A typical hustle: A man walks up to you and says, "Don't you remember me from the hotel? I'm the bartender." This is to open up a dialogue during which he will propose to "show you around," for a large tip. Ask him which hotel he is referring to, and he'll either know because he is telling the truth, or will have to guess from dozens. End of game.

In conversation, Jamaicans are less quick than Americans to start using first names. Using "mister" and "missus" or "miss" helps in establishing rapport.

It is not unusual for people, especially children, to shout at passing cars and buses, usually in the country. At Caucasians they might shout "white" or "white boy," and this shouldn't be cause for alarm. Overweight people might be identified as "bigger" or the succinct "fat." It is not always meant as an insult (although of course it can be), rather just as recognition. And it's something to shout.

You are free to bargain in street-vending situations. However, the women in fruit- and vegetable-market stalls are generally asking a fair price and won't try to rip you off (see "Shopping," p. 74; and "Getting Around," p. 88).

You will notice that most men and women in Jamaica dress conservatively, even at the beach. Skimpy bathing suits in public will only engender stares and cat-calls. Some restaurants have dress codes that are generally of the "shirts, shoes, no bathing suits" type. Topless and nude sunbathing is ostensibly restricted to certain beaches, though topless is tolerated in many places.

Tipping is expected and appreciated in all the same places it is at home. Usually 10-15%

will cover it, but be sure to read the menu or hotel bill for this: "A 10% service charge is included in the price." That 10% is a tip. You can add more if you feel the service warrants it. At Sangster International Airport in Montego Bay, where you will likely arrive, there are scads of porters who will carry your bags. If you change your money at the airport (you should do this as soon as possible), about US$1 should be plenty.

Jamaicans are understandably wary about having their pictures taken—too many anthropologists and travel-book writers over the years. Please ask first. Some people want money and if the photo means enough to you, pay for it.

Begging is common in towns and contributing to this is a personal choice. For some hustlers it is a game to play with tourists; for others it's a way of life. It is a harsh reality, but giving money to a beggar will do the same for Jamaica's poverty that spitting into the ocean will do for the tide.

LANGUAGE

Languages are the pedigree of nations.
  —Samuel Johnson (1709-84), British lexicographer, Tour to the Hebrides

Mek wi go.

  —"Let's go," an example of Jamaican Patois

Jamaica isn't in any danger of losing its language; rather, the *language* is in danger of losing the visitor. The rapid tongue- and grammar-twisting turns and dips of the language you hear occur just prior to the final "mon," possibly the only word you will understand in the phrase. But Jamaican Patois is a lyrical, very listenable language with color and depth, and no little history.

Again, slavery sets the tone, so to speak. English evolved as the pragmatic plantation language, but slave pidgin developed over generations to include bits of Portuguese, Spanish, and the West African languages Twi, Ewe, and Akan, an Ashanti language. English dominates Patois, but its grammar and vocabulary are far from today's standard English.

Pronunciation and intonation of English words emulate West African languages. The "th" sound becomes "d" or "t." Then "that" becomes "dat," or "three" becomes "tree," which is also a "tree." Thus, the "rat of God" is not our heavenly rodent friend, but the rage of the Almighty.

"Dem," as in "them," is added to a noun to make it plural as in "de pen dem," or "the pens." The "tl" sound in "bottle" becomes "bokkle." At times the "w" and "h" sounds are dropped from the beginning of a word, and "woman" is said "ooman," "him" becomes "im."

The pronoun "me" simplifies English's "I" and "me" and the possessive "my" to standard usage. "Me broke me toot" is "I broke my tooth." In the same manner "him" is "he," "she," or "it," and the possessives "his" or "hers."

Try this: "Me put 'im likkle bokkle ina cyar over dere" ("I put his/her little bottle in the car over there").

Jamaican Patois did not evolve as a written language but is now often written in novels, plays, *anancy* tales, and songs. The spelling leans toward the phonetic, but that is not always the case—"de bway" or "di bwoy" are both "the boy." In spelling, as in the language, the real rule is that personal preference dictates usage. Jamaicans can and will use varying degrees of Patois depending on those they talk to or, more accurately, those they want to understand them. In the hills and rural areas, Patois is deep; some people speak little or no stan-

SAMPLE JAMAICAN VOCABULARY

Jamaican Patois, like any language, is dynamic and prone to regional influences. Therefore, not all the sample words below are in use in all social situations, nor in all parts of the country.

Many Jamaican words are juxtapositions or variations in spelling and pronunciation of standard English. For example, "fambly" for family, "flim" for film, "dung" for down, and "cerfiticket" for certificate are often, but not always, discernible in the context of the sentence.

Bold italics are words used primarily by Rastafarians. Some standard English spelling is used here for purposes of comprehension, but keep in mind that the often wildly variable phonetic spelling is more common throughout the country.

arm-stick—crutch

backra, buckra—white person; whites; in slave days, term used to address white master

bankra—basket

banggarang—great noise or disturbance

batty—backside, anus

belly-god—glutton

bex—vex or vexed

big-belly—reference to the condition of being pregnant ("belly," "belly woman"); greedy

blind oat(h)—a lie

blood clot(h)—sanitary napkin

bra—brother

bredda—brother

bredren—brothers, not necessarily blood brothers but in the faith

bride—woman about to be or newly married, but can also refer to the bridegroom

bring come—bring it here

bulla—small sugar cake

bumbo— a strong invective referring to the backside, bottom

chalice—chillum, pipe used to smoke ganja

coodeh—exclamation meaning "look at that!"

cranky—sickly, in poor health

cris—"crisp," top-notch, superlative

cutchie—communal smoking pipe

cut-eye—the act of "cutting" one's eye at someone as an act of scorn or insult

daughter—said by a male to mean either daughter or woman friend

dig second—put a car into second gear to get up a hill, etc.

dege-dege—small, skimpy, as in portions

downpressor—oppressor

drunk, drunken—as well as usual meaning, to drown or half-drown by keeping in water too long

dutchie—heavy cooking pot

continued

dard English. In towns and business, especially among tourists and upper-class Jamaicans, Patois loses its edge; decreolization, or varying degrees of reverting to English, takes place as Jamaicans move toward social situations where the use of standard English is expected.

The vocabulary of Patois incorporates some English of the 17th century, words that the English themselves no longer use. A goblet? A large drinking glass. A chain? If a Jamaican says something is a chain or two down the road, it is not in reference to supermarkets. A chain is an Old English unit of measurement used by surveyors (66 feet, or 22 yards).

Unlike North American culture, polite discourse with a married woman often begins with "mistress," not "missus," even though "Mrs." is an abbreviation for "mistress." Confusing? Of course.

Hundreds of words with African origins have been recorded in Jamaican Patois. Many, like *duppy* and *anancy,* refer to spirits and the supernatural. *Jonkanoo* refers to the custom of masquerade dances. The word for "mud" is *putta-putta,* and some use *nyam,* possibly from the Fulani or Wolof languages of West Africa, meaning "to eat." A person who is a *quashie* is a fool. Place-names like Accompong and Naggo Head (the tribal name of a Yoruba-speaking people) owe their origins to Africa.

Phrases popularized by the tourist industry to project the image of the laid-back, nonchalant Jamaican, such as "soon come," "boonoonoonoos" (a big party), and "no problem" do have

---

fenky-fenky—finicky, fussy

foot—can refer to any part of the leg from the foot to the thigh

galliwasp—lizard that was often the subject of folk tales, incorrectly assumed to be poisonous

ginnal—huckster, untrustworthy person

good-belly—good-natured, kindly

gravalishus—greedy

hackle—hassle, worry

hard—old; also skilled

herb—ganja

hot belly—pain in the belly

I and I, I'n I—we

in (one's) ackee—feeling fit, energetic

irie—state of goodness, something good; now commonly used throughout the country to mean "fine" or "wonderful"

I-tal—natural foods and method of preparing food; natural life

Jah—God; deity referred to by Rastafarians and, in the past, some Maroon and other groups

janga—shrimp or crayfish

kiss me neck—exclamation of surprise; something like, "I'll be darned!"

labrish—gossip

liad—liar

lick—a hit, blow

long-belly—greedy person

maga—thin

make—allow, permit, as in "make a see," or "let me see"

mash—smash, crush, destroy

mashait—machete

natty—dreadlocks, as in "natty dread"

nyam—eat

ongle—only

pear—avocado pear

pickney—child, derived from pickaninny, a denigrating word used for black children in slavery days

quashie—foolish, stupid person

rass—an invective, one of the strongest in the language; also an exclamation of surprise; bottom, backside

ratchet—knife

roots—natural, approved African ways and values; the common people

screw, screw-face—angry; angry face

site up—to see

slack—bawdy, lewd

spliff, skliff—ganja cigarette

waters—drunk, as in "in him waters"

wolf—Rastafarian imposter

their basis in Jamaican Patois. Expressions, proverbs, and uniquely Jamaican place-names have evolved into colorful additions to the language. "Walk good" (standard English spelling) can be said as a farewell. "Cockroach no business a chicken yard" is telling someone to mind their own business. The small towns of Wait-A-Bit (from the wait-a-bit thorn bush of Africa, thought to have been brought by slaves), Quick Step, and Big Bottom tell their own stories.

One of the more versatile Jamaican words is *rass*, a good one to use judiciously. Originally it was derriere, and it still is, but it now can be a superlative ("a rass of a boat"), a term of endearment among friends ("Hey, rass, buy me nex drink"), or a straightforward cuss ("him a lying rass," or "dat rass dog"). It has, of course, an obvious English equivalent.

The special language of the Rastas has contributed more than a few words to Patois. A basic and central principle for this language, which has no definitive rules, is the emphasis of "I" for "I" and "me," and "I and I," sometimes "I 'n I," for the plural "we." The use of "I" establishes a relationship with both Haile Selassie—the Rasta greeting "Haile" is pronounced "eye-li"—and the self. Hence I-tal, or natural food preparation. Bob Marley's female backup group, featuring his wife Rita and two others, was called the I-Three's. The "I" is often substituted in words for emphasis, as in "I-thiopia." Rastas may refer to themselves or to Rastafarianism as "Rastafar-I." The ubiquitous *irie*, meaning "great, wonderful," has found its way into mainstream Jamaican conversation and onto almost half of the T-shirts in the country.

See the Jamaican vocabulary primer, p. 44, for a longer list of key Jamaican and Rastafarian vocabulary. A number of good language books are available in bookstores throughout the country, some funny, some profane, others serious studies. One of the best, though academic and expensive to boot, is *A Dictionary of Jamaican English* by Frederic Cassidy and R.B. LePage. The best current treatment, written in layperson's terms, is *Understanding Jamaican Patois* by L. Emilie Adams, available in most Jamaican bookstores (see the "Booklist," p. 211, for others).

RELIGIONS

Religious activity, in both the loose and strict sense of the word, is vigorously alive in Jamaica. From the days the Arawaks had their *zemis* (personal spirits) replaced by the preferred spirits of the Spanish, the Holy Trinity et al., religion has been the mover and, in many cases, the potent shaker of lives in the bizarre balance between ancient beliefs and the new.

Faith moves Jamaicans. On Saturdays and Sundays the churches fill to capacity; it is a spectacle of bright colors, pulpit fury, Bible-waving, and sonorous, exuberant walls of sound that would gratify any god.

CHRISTIANITY

More than three-fourths of Jamaica's population claim membership in a Christian religion. The Anglican Church of Jamaica, formerly the Church of England, has one of the highest totes on its tally board. It is also one of the oldest established religions in the country. Since 1655, when the British ousted the Spanish and their Catholicism, the Anglican Church has dominated. The country was divided into parishes by the Anglicans, who were also the ruling class. Each parish was given a church, sometimes one of the largest structures in the division. Although many parishes have replaced and modified the churches, today they can still be seen towering over buildings in the parish capitals.

Baptists

The Baptist Church first came to Jamaica after the American War For Independence, when defeated Tories came to settle in Jamaica during the 1780s. Former slaves from America came with them and brought their own brand of anti-slavery Baptist preachers, adding to the anxiety of the plantation class. The first mission to minister to slaves was set up at Adelphi village in St. James, at the invitation of a Quaker plantation owner. Because of its antislavery stance, the Baptist Church grew quickly in popularity among slaves and free blacks. Today, the church and the offshoot Native Baptist Church boast high membership.

Catholicism

The Roman Catholic Church arrived with Columbus in 1494, becoming the first established Christian religion in the country. With the British takeover of 1655, Catholicism went underground and didn't resurface until 1792, when Catholics were allowed to practice again. Today Roman Catholic churches can be found in almost every major town, and certainly in every parish.

Others

Several churches are represented: Methodist and Moravian (which began its ministry in Jamaica attending to mainly slaves and nonwhites), Quaker, Seventh-Day Adventist, Assemblies of God, and the United Church of Jamaica, to name a few. While these churches are not found in every town, they are adequately represented throughout the country.

CULTS

The slaves, of course, had brought their own religions with them from West Africa. Most were animistic, a word derived from the Latin *anima*, or soul. Popular in Africa and parts of Asia and the South Pacific, animism is a loosely defined set of practices based on the belief that spirits and souls are quasi-physical entities that can exist independent of human bodies and experiences. Animists believe that this root life-form is everywhere, inhabiting "inanimate" objects such as stones, water, and the sky. They also believe that spirits of their ancestors, once relieved of their temporal bodies, continue an earthly existence and might inhabit or repossess the living.

Many of the old religions have evolved into syncretic faiths that marry primal beliefs to modern creed and often defy categorization. In 1860-61, the so-called Great Revival swept Jamaica and attracted thousands of converts to Christianity, but in fact fortified religious syncretism. Slaves from different parts of the old country blended their practices with each other and with the rules of the mystical and angry god of the whites, Baptists in particular. The end goal is still redemption and salvation, but the road traveled is uniquely Jamaican.

Revivalism

Revivalism is a generic term for cults that combines the basic tenets of animism with Christianity. It is not spirit worship, but rather the process of using spirits to enhance life. Revivalists meet in small "bands" to perform ceremonies with the hope that worshippers will be possessed by spirits who guide and advise them. The spirits and possessions are brought on by elaborate ceremonial preaching, drumming, frantic dancing, and singing (often Christian hymns). The possessed are known to have seizurelike symptoms: shaking, falling, groaning, and speaking in tongues.

Two popular Jamaican Revivalist cults are the **Pocomania** and **Revival Zion** groups. Though similarities do exist, their differences lie in the spirits they attempt to summon. Pocomania (also Pukkumina and Poco) invokes earthly spirits, while Revival Zion looks to the heavens for spirits, such as angels, saints, and the Holy Spirit. Both cults have leaders: a "captain" in the Revival Zion group and a "shepherd" in Pocomania. If the leader is a woman, she is called "mother" in both groups. The leader of the group can also serve a secular role as an herbalist or magic practitioner. Ceremonies are conducted at "mission," or "seal" grounds, often privately, and for days at a time. Revivalists consecrate mission grounds with candles and food items. Pocomaniacs celebrate feasts at their ceremonies and often use rum and ganja ritually. Because Poco ceremonies are marked by loud and somewhat odd behavior, they are often disdained by other Revivalist groups and, in general, the rest of society.

A well-known Revivalist leader of modern times was the late Kapo, originally Mallica Reynolds, a major Jamaican intuitive artist. He died in Feb. 1989. An eccentric man and fascinating artist, the largest single collection of Kapo's work (65 paintings and sculptures) can be viewed at the National Gallery (see "Kingston," p.141).

Kumina is a Jamaican ancestral-spirit cult believed to be closer to its African roots than any other. The word *kumina* has Bantu language origins, and the words of the ceremony seem to have originated in the Congo region of central and west Africa. Kumina is thought to have been brought by the free Africans who made their way to post-emancipation Jamaica to work the cane fields. This group settled mainly in the eastern parish of St. Thomas, where Kumina is strongest.

Members invoke the spirits of their families as well as other deities, including earth and sky spirits. Spirits in Kumina ritual are sometimes referred to as zombies. Of the hundreds of Kumina spirits at least one, Shango, appears to have the same name as its African counterpart. During the ceremony, members can be possessed by ancestral or other spirits, invoked by ceremonies involving dancing, drumming, and singing. The ceremonies are held to pay respect to dead family members as well as to accompany important family events such as births, marriages, and baptisms. Kumina dances are also held publicly at events such as Independence Day celebrations.

A number of instruments accompany the ritual singing, such as scrapers and shakers. But drumming is most important in Kumina rituals, as the drums are considered to control certain spirit activity. Kumina drumming is today credited with laying down the basic beat that evolved into Jamaica's famous reggae.

Convince

The Convince cult is self-perpetuating in that its practitioners invoke spirits of past persons who belonged to the cult. Spirits, called *bongo* ghosts, may come from Africa or from ancient Jamaican slaves or Maroons. The older the spirit, the more powerful, more so if the spirit practiced obeah (magic) during his or her lifetime. Convince devotees are known as *bongo* men, and are said to hold at least one sacrificial animal ceremony yearly.

Prior to the spirit ceremony, *bongo* men may read Biblical passages, sing Christian songs, and pray. Later, spirits are invoked through dancing and song. Later still, a rather rigorous possession by spirits occurs, with attendant swooning and very physical dancing.

Magic

An underlying ingredient common to all Revivalist and spirit cults is the use of obeah and myal. Both are roughly magic or sorcery through spells, control of *duppies* (ghosts), and the use of herbs and concoctions. Obeah is possibly derived from the West African word *obayi*, meaning sorcerer. The practice has been around since the beginning of slave days, and is today practiced or "worked" illegally, having been banned by the government. Both men and women practitioners are consulted by believers to fix anything from illness to business arrangements to shattered love. If, in the believer's mind, illness and shattered love are in fact caused by supernatural forces, to counteract with the supernatural is only reasonable. But obeah has also been used, by believers, to cause bad luck and even death in enemies. Unless, of course, the enemy fights back with stronger obeah. That is why it's illegal, though there is no practical way to enforce such a law.

Obeahmen and women are sometimes herbalists who work with natural potions and root concoctions. Others are of the "hank of hair, eye of newt" school who hide their bones and blood and practice more surreptitiously. Obeah and a more recent and incongruously named offshoot called "Science," which uses manufactured medicines, are widely practiced, though true numbers of devotees are not available.

Myal is considered to be good magic, where obeah has had a reputation for resulting in evil. That distinction has become less defined over the years as *myal* seems to be dying as a skill. *Myal* was first practiced as almost strictly herbal-based healing by "doctors" who administered to slaves. Later, the solicitation of *duppies* figured strongly in *myal* ceremonies. Today *myal* seems to have been incorporated into the larger revivalist cults, and has largely disappeared from the Jamaican scene.

RAS TAFARI

Princes shall come out of Egypt;
Ethiopia shall soon stretch out her hands unto
*   God.*

—Psalms 68:31

By the rivers of Babylon, there we sat down
And there we wept, when we remembered
*   Zion.*
For the wicked carried us away in captivity
Required of us a song,
But how can we sing King Alpha's song
In a strange land?

—Psalms 137:1-4,
adapted and set to a traditional folk tune

NATIONAL LIBRARY OF JAMAICA

dreadlocked Rastafarian

The uniquely Jamaican Rastafarian movement (sect, religion, cult, political entity) is often maligned, often misunderstood, but definitely popular. Rastafarianism's close associations with ganja and the rhythmic beat of reggae make it attractive to fringe observers with a penchant for partying, who claim membership by growing dreadlocks and lighting the quotidian pipe. Don't be fooled: A good book has more than a cover. The higglers and hustlers you see on the streets draped in Ethiopian national colors, their eyes perhaps a slightly deeper shade of red, may or may not be true Rastas.

The true "brethren," conservatively estimated at over 200,000 worldwide, are a much more complex crowd with a history that has its roots in the earliest days of West Indian slavery. The dreadlocked, serene, Bible-carrying Rasta is the reality of Rastafarianism, as is the militant black consciousness that forms the core of Rasta philosophy. The reggae beat, hip dreadlocks, and ganja may be party material for some, but true Rastas display a keen disregard for "wolves," or Rasta imposters. Rastafarianism is about the Africanism of a displaced people. To understand Rastafarianism, it is necessary to look to a time in Jamaican history when blacks

began, out of necessity, to flex some political muscle.

Black Nationalism And Marcus Garvey

Black nationalism, or the struggle of displaced blacks to find dignified social status, commensurate economic opportunities, and even simple happiness in their countries of forced adoption, is a movement as old as Western slavery itself. From Maroon independence to Paul Bogle's Morant Bay Rebellion, Jamaican blacks have fought with a mixture of political savvy, mystical zeal, and inevitable violence. But long before the Black Consciousness, Black Pride, and Black Power movements of the turbulent '60s, and before inspirational leaders such as Martin Luther King, Jr., and Malcolm X fomented cohesive movements and radical philosophies concerning the future of blacks, one man articulated an awareness movement that was both elementary and doomed. He stands as the philosophical father to all that have followed. His name was Marcus Garvey, and he was Jamaican.

Marcus Moziah Garvey was born in St. Ann's Bay, west of Ocho Rios, in 1887, reportedly the son of a Maroon. The fifth of 11 children, he had an early childhood of almost stultifying poverty, not unlike the lot of most blacks in Jamaica at the time. Yet Garvey showed a talent for writing and public speaking at a young age. In his early teens he moved to Kingston (a move impoverished rural dwellers still make today), where he apprenticed as a printer. In a few years he was considered a master of the skill, knowledge that would serve him well in the heady days of his movement. Garvey was a follower of Ethiopianism, and it was in his early Kingston days he formed his theories of militant black nationalism, the cornerstone of which was redemption of Africans through repatriation to Africa.

Garvey's inspiration and the roots of his "Back To Africa" movement date back to a long history of mixing political and religious thought in Jamaica. Paul Bogle was a Native Baptist preacher who had organized his rebellion under the guise of conducting religious meetings. Sam Sharpe, the leader of the 1831 slave rebellion, inducted his followers into the *myal* cult.

But it was Ethiopianism that became the platform from which Garvey later launched his larger movement. Ethiopia had long held a fascination for displaced Africans in both the U.S. and the Caribbean, with great attention, even obsession, paid to it both historically and in biblical references.

Ethiopia, with Jordan, Palestine, Syria, and Egypt, formed the greatest block of land in which the biblical saga evolved. For centuries Europeans referred to the whole of the African continent as Ethiopia, and to the land now called Ethiopia as the Kingdom of Abyssinia. African fascination with Ethiopia started in the early days of slavery; the first Baptist church in Jamaica, established in 1784, was called the Ethiopian Baptist Church. The fascination grew to embrace all things Ethiopian, including the eventual development of the U.S.-based Ethiopian World Federation and its newspaper, the *Voice of Ethiopia*. It was a fascination that held hope for blacks, a vicarious association with a free and stately place that promised, for some, the only real freedom and heaven on earth.

By 1914, Garvey had established the Universal Negro Improvement Association (UNIA) to promote "the hopes and aspirations of the awakened Negro." He stressed that blacks needed to overcome feelings of inferiority and build upon their own unique and evolving culture, and ultimately return to Africa to redeem their homeland and build a future. Through his weekly newspaper, the *Negro World,* he reached an estimated two million UNIA members in the U.S., in the Caribbean, and around the world. His strong and often eloquent editorials consistently referred to Ethiopia, the land to which blacks should look for redemption. His releases and slogans showed a penchant for directness and modern-day public relations: "One God! One Aim! One Destiny!" and "Africa for Africans At Home and Abroad."

By 1919, Garvey had taken his headquarters to the U.S., where UNIA enjoyed greater support and numbers than in Jamaica. There he launched the Black Star Line, a steamship company to trade between various predominantly black areas, which had the ultimate task of repatriating blacks to Africa. This it did, transporting blacks to join established colonies in Liberia (founded by freed U.S. slaves in 1822), though Garvey himself was never able to make the trip.

Garvey enjoyed many successes. He established the Negro Factories Corporation to aid the development of black-owned businesses. He presided over a 1920 international convention in New York, where he was elected provisional president of Africa and given a somewhat imprecise mandate to end white domination of the continent. He formed the symbolic People's Political Party (PPP), which called for a minimum wage for blacks, social security, land reform, and a Jamaican university, among other goals. It can be said that he formed the first cohesive black-awareness movement of this century. The Black Star Line, however, initially successful and an inspiration to blacks worldwide, eventually became the albatross that dragged him down—to prison, in fact.

Garvey's successes had engendered hostility and fear among both whites and blacks. To whites he was possibly seditious, mobilizing the black race for all manner of mayhem. The *Negro World* newspaper was feared by racists the world over, and in some colonial countries possession of the paper was a crime. On the other hand, to some blacks—integrationists—his repatriation theories were radical and unworkable. To more militant black groups, he was a tepid capitalist. To the trumped-up charges of mail fraud involving the sale of Black Star stock, he was fodder for a racist system.

In 1923 Garvey was jailed in the U.S. after his conviction on the mail-fraud charges. He became both a victim and champion, as there has been little doubt about his innocence, yet UNIA suffered in his absence. The Black Star Line failed and he was ridiculed in both the white U.S. and Jamaican press, which portrayed him as a megalomaniac and addled. Upon his release from prison in 1927, he was deported to Jamaica. By 1934 he had moved his UNIA headquarters to London, where he observed world events such as the Great Depression and the rise of the working classes, including the Jamaican worker riots of 1938. He died in London in 1940, relatively obscure, and his body was returned to Jamaica where he was given a hero's welcome and interment. Garvey is now recognized as a national hero, and the Marcus Garvey Monument stands at the St. Ann's Bay parish library.

The Garvey legacy shows his pride in Africa and Africans. Though he failed in his ultimate goal of repatriating blacks, he kept alive a sub-

*His Imperial Majesty Haile
Selassie met by Mortimer Planno*

the Ethiopian savior. One such reference, found in Revelation 19:16, states, "He has a name written on his cloak and on his thigh, King of Kings, and Lord of Lords." The time had finally come, thought the Garveyites, to place themselves in the hands of their true ruler. His unintended influence was so strong that the first Jamaican followers adopted Selassie's pre-coronation name and called themselves Ras Tafari. Today, members are known as Rastafar-I, Rastafarians, or simply Rastas.

The first organized groups of Rastafarians appeared at a time when those at the bottom of the Jamaican economic heap were struggling for mere survival. The issues confronting poor Jamaicans in the '30s were exorbitant rents, severe economic depression, and a society dominated by race. Rastas were looking toward Haile Selassie for redemption and an end to exploitation during a troubled time ripe for the continued growth of a black-consciousness movement. At the time of Jamaica's independence, virtually all Rastafarians were in the 80% of the population termed as lower class.

One of the first acknowledged Rastafarians was Leonard Percival Howell, a charismatic laborer from West Kingston. He built a substantial following in the capital, then set about the island preaching the emergence of the Redeemer, financing his trip through Haile Selassie photograph sales. His message that Jamaicans' allegiance should be to the King of Kings and not to the King of England inevitably earned him a sedition charge and a two-year jail term. His followers, however, were not deterred and continued meeting under cover. By 1940, the first Rastafarian commune, Pinnacle, was established under the leadership of Howell in an area near Kingston. Howell is credited with much of the early development and determination of the movement from 1930 to 1960. Today, West Kingston is considered the birthplace of Rastafarianism.

Because of their clear anticolonialism message (some Rastas had begun to call themselves Nya men, after the Ugandan anticolonial movement, Nyabingi, which used the slogan "Death To Black and White Oppressors"), the commune suffered raids and police harassment. When several members were imprisoned, the commune was revived and men began to wear their hair like the Masai tribesmen of Kenya,

stantial, organized Jamaican resistance to white domination. He is also credited with the prophecy that kept alive Jamaica's beguilement with Ethiopia. Before he left Jamaica, he is alleged to have told a Kingston crowd to look to Africa, where a black king would be crowned. This man would be the Redeemer.

Rasta Origins

As it happened, in 1930 a black king was crowned not only in Africa, but in Ethiopia. He was Tafari Makonnen, or Ras Tafari ("ras" is an honorific title), prince regent of Ethiopia and son of Ras Makonnen, alleged descendant of King Solomon and the Queen of Sheba. Ras Tafari took the coronation name King Negus Negusta, and later that year, when crowned emperor, he took the throne name Emperor Haile Selassie I, as well as the traditional titles "King of Kings, Lord of Lords, Conquering Lion of the Tribe of Judah."

Selassie's coronation was well publicized and met with profound interest in Jamaica. Followers of the Ethiopia creed found multiple biblical references, as well as Garvey's prophecy, to support their emerging claim that Selassie was indeed the Redeemer, the king of all Africans,

uncut and uncombed. This appearance, both dignified and fearsome, began to earn Rastas the reputation of mystical wildmen, yet their influence and following grew steadily. The term "dreadlocks" was used to describe their matted hair. (Today the term "dread" can also describe a Rasta imposter.) This first commune also began to use ganja ritually and grew it as a cash crop.

Beliefs

A document that found its way into circulation around Kingston in the late '50s, called "The Foundation of the Rastafarian Movement" or simply the "Twenty-One Points," outlines the basic thoughts and philosophy of the Rastas. Since Rastafarianism is largely unorganized, neither a church nor a political party, it relies on these few central beliefs to adhere the faithful to the process. Two central beliefs are: that Haile Selassie, Ras Tafari, was divine, the living God, and chosen to lead Africans throughout the world; and that the African race is Jah's preferred race, and holds a special significance in the world and the Bible.

Haile Selassie—the man—was not without his faults. He was recognized as a harsh despot and his human rights record has been widely criticized. Yet despite this and his exile during the 1936-41 Italian occupation of Ethiopia, and, in fact, despite his overthrow in a 1974 coup and his subsequent death a year later, Rastafarians are unequivocal in their belief that he was the living son of Jah—Jehovah—and that Rastafarianism lives spiritually through his memory. Even his apparent rejection of throngs of chanting Rastas during a state visit to Jamaica in April 1966—he is said to have observed, uncomprehending, the dreadlocked legions from his airplane, and refused to disembark until his safety was guaranteed—did not deter the faithful. Many Rastas believe he was simply overcome by their joy and adulation. The point is, what mattered about Selassie was and remains his fulfillment of the prophecy.

Some Rastas believe that the Bible is the abstracted history of Africans, stolen at the time of enslavement and altered by white masters to deliberately fool and subjugate their slaves. This has led to a profound distrust of Christianity and, of course, white dominance, though some whites have been accepted into some Rasta groups. Especially distasteful to Rastas is the Christian concept of heavenly redemption, or waiting until after death for the rewards of a good life. Rastas believe in heaven on earth.

The expressive and symbolic dreadlocks are the most obvious Rastafarian emblem. Biblically justified by the laws of the Nazarites, which forbade the cutting of hair, and culturally significant among some ethnic groups in Ethiopia and Kenya, dreadlocks are worn by both men and women. The lion image, also an important Rasta symbol from Selassie's title "Lion of the Tribe of Judah," is reproduced by the flowing Rasta dreadlocks and beard.

The ubiquitous Ethiopian national colors—red, gold, and green—are another visible symbol found in clothing, street signs, and on homes throughout Jamaica. True Rastas eschew complicated lifestyles and adhere to dietary laws that stress the natural, or I-tal. The brethren place great significance in the Bible, albeit exercising their prerogative to interpret the book, especially the Old Testament, in a uniquely Rasta way. Rastas consider themselves to be one of the 12 tribes of Israel, descendants of the ancient Hebrews and a chosen people. Ethiopia is "Zion," or heaven. Jamaica and anywhere else not in Ethiopia, as well as the police, the church, and the established order, are collectively "Babylon."

Though Rastafarians are philosophically anti-establishment, some have entered the political arena in recent years. In 1962, Samuel Brown, a Rasta candidate for a West Kingston Parliamentary seat, ran and soundly lost. Ironically, his constituency was among the poorest and most heavily grounded in Rastafarianism, and the winner of the election was white. Yet the election did serve to trigger awareness of Rastafarianism in Jamaica. More recently, the late Rasta reggae great, Bob Marley, himself a victim of politically triggered gunshot wounds, helped conciliate the turbulent politics of 1976 by conducting a "Smile Jamaica" concert. Two days before the show, gunmen burst into his home and shot Marley and members of his entourage with machine guns. The show did go on, and Marley managed to bring candidates Seaga and Manley together later for a peace meeting. Again, when tensions and violence ran high in 1978, Marley brought Prime Minister Manley and JLP leader Seaga together on stage for the "One

Love" concert, a show commemorating the 12th anniversary of Selassie's visit to Jamaica.

Although Rastafarians constitute a small percentage of Jamaica's population, most are young (18-35) and therefore important to the country's politicians. The use of Rasta symbols such as reggae, colors, language, and the championing of radical black nationalism has become standard among campaigning politicos regardless of race.

Some Rastafarian groups reject Western medical treatment, contraception, and legal marriage. Others reject all magic and witchcraft, the eating of pork, secondhand clothes, and physical contact with whites.

The ritual use of ganja is one of the most widely known and controversial Rastafarian symbols. The "herb" is illegal, yet that hasn't deterred Rastas from using it in a sanctified rite. From growing it to preparing it to smoking it through a goat's horn or bamboo pipe known, not surprisingly, as a "chalice," ganja is part of the Rasta image and reality. Yet ganja smoking, ritual or otherwise, does not a Rasta make; just as all ganja users are not Rastas, not all Rastas use ganja.

The special language of the Rastas (see "Language," p. 43) has come to international attention since the '60s in the form of reggae music. Reggae, a product of (among other musical forms) the fast, rhythmic beat called *ska,*

achieved international popularity in the '70s through the music of such reggae stars as Jimmy Cliff and the late Bob Marley and Peter Tosh (see "Music," below).

Sects

Inevitably, ideological differences have contributed to the evolution of Rastafarian sects. The older, more traditional sect, descendants of the first communes, continue their "culture of poverty" and live in the hills around Kingston. Strict followers of dietetic and other biblical law, these turbaned, dreadlocked Rastas are often seen in Kingston carrying Bibles.

A younger, more political group, called the **Twelve Tribes of Israel,** consists primarily of middle-class Jamaicans who often are well-educated professional people. They have branches in Jamaica and other countries, including a large following in Brooklyn, New York. Bob Marley was a member of the Twelve Tribes, and took the tribal name Joseph.

The **Ethiopian Zion Coptic Church,** a third, controversial fringe sect, seems to be rooted in a capitalist philosophy based on the sale of ganja. Allowing white members (who are said by some to control the organization) and basing the operations of the group in Florida has not endeared them to Jamaican Rastas, many of whom think of the Coptics as "wolves," pseudo-Rastas intent on profit, not prayer.

MUSIC

But my hand was made strong
By the hand of the Almighty
We forward in this generation triumphantly
—Bob Marley, "Redemption Song"

One of the most recognizable and popular music forms to emerge from Jamaica has been reggae, the lilting and tough beat that sprang from the Kingston ghetto yards in the early '70s and has held Jamaica and much of the world captive ever since. For many, reggae was and remains the domain of Bob Marley, the undisputed king of reggae. But the form has evolved as it would have had Bob Marley lived and continued his creative dominance. Jamaican music constantly changes, often influenced by popular trends throughout the world such as jazz, swing,

rhythm and blues, and today's lyric-heavy rap. But one constant is ever-present in Jamaican popular music: its African origins, particularly the drumming tradition.

Early Music

Slaves brought with them their drumming traditions and the knowledge to fashion instruments in their new environment. *Burru* drums, an arrangement of "talking" drums originating in West Africa, were used in celebration. Later, the Rastafarians adopted the *burru* style of drumming with their *akete* drums, used in prayer and chanting. The emergence of Kumina, the spirit-ancestor cult of early slave days and today, produced the accompanying drumming and shaker rattling that strongly influenced the beat that later became reggae.

Slave celebrations, though few and far between, were always accompanied by music and dancing with a singular African influence. The early Jonkanoo (also Jonkonnu) celebrations, an amalgam of African, European, and what was evolving as Jamaican cultural activity, utilized drumming, rattles, and conch-blowing in elaborate bands of masqueraders who appeared at Christmas. The masqueraders, usually men, dressed as animals, devils, and women, and marched in a riotous parade that was no doubt made more riotous by the anonymity of the paraders. Jonkanoo celebrations were at first encouraged by planters, until they realized that slaves were communicating with their drums and conch shells. Such was the paranoia of the times that Jonkanoo celebrations were soon curbed. Yet the tradition continued and was later accompanied by fifes and flutes, and eventually by larger bands. The custom, and the music, began to die after emancipation, when slaves dispersed and the churches of the era saw the need to clamp down on African ritual.

In 1951, when the *Daily Gleaner* newspaper sponsored a Jonkanoo costume and dancing competition, the huge turnout implied that the tradition hadn't died completely. Jonkanoo has seen greater popularity in recent years, the result of increased awareness of and interest in African cultural heritage (see "Festivals and Events," p. 61).

Later, slaves began to imitate, often with heavy irony but with the blessings of plantation masters, the dances and customs of genteel English society. Reels, Morris dancing, the French quadrille, and polkas became incorporated into the growing body of amalgamated culture. Bands grew to include fiddles and horns.

The Maroons also had developed a musical history not entirely apart from their enslaved brethren. Theirs was rooted, again, in African tradition; the *abeng* (cow) horns were also instruments for war and warning.

Mento

By the turn of the century, Jamaicans were more mobile and tuned in to the sounds of the Caribbean—they'd often worked there as migrant laborers. The calypso of Trinidad and Tobago combined with the tango and samba of Central America to create a simple musical form that, once again, retained African influence.

Mento, origins of the word unknown, became a staple of small gatherings and dances throughout the country. *Mento* refers not only to the musical form, but to the styles of dance that accompanied it, with roots in maypole and Jonkanoo dancing.

Mento is simple music, often humorous, often bordering on the profane, played in 2/4 rhythm with a guitar, a banjo, or both; a tambourine, scraper, or shaker; and a rumba or bass box. The rumba box strongly resembles the African traditional thumb piano, though the box is hollow and larger. *Mento* remained popular throughout the '20s and '30s, and was the first popular Jamaican music form to gain attention outside the country.

The fast beat and island-mellow sound of *mento* gained new ground as the Jamaican tourist industry blossomed in the '40s, and as Trinidad's calypso, by now a sort of generic island sound, took the world by storm. Oddly enough, one of calypso's most famous artists, Harry Belafonte, was not Trinidadian but Jamaican. Belafonte's popularity spread to the U.S. with the 1957 release of his "Banana Boat Song" ("Day-O"). A Jamaican calypso spin off, called *soca,* still enjoys popularity in the country.

Today *mento* is seen often in the tourist industry. Some small bands play at hotels, and occasional compilation recordings are released to the delight of often older Jamaicans whose sentimental support of the music keeps it alive. Occasionally, reunions of *mento* bands are held in large arenas for day-long festivals.

Ska And Rock Steady

The larger influences of swing and the U.S. rhythm and blues of the late '40s and early '50s combined with *mento* to create *ska,* a big-band sound that emphasized lush horn arrangements, piano, and a bop-influenced quick beat. It's said that the word *ska* is an onomatopoeic response to the "skat, skat" sound of the music's rhythm guitar (some claim it was the piano). *Ska* was easy to move to, and created the same-named dance sensation of the '60s, also called "skanking." Popular culture combined with radio to begin the process of creating Jamaica's first pop stars and legends. Among them were The Vikings, Carlos Malcolm, and the famous Skatalites, from whose ranks many of the stars of the era emerged. One of the Skatalites' founding

top: Fern Gully, south of Ocho Rios (Jamaica Tourist Bureau)
bottom: Montego Bay (Jamaica Tourist Bureau)

Sista P on her farm at Hope Bay (Karl Luntta)

members, the talented and troubled Rastafarian trombonist Don Drummond, caused the breakup of the band with his 1965 conviction for the murder of a woman friend.

The dance craze and popularity of *ska* begat a new and enduring method of bringing the music to the people. Enterprising and eccentric, mobile DJs, called "toasters," would load breathtakingly large speaker systems onto the backs of trucks and, armed with a stack of the latest *ska* and American rhythm-and-blues cuts, move out to the townships armed for dance and trouble. "Toasting" can be compared, roughly, to the rap patter of today's DJs.

The rivalries and competition among these DJs for the latest music and best venues created the stuff of legends. With names like Sir Coxsone Downbeat, Count Machukie, King Stitch, and Lord Comic, these men who would show up at dances in capes, swords, and masked costumes, spinning with a wild look in their eyes, "toasting" between cuts. Often, they were guarded by a coterie of pistol-toting bodyguards. The DJs went on to become recording artists in their own right (in 1968-69 DJ toaster Hugh Roy had the first three hit songs on the Jamaican charts), and today's internationally known, reggae-inspired rapper/DJ/dancehall artists such as Yellowman, Shabba Ranks, and Ninja Man owe their success to these early innovators.

In Great Britain, where Caribbean music has traditionally had a strong following among immigrants and locals, *ska* was called "bluebeat," deferring to the major British music label Blue-Beat. A smash 1964 bluebeat hit by Jamaican Millie Small, "My Boy Lollipop," sold over six million copies in that country and established the sound as universal. The song was produced by another Jamaican, Chris Blackwell, founder of the musical phenomenon Island Records. Back in Jamaica, a group led by a young Bob Marley was chalking up early *ska* hits like "Maga Dog" and "Rude Boy." Rude boy was the popular slang at the time for Kingston ghetto toughs who ruled the streets.

The beat of *ska* slowed in the mid-'60s and a form with a dominant bass emerged. It was "rock steady," and is credited with laying down the basic bass line for reggae. Most credit the birth of the style to bassist Leroy Sibbles, now a Canadian, who pioneered the sound with his band The Heptones in the late '60s.

By the early '70s, U.S. and U.K. record producers and companies had their ears cocked to the Jamaican music scene. Texan Johnny Nash had scored hits with his album *I Can See Clearly Now,* which included the Bob Marley tunes "Stir It Up" and "Guava Jelly." Singer Paul Simon traveled to Jamaica to record his reggae-inspired "Mother And Child Reunion." Jamaican Desmond Dekker scored a hit with "Israelites" in March 1969. Jimmy Cliff, the then-reigning king of Jamaican pop and today one of Jamaica's best-known singers, had put the singles "Wonderful World, Beautiful People," "Wild World," and the wildly popular "You Can Get It If You Really Want" on the charts in 1969 and 1970 respectively. Cliff would later star in one of the few Jamaican films to be internationally known, *The Harder They Come,* a story about the "rude boy" underworld and music scene of Kingston.

Birth Of Reggae
No one can say for sure when or from what the term "reggae" originated. Some posit that it

BOB RACE

came from the slang terms *rege rege,* meaning "rags or ragged clothing," or *raga raga,* meaning "ragamuffin." According to the official biography of Bob Marley, *Catch A Fire* by music writer Timothy White, the word apparently first appeared in print in 1968, on a single by legends Toots and the Maytals called "Do The Reggay." Some credit Frederick (Toots) Hibbert with originating the form. Whatever the word's origins, however, most would agree that reggae's spokesperson and premier performer, without whom reggae might have ended its days as a standard on Jamaica's oldies charts, was Bob Marley. In fact, still *is* Bob Marley, more than 10 years after his death.

Marley was born Robert Nesta Marley in the town of Nine Miles, St. Ann, to a British functionary, Norval Marley, and his wife Cedella. His father later deserted Cedella and the family. Marley grew up with lifelong friend Neville "Bunny" Livingston, soon to become Bunny Wailer and one of the founding members of Marley's band, the Wailers. After their move to Trench Town, one of Kingston's most desolate and poverty-ridden areas, Marley began to play and write music, and formed a band with Livingston, Junior Brathwaite, and Peter Tosh. Originally called The Wailing Wailers, the band added backup singers and dabbled in *ska* and rock-steady tunes, with Marley and Tosh providing much of the writing talent. Later, the Wailers added Marley's wife, Rita, a singer in her own right, as leader of a backup group called the I-Threes. The other members were Judy Mowatt and Marcia Griffiths.

The Wailers' first albums sold well in Jamaica, but it wasn't until they signed on with Island Records that their careers took off. In 1973, Island released the albums *Catch A Fire* and *Burnin'* with the classics "Stir It Up," "Get Up, Stand Up," and "I Shot The Sheriff." When British rock legend Eric Clapton released his version of "I Shot The Sheriff" in 1974, it put reggae on the map for scores of nouveau listeners. Other Wailers albums and world tours followed, and reggae became the behemoth of the Jamaican music scene. The music of the Wailers is glib and demanding, commenting on the social and political arena of the day in linear Rasta terms. As a spokesman for Rastafarianism and worldwide black unity, Bob Marley attracted a solid following in third-world nations, particularly in Africa, where he is emulated through imitation and some adherence to a modified Rasta creed. In West Africa, due to the influence of Marley, reggae artists such as Majek Fashek have become popular, and have even had hits on the Jamaican music charts.

In Jamaica, however, Marley is regarded as no less than a mystic, and spoken about in almost mythical terms.

Peter Tosh and Bunny Wailer left the Wailers to pursue solo careers, and Bob Marley reformed the band in the late '70s to even greater success. *Natty Dread* and *Rastaman Vibration* followed to great acclaim. At the zenith of his career, Marley was struck down by cancer, a

Burning Spear

cancer he refused to take steps to eliminate in its early stages because of his Rasta beliefs. He died in May 1981 at age 36, after having been awarded Jamaica's third-highest civil honor, the Order of Merit. The funeral procession that carried him to a hillside mausoleum at his birthplace in Nine Miles stretched over 50 miles.

Reggae Today

Reggae is a worldwide music form that's shown no sign of abating in the years following Bob Marley's death. Many successful musicians have taken up the mantle and brought reggae into the '90s, although none yet with the staggering success of the Wailers.

Freddie McGregor, Dennis Brown, and Gregory Isaacs (the Cool Ruler), all consistently well received, have kept the standard high. Bands like Black Uhuru and Third World, after personnel changes and career dips, have reformed and continue to make albums. The venerable Burning Spear continues to record. Peter Tosh, after a successful solo career, seemed like the one to carry the reggae torch in the years after Marley's death. Tosh was tragically murdered in a 1987 attack at his Barbican, St. Andrew home by a self-styled dub poet. The mercurial Bunny Wailer has had flashes of brilliance, but performs irregularly. He is currently working on what may turn out to be the definitive Wailers story, his biography, called *Old Fire Stick*. A 1991 release of 11, including one previously unreleased, Wailers tunes called *Talkin' Blues* has been met with critical acclaim and commercial success, proving once again that the original is still the best. A 1992 compilation, called *Songs of Freedom*, contains 78 of the Wailers' tunes, some dating from 1962, others previously unreleased. Accompanying the package is a 64-page color booklet that traces Marley's career. For Bob Marley and reggae fans, this is possibly the to-date definitive release.

Rita Marley has taken over the Marley family affairs and continues to produce albums and perform. The Melody Makers is a Grammy-award-winning group consisting of four of Bob and Rita Marley's children (Marley had more than 10 legally acknowledged children), and is led by Ziggy Marley, bearing an eerie resemblance to his father in stature, voice, and talent. Even Cedella Booker, Bob Marley's mother, has cut an album of reggae-gospel

tunes entitled *Awake Zion,* as well as several children's albums.

Other currently popular reggae performers, many based in the U.S. or the U.K., include Maxi Priest, Shinehead, John Holt, and the Ryddim Kings.

Dancehall

A popular aberration of reggae began as "dub," originally a method of cutting out the vocals on the B side of a single, leaving the heavy bass and drum line open for singers to dub over with their own lyrics. One of Jamaica's more popular and thoughtful dub poets is Mutabaruka, whose distinctive voice and lyrics have gained him popularity around the world.

"Dancehall" music, however, has become today's music for the masses. The term originated as a description of the venues in which DJs set up their candle-snuffing, seven-foot speakers to blast dance music. The tradition of DJs becoming stars in their own right had preceded this form, but new artists have taken the part-rap, part-reggae form to larger dimensions. Artists like Ninja Man and U Roy dominate the scene, and one of Jamaica's best-known DJs today is Yellowman, so named because of his albino pigment. Yellowman, the bawdy boy of the dancehall, describes in his music the joys of hedonism and partying. He is the king of "slack," Jamaica's term for that which borders on the graphic.

The U.S.-dominated hip-hop scene has fused on many levels with the dancehall reggae arena of Jamaica to produce crossover hits and artists. The dancehall king today is probably Shabba Ranks, whose urban, rapid-fire, sexually roughneck style of rapping has caught on throughout the world. Shabba Ranks has won two Grammy awards and even scored a U.S. number-one single, something Bob Marley was never able to do in his lifetime. Other dancehall denizens include Mad Cobra, CuttyRanks, Super Cat, Papa San, and Daddy Freddy. The singer Buju Banton is notable for the furor his single "Boom Bye Bye" caused in both the U.S. and Jamaica. The popular single, a mostly homophobic rant that in fact advocated the killing of homosexuals, created a controversy that is typical and reflective of the hubbub surrounding American hip-hop, some of which is judged to be sexist and violent. There is no doubt that dancehall can be a raw, even cruel music, but no one would argue that it does not reflect the raw social environment from which it springs.

Concerts

The annual **Reggae Sunsplash,** now a tradition for years, attracts reggae performers and fans to Montego Bay from the world over for a week of dancing and rapture. The concert, held in July, is booked well in advance. It's best to get tickets and book a hotel room *now* if you want to go. For ticket information contact Synergy, tel. 924-3730/1, or the Jamaica Tourist Board (see "Information and Services," p. 80).

The **Reggae Ram Jam** is attempting to become a annual event, and definitely one to look out for. Held just after Christmas in Kingston or May Pen, the show has featured Dennis Brown,

Frankie Paul, Freddie McGregor, Junior Reid, Professor Nuts, and others. Call the Jamaica Tourist Board for information.

The **Jamaica Musical Theater Company (JMTC),** now over 30 years in existence, puts on a series of concerts and opera performances every year. Find them generally at the Terra Nova Hotel in Kingston, tel. 926-1430 or 929-3113.

Jazz has its aficionados throughout Jamaica, and some hotels have resident jazz bands. Try the Jamaica Pegasus in Kingston, tel. 926-3690/9, for weekly outdoor jazz nights. Also, the **Crystal Springs Jazz Festival,** held annually in late October at Crystal Springs near Buff Bay in Portland, draws talented jazz musicians from Jamaica and abroad; tel. 929-4222/5.

THE ARTS

THEATER AND DANCE

The painting, sculpture, theater, and crafts of Jamaica are vibrant and sophisticated, and accessible in most every large town in the country. Most towns have a theater or place that's used as a theater (school, hotel stage, etc.), commercial art galleries, and the ubiquitous crafts sellers.

Large theatrical productions often start their first run in Kingston. From there they make the rounds to the larger towns, usually easily accessed areas along the coast and interior. A play in Kingston or the rural areas can be an inexpensive night out, and a fascinating insight into a culture at work and, well, play.

The 1,000-seat **Ward Theater** (North Parade, tel. 922-7071) of Kingston hosts the annual **Little Theater Movement Pantomimes,** one of Jamaica's more popular events. Far from being the silent performances the name suggests, the 40-year-old pantomime group uses Jamaican Patois, jokes, and audience participation in their send-ups of life, politics, and historical characters. The characters inevitably include Anancy, protagonist of African folktales. The pantomimes start every year on Boxing Day, 26 Dec., and run until mid-April.

Kingston's **The Little Theater** (4 Tom Redcam Ave.; tel. 925-6129 or 926-6603) is home to

the Secondary Schools Drama Festival, held annually in November. It also hosts many performances of the active National Dance Theatre Company (NDTC). The NDTC, a troupe of dancers, singers, and musicians, performs folk dances, Kumina, and contemporary dance in wildly imaginative costumes. Its performance season is mid-July to mid-Aug., yearly. In November and December it also hosts annual week-long mini-seasons.

The Little Theatre also hosts performances by the Jamaica Musical Theatre Company, and performances in conjunction with the Jamaica School of Drama's Studio Theatre (2 Arthur Wint Dr.).

Other Kingston theaters include **The Barn** (5 Oxford Rd.; tel. 926-6469), **The New Kingston Theatre** (Altamont Cres., tel. 929-2618), and **The Theatre Inside** (6 Cargill Ave.; tel. 926-6711).

A personal favorite is the theater company **Sistren,** a group of women who perform around the country and internationally. Their plays often deal with the plight of women in the Caribbean, and manage to be poignant, scathing, and more than just a little funny. All actors are women. Keep your eye on the newspapers for performance dates.

Although it is not exactly theater, many of the large tourist hotels feature true Jamaican dance and folk performances by local artists. Keeping in mind that these performances are geared toward tourists and therefore toned down, many of them are actually quite good. But also keep in mind that fire-eating, limbo dancing (as it appears today), and walking across beds of nails are not Jamaican customs.

Many plays are performed in Patois, unfamiliar to non-natives. The language may be difficult to understand at first, but the context and crowd reaction should keep you clued in to what is happening. Even if you don't understand completely, plays are still great fun for the often raucous ambience. Jamaican plays are often heavy on comedy, sexual innuendo and the struggles of the working class—imagine often-bawdy versions of "The Honeymooners" in Patois. Call or visit the theater to find out how the play will be performed.

ART

Jamaican art has long dealt with the themes of slavery, race, nationalism (note the large number of honorific statues all over the island), Rastafarianism, poverty, and the more sensuous themes of love, family, and the human form. There is no one way to characterize Jamaican art except to say that its themes parallel the development of the nation and the sophistication of art both worldwide and in the country. The history of Jamaican art is not as old, for instance, as that of neighboring Haiti, which achieved autonomy and freedom of self-expression earlier.

Galleries in Jamaica carry everything from schlock paintings of women with bananas on their head (the Jamaican equivalent of a velvet Elvis) to truly moving pieces. Half the fun is looking, and you should do just that. But for a succinct, overall view of the development of Jamaican art, there is really only one place to go. **The National Gallery** (12 Ocean Blvd.; tel. 922-1561) in Kingston houses the largest collection of historical and contemporary Jamaican art in the country. It is a large museum, worth several hours of browsing, and is dominated by a statue of an over-dreadlocked Bob Marley as you enter the first floor.

The Edna Manley Exhibit occupies virtually the entire first floor. Manley was Jamaica's leading sculptor until her death at 86 in Feb. 1987. She was married to Norman Washington Man-

ley (who was also her first cousin), the architect of Jamaica's independence. Their union produced former prime minister Michael Manley. A fascinating woman and artist, she was one of the founders of the Jamaica School of Art.

The early "intuitives" of Jamaican art are included in work by sculptor John Dunkley and the famous Kapo (Mallica Reynolds). Kapo's exhibit, including paintings, sculpture, and carving, spans 26 years of his life (1949-75) and is the largest single collection of his work—65 pieces. Note the gray and foreboding painting *Silent Night.* Kapo, entirely self-taught as an artist, was also a major spiritual Revivalist cult leader. He died in Feb. 1989, some years after losing both legs, which he attributed to loss of circulation due to the heavy wood, usually lignum vitae, that he rested on them during carving. In 1981 the Jamaican government presented one of Kapo's works, *A New Spring,* to British royals Charles and Diana as a wedding gift. (Wonder if they gave it back?)

Also on exhibit is "Jamaican Art, 1922-Present," featuring the work of Karl Parboosingh and the surrealist Colin Garland among many others. A must-see is the "participatory" exhibit by Dawn Scott, her 1986 "A Cultural Object." It features her rendition of a walk through a Kingston ghetto yard. The National Gallery is open Mon.-Sat. 1000-1700. A small donation is expected.

Other smaller museums and galleries are indicated in the destination sections of this book. Most are commercial galleries, and some hold very fine paintings and art. Do not discount, however, some of the roadside art stalls and huts that you see along any major road around a tourist center. These stalls may have something you've been looking for, at a fraction of its cost in a commercial gallery.

CRAFTS

The largest and possibly most labor-intensive Jamaican craft enterprise is woodcarving. Don't be fooled or assume that *all* Jamaican carvers are from the "naked-man-in-a-barrel-with-a-big-surprise" school of carving—though *some* are. In major towns and along major roads, woodcarvers ply their trade in crafts markets or independent stands. The road along Fern Gully south of Ocho Rios has some ramshackle stalls and a host of good buys. Some carvers sell in galleries, but you can be sure you won't get any deals there. Try the crafts stalls; the pressure is generally not high but the quality can be, and you can look through quite a bit of work before buying. Inquire about the wood; lignum vitae is strong, heavy, and the best, but other types of wood suit some carvings. Prices can range from US$20-US$200 for the larger pieces. Carvers will bargain. Galleries, often, will not. If you are on the north coast, stop in to see Trevor Fairclough at the Cozy Alcove Guesthouse. Unassuming and modest, Mr. Fairclough is an award-winning carver, one of the best in the country, and always has several pieces around that you can see or buy.

Most other Jamaican crafts are tourist-oriented. Straw hats, figurines, baskets, hammocks, beadwork, shells, and shell art are normal fare, and some of it is nice. Along the north coast, wicker work is sold in roadside stands—often as furniture and mats. It is strong and well crafted, and you can bargain, but the practicality of shipping a wicker rocking chair overseas is something you will have to work out.

A small note: Remember that most roadside stalls deal in cash, officially in Jamaican dollars, unofficially in whatever currency you might have. They will most likely not be able to deal in credit cards or, in some cases, in traveler's checks. And they will probably not be able to ship your items home for you.

FESTIVALS AND EVENTS

Jamaica's roster of annual events is an amalgam of Caribbean folk tradition and other eccentricities gathered from around the world. The **Reggae Sunsplash,** which is just what it says—the world's best reggae, sun, and splashing—is one of the biggest events of the year. The **Jamaica Carnival,** the newest of Jamaica's carnivals, recently managed to attract nearly a quarter of the country's population to Kingston for seven days of costume parades; soca, calypso, and reggae parties; and the generic sorts of debauchery that accompany this most ancient of festivals. Jamaica Carnival is also held in Ocho Rios and Montego Bay.

The following is a short list of Jamaica's more popular annual events. Since some of these events happen on the cusp of the month, the dates may change from year to year. For precise information about Jamaica's festivals and events, contact the Jamaica Tourist Board (JTB) offices anywhere in the world (see "Information and Services," p. 80). The area code for Jamaica is 809.

January
The Little Theatre National Pantomime, held at the Ward Theatre, Kingston, has been an event for over 50 years. It's a musical spoofing Jamaican politics, current events, and life. Contact JTB offices for information.

The **Tryall Tennis Classic** (tel. 952-7950), held annually at the Tryall Tennis Club at Sandy Bay, is one of Jamaica's largest competitions. Tennis pros are from Jamaica, Canada, U.S., Europe, and the West Indies.

The 6 Jan. **Accompong Maroon Festival** (tel. 952-7950) celebrates Cudjoe's victory over the British with reenactments of war dances and treaty songs, local food, and marching. Celebrations take place at the *Kindah* (we are family) area and the Peace Cave. Only Maroons are allowed in the Peace Cave.

The **Jamaica Classic Golf Tournament** is the first event of the LPGA calendar. A pro-am tournament is followed by the professional contest, and features some of golf's top players. The event is sponsored by the JTB and the Tryall Club of Sandy Bay, near Montego Bay. Contact JTB offices worldwide for information.

The **Jamaican Musical Theatre Junior Company** (tel. 924-1430) presents their annual season. Youngsters perform at the Creative Arts Centre, Kingston.

The **Jamaica Sprint Triathlon,** held in Negril, features a half-mile swim, a 15-mile bicycle ride, and a three-mile run. Not for the faint of heart. Contact the JTB for information.

The **Mutual Life Jazz Festival** brings international musicians to the Mutual Life Building, Kingston. Contact JTB offices. *This event is held once per month, year-round.*

The **Red Stripe Cricket Competition,** named after Jamaica's most popular beer, features Jamaica's best playing teams from around the Caribbean. Held at Sabina Park, Kingston.

The **White River Reggae Bash** (tel. 929-4089), held in St. Ann's Bay's White River Reggae Park, is a jam featuring some of Jamaica's best reggae musicians.

February
The **Miami to Montego Bay Pineapple Cup Yacht Race** (tel. 952-6101), one of the world's longest races, has been held for over 40 years. The 811-mile course begins in Miami and sails around the Bahamas and Cuba before ending in Montego Bay. Spectators can observe the final leg in Montego Bay, as well as the award ceremonies.

The annual **Bob Marley Birthday Bash** (Tuff Gong International, tel. 923-9380 or 923-9384), 6 Feb., is now a national holiday, and the four-day party that surrounds it consists of performances by Jamaica's top reggae artists, including Ziggy Marley, the I-Threes, and Burning Spear. The venue changes: The event has been held at Nine Miles, St. Ann (Marley's birthplace), as well as at the Bob Marley Museum in Kingston.

The **Stowe Polo Club Polo Tournament** (tel. 972-2506) is held at Chukka Cove, St. Ann. Later in the month, the **Chukka Cove-Appleton Polo Tournament** is held at the same venue.

The **University of the West Indies (UWI) Carnival** is an almost two-week-long event that includes fashion shows, reggae and calypso competitions, parades, and all-night dances. Contact JTB offices for information.

Red Stripe Cricket Competition, Sabina Park, Kingston is a continuation of January's contests. If you're not familiar with the game, you'll be a little lost. Ask a Jamaican friend. Matches last for days.

The Jamaica Music Industry (JAMI) Awards is hosted by Kingston and features the best of reggae, folk, and classical. Call JTB offices worldwide for information. *Sometimes held in March.*

March
The **Miss Universe Jamaica Beauty Pageant** winner represents Jamaica in the Miss Universe contest. The final event is often held in Kingston. Contact JTB offices for information.

The **Jamaica Musical Theatre Company** (tel. 926-1430) starts its spring concert season in Kingston.

The **Port Antonio International Spring Fishing Tournament** (tel. 923-8724) is host to anglers pursuing all categories of fish.

The **Montego Bay Song Festival** competition includes *mento,* reggae, *soca,* and other sing-offs. Contact JTB offices for details.

April
Expo '94 (tel. 926-6740) is a biennial, five-day trade exhibition held at the National Arena, Kingston, and sponsored by the Jamaica Manufacturers Association and the Jamaica Exporters Association. The show features representatives from food, garment, furniture, textiles, and other leading industries. Nightly entertainment.

The **Jamaica Musical Theatre Company** (tel. 926-1430) kicks off its concert season in Kingston.

The National Dance Theatre Company (NDTC) **Easter Sunrise Concert** (tel. 922-0260) is held on Easter Sunday, 0600-0700, at the Little Theatre in Kingston.

The Montego Bay Yacht Club's **Easter Regatta** (tel. 952-6101) has been held for over 50 years, and is a five-day series of yacht races and parties.

For over 18 years, the **Orange Carnival,** held in Kingston and Port Royal, has been inspired by the famous Trinidad carnivals and features beach parties, calypso, and bacchanalia.

The big **Jamaica Carnival** is Jamaica's contribution to the world of mayhem. This post-Lent, week-long event features parades, reggae, calypso, and *soca* parties, and is getting bigger every year. Contact JTB offices worldwide for information on both carnivals.

The **St. James Agricultural Show** (tel. 922-0610) is held at the Jamaica Defence Force camp in Montpelier, south of Montego Bay.

The **St. Elizabeth Horticultural Society's Annual Show** (tel. 965-2203) is held in Black River.

The **Annual Red Stripe International Tournament and Horse Show** (tel. 972-2506) is held in late April at Chukka Cove, Ocho Rios. The event is a combined grand prix with top riders from Jamaica, the U.S., and Europe.

The University of the West Indies (UWI) **Dance Society** season starts in late April or

outdoor Pantomime in Port Royal, Kingston

PHYLLIS LUNITA

Carnival

BOB RACE

early May. Call the UWI Creative Arts Centre, tel. 927-1456, for details.

May

The University of the West Indies (UWI) **Pop Society Concert Season** (tel. 927-1456) kicks off in early May with performances of jazz, reggae, calypso, and *mento,* at the Creative Arts Centre, UWI, Kingston. (See also "April" listing.)

The **Jamaica International Hot Air Balloon Festival and Air Show** has been an event since 1988 and features balloons from all over the world. The three-day event is held at Montpelier, near Montego Bay. Contact JTB offices for details.

The **Manchester Horticultural Society Show** (tel. 962-2328), Mandeville, features exhibits of flowers and foliage plants, as well as demonstrations. The Society, one of the oldest in the Caribbean, is more than 125 years old.

The **Negril Carnival** (tel. 957-4437), held late in the month, includes the Jamaica Police Band performances, Jonkanoo dancing, parades, and *mento* band competitions.

June

The **Caymanas and Constant Spring Golf Club Tournament,** Kingston, is an open week of golf with competitions for men and women. Contact JTB offices for information.

The **All-Jamaica Junior and Open Tennis Championships** (tel. 929-5878), held every year at the Eric Bell Tennis Complex, Kingston,

has been around for over 85 years. It's open to Jamaican nationals, and winners become Jamaica's champions.

The **Junior Miss & Mr. Bodybuilding Competition** (tel. 929-5193), held in Kingston, is the venue for the smaller flexologists of Jamaica.

July

Manchester Golf Week (tel. 962-2403), Mandeville, is Jamaica's oldest golf tournament. Visitors are welcome to watch or play.

The National Dance Theatre Company's (NDTC) **Season of Dance** (tel. 926-6603) kicks off in Kingston, at the Little Theatre.

The **Pushcart Derby Semi-Finals** (tel. 973-3351/3), sort of like soapbox derbies, are held in towns countrywide. Finals are in August at Kaiser Sports Club, Discovery Bay.

August

The annual **Reggae Sunsplash** (tel. 924-3730 or JTB offices worldwide), virtually a mecca to reggae fans, is held at the Bob Marley Centre, Montego Bay. Book rooms early for this very packed, five-day event. *Sometimes held in July—call ahead.*

The **Independence Festival** is an annual showcase for talented Jamaicans in dance, drama, literature, fine arts, and music. Competitions are held islandwide during the year; during the week prior to Independence Day, finals are held in Kingston. Contact JTB offices for information.

Mello Go Roun is a variety concert featuring

winners of Independence Festival events, held in Kingston at the National Arena. Contact JTB offices for details.

Independence Day, officially 6 Aug., is celebrated the first Monday of the month throughout Jamaica. Kingston has the gala events. Festivals, parades, historical reenactments, speeches, and bands islandwide are featured. Contact JTB offices for information.

Great Bay Carnival, Treasure Beach, has boat regattas, traditional dancing, and Maroon cultural events. Contact JTB offices for details.

September

The **Montego Bay International Marlin Tournament** (tel. 952-6101) attracts sports fishermen from the world over.

The **Miss Jamaica Beauty Contest Coronation Show** (tel. 927-7575) is held in Kingston. The winner represents Jamaica in the Miss World contest. Jamaica has had two Miss World winners.

October

The **Ocho Rios International Marlin Tournament** is held in early October, and features prize money and a local canoe fisherman's tournament. Contact JTB offices for entry information.

The **Port Antonio International Marlin Tournament** (tel. 923-8724) has been held since 1963 and is one of the oldest and most prestigious in the Caribbean.

The **Jamaica Open Golf Tournament** (venue varies, has been held at the Wyndham Rose Hall Beach Resort in Montego Bay) is one of Jamaica's biggest golf tournaments. Contact JTB offices for information.

November

Some of Jamaica's ethnic groups still honor their customary festivals. East Indians celebrate Hussay and Deewali (Festival of Lights), though the customs seem to be dying. The Chinese community is now largely Christian. The small Jewish community celebrates its own religious and commemorative holidays.

Often festivals and events are staged on short notice and might be missed if you don't keep an open eye. Read the newspapers and billboards for announcements, and listen to Jamaica's radio stations.

ACCOMMODATIONS

No shortage of accommodations exists on either end of the scale in Jamaica; you can find grubby rooms with broken doors, or rooms where a maid floats hibiscus petals in the toilet before she turns down the satin sheets. Choose from US$10-20 per night for guesthouse rooms that are clean, secure, and a tremendous value, to over US$300 per night for exclusive resorts, some very good and some not worth a fraction of that amount. Then again, the bulk of the hotels in Jamaica are medium-sized, medium-priced, comfortable, and appealing not for their amenities but for their location along beaches or in the cool hills. How do you sort it all out?

Start with yourself, of course, your budget, and your personal style of travel. If you are an independent traveler who wants to mingle with Jamaicans, and do it cheaply, Jamaica has plenty to offer. If you want to be pampered and stay sequestered inside resorts, Jamaica has that experience, too. You'll pay for it, but will get all the sun and sand you need.

Hotels And Resorts

The **Jamaica Tourist Board** (JTB) publishes a list of over 120 approved hotels and resorts throughout the country, a list that can be very helpful in planning a trip. In addition, over 300 small guest cottages are approved. When a hotel is approved by the JTB, rest assured you will have a good standard of cleanliness, security, and amenities. Yet there are several hundred hotels and cottages, some also perfectly fine, that operate outside the JTB licensing system, either by choice or because they have not met the JTB standards (some of which regulate trivial items such as wall art). Many nonapproved hotels and guesthouses are clean, comfortable, and excellent deals.

Jamaica is probably the premier purveyor of all-inclusive resorts in the Caribbean. All-inclusives are just what they say they are—you get the room, all meals and snacks, transfers from the airport, drinks, tips, some tours, water sports, and resort facilities for one price. They advertise that one need only bring money for incidentals and shopping. Some even include airfare. Two major chains, **Sandals** and **SuperClubs,** control the largest and most popular all-inclusives on the island. Sandals is for couples only, SuperClubs caters to singles, couples, and families. Other independent, smaller all-inclusives also operate throughout the island. Sandals has resorts in Montego Bay, Negril, Ocho Rios, and Dunn's River (U.S.A. and Canada tel. 800-SANDALS, U.K. tel. 071-581-9895, Jamaica tel. 809-952-6610). SuperClubs has resorts in Negril. Ocho Rios, Discovery Bay, and Oracabessa (U.S.A. tel. 800-858-8009, Canada tel. 800-553-4320, U.K. tel. 992-447420, Jamaica tel. 809-957-4010).

The advantage to all-inclusives is that they eliminate travel hassles (if you are hassled by travel) and give you a certain vacation experience under one roof. They bus you out to shopping, tours, and the like, but everything else takes place at the hotel. This approach appeals to quite a few vacationers, as JTB statistics bear out. The all-inclusives claim over 70% occupancy year-round, while the rest of the island's hotels average 50% occupancy.

The disadvantage is cultural. While you are not restricted to hotel grounds, the tendency is to stay there if all meals and activities are close by and already paid for. You may lose the impetus to go out and search and talk to Jamaicans in the towns. Instead, you meet other tourists.

All-inclusives are a good deal if you have the money (from about US$100 pp p/d, based on double occupancy) and want that type of experience. They are recommended for those who want to escape completely and forget about carrying money. They aren't for the independent traveler who wants to see as much of Jamaica as possible, who doesn't need frills, and who is on a limited budget. **Note:** Many all-inclusives do not accommodate children under 16; some do not accommodate children at all. Check first.

Most other hotels in Jamaica run on the European plan, although many are willing to work out meal plans for you if that is your desire. European plan refers to the type of hotel where you pay separately for room, meals, and extras. Variations include the continental plan (breakfast), the modified American plan (breakfast and dinner), and others.

Villas And Apartments

The **Jamaica Association of Villas and Apartments (JAVA),** an organization working in conjunction with the JTB, lists over 300 properties (about 80% of Jamaica's available villas) for the type of traveler who wants independence from hotels and the capacity to cook at home, and who might possibly stay for extended periods. These villas inevitably include a pool, maid, gardener, cook service, and other amenities you may not need or want. But you can often negotiate price along an "a la carte" type of arrangement, choosing what you need. Price is also based on the number of bedrooms in the apartment or villa, and on its location—generally the closer to seaside, the more expensive. Prices range from US$200 per week for studios to US$12,000 per week for six-bedroom luxury villas. Average is about US$40-50 per bedroom per night, based on weekly occupancy. Villas can be cost effective if you're traveling with a small group, and they are generally in very pretty areas. See "Information and Services," p. 80, for JTB and JAVA office locations throughout the world.

You need not go through JAVA to find good deals on villas and apartments. Check the classifieds in the travel sections of large metropolitan newspapers for private rentals and rental companies—the *New York Times,* for instance, often has a beefy Jamaica listing in its Sunday travel section. Travel magazines such as *Caribbean Travel & Life* also carry advertisements, though they tend to offer the higher-priced villas.

In addition, try **Sunshine Villas** (257 S. 16th St., Philadelphia, PA 19102; tel. 215-790-1190 or 800-346-5897, fax 215-790-0064) and ask for Jackie Waite or Parchi Parchment. Tell them your desired location and price range, and they will try their best to find a place for you.

Other villa rental agencies include **Villa Leisure** (P.O. Box 1096, Fairfield, CT 06430; tel. 203-222-9611), **At Home Abroad** (405 E. 56th St., Apt. 6H, New York, NY 10022; tel. 212-421-9165), and **Condo World** (tel. 800-521-2980).

For all kinds of bookings, though often on the high end of the scale, contact the **Jamaica Reservation Service** (1320 South Dixie Hwy., Suite 1180, Coral Gables, FL 33146; tel. 305-666-0447 or 800-JAMAICA).

Camping

No camping facilities are currently recommended by the JTB. But there are a few, particularly in the Blue Mountains, Montego Bay, Negril, and Ocho Rios, that are safe and do the job. Some are attached to hotels and will even rent tents if you don't want to carry your own. Others are bona fide campgrounds, and still others are guesthouses that will allow you to set up your tent on their grounds. Virtually all have water and bathing facilities, and most offer restaurants or kitchen facilities. Average cost is US$5-10 per tent per night.

Camping on private grounds is more involved. It is possible but needs negotiation with landowners, and safety is not ensured. Camping on government property, some beaches for instance, is not allowed. With the number of good, inexpensive guesthouses available, including those that will let you pitch your tent on the grounds, it is better to stick to those or bona fide campgrounds.

Campsites are listed in the destination chapters of this book.

Staying With Families

It is possible to stay with Jamaican families. This type of arrangement may take some time to organize. If you meet someone with whom you have developed rapport and trust, it's not unusual to ask them about staying with a family (possibly their own or one they know). Many Jamaicans would warmly welcome a visitor, and rich relationships can develop. Of course, you'll pay for your board, but will learn a great deal from this intimate exposure to family life.

Some visitors to Jamaica have found success in simply pulling into the area where they would like to stay, and asking around for someone who will rent a room. You will, with persistence, find a place. This practice, while certainly the most adventurous, takes a certain type of person to do it. You are the best judge of whether you are that type of person. Your security is not assured, and there are dangers involved to you and your property if you go about it blindly. However, in some towns, mostly coastal, Jamaicans have rented to visitors in the past and have the routine down.

The JTB operates a program called "Meet The People," which places visitors with Jamaicans of similar age and often professional background. The visits can be as simple as lunch or dinner, but in the past they have had success in placing visitors for overnight stays with Jamaicans. The program has started and faltered due to logistical problems, and has been for the longest time in the process of being redeveloped. Nevertheless, it is worth an inquiry.

A similar concept, called "Community Tourism," operates from the south-central town of Mandeville. It enables tourists to meet local hosts at work, at social events, and at home. These host families are usually operators of their own small "bed and breakfasts." Contact the ever-dynamic Diane McIntyre-Pike, who organizes the program from her Astra Country Inn (62 Ward Ave., Mandeville, Manchester Parish, Jamaica, W.I.; tel. 962-3265).

Rates And Seasons

Jamaica's busy tourist season lasts from mid-Dec.-March or mid-April, or roughly the winter. The summer is off-season and, as such, off priced. You can count on room rates being 20-40% cheaper then, and you'll have the added luxury of traveling in uncrowded areas. Some hotels retain the same rate all year, and others have three or more different rates depending on the season. During the summer many small hotels are short of guests, and substantial rate reductions can often be negotiated no matter what your length of stay. Talk to the manager.

Many hotels do not fill up, even during the high season. Rather than letting empty rooms sit, where no money is earned, hotels often shift a certain percentage of their business to hotel wholesalers at bulk rates. They in turn offer these accommodations to the public at significant discounts. One such wholesaler is **The Room Exchange** (tel. 800-846-7000, fax 212-760-1013). They book over 50 properties, primarily hotels and all-inclusives. Some rooms may be available for as much as 25% off in the high season, and up to 50% off in the low season.

A rule of thumb in looking for discounts: In all cases it is best to call the hotel or guesthouse directly, and ask if they are offering any deals, discounts, or packages. If not, suggest one yourself.

A room tax is often added to bills, so you should check to see if the tax is included in the rate or will be added later. The tax, which is causing all sorts of consternation throughout the country—primarily because no one understands it—was enacted in Oct. 1991 and is called the **General Consumption Tax (GCT)**. This tax is generally 10%, although some smaller guesthouses charge 5% if they charge it at all. Items that are "zero-rated," which means that they are tax-free to the consumer, are: raw foods such as fruits, vegetables, onion, garlic, meat, poultry, and fish; processed foods such as rice, brown sugar, bread, "patties" (spicy ground meat in a pastry shell), milk, and flour; books, newspapers, and stationery; and train or bus fares, ice, postage, and utility bills. Items that are taxed include hotel rooms, restaurant meals, alcohol, and much of what you'd buy in a tourist shop that is not duty-free.

An additional charge you might see on a hotel bill is a 10% service charge, which is meant to be a tip for services rendered at the hotel. Ostensibly, this tip is divided among the hotel staff. If you feel like giving chambermaid or porter more, feel free to do so.

Most hotels in Jamaica will accept major credit cards (Discover Card is gaining acceptance). Smaller hotels will accept traveler's checks, but for most guesthouses, you will have to pay cash.

Disabled Travelers

Jamaica's tourism infrastructure has a little bit for everyone, but specialized travel situations may need some research.

Disabled travelers will not, unfortunately, find much in the way of accessible facilities in hotels and general transport systems throughout the country. In particular, wheelchair-bound visitors will have to plan well in advance to ensure that their needs are met. Some hotels have accessible first-floor rooms, but not all have accessible bathroom facilities.

In Jamaica, the best source for information regarding facilities for disabled travelers is Derrick Palmer, director of **Disabled Persons International** (P.O. Box 220, Liguanea, Kingston 6, Jamaica, W.I.; tel. 929-2073 or 926-6776). Palmer and his organization have worked hard to promote disabled-accessible facilities in Jamaica and throughout the Caribbean. He regards Sangster International Airport in Montego Bay as one of the best facilities for the disabled in the English-speaking Caribbean. Because of his lobbying, many of the shopping plazas in Kingston now

have ramps. Parking spots for the disabled are now part of the country's building code. Alas, however, he cannot yet recommend many hotels that are truly accessible. The bottom line for Jamaica: Decide on the hotel you would like to visit, and call ahead for information on their facilities. Be specific in your questions.

For general information regarding travel for disabled persons, contact *The Wheelchair Traveler*, a newsletter issued by Douglass R. Annand (123 Ball Hill Rd., Milford, NH 03055; tel. 603-673-4539).

Senior Travelers

Older travelers will find Jamaica an easy and rewarding trip. For those who want to relax and stay by the sea, that is where the majority of hotels and other accommodations are anyway. For those who are prefer mountain hiking, biking, and the outdoors, that experience is available as well. Since seniors are often retired and unencumbered by job obligations, they can travel at their leisure and take advantage of off-season rates and uncrowded streets. By and large, however, Jamaican hoteliers and restaurateurs have not adopted the custom of giving discounts to seniors. Some do, but not as a rule. Still, bring identification for proof of age if you intend to seek out senior discounts.

Traveling with senior groups on charters or special cruises organized by senior travel programs may be helpful. Contact the **American Association of Retired Persons (AARP)** (601 E St. NW, Washington, DC 20049; tel. 800-441-2277 or 202-434-2277; annual dues US$8) for information about joining the organization. Also try the **National Council of Senior Citizens** (1331 F St. NW, Washington DC 20004; tel. 800-322-6677 or 202-347-8800; annual dues US$12).

Student Travelers

Students on spring break are given, well, a break in selected hotels, restaurants, shops, and nightclubs in Montego Bay, Negril, and Ocho Rios. One program is sponsored by the JTB from mid-March through mid-April, and the discounts range 10-50%. The 50% doesn't often apply to rooms. Look at rates carefully and compare to normal rates in other area hotels—you may find that shifting to a different hotel would be cheaper anyway. Call the JTB for details.

One of the larger U.S.-based travel agencies that deals with student travel to Jamaica is **Student Travel Services** (120 N. Aurora St., Ithaca, NY 14850; tel. 607-272-6964 or 800-646-4849, fax 607-272-6963). They often go as far as booking out entire hotels for their groups, and offer packages that include charters from around the country, airfare to Jamaica, selected tours, and mega-parties. Be clear about how many people you want to room with, however. Some of the hotels used by this tour allow up to four in a room, which is why accommodation is so inexpensive.

Family Travelers

Families are generally accommodated without a problem in Jamaica. Most hotels offer free rooms or discounts to families with children under 12 or so, as long as child and parents stay in the same room. Several hotels, including the all-inclusive SuperClubs' **Boscobel Beach Resort** in Oracabessa and **Franklyn D. Resort (FDR)** in Runaway Bay, are geared expressly toward families. They offer all sorts of services such as game rooms, baby-sitting, children's beach activities, children's talent shows, and so on.

Other resorts, particularly some of the other all-inclusives, do not accommodate children under 18, or in cases, under 16. These include the other SuperClubs resorts. Sandals does not accommodate children at all.

Dozens of guidebooks on the market deal specifically with family travel. Recommended is *Best Places to Go, Vol. I,* by Nan Jeffrey (San Francisco: Foghorn Press, 1993).

Villas are a good bet for families because of the autonomy they afford. You can cook, eat, see the sights, and sleep at your leisure. Most come with cooks and household help, which gives you the chance to relax a bit and let someone else do the work. For a large family, or for two families, villas can be very cost-effective.

Single Travelers

Singles have the widest range of possibilities in Jamaica, for the obvious reasons. Remember, most hotels give rates for single and double rooms, but others give rates per person based on double occupancy, which may not be the same as single occupancy. This is particularly true in the all-inclusive resorts that allow singles. Some all-inclusives will book single travelers into a room with someone of the same sex, unless a "guaranteed single" fee is paid, sometimes as much as US$75 per day. Some all-inclusive hotels allow couples only; singles need not apply. Check in the destination sections of this book.

Gay And Lesbian Travelers

Gays and lesbians will find Jamaica a culture that does not embrace homosexuality. While obviously homosexuality does exist in the country, it is not a life that is accepted enough or even tolerated on a level that would make openly gay visitors comfortable in all situations. This is not to say that gay and lesbian travelers should avoid Jamaica—the issue, rather, is one of your own comfort level in being open. For more information about Jamaica and other destinations, contact the **International Gay Travelers Association** in Key West, Florida, tel. (800) 448-8550.

Specialty Travel Index

An extremely useful publication for all travelers is the *Specialty Travel Index* (305 San Anselmo Ave., San Anselmo, CA 94960; tel. 415-459-4900, fax 415-459-4974). The magazine comes out twice per year and lists over 620 tour operators and outfitters that cater to special and not-so-special interests. Entries are cross-referenced by geographical region, personal interests, activities, and more. Cost is US$6 per issue, or US$10 per year.

EATING AND DRINKING

Jamaicans love a good meal and good meals are here to be had. Primary ingredients of the island's diet are fish, chicken, vegetables, exotic fruit, and pepper-based spices, either light or flame-throwing. The diet is truly Jamaican these days, with traces of African and post-British colonial influence mixed throughout.

Eating Out

Jamaica is not really an "eating out" society, and the consequence is a lot of small restaurants competing for the local dollar—great places for anyone to eat. The hygiene is generally acceptable, and the no-frills, swinging-door ambience of these places makes for distinctly Jamaican and very reasonable meals.

Breakfasts might be a surprise. The fare in small restaurants is generally solid. Favorite dishes are liver and boiled green bananas, or beef stew, or possibly tripe and beans. The famous national dish of *ackee* and saltfish is also popular any time of day. *Ackee* is the small fruit that, when ripe, bursts through its skin to expose the yellow flesh inside. Take care not to eat *ackee* before its ripened-burst phase—if cooked before it opens naturally, it can be toxic. The fruit blends well with salted cod to create the national dish, and resembles spicy scrambled eggs.

In and around tourist areas, restaurants become more expensive and more exotic. The food is likely to be French, Italian, Chinese, and I-tal (vegetarian prepared by Rastafarian code.) It also becomes fast food, and you can find Kentucky Fried Chicken, Shakey's Pizza, the Jamaican chains of King Burger and Mother's, and others serving burgers and yam chips (fries), goat curry, and the Jamaican favorite, "patties"—spicy ground meat in a pastry shell.

Some of the best restaurants in the country are found in Kingston, Montego Bay, and Ocho Rios. Negril, Mandeville, and Port Antonio also have some very fine restaurants, often attached to hotels.

Seafood

Seafood is a natural Jamaican favorite. Lobster, the clawless variety which is really crayfish, is often curried or grilled with butter and garlic. In restaurants it can be expensive, up to US$20, but at beach kiosks it can be had for as little as US$5. Pepper shrimp, a tiny and spicy snack, is sold at roadside stands around the Middle Quarters area north of Black River in St. Elizabeth (J$20 a small bag). Another favorite is *escoveitch* fish, from the Spanish *escabeche,* meaning pickled. At kiosks, fish is often served with "festival," a deep-fried, sweet cornbread. Fish is also served "run down," or "run dun," a method of preparing it with coconut milk and spices.

Popular fish used for cooking include grouper, one of the more common catches; kingfish, a large, meaty fish; marlin, which produces thick steaks; mullet; a freshwater fish; parrot fish; and snapper, perhaps the most common found in restaurants.

Fresh-water and ocean crabs are also used in dishes, as is conch and *janga* (small crayfish).

Jerk

A well-known Jamaican preparation is "jerk" meat, either pork, chicken, or fish. The word is said to have originated from an indigenous South American language, and traveled to English via Spanish and, possibly, the Arawak language. It does *not,* as some jerk vendors will tell you, refer to the reaction of your central nervous system as you eat this spicy preparation. The Maroons, ever on the run, are believed to have preserved and perfected the cooking method during their many years ensconced in the Blue Mountains and Cockpit Country. Today, jerk chicken or pork can be found at most roadside stands throughout the country. The best can be found at Boston Beach, located east of Port Antonio in Portland. There, the vendors will not only sell the meat, but the jerk seasoning as well.

The "jerk" method involves preparing the meat with a mixture of pepper, pimento, nutmeg, cinnamon, possibly garlic, scallions, salt, and the cook's secret ingredients (one has claimed over 35 ingredients in his sauce). The seasoned meat is grilled slowly over coals from hardwood while covered with mahoe wood slats or even corrugated tin sheets. Small roadside vendors often jerk their pork or chicken in colorful ovens

THE STORY OF RUM

The Three "R's," rum, reggae, and Rasta, form the triumvirate that rules Jamaica's identity throughout the world. Of the three, rum has been around the longest.

Rum is *the* Jamaican drink, used in everything from Revivalist ceremonies to herbalist medicine to house parties, and Jamaican rum is some of the best worldwide. Jamaica was the first to produce it commercially, and still does to worldwide acclaim.

The origins of the word are uncertain. Some believe "rum" is derived from the botanical name of sugarcane, *Saccharum officinarum*, from which rum is produced. Others believe the word originated among the planters of Barbados, where it was originally called "rumbullion" for the escapades it induced.

During Columbus's third voyage of discovery to the West Indies, he planted sugarcane on the island of Hispaniola. The Spanish colonists soon found that a sweet liquor could be made by distilling the heavy residue, molasses, from cane processing. Sailors and buccaneers soon discovered the drink, and it became indentified with life on the seas, as in "yo ho ho and a bottle of rum."

In the 1600s, the British began to make excursions into the West Indies, and sugarcane production on massive plantations became a way of life. Rum was produced on a large scale in Barbados, and was first produced commercially in Jamaica. Still, rum was considered a drink of ruffians, of the lower class, and did not gain wide acceptance as proper drink in polite European society for centuries. It wasn't until the early 20th century that rum came into its own as a cocktail ingredient.

The original distilling process is still the basis for rum production today. Sugarcane is pressed and produces cane juice, from which both sugar and its by-products such as molasses emerge. Water is added to the molasses to reduce the sugar content, and the mixture is pasteurized. Yeast is added to the molasses mix, and the fermentation produces alcohol. The alcohol in turn kills the yeast; the resulting "dead wash" is distilled to produce rum.

Traditionally, the rum was then aged in oak casks for at least three and as many as 20 years. The casks produced both the colors and flavors of the various rums you see on the market. Today's rum is still aged, but often in vats, for up to three years. Caramel is added to produce the darkest of rums.

Rums run the gamut from the smooth, amber drink to the darkest rum, which is richest in flavor. Jamaica's famous "overproof" white rum, a favorite in folk medicine and among certain religious groups, is the strongest of the lot—you've been warned. It'll put the heartiest of imbibers under the table in a New York minute.

Rum drinks are very popular in the tropics, as much for their attendant fruit mixes and frothy daiquiri-style additions as for the rum itself. One of the oldest mixed rum punches originated during the heyday of sugarcane plantations. Its recipe, in this order, was simple: sour, sweet, strong, and weak. Translation: One part sour, or lime juice; two parts sweet, or sugar; three parts strong, or rum; and four parts weak, or water or fruit juice.

made from cut drums, and the smell will lead you to them. Jerk pork, sausage, and chicken are sold by the pound, or by the section. Chicken is about J$90 (US$4) for half of the bird, pork and sausage about US$5 per pound.

Market Vegetables

Jamaican vegetables include *cho-cho* (also *christophine*), a squashlike, pulpy vegetable with a white center. *Callaloo,* also *calalou,* is a Jamaican spinach and the principal ingredient of the island's famous pepperpot soup (see below). Jamaicans use the terms peas and beans interchangeably, and the popular dish of rice and

peas, usually *gungo* beans, is served in most restaurants. Okra, potatoes, yams, and the root crop cassava are also grown. Cassava, which was grown by the Arawaks, is pounded and prepared to make another national favorite, *bammy,* a heavy but tasty starch cake. Plantain, a member of the banana family, is a favorite with carbo-loaders and is often eaten as a side dish. It needs to be cooked. Breadfruit, which is actually a fruit transplanted from Polynesia by Captain Bligh in 1793, is served either boiled, baked, or, a personal favorite, deep-fried. *Bulla,* a ginger sweetcake, is a favorite in Jamaica.

RECIPES

A few of Jamaica's favorite recipes, personally sampled:

Pepperpot Soup
Louis Kennedy, chef
Triff's Inn, Port Antonio, and The Admiralty Club, Navy Island, Port Antonio

- one "bundle" *callaloo* or spinach (about one-half pound)
- one meatbone, about one-half pound (can use salt beef)
- one pint condensed milk
- two tablespoons flour
- two stalks scallions
- one small bunch fresh thyme
- pinch M.S.G. (optional)
- coarse black pepper

Boil two quarts of water and toss in the meatbone or salt beef. Tie up the *callaloo* and throw it in with the bone. Boil for one hour, or until the *callaloo* is soft. Remove the bone and *callaloo* and strain off the water, placing it back on the stove. Finely chop the *callaloo* and toss it back into the water. Add the scallions and thyme. Add the milk and M.S.G. and stir. Mix the flour with a little water and add. Add milled black pepper and salt to taste. Simmer until you have a good feeling about it. Serves six.

Escoveitch Fish
Lloyd Corwell, chef
Pine Grove Guest House, Kingston

- one snapper, or ocean fish (freshwater fish will also work, but requires more salt)
- a few carrots
- a few *cho-chos*
- a few sweet peppers
- an onion
- vinegar (not too much, not too little)
- black pepper
- pimento seeds
- onion powder
- garlic powder
- coconut cooking oil

Clean the fish. Season with black pepper, onion powder, garlic powder, and salt. Heat a dutch pot (frying pan) until it's "well hot," otherwise the fish will stick to the bottom or get mushy. Add a small amount of oil and fry the fish on both sides until it's almost done. Remove from the pan. Slice the carrots and *cho-cho* into strips and add to the oil. Add two or three pimento seeds, the vinegar, sweet pepper, and sliced onion to sauté. Place the fish in a deep pot and cover with the carrot, *cho-cho*, and vinegar mixture. Steam for 5-10 minutes, and the kitchen is now smelling nice. Add a pinch of sugar to cut through the vinegar.

Grilled Lobster
"Rick" Fitzroy Campbell, chef
Seafood Giant, Runaway Bay

Mix pimento, crushed ginger, black pepper, crushed garlic, onion powder, and salt to taste. Parboil the lobster. Cut it in half lengthwise and rub liberally with the season mixture. Place fleshy side down on a medium barbecue and grill for 10-15 minutes. Serve with butter and a cold Red Stripe beer—maybe two beers.

Ackee and Saltfish
Pam Chong, owner
Egbert Gibbs, chef
Harmony Hall Restaurant, Ocho Rios

- one dozen *ackee* pods or one can *ackee*
- three ounces codfish (salted cod)
- one small onion
- one small tomato
- black pepper
- Scotch Bonnet brand hot pepper

Soak the codfish overnight or boil to eliminate salt. Flake the fish and set aside. Discard pod, seed, and pink membrane from the *ackees*. Add the *ackees* to water and boil until tender. Drain and set aside. Sauté the sliced onion, tomato, and other ingredients. Add the fish and cook for about 10 minutes. Add the *ackees*, taking care not to damage them, and cook for an additional 10 minutes. Can be served on an open-faced bun sprinkled with raw scallions, or as a side dish.

Jerk Chicken
Laurence Sombke, author
Fearless Entertaining

- 8-12 chicken thighs
- two tablespoons ground pimento (allspice)
- three to four hot green chili peppers, Scotch bonnies, jalapeños, or long green cayenne peppers, chopped
- three scallions, trimmed and chopped
- one-quarter cup light soy sauce

continued

RECITES *(cont.)*

- one tablespoon fresh ginger, peeled
- one-quarter teaspoon each cinnamon and cloves
- one-half teaspoon each salt and black pepper

Place the thighs in a large glass or ceramic cake pan or casserole dish. Place the remaining ingredients and one-half cup of water in a food processor and whir until smooth. Pour the sauce over the chicken, coat the pieces thoroughly, and let marinate for at least one hour at room temperature or overnight in the refrigerator. The most authentic and flavorful way to make jerk chicken is to cook it over a slow smoky fire outdoors. Build a charcoal or wood fire in a hooded barbecue grill. When the coals are gray, move them all over to one side of the grill. Place the chicken pieces on the side of the grill opposite the coals and at the highest point away from the fire. Cover the grill, close all vents and let the meat roast 30-40 minutes. If you are using your inside oven, preheat to 325° F. Drain the marinade from the chicken and place the thighs in a roasting pan. Cover with foil and roast for one hour.

Crabcakes
Robert Hall, Food and Beverage Manager
Trident Villas and Hotel, Port Antonio

For every pound of crabmeat:
- four slices white bread, crust removed, chopped into bread crumbs
- one tablespoon butter
- one tablespoon flour
- one-half cup milk
- one-half teaspoon chili flakes
- scallion
- one tablespoon parsley
- one teaspoon thyme
- one clove garlic, finely chopped
- one teaspoon Dijon mustard

Pick over the crabmeat and combine with bread crumbs, scallion, parsley, and thyme. In a saucepan, melt the butter and add the flour. Cook for two minutes, then add the garlic, chilies, and milk. Stir until thick. When that cools, add the mixture to the crab. Season with salt and pepper. Chill. Portion the mix into one- or two-inch balls, and pat down to form cakes. Dredge in seasoned flour, dip into beaten egg, and coat the cake with dry bread crumbs. Fry in hot oil until golden brown. Make a dip with mayonnaise, Dijon mustard, Scotch Bonnet brand hot pepper, lime juice, and salt and pepper to taste. Goes well with crisp white wine.

Cream of Pumpkin Soup
Dian Myers, chef
Treasure Beach Hotel, Treasure Beach

- chicken pieces
- two pounds pumpkin
- two ounces flour and two ounces butter to make roux
- scallions
- pinch parsley, thyme
- pinch M.S.G. (optional)
- carrots, *cho-cho,* turnips
- chicken base spice
- heavy cream

Make a chicken stock by combining four pints water, chicken bones and pieces, scallions, carrots, cho-cho, turnips, parsley, and thyme. Simmer four hours, then strain. Boil the pumpkin in the stock until it is soft. Mash it well or put it in a blender, then bring back to boil. Melt the butter in a saucepan and add flour lightly while whisking until smooth. This is called "roux." To the pumpkin, add chicken base seasoning, roux, and cream while whisking. Do not boil, just simmer. Season to taste. A very smooth treat.

Tilapia Snapper in Herbed Egg Jacket Over Pink Grapefruit and Lime Vin Blanc (serves four)
Grand Lido, Negril

Ingredients
- eight pieces freshwater snapper
- four eggs
- one teaspoon each fresh dill, fresh tarragon, fresh fennel tops, chopped
- three ounces flour
- four ounces butter
- salt and pepper to taste

Sauce
- three ounces heavy cream
- three ounces dry white wine
- three ounces fish stock
- two ounces grapefruit juice
- one ounce lime juice
- salt, pepper, and cayenne to taste
- 1.5 ounces beurre mané (one part flour and one part butter mix)

Start with the sauce first. In a saucepot, add the heavy cream, wine, and fish stock, and reduce by half. Add the remaining ingredients and thicken with the beurre mané. Simmer slowly for 15 minutes. For the fish, put the flour in a bowl and season with salt

continued

RECIPES (cont.)

and pepper. In a separate bowl, vigorously whisk the eggs and add the fresh herbs. Take the snapper filets and dredge in the flour mixture, pat off excess flour, and then dredge in the egg mixture. The fish then go directly to a hot frying pan with melted butter. Fry to a golden brown and turn. Serve fish over sauce on a plate, topped with grapefruit, orange, and lime sections, and fresh dill. Nice served with wild rice and asparagus.

Fruit Punch
Richard Walker, barman
Admiralty Club, Navy Island, Port Antonio

• pawpaw
• pineapple
• banana
• pineapple juice
• evaporated milk
• clear cane syrup or strawberry syrup
• nutmeg
• cinnamon
• vanilla

Add fresh fruit ingredients to a blender in equal amounts. Add the pineapple juice and a dollop of cane syrup. Blend. Splash in enough milk to give a pastel color, but not too much or it will curdle because of the citrus. Add dashes of nutmeg, cinnamon, and vanilla. Can blend with ice or serve over the rocks. Stick one of those tiny umbrellas into it. A small bit of rum wouldn't hurt, either.

Pimento Liqueur
Leila Rutty, owner
Pentus Guest Villa, Ocho Rios

• three pints fresh pimento berries
• one-half pint fresh lime juice
• one-quart bottle white rum
• 1.5 pounds sugar
• cinnamon sticks

Combine the pimento berries, lime juice, and rum in an earthenware or glass pot and cover for three to four days. Combine the sugar and a couple of cinnamon sticks with water and boil until it becomes syrupy, not sticky. Strain the pimento mixture and discard the berries. Add to the syrup, mix, bottle, and chill if you prefer.

For a quick and exotic snack, turn to the markets for fruit. Bananas, mangoes, pawpaws (papayas), oranges, *ugli* fruit, naseberries (resemble kiwi fruits), *otaheite* apples, June plums, soursops and sweetsops (both sweet, it's just that the sweetsop is sweeter—if you have a fridge try it frozen for a custardlike treat), *guineps,* and star apples can all be had for pennies and small talk.

Coconuts and raw sugarcane are favorites of street vendors. Drink the green nut and have the vendor cut it open for the jelly inside. Sugarcane is well worth trying, again for pennies, but is sort of like eating a fistful of sugar cubes. Tamarind candies, a mixture of the tart fruit's syrup and sugar, will be a big surprise if you don't take a nibble at a time.

BOB RACE

taro

Tea, Beer, And Liqueurs
Tea in Jamaica means anything hot and brothy, including tea. Fish tea is advertised at roadside stands, and ganja tea, ginger tea, and mint teas are used for pleasure and in folk medicine. The amazing Irish moss is popular as a drink. Irish moss, said to be an aphrodisiac, is a gelatinous extract of seaweed which can be mixed with milk, nutmeg, or rum and used as a drink or jelly.

Red Stripe Beer is the local suds and can be found in every roadside stand throughout the country. The thick Dragon Stout is also popular and a meal in itself (sort of like drinking a loaf of bread), and Heineken beer is brewed locally.

Jamaican liqueurs are available, among them the famous Tia Maria, made from Jamaica's equally famous coffee. Try pineapple liqueur or pimento liqueur for a sweet and powerful drink.

SHOPPING

If you are interested in collecting Jamaican crafts, you'll sift through the bad to get to the good. Jamaica has some exceptional arts and crafts, as well as duty-free deals and specialty items.

Where To Shop

The cheapest shopping, duty-free or otherwise, is outside of the hotels. Hotel boutiques have fine items, and their prices reflect that. The advantage to hotel boutiques is that they carry familiar items that you may want, such as international newspapers and magazines, not to mention M&Ms, and they are often open on Sundays, when the rest of Jamaica shuts down.

Montego Bay and Ocho Rios undoubtedly have some of the best shopping in the country. Montego Bay and Ocho Rios are geared up in the biggest way for tourists, so many of the shops you'll find are reflective of that. Still, there are plenty of shops that sport nice items at inexpensive prices.

If you happen to find yourself in Kingston, you'll find dozens of shopping plazas and malls that carry fine arts and crafts and other items. Kingston is where the elite of Jamaica shops, so you'll find a more eclectic array of things to buy than in tourist shops.

The least-expensive items in the country, relative to what you'd pay at home, are locally produced items such as Blue Mountain and other coffees, rums, Tia Maria and other liqueurs, cigars, and crafts. More expensive, but still cheaper than at home, are duty-free items.

Duty-free

Montego Bay, Ocho Rios, and Kingston are undoubtedly the best towns to shop for duty-free items and crafts. Gold, silver, crystal, and china will often be up to 30% cheaper than the same items elsewhere. Leather goods such as designer luggage, purses, and footwear were taxed until recently. Now you can save 10-30% on these items over prices at home. Linens, silks, some clothing, watches, perfumes, and other items also fall into the duty-free category, and will be cheaper than at home. Still, don't walk into a shop and expect that because it is a duty-free store it has the best prices in town. Poke around, compare prices; for some people that is half the fun.

Swiss Stores, one of the largest but certainly not the only duty-free emporium, has branches as in all three towns, and has a wide range of the duty-free items available in Jamaica.

The current law requires that all duty-free items be paid for in foreign currency, preferably U.S. dollars. This of course conflicts with laws stating that the Jamaican dollar is the only acceptable currency in the country. So be it; life is full of contradictions. The point is, it is best to use credit cards or traveler's checks when shopping duty-free. Even better, use credit cards when possible to help facilitate returns or exchanges. All duty-free stores in Jamaica accept most major credit cards. The Discover Card hasn't yet been wholly discovered, but is accepted by a few businesses.

The 10% GCT, or sales tax, is not charged on duty-free items.

Crafts

Many fine, handmade crafts can be found on roadsides throughout the country. As well, town markets often have numerous crafts booths—many selling the same sorts of things—where good-value deals can be found. It's okay and expected to haggle a bit over crafts. The biggest crafts markets in the country are in Kingston, Negril, Montego Bay (which has several outdoor craft markets), and Port Antonio. See the chapters on these destinations for more thorough descriptions.

Crafts are generally carvings, colorful baskets, straw hats, dolls, T-shirts, velvet country maps, and the usual suspects. Carvings are the most crafted of all, and some exhibit a high degree of workmanship and value. Many carvings are made from mahoe, lignum vitae, and mahogany.

Local art is colorful, vibrant, and often well done. Some very fine paintings can be found in small roadside stands and crafts markets.

Seashell and ocean-derived crafts are pretty but keep in mind that the reef, especially black coral, is often vandalized for the sake of coral jewelry and other coral crafts. It takes years for a piece of coral to grow, and only seconds to break it down. Further, black coral and white coral are protected by law, and it is illegal to sell or buy them.

Groceries

If you have access to a kitchen, you'll find that the larger towns have a variety of food items for sale. Most have full-line supermarkets, and you can find most anything you'll need or want, including beer, wine, and liquor. Bottled water is expensive and not necessary in Jamaica—in general, the water is fine throughout the country. You'll also find gourmet and health-food stores in Kingston, Montego Bay, and Ocho Rios. For fruits and vegetables, the farmer's markets have better selections and better prices, and are more fun.

Books

Bookstores are usually well stocked. **Sangster's,** with stores in Montego Bay and Kingston, is one of the better chains in Jamaica. All major towns have several bookstores, selling everything from novels to newspapers to tourist books and Christian tracts. Duty-free stores and hotel shops also stock a wide array of books, most of which are guide books and photo-essay-type, coffee-table books. No tax is levied on books or stationery.

Hours

Most businesses are open Mon.-Sat. 0900-1700—though on days when cruise ships arrive in town, businesses will accommodate their schedules. Market days are heaviest on Friday and Saturday. On Sunday most of Jamaica rests, save for a few small roadside shops and convenience stores.

Bringing It Home

Americans are allowed to bring home US$400 of purchases per person before tax is charged, after staying in excess of 48 hours. You can mail an unlimited number of gifts of up to US$50 per day to any single address, with the exception of perfume, tobacco products, or liquor. Jamaican rums and liqueurs make nice gifts to carry home. Persons age 21 and over can carry one liter each, or buy more and pay customs on arrival. For customs regulations not specific to the U.S., check with the individual country's customs department.

HEALTH

Jamaica is generally a healthy place. The only problems most visitors encounter are overexposure to sun, rum, and spicy foods, all preventable by common sense. It's always wise to increase your intake of nonalcoholic fluids in a tropical environment—you'll lose quite a bit through sweat. Doctors recommend at least eight large glasses of water per day. Coconut water is a healthy and inexpensive alternative to soft drinks, and more fun to drink.

Sun Exposure

The sun in Jamaica is strong, even when it's cloudy. Use your brand of sunscreen (all brands are available in the country), and try to take it easy on the tanning process for the first few days. Aloe vera is good for a sunburn, but it doesn't replace the best cure: shade. If you are light-skinned and snorkeling for any length of time, you might want to wear a T-shirt to guard against overexposing your back.

Cuts, Scratches, And Bacteria

New environments and bacteria can contribute to slower healing of cuts and scratches; they become infected more easily and linger. Scratched mosquito bites are prime offenders, as are small rock scrapes or other skin breaks. Wash, disinfect, and cover all cuts as soon as possible. Try not to scratch bites. It is *not* true that salt water is a good healer for cuts, especially cuts in their early stages. Salt water carries enough bacteria to give you a nasty infection.

Vaccinations And Prescription Drugs

Smallpox and yellow fever have been eliminated in the country. Recent isolated outbreaks of typhoid on the southwest coast were attributed to contaminated dairy products. Drinking water is filtered, chlorinated, and safe throughout the country, except for periods immediately after hurricanes or high-water situations. Vaccination certificates are not required of North American or European travelers. Travelers originating from other Caribbean countries, Asia, Africa, and other parts of the world should check regulations before departure.

If you need prescription drugs don't count on

them being readily available in Jamaica—bring enough to last your trip. Bring an extra pair of glasses or contacts.

Sexually Transmitted Diseases
Jamaica has not escaped the worldwide proliferation of sexually transmitted diseases. Herpes, gonorrhea, and other venereal diseases exist. Unless you want to take home more than just a tan, use condoms; they're available in all pharmacies and hotel shops. *Check their expiration dates.*

Sadly, AIDS is a major problem throughout the Caribbean, as it is throughout the world. A recent conference of health officials from Antigua, the Bahamas, Barbados, Cuba, Dominica, the Dominican Republic, Grenada, Guyana, Haiti, Jamaica, and Trinidad and Tobago established that those countries account for over 15,000 confirmed cases of AIDS. Given the numbers of tourists that move through Jamaica yearly, as well as the number of Jamaicans who travel regularly between North America and Jamaica and the virtual explosion of the disease worldwide, it would be foolish to engage in unsafe sex. Take that initiative yourself. Even though great strides have been made in public education in the country, there are taboos about wearing condoms and engaging in other safe sex practices.

Medical Care And Insurance
Most resorts have a resident nurse or doctor, and hotels have a doctor on call. (A hotel nurse, when asked what the most common complaint among tourists is, replied, "the morning after".) There are over 20 clinics and small hospitals in the rural areas, and the major towns have large medical centers. Among them are: **Kingston Public Hospital,** North St., Kingston, tel. (809) 922-0210, or 922-0227/9; **Nuttall Memorial Hospital,** 6 Caledonia Ave., Kingston, tel. 926-2139; **University Hospital of the West Indies,** Mona, Kingston, tel. 927-6620; **Doctor's Hospital,** Fairfield, Montego Bay, tel. 952-1616; **Port Antonio Hospital,** Naylor's Hill, tel. 993-2646; **Mandeville Hospital,** Hargreaves Ave., tel. 962-2067; **Savanna-la-mar Hospital,** tel. 955-2533.

Check your health insurance to see if you're covered overseas, and what the coverage entails. If you want to purchase more, the following offer treatment and evacuation coverage, as well as hard-to-find protection for scuba-diving injuries. Payment is determined by the length of time you travel, and by the coverage you need. Price is about US$80-90 per week for a package of medical, evacuation, accident, and loss of life coverage. Try **American Express Travel Protection Plan,** 6440 Lusk Blvd., Suite D205, San Diego, CA, tel. (800) 234-0375; or **Access America International,** 600 Third Ave., New York, NY 10163, tel. (800) 284-8300.

Personal Safety
Women traveling alone are taking a chance, not unlike in many parts of the world, of incurring some verbal harassment. Staring, whistling, and getting hit upon are not uncommon—remember, tourists often represent people out for a good time. That may not be you, but it is some people, and you'll have to put up with the behavioral flotsam left in their wake. Women traveling in groups or with a companion are in a better position to avoid it.

Jamaica is, in general, a conservative society, but the proximity of tourist activity lends a looseness to the social atmosphere, which can send the wrong signals. Women *and men* should not wear skimpy bathing suits in the streets or markets—note that Jamaicans do not. Topless and nude sunbathing is generally regulated, and doing it outside of certain areas will cause a stir. Avoid walking along deserted beach stretches at night, or getting into unmarked cars declaring themselves taxis. Areas in Montego Bay, Ocho Rios, and Kingston can be dangerous at night, both for Jamaicans and for visitors. Ask Jamaican friends what places they avoid and do the same.

Be street smart as you would in any major city worldwide. Lock your rental car. Carry your wallet or purse in a pouch or front pocket. Avoid basket-type or open handbags; they're easy targets for pickpockets. Pulling large wads of cash out to buy things sends a signal as bright as a lighthouse beacon. Don't leave bags unattended at the beach.

With a little world-wise common sense, Jamaica is as safe as where you've come from.

MONEY, MEASUREMENTS, AND COMMUNICATION

Jamaica's monetary unit is the Jamaican dollar, split into decimal units. The coins are 1c, 5c, 10c, 20c, 25c, and 50c. The bills are color-coded and bear the likenesses of Jamaica's national heroes, except for the J$20 note portraying Noel Nethersole, the Bank of Jamaica founder. Prior to Sept. 1969, Jamaica used the British pounds and pence system.

EXCHANGE RATES AND MONEY MATTERS

A recent deregulation of exchange rates and banking hours as well as a liberalization of foreign-exchange restrictions sent commercial banking institutions into a mild schizophrenia of barter and rate fluctuations in competition for foreign exchange. The Jamaican dollar exchange rate, unstable for several years, climbed as high (or as low, depending on your point of reference) as J$28 to US$1. It has since stabilized, but remains high at over J$20 to US$1.

There are numerous ways to change your money. Commercial banks include CIBC Jamaica Limited, Century National, Citizens, Jamaica Citizens, National Commercial Bank (NCB), and Scotiabank, among others, with branches in every major town in the country. Their rates are competitive. Most commercial bank hours are Mon.-Fri. 0900-1500. Others are Mon.-Thurs. 0900-1400, and Fri. 0900-1500. Banks in the rural areas vary their hours slightly.

Most banks also operate Bureaux de Change that handle foreign exchange only. A Bureau de Change is usually set up along the main street of a tourist center, for the convenience of visitors. Upon arrival at the airport, at any hour, a Bureau de Change will be open to change your money, and you ought to do this as soon as possible. It is always best to carry and exchange traveler's checks, if only for security reasons.

Money can also be exchanged in hotels, though the rates will not be as good as in banks. In all cases, save the exchange control receipt; you may have to produce records of your exchanges when departing Jamaica in order to change money back. It is illegal to export or carry Jamaican currency out of the country.

Tourist shops will change money, as will numerous young men on the streets, hungry for foreign exchange and profit. The black market has the best exchange for your money, about 10-15% higher than the bank rate—but it is not recommended. By usurping the banks, no matter what you think about big business profits and all that, you are undermining the system that has been instituted to try and correct the profound foreign exchange problem that afflicts Jamaica. By buying a few more Jamaican dollars for your dollar, you are helping to drive down the value of the Jamaican dollar, and are indirectly inflating prices. You might not suffer from using the black market, but locals who do not have access to foreign-exchange might.

The official position of shops and the government is that Jamaican dollars are the only legal tender for exchange. (The exception is duty-free shops, where all purchases must be made in foreign currency.) Yet the wildly oscillating Jamaican dollar has so frustrated hotel owners and shopkeepers that many list their rates in both Jamaican and U.S. dollars (or just U.S. dollars) to stay abreast of the exchange rates. Some also list prices in pounds sterling, Canadian dollars, and others. This means that they'll accept payment by U.S. dollars (and often other currency) and traveler's checks. Some will also exchange cash under the table—again, the choice is yours.

In this book, prices will be given in U.S. dollars if they were quoted that way by Jamaican hotels, restaurants, and businesses. In all other cases, the current, somewhat stabilized, exchange rate of J$22 to US$1 has been used. As well, prices under US$1 will be expressed in Jamaican dollars (J$). Holders of Canadian dollars and British pounds sterling will be able to calculate their exchange rates by going through the U.S. dollar exchange rate. Remember that *exchange rates are subject to change at any time.*

Major credit cards and **traveler's checks**

are accepted at major businesses in the larger towns. If you are unsure of which form of payment is acceptable, ask ahead of time. In the rural areas, make sure you have ready cash for exchange. In most gas stations, only cash is accepted. **Note:** For lost or stolen American Express credit cards or traveler's checks, contact representatives in: Montego Bay, tel. 952-4350/3; Ocho Rios, tel. 974-5369; Kingston, tel. 929-3077; or Port Antonio, tel. 993-2609.

Tipping, by the way, is expected and appreciated in Jamaica. Tip 10-15% but check the restaurant or hotel bill to see if a service charge, the tip, hasn't already been included.

A 10% General Consumption Tax is levied on selected items throughout the country. These items include accommodation and restaurant bills.

When leaving Jamaica, a departure tax of J$100 per person is payable at the airport—about US$5. It is possible to pre-pay departure tax when purchasing your ticket, so you'll only have to produce the receipt when departing. Consult your ticket vendor.

MEASUREMENTS

Jamaica is a country caught between the imperial and metric systems of measurement, but at this point the imperial system wins by a mile, so to speak. Street signs and maps are in miles and inches, though some grade-school textbooks are beginning to use kilometers and centimeters. Some Jamaicans still refer to the old English "chain," a unit of length equal to 22 yards. Liquid is measured by pints, quarts, and gallons. Mass is in grams and pounds. Temperature is Fahrenheit. See the conversion table at the back of this book.

In this book, time is indicated by the 24-hour clock, i.e., 0900 is 9 a.m., 1200 is 12 noon, 2100 is 9 p.m., and so on. Jamaicans, however, do not refer to time that way. Jamaica functions on **Eastern Standard Time** year-round, or five hours earlier than Greenwich Mean Time. **Electricity** is 110 volts AC, 50 cycles. Some hotels have 220-volt outlets available (and plugging your 110-volt appliance in to a 220-volt outlet will *not* make it run twice as well). If you need a converter it's best to bring it, though some of the large hotels will have them. If you are oper-

ating a portable computer or appliance, bring a surge protector and a small extension cord—it sounds odd, but many hotels have exactly two outlets, both behind the headboard of the bed. Bring plug converters if your appliance has round prongs.

POST

Every town in Jamaica has a small post office or postal agency. Full-service post offices send and receive parcels and letters, operate philatelic bureaus, send telegrams, and even have small bank or postal-savings services. Smaller postal agencies send and receive letters and parcels, but are unlikely to have all of the other services. When sending letters and parcels, airmail is the quickest, taking as little as one or two weeks to North America, longer to Europe. Surface mail is excruciatingly slow, and can take one to three months before arrival. Sending mail *to* Jamaica tends to take much longer for both letters and parcels.

Airmail parcels to the U.S. or Canada cost J$13.80 per pound or part thereof. To Europe the airmail rate is J$26.40 for the first pound and J$8.80 for every additional pound. The cost of sending parcels by surface is considerably cheaper, but weighed against the time and possible damages (surface mail tends to get battered), it's safer to go with air.

You might find Federal Express a swift and sure way to send small packages home. It's more expensive than regular post, but it's reliable. Find them at 20 Sunset Blvd., Montego Bay, tel. 952-0411; or 75 Knutsford Blvd., Kingston, tel. 926-1456.

Post offices are open Mon.-Fri. 0800-1700.

CURRENT POSTAL RATES

LETTERS	TO U.S. AND CANADA	TO EUROPE
Airmail, per half ounce	J$1.10	J$1.40
Aerogram	J$.80	J$.80
Postcard	J$.90	J$.90
Surface, per half ounce	J$.50	J$.60

Postal agencies keep more irregular hours, and open Mon., Wed., and Friday. Check each agency for times.

When addressing a letter to Jamaica, include a name, box or street number, town or postal district, "Jamaica," and "West Indies," or "W.I."

Jamaican stamps from the philatelic bureau are quite colorful and make nice souvenirs or gifts for stamp collectors. They also make a fair bit of revenue for Jamaica's postal system.

TELEPHONES

As of a 1987 poll, there were 152,000 telephones in Jamaica. There are probably half again as many today. Most are private, of course, but Jamaica has a good system of pay phones that will get the job done. To use a public phone, pick up the receiver and wait for a series of curious noises before you dial. Then a connection is made and you deposit coins before you can talk.

The best way to call overseas is to reverse the charges. Bring your calling card, but be aware of two problems. There is some confusion, even among operators, about whether AT&T and other calling cards are usable from Jamaica. When trying to connect, some operators will tell you that you cannot use the card from Jamaica. Other times you will be connected instantly. Calling cards work most often when you are able to use them in a direct-dial situation, such as calling from a hotel that has a direct-dial system. If you must call an operator first, that's when things break down. This situation occurs sporadically and inconsistently all over the country, so bear with it.

Secondly, whichever situation you encounter, it is not wise to give your card number to anyone but the overseas or hotel operator. Calling-card scams are not unknown in Jamaica.

The area code for Jamaica, as well as for most of the Caribbean, is 809. This means you can dial Jamaica direct from North America. The connection sometimes crackles and echos. If you are communicating with Jamaica by facsimile machine, the area code is the same. Faxing Jamaica for current hotel prices and other information can save time and money when researching your trip.

MEDIA

As of 1987, Jamaica had 387,000 televisions and 910,000 radios, and daily newspapers circulated to 4% of the population. Two local television stations, the Jamaica Broadcasting Corporation (JBC) and CVM Television, plus hundreds of satellite dishes in hotels and private homes, provide the country with television imagery. U.S.-based network programming such as CNN and others is available. Radios pick up eight main local FM stations, including FAME-FM (Fraternity of Amazing Musical Expressions), RJR (Radio Jamaica Rediffusion), JBC Radio One and JBC Radio Two, KLAS-FM, IRIE FM (the reggae station), Radio Mona, and Radio Waves. JBC and RJR also operate AM stations.

The Gleaner Company Limited prints Jamaica's premier newspaper, *The Daily Gleaner.* The paper is the oldest in the nation, having been continuously published since 1834. It is also the country's best paper, and carries a fair section of international as well local news. The Gleaner Company also prints *The Star,* a raggish tabloid filled with steamy scandal and advice columns; and *The Sunday Gleaner,* big enough to relax with by the pool on a lazy weekend morning. *The Record* is the largest rival paper and worth looking at, though its print and paper quality are erratic. *The Record* also prints a Sunday paper. Other local newspapers include *The Vacationer,* a tourism newsletter, the *Jamaica Observer,* and the *Western Mirror,* printed in Montego Bay. All local papers are fine for keeping up with the news and cost J$4-5 for the daily paper. *The Sunday Gleaner* and *Sunday Herald* each cost J$8. In large hotels and tourist shops, you can find *USA Today, The New York Times,* the *Miami Herald, The International Herald Tribune, The Times* of London, *Le Monde,* and others, sometimes only a day late, for up to 10 times the cost of a local paper.

INFORMATION AND SERVICES

TOURIST INFORMATION CENTERS

The **Jamaica Tourist Board (JTB)** maintains six main offices in Jamaica and numerous overseas branches. You'll also find JTB information booths at both major airports in Montego Bay and Kingston. Call or fax for information and brochures prior to your departure; they are generally a very congenial and helpful outfit. While in the country you can drop by the office with questions but remember, the JTB is not a booking agency. In an emergency, they will allow you to use their phones to call (for a fee) hotels or home. Brochures and maps are available (road maps cost US$1). In addition, in major towns the JTB maintains information kiosks where you can obtain brochures and ask questions. JTB offices are listed below.

The **Jamaica Association of Villas & Apartments (JAVA)** is also very helpful and they'll point you in many directions for an apartment or a villa. In Jamaica, contact JAVA, Pineapple Place, Box 298, Ocho Rios, Jamaica, W.I.; tel. 974-2508, fax 974-2967. Ask for Mrs. McKnight, whose broad knowledge of the island can be very helpful in getting you into the environment you want.

In the U.S. or Canada, call Vacation Network, tel. (800) 423-4095 or (312) 883-1020, fax (312) 883-5140. They are the North American reps for JAVA. But remember, these are *for profit* organizations, and they do not represent every villa or apartment on the island.

Another source for information is the **Jamaica Hotel and Tourist Association (JHTA),** at 2 Ardenne Rd., Kingston 10, Jamaica, W.I.; tel. 926-3635. They serve as an umbrella agency for their member hotels and tourist facilities. They do not represent every hotel on the island.

If you already have a solid itinerary and know where you are going to stay, you can book it directly through the **Jamaica Reservation Service,** tel. (800) JAMAICA. They will book and confirm everything from your rooms to cars. This is not the cheapest way to go, however. Also, while they will make suggestions, they won't shop for you. As in most cases, the best place to shop for deals is on the island itself.

National Library Service

A unique and inexpensive way to learn more about Jamaica during your visit is to join the national library service. A visitor pays a small deposit and can check out up to three books at a time. When you return the books, you get the money back. Every parish capital has a decent library, usually with an in-depth West Indies section. Libraries are generally open Mon.-Fri. 0900-1800 and Sat. 0900-1300. Jamaica Library Service headquarters are in Kingston, tel. 926-3310.

USEFUL TELEPHONE NUMBERS

Area Code 809

Customs and Excise Dept., Newport East, Kingston, tel. 922-5140

Ministry of Foreign Affairs, 85 Knutsford Blvd, Kingston, tel. 926-4220

Geological Survey Dept., Hope Gardens, Kingston, tel. 927-1936/7

Ministry of Health, 10 Caledonia Ave., Kingston, tel. 926-9220

Jamaica Council for the Handicapped, 92 Hanover St., Kingston, tel. 922-0585

Jamaica Information Service, 58a HWT Rd., Kingston, tel. 926-3740

Police Emergency, Kingston, tel. 119

General Post Office, 13 King St., Kingston, tel. 922-2120

Prime Minister's Office, 1 Devon Rd., Kingston, tel. 927-9941

Ministry of Tourism, 36 Trafalgar Rd., Kingston, tel. 929-8990

EMBASSIES

Area Code 809

American Embassy, 2 Oxford Rd., Kingston, tel. 926-3781/3

Australian High Commission, 64 Knutsford Blvd., Kingston, tel. 926-3550/2

Belgium Embassy, 6 Oxford Rd., Kingston, tel. 926-4925 or 926-6589

Embassy of Brazil, 64 Knutsford Blvd., Kingston, tel. 929-8607/8

British High Commission, Trafalgar Rd., Kingston, tel. 926-9050

Embassy of the People's Republic of China, 8 Seaview Ave., Kingston, tel. 927-0850

Colombian Embassy, 53 Knutsford Blvd., Kingston, tel. 929-1702

Canadian High Commission, 30 Knutsford Blvd., Kingston, tel. 926-1500

French Embassy, 13 Hillcrest Ave., Kingston, tel. 927-9811

Embassy of the Federal Republic of Germany, 10 Waterloo Rd., Kingston, tel. 926-6728/9 or 926-5665

Indian High Commission, 4 Retreat Ave., Kingston, tel. 927-0486 or 927-4270

Israeli Embassy, 60 Knutsford Blvd., Kingston, tel. 926-8768

Japanese Embassy, 32 Trafalgar Rd., Kingston, tel. 929-7534 or 929-3338/9

Republic of Korea Embassy, 60 Knutsford Blvd., Kingston, tel. 929-3035/7

Mexican Embassy, 36 Trafalgar Rd., Kingston, tel. 926-6891

Netherlands Embassy, 53 Knutsford Blvd., Kingston, tel. 926-2026

Embassy of Spain, 25 Dominica Dr., Kingston, tel. 929-6710 or 929-8575

Trinidad and Tobago High Commission, 60 Knutsford Blvd., Kingston, tel. 926-5730

Venezuelan Embassy, 36 Trafalgar Rd., Kingston, tel. 926-5510 or 926-5519

In addition, the U.S. maintains a consular agency in Montego Bay at the Blue Harbour Hotel on Sewell Ave., tel. 952-0160 or 952-5050. The Canadian government maintains a consulate at 29 Gloucester Ave., Montego Bay, tel. 952-6198.

JAMAICA TOURIST BOARD OFFICES

JAMAICA

Area Code 809

The Tourism Centre, 21 Dominica Dr., P.O. Box 360, Kingston 5 tel. 929-9200/19, fax 929-9375, airport tel. 924-8024

21 Ward Ave., Mandeville tel. 962-1072, fax 962-2762

Cornwall Beach, P.O. Box 67, Montego Bay, tel. 952-4425/8, fax 952-3587, airport tel. 952-2462

Adrija Plaza, Shop No. 9, Negril P.O., tel. 957-4243, fax 957-4489

Ocean Village Shopping Center, P.O. Box 240, Ocho Rios tel. 974-2582/3, fax 974-2559

City Centre Plaza, P.O. Box 151, Port Antonio, tel. 993-3051 or 993-2587, fax 993-2587

UNITED STATES

Toll-free, tel. (800) 847-4279

300 W. Wienca Rd. NE, Suite 100A, Atlanta, GA 30302, tel. (404) 250-9971/2, fax (404) 252-7029

21 Merchants Rowe, Fifth Floor, Boston, MA 02109, tel. (617) 248-5811, fax (617) 367-2438

36 S. Wabash Ave., Suite 1210, Chicago, IL 60603, tel. (312) 346-1546, fax (312) 346-1667

1320 South Dixie Hwy., Suite 1100, Coral Gables, FL 33146, tel. (800) 327-9857 or (305) 665-0557, fax (305) 666-7239

8214 Westchester, Suite 500, Dallas, TX 75225, tel. (214) 361-8778, fax (214) 361-7049

26400 Lahser Rd., Lahser Center One, Suite 114A, Southfield, MI 48034, tel. (313) 948-9557

3440 Wilshire Blvd., Suite 1207, Los Angeles, CA 90010, tel. (213) 384-1123, fax (213) 384-1780

(continued)

JAMAICA TOURIST BOARD OFFICES *(cont.)*

801 Second Ave., 20th Floor, New York, NY
  10017, tel. (212) 688-7650, fax (212) 759-5012

1315 Walnut St., Suite 1504, Philadelphia, PA
  19107, tel. (215) 545-1061

CANADA

1110 Sherbrooke St. W, Montreal, Quebec H3A
  1G9, tel. (514) 849-6386/7, fax (514) 849-4260

1 Eglinton Ave. E, Suite 616, Toronto, Ontario M4P
  3A1; tel. (416) 482-7850, fax (416) 482-1730

U.K. AND EUROPE

Schmidftrasse 12, 6000 Frankfurt Main 1,
  Germany, tel. (069) 75-80-03-17/8/9

111 Gloucester Place, London W1H 3PH, England, tel. (071) 224-0505, fax (071) 224-0551

c/o Target International, 52 Avenue des Champs
  Elysees, 75008 Paris, France
  tel. (01) 45-61-9058, fax (01) 42-25-6640

c/o Sergat Italia S.R.L., Piazza dei Cenci 7/A,
  00186 Rome, Italy, tel. (06) 686-9112 or 654-
  1336

JAPAN

c/o The Carrington Group, Ginza Yamato Building,
  Ninth Floor, 7-9-17 Ginza, Chou-Ku, Tokyo 104,
  Japan, tel. (03) 289-5767, fax (03) 289-5769

LATIN AMERICA

c/o TRAC, 6595 N.W. 36th St., Suite 109, Miami,
  FL 33166, tel. (305) 871-7820 fax (305) 871-
  7833

MEXICO

535 Xola Ave., 12th Floor, 03100 Mexico City,
  Mexico, tel. 660-4453, ext. 2663

BEFORE YOU GO

VISAS, PASSPORTS, AND OTHER DOCUMENTS

U.S. and Canadian citizens can enter Jamaica with only a passport, or with the combination of a birth certificate and driver's license with photo, or with a residency or naturalization certificate. Travelers from most other countries are *required* to carry passports—check with your respective country's authorities regarding visa requirements. All passengers may be required to show a ticket as proof of departure.

Photocopy your proof of citizenship and keep your passport number written somewhere or commit it to memory.

Keep a list of your traveler's checks by number, separate from the checks themselves.

Bring your driver's license if you want to rent a car or motorcycle.

If you are a diver, don't forget your certification card.

WHAT TO TAKE

If it doesn't fit in your seabag, you don't need it.

—sailors' axiom

Luggage
Consider your clothes laid out on the bed, ready to be packed. Consider your billfold, filled with traveler's checks. Now, put half the clothes back and go out and get some more money. It's not that Jamaica is expensive. With effort, and aside from airfare and a rental car, you can cover it on US$40 per day. You might also spend up to US$300 per day and any amount in between; it all boils down to elective lifestyles.

Generally, people bring too many clothes, accessories, knicks, and knacks—and get bogged down with lugging the beasts all over the country. Travel lightly and efficiently. Efficiently in this case means that you are able carry it yourself, be it a backpack or suitcase. For some, efficiency means taking only carryon luggage, in which case you'll have no lost luggage ending up somewhere in French Guiana, and you'll be among the first in and out of customs lines. Check with your airline regarding baggage allowance. Most allow two or three checked bags and one or two carryons. Typically, the carryon allows for 45 linear inches in total dimensions (add the length, width, and depth of your bag) and up to 70 pounds in weight. Pocketbooks, purses, and small briefcases are not, in practice, considered carryon luggage, so you can take them on as well. Checked bags are typically 62 total inches in dimension and 70 pounds each. It sounds technical, but in practice these allowances cover just about any standard suitcase or backpack available. Additional bags are charged by weight. But you'd be surprised how much you can fit in a carryon bag. Remember, in these days of tight airport security, all bags must be tagged with your name and address. It's a good idea to keep an ID label inside the luggage as well for further identification if it's lost or stolen.

Clothes And Toiletries

Think "light" for clothes: light cotton shorts, T-shirts, and tops for both men and women. Take one set of evening wear—**men note:** Some, but not many, hotels and restaurants require a jacket and trousers at dinner. Consider prints, which don't show wrinkles readily, and drip-dry-type clothes. Unless you want to take out a series of small loans to pay for hotel laundry services, you'll be doing your own washing. Coin-operated washing machines are not readily available in Jamaica, but you can drop off your clothes at cheaper, independent laundry services.

Take two bathing suits. Many endeavors in this world are more unpleasant than putting on a wet bathing suit, but they just don't come to mind right away.

A lightweight jacket or sweater will be important in the cool mountains and even by the beach on some evenings. To save luggage space, wear the sweater on the trip. Airplanes tend to be cool anyway, and if you've just flown out of Toronto in sub-zero weather, you'll need something to get you to the airport. You'll not want to carry a heavy winter coat to Jamaica.

Flip-flops are fine most of the time. Consider your intended activities, whether they'll be hiking, sports, dancing, or dining in nice restaurants, and bring the proper footwear.

All basic toiletries are available in Jamaica, but many are expensive. You have your own preferences, so bring your deodorant, toothpaste, floss, and shampoo, as well as makeup, skin cream, contraceptives, tampons, and other items you'll need to stay comfortable.

Take your prescription drugs, glasses or contacts, vitamins, aspirin, antiseptic cream or spray, sterile strips, lip protection, something for diarrhea, insect repellent, medicinal charcoal tablets, and, if you're prone to it, motion-sickness medication. (There are nondrug products on the market to prevent motion sickness. One, a wristband that controls nausea by applying acupressure to specific points on the wrist, costs about US$15-20 for a set of two. They're called Sea Bands and can be found at health stores, sporting-goods stores, or through various catalogues.) As well, most of the items above are available in Jamaica but are more expensive.

Hiking And Camping Supplies

Most campers and hikers have a fair idea of what kind of gear they'll need. Bring it. A few camping spots rent tents, but don't count on it. Make sure your tent is secure, mosquito proof, and waterproof. If you can lock the zippers or flaps, then do so. Bring cooking utensils, but keep in mind that many camping areas have kitchen facilities or restaurants nearby. Do bring a can-and-bottle opener (or ask a Jamaican to show you the astonishing local method of opening beer bottles). A flashlight, pocketknife, corkscrew, canteen or water bottle, and compass will come in handy. Of course, your best hiking shoes, shorts, sunglasses, and a sun hat are must-brings. Bring food containers, insect repellent, a small first-aid kit, and a light sleeping bag or sheets.

A day pack is good for shopping and going to the beach. Waterproof matches are important, even when it's not raining. Humidity has been known to reduce match heads to feckless lumps.

A poncho or good umbrella will be very useful. Dried food is your call; there are enough fresh fruits, vegetables, and good restaurants everywhere to warrant leaving the astronaut stuff at home. Extra twine comes in handy for clotheslines and tying things to your pack.

Cameras

Jamaica was made for the camera's eye—it would be a shame not to capture the island's beauty on film. You know your camera, filters, and accessories best, but always pack them with silica-gel bags to beat the humidity. Bring enough film for the entire trip, and consider having it processed back home. Film is expensive in Jamaica, and although developing is comparable, not all processes are available everywhere. If you have an instant camera, it's a great way to give photo gifts to people. If you want to take photos of Jamaicans, please ask first. They may want one for themselves, which is where the instant can be fun. They may also want money, and if the photo means enough to you, please respect that. Bring photos of yourself and fami-

ly if you plan to spend time in the rural areas—people love to see and talk about them.

Incidentals

If you have specialized sports gear, bring it along. This includes golf equipment (though the courses rent their own), tennis and other racquets, extra balls, and specialty shoes. Scuba divers can bring their regulators and buoyancy compensators, and all divers might want to bring their own masks, fins, and snorkels. Diving equipment, however, can be rented at hotels and dive centers. Reef-walking shoes are a nice plus if you intend to spend time walking along the reef and rocky shorelines.

Don't forget your address book at home or at the hotel (one of the most common "left behind" items). Bring pens, stationery, and envelopes. Plastic bags come in handy for storing wet or dirty clothes.

Jamaican customs allows you to carry in one carton (200) cigarettes and one pint of liquor, provided it's not rum, as well as a half pound of tobacco and one quart of wine.

GETTING THERE

BY AIR

Most visitors to Jamaica fly into Sangster International Airport (named after a former prime minister, Sir Donald Sangster) in Montego Bay. If your final destination is Port Antonio or the east coast of the island, you can fly on to Kingston and get transport from there. Flights to Montego Bay from various points in North America take approximately the following amount of time: Boston, 4 hours; Chicago, 3 hours and 45 minutes; Dallas, 4 hours and 50 minutes; Los Angeles, 5 hours and 20 minutes; Miami, 1 hour and 20 minutes; New York, 3 hours and 30 minutes; Philadelphia, 3 hours and 20 minutes; Toronto, 4 hours.

For flight departure information while in Jamaica, try **Sangster International Airport,** tel. 952-5530, or call your airline direct. At **Norman Manley International Airport** in Kingston call 928-6077, or contact your airline.

Shopping For Flights And Fares

Shopping for flights can be frustrating because of the sheer numbers of airlines and charter companies that service Jamaica. Some travelers prefer to find their own flights, but it may be worth your while to go to a trusted travel agent. A good one will do your shopping for you, while others might try to sell you expensive packages that lock you into one place and time.

You can shop for flights yourself, using the toll-free numbers (see chart, "Major Airlines Serving Jamaica"). If you are traveling on a budget, ask for the lowest fare and inquire about restrictions, including minimum and maximum stays and cancellation policies. Air Jamaica, for instance, sometimes offers a discount fare if your hotel stay is pre-paid (your choice of hotel for a minimum of three days) and you present a voucher to prove it. Call the airline of your choice more than once; odds are you'll get a different agent each time, and ask the same questions to see if the answers are the same. There are too many variables in international travel to try it only once.

Airfare to Jamaica goes up in the winter season, so if time is not an issue it's better to travel from mid-April to mid-Nov. or so. Different airlines define the heavy season by slightly different dates. The difference between on- and off-season flying can be as much as 15-20%. Traveling Mon.-Thurs. is often cheaper than traveling on weekends, by as much as US$100 for the roundtrip.

Currently, roundtrip fares start about US$400, high season, from the U.S. East Coast. Off-season fares are as low as US$280. These are basic rates; variations exist depending on how long you stay, how far in advance you pay, airfare battles currently underway, etc. Fares from the U.S. Midwest or West Coast need not be much more expensive if you've shopped for inexpensive connecting flights.

In general, the earlier you can decide, book, and pay for your flight, the cheaper it will be. On the other hand, good deals sometimes come up only a month before they're effective. Check for special rates around spring break for North America's colleges. Some airlines require payment up to three weeks beforehand, and will penalize for flight changes after payment.

When you leave Jamaica, a departure tax of J$100 (about US$5) pp must be paid at the airport. Consult your ticket vendor about prepaying the departure tax when purchasing your ticket—it will save time as well.

Flights From North America
Air Jamaica has the most gateways to Mon-

tego Bay from North America, flying from Atlanta, Baltimore, Los Angeles, Miami, New York, Orlando, Philadelphia, Tampa, or Toronto. Air Jamaica offers charters from Chicago and Cleveland.

American Airlines has gateways to Montego Bay from Miami and JFK in New York, and flies two to three times daily. An advantage with American is that their connections to those cities from the rest of the country, especially to New York, are frequent.

Air Canada leaves Montreal, Toronto, and Winnipeg nonstop for Montego Bay, the best bet for Canadian travelers.

Continental Airlines flies from Newark and other eastern points. **Northwest Airlines** flies nonstop out of Boston and other eastern points.

Flights From Around The World
From Europe, a flight to London or Gatwick will send you directly to Jamaica via **British Airways.** Otherwise, a flight to North America and a connection with one of the airlines mentioned previously will get you there. British Airways also connects the Bahamas to Jamaica, out of Nassau.

For interisland travel, one of the airlines of the Caribbean, **British West Indies Airways (BWIA),** connects to Antigua, Barbados, Haiti, Puerto Rico, and Trinidad.

South American travelers will want to connect with **ALM Antillean Airlines,** which flies in from Aruba, Bonaire, Puerto Rico, St. Maarten, Medellin, and Panama, as well as others, via their gateway to Jamaica, Curaçao. **COPA**

MAJOR AIRLINES SERVING JAMAICA

Area Code 809

Air Canada, Kingston, tel. 924-8211; Montego Bay, tel. 952-5160; U.S.A., tel. (800) 776-3000.

Air Jamaica, Kingston, tel. 922-4661; Montego Bay, tel. 952-4300; Ocho Rios, tel. 974-2566; Negril, tel 957- 4210; U.S.A., tel. (800) 523-5585.

ALM Antillean Airlines, Kingston, tel. 926-1762.

American Airlines, Kingston, tel. 924-8305; Montego Bay, tel. 952-5950; U.S.A., tel. (800) 433-7300.

British Airways, Kingston, tel. 929-9020; Montego Bay, tel. 952-3771.

British West Indies Airways (BWIA), Kingston, tel. 929-3771/3; U.S.A., tel. (800) 327-7401.

Cayman Airways, Kingston, tel. 926-1762/4.

Continental Airlines, Kingston, tel. 924-8271/2; Montego Bay, tel. 952-4460; U.S.A., tel. (800) 231-0856.

Northwest Airlines, Montego Bay, tel. 952-5531; U.S.A., tel. (800) 447-4747.

(Compañia Panamena de Aviación) connects from Panama. **Cayman Airways** flies from Grand Cayman, and **Cubana** makes the Havana-to-Jamaica connection.

BY WATER

Cruises

Over a dozen cruise companies visit the ports of Montego Bay, Ocho Rios, Port Antonio, and Kingston. Ocho Rios takes in the largest numbers, with 75% of the cruise business docking there. While this is certainly one way to get to Jamaica, it is not really a Jamaican vacation. Your few hours in each port is balanced by many more on the ship—those who cruise do it for the ambience on board, not to truly experience of the countries they visit. For more information, try **Carnival Cruise Lines,** tel. (800) 327-7373 in the U.S. except Florida, tel. (800) 325-1214 in Florida; **Crystal Cruiselines,** tel. (800) 446-6645; **Royal Cruise Lines,** tel. (800) 227-4534; or **Royal Viking Line,** tel. (800) 422-8000.

Yachtsmen cruising to Jamaica from the U.S. find southern Florida an ideal place to begin the trip. Taking advantage of strong northeasterly winds, the cruise passes through the Bahamas (an ideal place to refuel and replenish supplies) to Grand Inagua and the Windward Passage, between Cuba and Haiti. From there it's a straight and easy shot to Jamaica's north coast, some 100 miles south. Generally, the northeasterlies are strongest in summer, an ideal time to sail. Keep in mind that the tail end of summer is also hurricane season, so keep abreast of weather reports.

Jamaica's ports and marinas are excellent for cruising the island, but if you are sailing a foreign registered boat, you must first enter Jamaica at ports where you can clear Customs and Immigration. These are: West Harbour in Port Antonio; Ocho Rios Bay or St. Ann's Bay in Ocho Rios; Montego Bay Yacht Club in Montego Bay; and Newport East, Royal Jamaican Yacht Club, or Port Royal in Kingston.

The Jamaican government, because of its stringent position on drug smuggling, requires that you clear customs at each individual port in the country. You will be issued a coastal clearance certificate, enabling you to leave one port and enter another, and your boat may be boarded by customs or Coast Guard officials for inspection. All firearms must be declared and surrendered for safekeeping while you are in port, and they'll be returned upon your departure.

Remember to fly your Jamaican courtesy flags when approaching port, and to contact the harbor master, who will direct you to Customs and Immigration.

Local charter boats, which offer packages from day-cruises to extended charters, can be found at marinas in major ports including Montego Bay, Falmouth, Ocho Rios, Oracabessa, Port Antonio, Kingston, and Negril. This type of traveling is perfect for the visitor whose appreciation of a country is enhanced by cruising—the Jamaican coastline is stunning, and distances between ports are not great. But it's not inexpensive. Depending on the size of the boat and crew, a charter can run several hundred dollars or more per day.

TOURS AND CHARTERS

Hundreds of companies operate tours to Jamaica. These include Jamaica-based tour operators, overseas tour operators, airlines,

PHYLLIS LUNTTA

hotels, airlines in conjunction with hotels, and permutations thereof. Tours have varying themes but the basics are a return flight, a certain number of nights at a hotel or resort, airport transfers, and guaranteed prices. Some include breakfast or all meals, and others include sightseeing tours. As has been mentioned, packages can be a good deal for those who are willing to commit to one hotel and one area for their stay.

In general, tours are less expensive per person if you go with someone else. Tour operators quote prices per person based on double occupancy. Make sure you find out what the price

is per person, *single* occupancy. It always involves a supplemental payment and will be more than the bold numbers on the brochure. Tour operators usually operate on charter flights, that is, flights that are leased from an airline to carry one group of people to one place. They often depart only once per week.

Of the charter companies flying to Jamaica, one of the largest is **American Trans Air** (7337 W. Washington, Indianapolis, IN 46251; tel. 800-225-9920). They operate twice per week out of Indianapolis, and if you catch the charter from there it'll be a good deal. In the past they have

THE GOLDEN CARIBBEAN

SCHEDULE FROM	SCHEDULE FROM
BOSTON	**PHILADELPHIA**
TO	TO
✤ **JAMAICA** ✤	✤ **JAMAICA** ✤
West Indies	West Indies

Leave
BOSTON
Long Wharf

Every
Wednesday
At 10 A. M.

From October to April

Leave
PHILADELPHIA
From PIER No. 5, NORTH

Every
Thursday
At 10 A. M.

From October to April

These Steel Twin-Screw American Steamers have first-class accommodations for passengers on main, upper and hurricane decks. Staterooms are all outside rooms, lighted by electric lights, located forward of the engines on main deck and removed from the noise of propellers, are especially well ventilated, of ample dimensions, and on the bridge deck passengers have ample room for promenade.

STEAMSHIPS
ADMIRAL DEWEY and
ADMIRAL SAMPSON
New American Twin-Screw Steamships
United States Mail Service

STEAMSHIPS
ADMIRAL SCHLEY and
ADMIRAL FARRAGUT
New American Twin-Screw Steamships
United States Mail Service

RATES OF FARE:
May 1 to November 1
Round Trip, $60.00;   One Way, $35.00
November 1 to May 1
Round Trip, $75.00;   One Way, $40.00
For return sailings and connections see pages 10 and 12

RATES OF FARE:
May 1 to November 1
Round Trip, $60.00;   One Way, $35.00
November 1 to May 1
Round Trip, $75.00;   One Way, $40.00
For return sailings and connections see pages 10 and 12

booked through tour operators out of Boston, Chicago, Dallas, Detroit, Houston, Indianapolis, Milwaukee, New York, and Fort Lauderdale, but flights on charters from those cities are comparable to regular airline travel. The disadvantage to charters is that they fly infrequently and impose monetary restrictions on changing your flight dates or cancelling your ticket. The advantage, if you can find one in your area, is that they're inexpensive.

Sunburst Holidays (4779 Broadway, New York, NY 10034; tel. 800-666-8346) deals exclusively in Jamaica destinations and operates a fairly extensive operation, chartering from gateways in Atlanta, Baltimore, Boston, Hartford, Los Angeles, Newark, New York, Philadelphia, and Washington, DC. They are the ones to start with when researching package vacations.

A travel agent will have specifics on available packages. Shop with bargain houses such as **Vacation Outlet** of Boston, Massachusetts, tel. (617) 267-8100. Again, peruse the travel classifieds of your Sunday paper or of travel magazines for deals.

GETTING AROUND

The most economical, but not necessarily the quickest, way to get around is to use Jamaica's public transportation. Plenty of buses, minibuses, and taxis are either in the towns or zooming along the major roads connecting the towns. However, their schedules and fares are decipherable only to a select few—which most likely won't include you. But they're fun, they're the way Jamaica moves, and, to understate it, they're an adventure.

Buses
Buses and minibuses leave towns from bus stands, often near the main market of town. Their destinations are marked on the window. You can catch them at their stands or flag them down *anywhere* on the road between points—stops are also designated along the roads. Fares are calculated on a "between stops" basis. When you get on, a "conductor" will collect your fare. You will probably sit next to a man who is wondering if his bananas on the roof rack are in peril. Reggae will blast from speakers. Children will stare. The driver will demonstrate a low threshold of fear as he accelerates around corners and simultaneously participates in three conversations with passengers. This is daily living. All buses have colorful names: "Jesus Is Lord," "Rambo," "The Exterminator," and "Irie-I" are typical. A personal favorite: "Crashless."

Minibuses are vans that pick up passengers around and between towns and operate like the larger buses. Identify them by the large number of arms dangling from their windows and by their red license plates. All public-transport vehicles carry red plates with the initials PPV (Public Passenger Vehicle).

Taxis
Taxis are often unmetered and fares should be discussed before entering one. Drivers are generally not out to take you for a ride, so to speak, but you should know how much they'll charge, especially if a return trip is involved. There are two types of taxis: the standard red-plate type and those licensed by the Jamaica Union of Travellers Association (JUTA). JUTA drivers do more tourism business than the rest, and are slightly more expensive. Maximum rates are suggested for all taxis by the government, but not always followed. Typical rates around Montego Bay and Sangster International Airport are J$20-50 and more. In and around the Kingston metro area, expect J$50 and more. But a Kingston-to-Montego Bay trip can run closer to J$1700. A long tour by taxi may pay off if you fill the car with people and split the rate. If you're interested, pick up a fare table of suggested rates (not always available) from any JTB office. Taxis can be hailed or found parked in front of your hotel. Many assemble at the bus stands in towns.

Some taxis, often minivans, operate like buses and pick up more than one passenger at a time, dropping them off around town. This is definitely the cheapest and quickest way to travel short distances, as they charge closer to bus rates than to taxi rates.

Vehicles with blue license plates also pick up passengers. The blue indicates that they've applied for a PPV.

Trains

After a series of stops and starts of track repairs due to aging and hurricane damage, the venerable Jamaica Railway Corporation (JRC) train is back in business. This is a fun and inexpensive way to traverse the country, and a way to see Jamaica's interior. The basic route is Montego Bay to Kingston and back, with stops at Catadupa, Appleton Estates, Williamsfield, May Pen, and Spanish Town. Currently, the train departs Montego Bay at 0900 and arrives in Kingston at 1335. The trip from Kingston departs at 0900 and arrives in Montego Bay at 1450. Cost is a bargain J$39.50 from Montego Bay to Kingston, less for stops between. For information contact JRC Kingston, 922-6620; or JRC Montego Bay, 952-4842.

JRC also operates a tourist train from Montego Bay to Appleton (see "Montego Bay," p. 92) and a few cargo routes in the southwest.

Car And Motorbike Rental

Possibly the best way to see the island is by renting a car. Unfortunately, it is not the cheapest way to see the island unless you are splitting the cost with several people. Rates vary with the model and season but average around US$50 per day, and US$350 per week for the economy models. Tax and insurance add another US$10-12 per day. You should be able to get out of paying insurance by producing your insurance contract from home, but in practice this is confusing and generally unworkable. Most car rental companies recognize that insurance can be waived if you rent with an American Express card. Many car companies will cut a deal in off-season for unlimited free mileage and reduced rates. Some give unlimited mileage as a matter of course. Cars rented at the airport tend to be the most expensive—if you can hold off, wait until you get into town to pick up a car. Better yet, call ahead to reserve the car, and make arrangements for the rental company to meet you at the airport.

Gasoline is in addition to the rental, and currently sells for about J$8 per liter, or US$1.40 per gallon.

Major international rental agencies such as Avis, Hertz, Thrifty, Dollar, and Budget Rent-A-Car operate in Jamaica, as well as hundreds of smaller companies in Kingston, Montego Bay, Ocho Rios, Negril, Port Antonio, and Mandeville. Smaller companies can be cheaper, and are usually reliable—just check to see that all mirrors

are in place, and that the car is equipped with a spare tire and jack. If you are traveling across the country, ask what policy the rental agency has should you break down in a remote area.

Cars are usually compact, and your choice will be automatic or standard shift, a/c or no a/c. Automatic is best for mountain driving, and a/c is a personal choice. You don't need a 4WD in Jamaica unless you plan to drive straight up the side of a mountain.

Jamaicans drive on the left, or the "wrong side" for North Americans—another reason to get an automatic, if shifting with your left hand is a problem. Practice in a parking lot before you pull out onto a road. Traffic circles or rotaries are tricky, so go slowly into them. The speed limit throughout the island is 50 mph on the highways and 30 mph in towns. That's in theory. In practice, Jamaicans seem to add another 10 mph or more.

The roads are usually in good condition. Jamaica's major highways (most often one-lane roads with some traffic lights near towns) circle the island and cut across at a few points, and are really quite good. The drive is breathtaking in places. In the mountains, the roads are less well kept, and you will need to worry a bit after a heavy rain. Mountains deposit piles of stone and dirt; roads buckle and are narrow enough in the hills to make passage impossible. Backing out can be a challenge. If you're in doubt about a mountain road, ask a Jamaican what it's like around the corner. If they say it's bad, it's pretty bad.

Highways are generally well marked and designated by an "A" or "B," as in, for example, A3 or B9. The "A" and "B" represent primary and secondary roads, respectively. You can expect both to be hard surfaced. In the rural areas, signs have disappeared or faded beyond recognition. The best way to navigate is to ask for directions.

Jamaicans use their horns liberally and with some abandon. Don't take it as an insult. It means someone is passing you or passing someone else and signalling it. In the mountains, the roads are so narrow that sounding your horn around a hairpin corner is an act of survival.

While you drive you will notice some people gesturing with an open hand, sort of a dramatic sweep of the arm toward the road ahead. They are hitchhiking, and you should do the same should you hitchhike. Hitching is as safe in Jamaica as it is anywhere else, so know your limits. You may be expected to pay for a lift, so clarify this before jumping in.

In resort locations, motorcycles, scooters, and mopeds can be rented by the day or week. A small 50cc bike goes for about US$30 p/d, up to a large 500cc bike for US$50 p/d. Again, these prices can be negotiated, especially during the off-season. In practice, you need not produce a motorcycle license from your home. Helmet laws are not enforced, but helmets are often available from the rental agency.

Note: In Jamaica you must be 21 years old and possess a valid driver's license to rent a vehicle.

Bicycle rentals are also available in tourist towns, particularly in Negril, which lends itself more readily to biking than to driving.

Air

A number of small airstrips throughout the country service Jamaica's internal airlines. **Trans Jamaican Airlines** flies to Kingston (Tinson Pen Aerodrome), Negril, Montego Bay, Ocho Rios, and Port Antonio several times daily in seven single- and twin-engined light aircraft. Fares are cheap enough if you're in a hurry to get somewhere. Typical costs are: Montego Bay to Port Antonio, US$70 OW; Montego Bay to Negril, US$50 OW; Montego Bay to Ocho Rios, US$60 OW; Kingston to Negril, US$60 OW; Ocho Rios to Negril, US$78 OW; Port Antonio to Negril, US$85 OW; Negril to Port Antonio, US$85 OW.

Contact: Kingston, tel. 923-8680; Montego Bay, tel. 952-5401/3; Ocho Rios, tel. 974-3254; Negril, tel. 957-4251; Port Antonio, tel. 993-2405. You can book your flights from North America by contacting Ticket Office, c/o Air Overseas Inc. (7800 Red Rd., Suite 114, South Miami, FL 33143-5523; tel. 305-665-8109 or 800-432-7724).

Timair (tel. 952-2516) is another Montego Bay-based internal airline that operates charters and some flights between Montego Bay, Negril, Port Antonio, Ocho Rios, and Kingston.

Alternative Tours

A number, in fact a large number, of tour companies offer tourist packages that will take you to some of the country's more well-known sights and activities, such as Dunn's River Falls and Rio Grande River Rafting. These orga-

nized tours are fine if your idea of experiencing the country is to pile onto buses filled with dozens of camcorder-toting passengers. The costs vary according to where you are going, but the tours generally pick you up at your hotel, and include lunches and drinks and so on. You can arrange this type of tour at the hotel.

Several unique tour companies, however, organize custom-built tours for travelers to alternative destinations, with the idea that natural beauty is one of the brightest stars Jamaica has to offer. Possibly chief among them is **Sense Adventures** (P.O. Box 216, Kingston 7, Jamaica, W.I.; tel. 927-2097, fax 929-6967), headquartered at Maya Lodge, Kingston. They are also the base for the **Jamaica Alternative Tourism, Camping and Hiking Association (JATCHA).** (See "The Blue Mountains," p. 162, for more information on Maya Lodge.) Sense Adventures offers a range of alternative tours, from canoeing adventures to Cockpit Country excursions to historical tours. Some are one-day trips; others last for nine days. The emphasis is on meeting and dealing with rural Jamaica, and the trips are custom-built around the size of your group. Contact founder Peter Bentley for tour information or for camping and other reservations.

A relative newcomer to the alternative-adventure scene is **The Touring Society of Jamaica** (5 Duke St., Kingston, Jamaica, W.I.; tel. and fax 968-5011). Lynda Lee Burks offers custom tours for birdwatchers, garden lovers, natural history enthusiasts, or architecture and art buffs. Tours are for one to four persons. Cost is about US$50-85 pp for a couple, or US$25-65 pp for groups of four. The Touring Society will also make hotel bookings and other reservations.

Write to the **Jamaica Government Forests Department** (173 Constant Springs Rd., Kingston 10, Jamaica, W.I.; tel. 924-2612) for information regarding hikes and alternative accommodations in the Blue Mountains and other government reserves.

One of the more interesting tours offered nowadays has nothing to do with Jamaica, except as a jumping-off point. Several tour companies offer day-trips to Cuba, only a 45-minute flight from Montego Bay. The tour includes the flight, visits to historical sites such as the Monacada Barracks (which has displays of weapons used in Fidel Castro's 1959 Revolution), and The Museum of Piracy at Morro Castle. Other tour companies offer weekend trips to Cuba, including visa arrangements, accommodation, Havana tours, and visits to beaches.

These tours are one of the many indicators that Cuba is beginning to dispossess itself of some of its previous anti-capitalist ideology in its desire for badly needed foreign currency. But *U.S. travelers please note:* Because the U.S. has no direct diplomatic relations with the Cuba and, in fact, still maintains an economic embargo, access to the country by U.S. citizens is limited. While Americans are not expressly forbidden to visit Cuba, they are in essence not allowed to spend money there. In addition to a valid passport and visa, a special permit to

spend money is required from the U.S. Treasury Department. Practically speaking, travel by Americans to Cuba is limited to some journalists, professional researchers, and U.S. government officials. American passport holders have been known to skip the required hoops and red tape by traveling to Cuba through Mexico or Canada, and now Jamaica. This practice is risky, and carries heavy U.S. prison penalties and fines if you are caught—an unpleasant way to end your Jamaica vacation.

For the day tour, contact **Sunholiday Tours** in Montego Bay (tel. 952-5629 or 952-4585, fax 953-2391). Cost is US$170 per person. For weekend excursions, contact **Caribic Vacations** in Montego Bay (tel. 952-5013), Negril (tel. 957-4760), and Ocho Rios (tel. 974-5741).

BOB RACE

MONTEGO BAY
INTRODUCTION

Montego Bay was first named El Golfo de Buen Tiempo, or "Fair Weather Gulf," by Christopher Columbus. Its current name, derived from the somewhat less charming Spanish word *manteca* (meaning "lard"), refers to the first commerce conducted in this soon-to-be-busy port; lard, or "pig's butter," was extracted from wild pigs and prepared for export. Early maps even show the area labelled as Lard Bay. After the heyday of lard, Montego Bay, or "MoBay" locally, became a major shipping port for sugar and bananas.

In the late 19th century, local doctor Alexander McCatty became convinced that the curative powers of seawater were particularly strong in Montego Bay. He acquired property, and Doctor's Cave Beach was born. Wealthy North Americans began to visit the area (and some built homes there) for the purpose of taking the restorative plunge for body and soul. McCatty

> *Jamaica is pleasing to the eye. But can it adequately provide for visiting American winter tourists? Assuredly, yes!*
> —Jamaica, Hayti and the Spanish Main, *a 1906 tourist brochure issued by the Hamburg-American Line*

donated the property to the town at the turn of the century, and hotels soon began to spring up in the area. The first became known as the Casa Blanca Hotel, built by the Ewan family, an updated version of which still stands today. Other larger hotels followed, visited by the rich and often famous who traveled to Montego Bay on banana boats. An airstrip built during WW II opened as a commercial strip after the war. This was the start of the Montego Bay tourist boom, which hasn't abated since.

Montego Bay is the center of tourism on Jamaica's north coast, and capital of St. James Parish. It's been officially a city since 1981. With a population of over 43,000, second in size only to Kingston, the town greets most of the over 1.5 million annual visitors to Jamaica. The town is unabashedly tourist-oriented, which some might find unappealing. Here, the hotels are often crowded along strips, the restaurants stacked, and the hustlers aggressive. At the height of the tourist season, the bay reverberates like a giant chainsaw, with ski- and parachute-pulling powerboats and jet skis cutting foam across the water. The glitz of some of the high rises is difficult to reconcile with the breathtaking poverty of the slums to which the menial hotel staff retire daily.

Yet the beauty of Montego Bay that first attracted all of this is hard to diminish, even in the face of overdevelopment. The half-moon bay itself is large and ringed with some of Jamaica's finest beaches. The hills behind it (to the east) are high and afford wide panoramas of the city and bay. The plethora of tourist-oriented energy in and around town doesn't mean that there aren't plenty of activities for the independent, curious traveler.

SIGHTS

The Montego Bay area—roughly from Falmouth, the capital of nearby Trelawny Parish in the east, to Sandy Bay in the west—is full of activity, some real, some created. Many local tour agencies operate islandwide tours from here, at premium cost. However, the area is *so* developed for tourism that it's easy to avoid the packed bus-and-camera tour scene in favor of more leisurely outings via the abundance of taxis or rental cars.

Anyone visiting Montego Bay or the western part of the island will fly into **Sangster International Airport.** Most international flights touch down in Montego Bay and go on to Norman Manley International Airport in Kingston, the only other international airport in the country.

DOWNTOWN

The Square
The center of town lies south of the airport, along Kent and Gloucester avenues, and into the fumed and frenetic **Sam Sharpe Square,** busy with taxis, shops, and street vendors. The square, once called Charles Square after a former governor, was renamed after a national hero, the former slave and church deacon Samuel Sharpe, who led the 1831 Christmas Rebellion. The slave uprising originated in Montego Bay as a nonviolent strike, but later turned surly and engulfed the western parishes of the island. In the aftermath of the rebellion hundreds of slaves, including Sharpe, were hanged in the square that now bears his name and monument. In a corner of the square is a small building called **The Cage,** a former jail used to imprison runaway slaves. The **Slave Ring** on Union St. was once the location of the slave market, later the venue for cockfights.

Architecture
The architecture around the square is a combination of plantation elegance and "nouveau mall." St. James St., the main drag downtown, is worth a walk, albeit harried, for window shopping and just breathing in the scene. Interestingly, this area is prime for information dissemination about what's going on in town. A dense number of street banners and posters slapped about announce reggae shows, dances, plays, and events.

West of the square, on Church St., is the **St. James Parish Church,** one of the finest

Sam Sharpe, national hero

NATIONAL LIBRARY OF JAMAICA

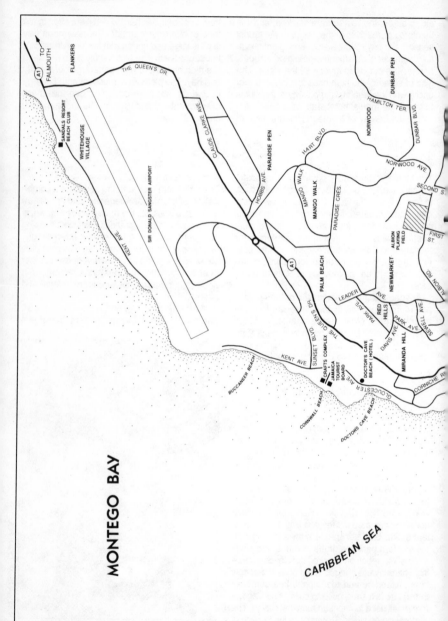

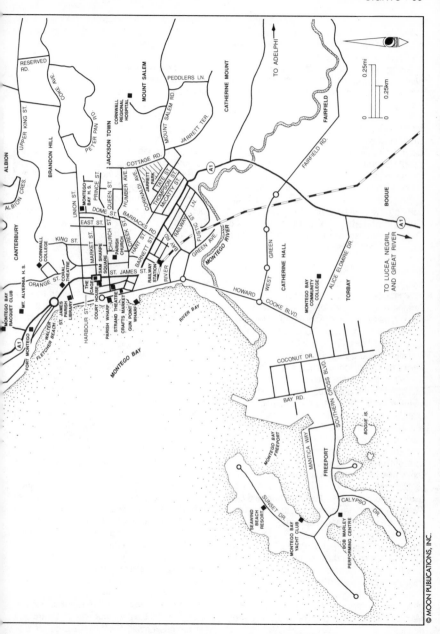

© MOON PUBLICATIONS, INC.

examples of mid-18th century architecture in Jamaica. The church, shaped like a Greek cross, was destroyed and rebuilt following an earthquake that rocked Jamaica in 1957.

Along Fort St. and up Miranda Hill on The Queen's Dr., you can see the remains of **Fort Montego.** Three of its original 17 cannons sit in battery, pointed toward the harbor. It's unclear when the fort was built, but its history of defending Montego Bay could belong to a Marx Brothers movie. The first recorded firing of its cannons was in celebration of the 1760 surrender of Havana; one old gun exploded and killed its cannoneer. Later, in 1795, the fort fired upon a vessel believed to be a French privateer attacking the harbor. It was, in fact, a British ship carrying a load of dogs and their handlers from Cuba, imported to root out the Maroons of Trelawny. No damage was done to the ship because the cannon missed.

To Market
South of the square, along shore-hugging Howard Cooke Blvd., is the town's crafts market. Among the items available are carvings, shell jewelry, baskets, hammocks, and T-shirts. Much of it is quite good, though it's fun enough to walk around and observe Jamaican entrepreneurs in action. If you want to buy, check prices at different stalls, talk to the vendors (often women), and return to the stalls you like. A certain amount of bargaining is accepted and expected. Also visit the **Fustic Market,** on Fustic and Barnett streets, for a taste of an old-style market. Here the women sell crafts as well as department-store items, fruits, and vegetables. It's a loud and energetic environment, busier toward the end of the week—a good taste of the hustle that's needed to make a living in Jamaica.

Along Howard Cooke Blvd. are the town's two commercial wharfs, **Parish Wharf** and **Gun Point Wharf,** where fruits, vegetables, and other goods are shipped and received.

Jarrett Park, along Cottage Rd., used to be the home of the annual **Reggae Sunsplash.** The event, held annually in July or August (see "Festivals and Events," p. 61), attracts over 35,000 reggae stalwarts and musicians for a five-day jam and dance jubilee. The event outgrew Jarrett Park and has moved to the **Bob Marley Performing Centre** in the Freeport district.

Freeport, located south of the Montego River, is a manmade peninsula and industrial area created during the '60s by private developers. It's mostly drab factories with a few exclusive townhouse and condo developments, as well as the anomalous **Seawind Beach Resort.** The **Montego Bay Yacht Club** is housed on the peninsula, as is the Marley Centre. In the free zone, export companies operate duty-free at the invitation of the government.

A drive through the hills surrounding the town gives you an idea of the disparity of lifestyles that exist side by side in this tourist area. The shacks and hovels along Upper King St. and **Brandon Hill,** where the annual income of their dwellers is perhaps 5% of what a visitor might spend in a week, are testimony to rough times in Jamaica.

BEACHES

North of Sam Sharpe Square and the town center is where the real tourist strip begins. Out with the quaint, in with the semi-high-rise hotels and stacked craft stores. Yet this is a happening area for tourism, full of bustle, including bars, things to buy, things to eat, and places to swim.

Walter Fletcher Beach on Gloucester Ave., one of the newer and more popular town beaches, has recreational facilities and a restaurant. Admission is J$5 for adults and J$3 for children, open 0900-1700, tel. 952-5783.

Doctor's Cave Beach, one of Jamaica's most famous, remains as much an attraction as it was when it started Montego Bay's tourist boom at the turn of the century. Despite one-time destruction by a hurricane, the beach is now 20 times greater than its original size and, yes, men and women can now swim together. Young men crowd the entrance hoping to sell rides, favors, and substances, but inside it's relatively hassle free. On Jamaican national holidays the beach is especially busy, and lines have been known to form along Gloucester Ave. while people wait to get in. Admission is J$20 for adults, J$10 for children under 12, plus the 10% general consumption tax. Open 0830-sunset, tel. 952-2566.

Cornwall Beach, also on Gloucester Ave., is located next to the **Jamaica Tourist Board** and a small crafts center. The beach is large, more or less the same beach as Doctor's Cave, and has facilities, a beach bar, and a small admission charge of J$5 for adults and J$3 for children 12 and under. Open 0900 until very late, tel. 952-5796.

Buccaneer Beach, a small, white-sand spit just north of Gloucester Ave. on Kent Ave., is wide open with no admission. The beach is right next to the road, and across the street from the Buccaneer Beach Hotel. You can't miss it. The hotel runs a small snack-and-drinks kiosk.

MONTEGO BAY AREA TOURS

The tour business profit is certainly evident, and if you don't mind packing it along with a group of people, there are some advantages to taking organized packages to sights. First, they're interesting, and people are bound to be around whether you pull up in a tour bus or not. As well, the bus will almost always bring you roundtrip from your hotel, a time-and-effort advantage, and the cost for the bus ride is generally included in the tour price. Since the days and times for these tours change with the seasons, it's best to call ahead for confirmation.

The places described in the following tours can also be visited on your own.

Appleton Express
The Appleton Express is a tourist passenger train that ambles through the mountains for a full-day tour of the **Appleton Estates,** one of the larger sugar factories and rum distilleries in the country. Appleton is located near Maggotty, deep in the interior, just south of the Cockpit Country. The ride is fun for those who like trains, and rum is served throughout for those who don't. The train stops at **Catadupa,** an unabashedly tourist-oriented village with a crafts-and-cloth market. Here, you can be measured for a shirt or blouse; on the return trip the train stops again, allowing you to pick up the completed garment. The return trip also includes a stop at **Ipswich Caves,** a short walk from the train. At US$60 per person, the trip is a little pricey, but it includes lunch, rum drinks, and attractive mountain scenery. It runs Tues. and Thurs. at 0850, tel. 952-3692.

Governor's Coach
The Governor's Coach tour is much the same as the Appleton Express tour, with the addition of limbo contests and a calypso band. Cost is about US$65 per person. It departs Tues., Thurs., and Fri. at 0900, tel. 952-1398.

Other Tours
Croydon Estate, situated in Catadupa, is a 45-minute ride south from Montego Bay. The 132-acre plantation is a working farm producing coffee, pineapples, and citrus. This was the birthplace of national hero Sam Sharpe. Since the terrain on the farm prohibits machinery, all work is done by hand. The tour is US$40 pp, including the bus ride and lunch on the farm. Open Tues., Wed., and Fri., 1000-1230; tel. 952-4137.

BOB RACE

Rose Hall

The **Rocklands Bird Feeding Station,** operated by Lisa Salmon for more than 30 years, is just southwest of Montego Bay near the town of Anchovy. The birds, just the other side of tame, arrive at about 1500 for hand feeding from bottles. They include doctor birds, mango hummingbirds, and the tiny bee hummingbirds, as well as other indigenous fowl. The outspoken Salmon, also an artist and writer, knows her birds and loves to discuss Jamaica's ornithological life; she has opinions on everything from conservation to tourism. Admission is J$50; open daily 1500-dusk, tel. 952-2009.

Rose Hall Great House, about eight miles east of town, is one of the area's more popular tours. The old plantation house, built in the 1770s, is regarded as one of the most elaborate in the country. The embellishment of the legend of Annie Palmer, the alleged "White Witch" of Rose Hall, no doubt helps bring in visitors. Palmer, the second mistress of the house, is said to have murdered three or possibly four husbands, taken countless lovers, and treated her slaves with vicious abandon. She was eventually murdered herself, some say by a Haitian lover, a slave with whom she'd dabbled in voodoo. The house has been restored by its current owner, John Rollins, a former lieutenant governor of Delaware. Admission is about US$10. Open daily 0900-1800; tel. 953-2323.

Every town along the north coast seems to have rafting tours. Montego Bay is no exception, with a few quiet rivers that flow nicely for this sort of thing. **Mountain Valley Rafting** at Lethe offers a one-hour drift down the **Great River,** starting just a few miles south of Montego Bay. The Great River forms part of the border between St. James and Hanover parishes; Lethe, once a large plantation, is now a small mountain village. The bamboo-raft ride ends with donkey rides and other activities, but the river-rafting itself is soothing. Cost is US$30 per raft (two persons) for the services of a licensed poler. Open daily 0900-1700; tel. 952-0527 or 952-4706.

Rafting on the **Martha Brae River** is more of the same, about 1.5 hours down the longest river (20 miles) in Trelawny Parish. The river, originating in the Windsor Caves deep in the Cockpit Country, is said to have been named after a legendary and supernaturally empowered Arawak Indian girl, Martha Brae. As the fable goes, during the Spanish occupation Martha was tortured by the conquerors for information that would lead them to a nearby mother-lode gold mine. She drew upon her powers to swell the river, causing it to flood and drown her, destroying the secret of the mine forever. Find the rafts just east of Falmouth, tel. 952-0889. Cost is US$30 per poled raft; open daily 0900-1600.

If you have a car, take a relaxing drive into the interior for some mountain views and village stops, and for a small tug at the heart of Jamaica. The roads are good and the villages receptive. **Adelphi,** formerly part of an estate named "Stretch and Set," presumably because of the treatment received there by slaves, was the first town on the north side of the island where slaves were allowed religious instruction. The second Baptist church on the island was established at Adelphi in 1788 under the ministry of Moses Baker, a free black from the United States.

About 20 miles south of Montego Bay, through chest-thumping mountain roads, lies **Seaford Town,** one of Jamaica's true sociological anomalies. Settled by indentured German peasants who were brought over as laborers during the post-emancipation period, the town has retained a certain degree of racial homogeny (see "Jamaica's People," p. 39). It's hard not to stare, but it's a shame not to see the town. While there has been some degree of racial intermingling in the more than 150 years of this community's existence, the 200 Germans of Seaford Town retain family names (Grosskopf, Kleinhans) and racial characteristics, but that's about it. Their language is Jamaican Patois, their customs are more Jamaican than German, and they live as poor Jamaicans in a rural town. Take a look at the **Seaford Town Historical Mini-Museum** for more history about these people. No set hours, just drive to the **Sacred Heart Mission,** tel. 952-0407, and ask Father Francis or Rita Wiedenhaupt for the key. A small donation is appreciated.

MONTEGO BAY VICINITY

Falmouth
The road to Falmouth is heavily traveled and laden with hotels and businesses. Falmouth, the capital and largest town in Trelawny, lies

Montego Bay

23 miles east of Montego Bay. Considered by many to be one of the few towns in Jamaica that is still an "original," having retained many of the characteristics of its colonial past, the town was built in the 1790s on land bought from the wealthy Barrett family, and was so intertwined with their business ventures that it was once called Barrett Town. At **1 Market St.** in Falmouth, you can still see the original stone-and-wrought-iron home of Edward Barrett, built in 1799.

Falmouth was once a busy shipping port for the area. Sugar, rum, and slaves all departed and arrived while the planned town thrived through the early 19th century. With the decline of sugar, the emancipation of slaves, and the advent of steamship carriers as well as the railroad constructed between Montego Bay and Kingston, Falmouth lost its luster and virtually became a ghost town in the 1890s. Town development ceased, only to be revived recently with the growth of tourism. Because of this gap in development, the town still retains much of its original, even decrepit, 19th-century Georgian architecture and detail.

On Duke St., stop at the **Falmouth Parish Church,** also called St. Peter's Anglican Church, a large structure dating from 1796. This is the oldest church in Trelawny Parish. Crafts vendors usually set up makeshift stands in the parking area in front of it. The **Falmouth Police Station** on Rodney St. dates back to 1814. The **Falmouth Courthouse** was built in 1815, then was destroyed by fire in 1926. The restored Georgian structure now houses the town council offices.

Along **Market St.,** vendors sell snacks and fruit.

This untraveled area is a unique and unperturbed experience for tourists. Don't miss it.

Just east of town, stop at the **Glistening Waters Inn and Marina,** a local hangout and a good place to try seafood.

PRACTICALITIES

ACCOMMODATIONS

Montego Bay has a total capacity of over 4,100 rooms—more than any one town on the island—so you shouldn't have any problem finding the right one for your style and budget. The general rule is that the bigger the place and the closer you are to beaches, the more expensive it will be. Remember that some hotel rates drop in the summer, or off-season, by as much as 20-40%, others less so. Again, off-season is roughly mid-April through mid-Nov. or mid-Dec., depending on the establishment. The 10% General Consumption Tax (GCT) is applicable year-round. Guesthouses generally (this is a gray area) don't have room tax, but in *all cases* it's best to call or write ahead to confirm current rates and incidentals.

Inexpensive

Ashanti Inn (50 Thompson St., Montego Bay, #2 P.O., Jamaica, W.I.; tel. 952-6389; U.S.A.: Sunshine Villas, tel. 800-346-5897 or 215-790-1190, fax 215-790-0064) is a 15-room inn in a great location downtown, just south of Jarrett Park. The rooms are basic and clean, and there are a comfortable lounge and small balcony on the second floor. Six rooms with a/c are US$40 in summer and US$50 in winter, s or d. Rooms with ceiling fans run US$10 less. Price is inclusive of all taxes and service charges.

Big Apple Hotel (18 The Queen's Dr., Montego Bay, Jamaica, W.I.; tel. 952-7240, U.S.A. tel. 212-465-1806) is located in The Queen's Dr. hills overlooking the ocean. All rooms have a/c and private baths, and there's a pool on the grounds. It's small, but the price is right: US$40 s and US$50 d, year-round; add 10% GCT.

Blue Harbour Hotel (Sewell Ave., P.O. Box 212, Montego Bay, Jamaica, W.I.; tel. 952-5445/6, fax 952-8930) sits in the hills above Montego Bay. The view is nice, the location is fine but it's a short hike to town and the beaches. Meals are basic but priced that way. Summer rates are US$29-46 s and US$38-50 d, winter US$46 s and US$50 d. Studio apartments are US$64 in summer. Add a 10% service charge and 10% GCT.

Caribic House (69 Gloucester Ave., Montego Bay, Jamaica, W.I.; tel. 979-0322 or 979-9387, fax 953-0981) is on Gloucester Ave. across from Doctor's Cave Beach, and is one of the better deals in town. It's small with only 17 rooms, some with a/c, some with fans. The hotel is easy walking distance to restaurants and town sights. Winter rates are US$35-50 s and US$40-55 d for standard rooms, to US$45 s and US$60 d for a "penthouse." Add 10% service charge plus 10% GCT. Summer, subtract about US$5 from all prices.

Comfort Guest House (55 Jarrett Ter., Barnett View Gardens, Montego Bay, Jamaica, W.I.; tel. 952-1238) is on Jarrett Ter., overlooking Jarrett Park. Great location near downtown. The house is clean and has a small balcony on top to take in the wide view. Rates are US$30 s and US$40 d in summer.

Irving Greystone Lodge is on Miranda Hill overlooking the bay, near the heart of the beaches and shops. John Irving has rooms and apartments, and a kitchen area for guests. Rates are US$25 s and US$40 d for a room, with two- to four-bedroom apartments for US$80-240 per night. He will give discounts for stays of a week or more. (U.S.A.: John Irving, 821 Riverside Dr. #1A, New York, NY 10032; tel. 212-927-2314. Jamaica: Vera Irving, White Sands Beach P.O., Montego Bay, Jamaica, W.I.; tel. 952-1894.)

Rose Green Guest House (Greenside District, Falmouth P.O., Trelawny Parish; tel. 954-3177) is out of town, a 15-minute drive east from the airport. A sign on the north side of the road marks the turnoff. Its location between Montego Bay and Falmouth takes it right out of the tourist mainstream, but still within access to beaches and either town. Thaydene Duncan and her husband recently opened the lodge, which is actually their house with rooms open for guests. Cost is US$30 per room or US$50 per room with breakfast, Jamaican style. Bathing facilities are shared.

Royal Court Hotel (P.O Box 195, Montego Bay, Jamaica, W.I.; tel. 952-4531, fax 952-4532) is on Sewell Ave., overlooking the bay. It's a simple place, with a pool, bar, restaurant, and free transport to the beach or to town. Suites, which really are just plush rooms, have TVs and refrigerators. In the summer, you'll pay US$40 s and US$45 d, plus 10% service charge and 10% GCT.

Verney House Hotel (P.O. Box 18, Montego Bay, Jamaica, W.I.; tel. 952-2857, U.S.A. tel. 800-JAMAICA) is five minutes from the airport, on Leader Ave. in Red Hills, another easy-access location. It has a heart-shaped pool and some a/c rooms. Winter rates are US$40 s and US$55 d. Summer rates are US$28 s and US$50 d. Add 10% GCT, and a 10% service charge.

View Guest House (P.O. Box 513, Montego Bay, Jamaica, W.I.; tel. 952-3175) is another downtown location, more of a hotel than guesthouse, but with guesthouse prices. It's on Jarrett Ter. overlooking Jarrett Park. It has a pool, bar, dining room, and a/c rooms. Winter rates are US$30 s or d; a/c is about US$7 extra per night. Discounts for extended stays.

Winged Victory Hotel (5 The Queen's Dr., Montego Bay, Jamaica, W.I.; tel. 952-3891, fax 952-5986), up in the hills overlooking the ocean, is worth a mention if only for its optimistic name. Actually, it's more than that. The Jamaican cuisine at the Calabash Restaurant is very good and inexpensive. The 22 rooms are pretty standard, and are either ocean view or the euphemistically named mountain view, which really means that you can't see the ocean. The rooms, s or d, range US$40-70 in summer and US$45-90 in winter. Deluxe rooms, suites, meal plans, and honeymoon packages are also available. Add 10% service charge and 10% tax.

YMCA Hostel (28 Humber Ave., Montego Bay, Jamaica, W.I.; tel. 952-5368) is about the cheapest you'll find in town. The location, near downtown, is good for getting around. The hostel is available to both men and women. The rooms are private but baths, which have cold water, are shared. Hostel rate is J$300 s and J$500 d (about US$14-23). Fans can be rented for J$15 per night (less than US$1).

Special mention should go to the **Orange River Lodge** (Montego Bay P.O., Montego Bay, Jamaica, W.I.; tel. 979-3294/5), opened in 1992. The Lodge, seven miles southeast of Montego Bay on 1000 acres of what used to be a sugar, cattle, and banana plantation, is definitely the nature lover's place to stay. You can go birdwatching, hiking, biking, horseback riding, and swimming in the Orange River, which cuts through the property. Trips to the Cockpit Country can be arranged. Accommodation is in one of the five rooms of the old great house, US$25 s, plus US$20 each additional person. Some rooms share baths, with hot and cold water. A large hostel accommodates about 22, and the rate is US$10 per person. The hostel has a dining area, washing facilities, and a kitchen. Camping is also available at US$5. Bring your own tent or call to find out if tents are available. Plans are afoot to expand the accommodation facilities. The advantage here is that you're close enough to Montego Bay to have some fun there, yet you're staying in a natural, inexpensive setting.

Moderate

Buccaneer Beach Hotel (7 Kent Ave., Montego Bay, Jamaica, W.I.; tel. 952-2694 or 952-6489, fax 952-7568) is on Kent Ave., right on the hotel-row beach. They have 70 rooms, a/c, bars, pool, game room, lounges, and some rooms with TV. The Dead End Bar, on the beach, is operated by the hotel. The advantage to this hotel is its location near the main strip and the beach. Rooms are US$66 s and US$72 d, winter rates. Summer rates are US$45 s or d.

Chatwick Gardens (10 The Queen's Dr., White Sands P.O., Montego Bay, Jamaica, W.I.; tel. 952-2147, fax 952-2447), on The Queens Dr. just south of the airport, is a little pricey for the location—the airport blast can rattle, and it's not a quick walk to anything except the airport. But the hotel itself has some charm, and is a good base for exploring both Montego Bay and Falmouth by car. Rates are about US$65 s, US$75 d in winter, about 20% less in summer. Room tax and service charges are included in the price.

Coral Cliff Hotel (P.O. Box 253, Montego Bay, Jamaica, W.I.; tel. 952-4130, fax 952-6532) is on Gloucester Ave., a two-minute walk from Doctor's Cave Beach. The location is central, and they've got a pool and balconies with ocean views. Winter rates are US$54 s, US$56 d, and US$62 t for standard rooms. Superior rooms, add about US$6. Summer rates, subtract about US$5. Add 10% service charge and 10% GCT.

The Gloucestershire Hotel (P.O. Box 86, Montego Bay, Jamaica, W.I.; tel. 952-4420/2, fax 952-8088)—you'd be hard pressed to find a better location for a hotel in Montego Bay. It's directly across from Doctor's Cave Beach and on the main strip of hotels, and has everything from pools to restaurants to little waterfalls here and there. It's an inviting place, sort of a big hotel with a small inn feeling. Rooms are standard, superior, and deluxe. Standard summer rooms are US$65 s and US$70 d, and US$90 s to US$95 d in winter. Meal plans are available. Add 10% service charge and 10% GCT.

Hotel Montego (P.O. Box 74, Montego Bay, Jamaica, W.I.; tel. 952-3286, fax 979-0351) is located on Federal Ave. just around the corner from the airport—so expect some noise. Rooms have balconies and a/c, and the pool is nice. Winter rates are US$62 s and US$73 d, all service charges and tax included.

La Mirage Hotel (6 The Queen's Dr., Montego Bay, Jamaica, W.I.; tel. 952-4435, fax 952-6980) is small with only 22 rooms, and located on The Queen's Dr. overlooking the bay. This is a quaint little place, one of the best medium-priced hotels in town. Walking distance to town and beaches. The rooms, standard and superior, are basic but have private baths, a/c, and TV, and there is a freshwater swimming pool on the premises. The restaurant offers healthy servings of European and Jamaican dishes, and has a bar. Winter rates are US$44-54 s, and US$54-64 d. Summer rates, as always, are the better deal at US$36-42 s, and US$46-54 d with service charge and GCT included.

Queen's Hotel (P.O. Box 923, Montego Bay, Jamaica, W.I.; tel. 952-3163), next to La Mirage on The Queen's Dr., is about as straightforward as they come, but clean and attractive. You'll find basic rooms (some with a/c or fan), a bar, restaurant, and pool. The advantages are the view and location near the center of things; and they negotiate prices during off-season. Rates are US$50 per room in winter, US$45 per room in summer, s or d, GCT included.

Seville Apartments (contact Mr. Easton Powell, tel. 952-2814) have three locations around town, and are generally cheap and negotiable. Ask for the guesthouse on Sunset Blvd.; it's the best and closest to the town center. The advertised apartments on Sewell Ave. have tiny kitchenettes. Prices range US$40-75 for the apartments, more for the villas.

Toby Inn (P.O. Box 467, Montego Bay, Jamaica, W.I.; tel. 952-4370/1, fax 952-6591, U.S.A. tel. 800-327-5767) is on the corner of Kent Ave. and Sunset, two blocks from Cornwall and Doctor's Cave beaches. The rooms are clean, each with a/c and patio. Two pools, a bar, and restaurant sit on the two-acre property, which has a large garden. The best thing about it is the location, near the main hotel strip and beaches. Winter rooms are US$50 s and US$75 d, summer US$40 s and US$65 d. Add 10% GCT.

The Wexford (P.O. Box 108, Montego Bay, Jamaica, W.I.; tel. 952-2854, 952-3679, fax 952-3637, U.S.A. tel. 800-237-3421) is another Gloucester Ave. hotel, within minutes of Doctor's Cave Beach. This one has the works, as well as a gaming room (slot machines), pool, and restaurant and bar. Rooms have garden

Optimist Club sign

OPTIMIST CLUB
OF MONTEGO BAY

MEETS EVERY 1ˢᵗ & 3ᴿᴰ WEDNESDAY
CLUB PARADISE

BOB RACE

views or ocean views, and prices range from US$80 s to US$100 d in summer, US$110 s to US$125 d in winter, taxes included. One-bedroom suites range from US$100 d in summer to US$130 d in winter. Meal plans are available.

Luxury

Half Moon (P.O. Box 80, Montego Bay, Jamaica, W.I.; tel. 953-2211, fax 953-2731, U.S.A. tel. 800-237-3237) is a golf and tennis resort, situated on 400 acres and about a mile of beach, just outside of Montego Bay. This is one of the nicer resorts in the area, and one of the Elegant Resorts of Jamaica—major amenities, maximum comfort. Rooms are superior to deluxe, and villas are one- to three-bedroom. Cost in off-season is US$120-300 s, US$150-330 d. In winter, figure on US$210-620 s and US$250-660 d, greens fees, health club included.

Jack Tar Village (P.O. Box 144, Montego Bay, Jamaica, W.I.; tel. 952-4340/5, fax 952-6633, U.S.A. tel. 800-999-9182) is an all-inclusive resort in the thick of it on the main hotel strip. The beach is long and pretty, and the hotel, though large, is more homey than other all-inclusives in the area. Excluding special packages, rack rates per person per night are US$200 s, US$170 d, and US$170 t in winter, and about US$20 less off-season.

Sandals Montego Bay, Sandals Royal Caribbean, and **Sandals Inn** are the three representatives of the Sandals all-inclusive chain here. For some reason they've built them all in the same town. But it works; they're full much of the time. Sandals Montego Bay has the longest beach in town, and there is no disputing the quality of the food and service. It is next to—we're talking right next to—the airport, and it gets noisy at times. Sandals Royal Caribbean has a rather upscale, plantation motif, and guests can use the facilities of other Sandals hotels. Sandals Inn is across the street from the beach on Kent Ave. Heterosexual couples only for all Sandals. Winter rates, depending on type of accommodation and length of stay, are US$300-600 per couple per night. (U.S.A.: Unique Vacations, 7610 S.W. 61st Ave., Miami, FL 33143; tel. 800-SANDALS, fax 305-284-1336. Canada tel. 800-558-0399. U.K.: 32 Ives St., London, England; tel. 71-581-9895. Jamaica: P.O. Box 100, Montego Bay, Jamaica, W.I.; tel. 952-6610.)

Sea Garden Resort (P.O. Box 300, Montego Bay, Jamaica, W.I.; tel. 952-4780/1, fax 952-7543, North America tel. 800-545-9001) is an all-inclusive hotel on Kent Ave. It has a good location on its own beach, a few minutes' walk to Cornwall and Doctor's Cave beaches, as well as to the tourist-strip shopping area. The hotel has pools, tennis, water sports, and lush gardens. The food is good and you don't have to limbo if you don't care to. Prices for singles start at about US$198-211 per night in the summer. Doubles are US$278-290 per couple in summer. Minimum stay is three nights.

Seawind Beach Resort (P.O. Box 1168, Montego Freeport, Montego Bay, Jamaica, W.I.; tel. 952-4874/6 or 952-4070, fax 979-8039, U.S.A. tel. 800-268-0424) might be classified as moderate to luxury. It's an alarmingly painted high-rise building, with pastel yellows and mauves that give it the look of an elaborate practical joke. But, as values go, it's a good one. In the Freeport area south of town, the hotel is isolated and on a superb beach. Winter rates range from standard singles at US$63, to two-bedroom suites with kitchens for US$200. Off-season is cheaper. Add a 10% service charge and 10% GCT.

Wyndham Rose Hall Beach Hotel (P.O. Box 999, Montego Bay, Jamaica, W.I.; tel. 953-2650/9, fax 952-2617, U.S.A. tel. 800-822-4200, Canada tel. 800-632-4100, Europe tel. 01-367-5175) is on an old sugar plantation next to Rose Hall Great House, east of town. It's a big attraction for golfers, as it includes an 18-hole golf course. It also features tennis, water sports, and three or four restaurants, including the **Ambrosia Restaurant,** serving one of the better Italian meals in the Montego Bay area. Pool and private beach. A drawback is that the hotel is a high rise. Rooms range US$160-190 s or d in winter, US$115-135 off-season, plus 10% service charge and 10% GCT.

Villas

Numerous villas line the coast or dot the mountainside in and around Montego Bay. Villas can be a good way to travel on a budget, particularly if you are sharing with one or more people. They can also be expensive, depending on their location and facilities. Several stand out:

Casaker Villa is located at Ironshore Estates, just north of town, and has two self-contained

Montego Bay

KARL LUNTA

studio apartments as well as a four-bedroom, three-bath villa with swimming pool. Studio rates are US$70 per night in summer and US$85 in winter, and the villa is US$214 in summer and US$285 in winter. The entire unit (six bedrooms) rents for US$308 in summer and US$428 in winter.

Davelyn Villa, also at Ironshore, is a comfortable four-bedroom, four-bath home with a huge kitchen and swimming pool that rents for US$287 per night in summer and US$375 per night in winter. It sleeps up to eight.

Carib Sands is an elegantly decorated home on the water next to the Sandals resort; it has three bedrooms and three baths with a/c in all rooms, TV, maid service, pool, and a private beach. The cost is US$1573 per week in summer and US$2220 per week in winter.

Windward Villa is another beachside home, with three bedrooms and three baths, phone, maid service, cooks, and all amenities. A balcony overlooks the pool and ocean, just feet away. Summer rate is US$2100 per week and winter rate is US$3150.

Leeward Villa is next door with much the same setup, only nicer. It's US$2200 per week in summer and US$3300 per week in winter.

For the above, contact Sunshine Villas at (215) 790-1189 or (800) 346-5897. In Jamaica, contact Andrea Bernard at 953-2387 or 953-2253.

As well, Vacation Network or the Jamaica Association of Villas and Apartments (JAVA) are helpful for local villa and apartment rentals (see "Accommodations," p. 64).

EATING AND DRINKING

Restaurants
The competition for tourist and local dollars has produced some fine restaurants in Jamaica, and Montego Bay has its share. For quick and easy, Gloucester Ave. has enough fast food of the Shakey's and KFC types to soothe a Western palate. Downtown, especially in the area of Barnett St. and the railroad station, small eateries feature Jamaican and Chinese cuisine.

Hotel restaurants, excluding the all-inclusives not open to the public, are generally good and open early for breakfast, as well as on Sundays. Many restaurants in town will pick you up and return you to your hotel free of charge. Ask when you make the reservation.

For inexpensively priced meals try **The Pork Pit** (tel. 952-1046) near the corner of Kent and Gloucester; possibly Montego Bay's best jerk pork, chicken, and sausage—and it's open late. **Tony's Pizza** (tel. 952-0346) on Gloucester Ave. is an outdoor stand open until 0200 daily, 0300 on weekends for post-reggae hungries. **Texas Tacos** on Gloucester Ave. has given the concept of drive-thru a strange twist, considering that most people are on foot, but they've persisted. **Patsy's Place** (tel. 952-0738) at 35 Gloucester Ave. serves bar food and light dinners, as well as highly recommended soups. **China Gate** (tel. 952-5847) on East St. downtown serves lunch and dinner, as does **China Doll** (tel. 952-43340) in Sam Sharpe Square. Both serve Chinese and some Jamaican. Try **Jimmy's Pastry** (tel. 952-0585) on Jarrett St. for pastries, sweets, and bread. **Zulu's Bar and Eatery** on Gloucester Ave. is a good place to have a beer and watch the parade go by.

Greenhouse Restaurant (tel. 952-7838) on Gloucester Ave. serves great coffee in bucket-size mugs—well, big mugs anyway—inside or out on a streetside patio, and lends newspapers to patrons on Sunday mornings. It also serves light lunches and dinners until 2300. **The Pelican** (tel. 952-3171) on Gloucester Ave. is a family-style, quasi-fast-food joint that has fine burgers and fried fish dishes. At the Pelican, the **Cascade Room,** so named because it features a tiny waterfall splashing in the background, serves more elegant fare in a subdued dining room—except, of course, for that waterfall. Both restaurants will pick you up at your hotel free of charge.

Ma Maison (tel. 952-5996) on Gloucester Ave. serves reasonably priced and good seafood. **Le Chalet** (tel. 952-5240), also on Gloucester, serves Jamaican, Chinese, and European, at moderate prices. For Asian, try **Rice Bowl** (tel. 952-6494) on Church St. downtown.

Marguerite's By the Sea (tel. 952-4277) on the ocean side of Gloucester Ave. is good for a casual meal or a beer and Jamaican peppered shrimp while watching the Caribbean slosh about. Try the crabcakes for a hot treat. Marguerite's is actually two restaurants in one: casual outdoor seating for lunch and drinks, and an enclosed dining room for evening eats.

The Dolphin Grill (tel. 953-2676) near Rose Hall is popular, but is a short drive north of town.

The Georgian House (tel. 952-0632) on Orange St. downtown is formal and famous for its antique elegance and extensive menu and wine list. They will pick you up from your hotel, free of charge. **Mario's** (tel. 952-7240) on The Queen's Dr. does not, contrary to its name, serve Italian. It serves inexpensive and delicious Jamaican food, with fish entrees ranging US$8-20. **Julia's** (Bogue Hill, tel. 952-1172) serves some of the best gourmet Italian in Montego Bay. The restaurant is located on a hill overlooking the town. They will provide transportation from your hotel.

The Montegonian (tel. 952-4159) is on The Queen's Dr. overlooking the bay and airport. The view is striking: airport lights in motion at night. A personal favorite, the restaurant is sometimes called Mickey's after a previous owner. Try the grilled garlic lobster or snapper for some of the best seafood in town. Nearby is **The Diplomat** (tel. 952-3353); it's ornate, distinguished by its seafood and steaks, and pricey. The view, however, is compelling.

In Falmouth stop at **7th Heaven Fish Pot** on the through road for grilled lobster or steamed fish and a cold Red Stripe.

USEFUL PHONE NUMBERS IN MONTEGO BAY AND VICINITY

Area Code 809

Air Canada, tel. 952-5160

Air Jamaica, tel. 952-4100 or 952-4300

American Airlines, tel. 952-5950

American Express, Stuart's Travel, 32 Market St., tel. 952-4350

British Airways, tel. 952-3771

Canadian Consulate, 29 Gloucester Ave., tel. 952-6198

Continental Airlines, tel. 952-4460

Doctor's Hospital, Fairfield, tel. 952-1616

Fire and Ambulance, tel. 110

General Post Office, Fort St. and North, tel. 952-2489

Immigration, Sangster International Airport, tel. 952-5645

Jamaica Citizen's Bank, 5 Gloucester Ave., tel. 952-6411

Jamaica Tourist Board, Cornwall Beach, tel. 952-4425

Northwest Airlines, tel. 952-5531

Police Emergency, tel. 119

Sangster International Airport, tel. 952-5160

Trans Jamaican Airlines, tel. 952-5401

United States Consular Agency, Gloucester Ave., tel. 952-0160/5050

Weather Information, tel. 952-0760

Markets

The **Fustic Market** off Barnett St. by the rail station is good for fruit, vegetables, and jerk meat. It gets busy on Friday and Saturday, traditional market days. Here, munch on sugarcane, coconuts, roasted peanuts, fresh bread, and seasonal fruit—and enjoy the pandemonium.

Parkway Supermarket, across from Doctor's Cave Beach, is convenient for basics such as coffee, rum, and, well, food, for that matter. Every takeout stand and convenience store sells beer and soft drinks.

ENTERTAINMENT

Shopping

For crafts and duty-free shopping, as well as sidewalk haggling, a walk down Gloucester Ave. will do the trick. If you can't find it there, you won't find it anywhere. Beware the sidewalk jewelry salesman or the fellow with Rolexes lining both arms. If the product was that good, it would be in a shop.

The **Crafts Market** between Harbour St. and Howard Cooke Blvd. sells crafts and those types of things, in an enclosed area. Tourists will be approached to have their hair braided, Bo Derek style, a spurious sort of look that's supposed to imitate African or Caribbean style. It only takes a couple of minutes on the island to realize, however, that only tourists braid their hair; Jamaicans don't. Even if they did, the practice strikes one as having the same sensitivity as donning a headdress and walking around a Native American reservation.

A mini-mall at the **Holiday Village Shopping Centre**, across from the Holiday Inn on Hwy. A1 east of town, is worth a look if you want crafts, duty-free items, or music. Have shopowners play the tapes before you buy them, as the quality can be poor—some are actually bootlegs. Other possibilities for tapes and CDs are **Federal Records & Electronics** (tel. 952-7541) on Market St. just off Sam Sharpe Square, and **Benny's Record Shop** (tel. 952-0506) on Church St. downtown.

Downtown, across from the St. James Parish Library on Fort St., is the **City Center Building** with shops and crafts. Farther south, across the Montego River, is the **Freeport** shopping area, with more duty-free and crafts.

In the square area you can find basics in clothes, photography, and miscellaneous items. **Salmon's** (tel. 952-4527) on St. James St. is the best spot for photography items and developing, though you might want to wait until you return home to develop photos, given the high cost in Jamaica. **Sangster's** (tel. 952-0319), also on St. James St., is one of the best-stocked bookstores in Montego Bay. The other is **Dominican Stationery,** St. James St., across from the post office. **Overton Plaza** on Union St. has **Hometown Supermarket** as well as shops that sell stationery, music, and videos.

The Bay Gallery (tel. 952-7668), at St. James Place on Gloucester Ave., features local and nationally known artists, including painters, sculptors, and potters. The **Gallery of West Indian Art** (tel. 952-4547) on Orange St. features work by artists from Jamaica and the Caribbean.

Sports And Recreation

Beachfront outfitters rent water equipment, and all hotels can arrange diving and water excursions for you. **Seaworld** (tel. 953-2180), located at the Cariblue Beach Resort east of the airport, offers snorkeling, diving and certification, water-skiing, and glass-bottom boat sightseeing. Dive packages start at US$199. **Poseidon Nemrod Divers** (tel. 952-3624 or 952-6088) operate boats out of Marguerite's Restaurant and offer underwater photography and snorkeling trips, as well as PADI training. The PADI Advanced Course is US$250. Open Water Certification is US$375. Rates start at US$35 for one dive, to US$225 for 10 dives. Snorkeling equipment can be rented for US$10 per day. Some say the **Airport Reef,** located southwest of Sangster International Airport, is the best diving in Jamaica.

Fishing can be arranged through hotels or by calling direct. Two charter boats are found at the Cariblue Hotel: *Fantasea* and the *Fansea Lady* (tel. 953-2022). The *No Problem* (tel. 952-1235) takes charters as far as Negril, in addition to daily charters out of Montego Bay. The *Calico* (tel. 952-5860) sails out of the Pier 1 Marina for snorkeling cruises (US$50), which include lunch and drinks, or evening cruises (US$25). Visit the **Montego Bay Yacht Club** (tel. 952-3028) at Freeport for charters or for cruise charters. The yacht club has been host to more than 29 **Montego Bay Annual Marlin Tournaments,** held every September. Half-day charters run US$250-300, while full-day charters run US$400-600.

Many hotels, except for all-inclusives, allow nonguests to use tennis courts for a fee. The **Montego Bay Racquet Club** (tel. 952-0200) on Sewell Ave. has seven lighted courts.

Horseback riding can also be arranged through hotels, generally at about US$10 per hour. Try **Rocky Point Stables** (tel. 952-2286) at the Half Moon Club, east of the airport.

Golfers love Montego Bay. Four major courses, one of them PGA-approved, attract tournaments and professionals year-round. Greens fees vary between summer and winter, and caddies, club rentals, and cart rentals run US$15-30 at each course.

Twelve miles west of town, **Tryall Golf and Country Club** (tel. 952-5110) is PGA-approved and home of the Jamaica Classic, an LPGA Tour event. It recently hosted the Johnnie Walker World Championship. Greens fees are US$50, additional for caddies and carts. Tennis is also available. **Ironshore Golf Club** (tel. 953-2800) is just north of the airport. Greens fees are US$25-35. **Half Moon Golf and Country Club** (tel. 953-2211) was designed by Robert Trent-Jones. Greens fees are about US$17. Tennis and squash are available. **Wyndham Rose Hall Country Club** (tel. 953-2650) is located at Rose Hall Estate, east of town. Greens fees are about US$25-35. Tennis is also available.

Nightlife

The Friday night reggae-and-dance show at Walter Fletcher Beach, called **"Boonoonoonoos,"** a little-used Jamaican word resurrected by the tourist board to mean "very big party," which, in fact, it is, features a live band, buffet, and bar. Cost is about US$30 including dinner and drinks. Hours are 1900-2300; tel. 974-2619.

Pier 1 restaurant and marina (tel. 952-2452) on the waterfront section of Howard Cooke Blvd. also has a Friday-night dance party. The **Cave**

MONTEGO BAY CAR RENTAL AGENCIES

Area Code 809

Anna Rent-A-Car, Holiday Inn, 953-2766; St. James St., 952-4585 or 952-5629

Avis Rent-A-Car, Sangster International Airport, 952-4543; Ironshore, 952-1481

Bargain Rent-A-Car, 26 Sunset Blvd., 952-0762

Budget Rent-A-Car, Sangster International Airport, 952-5061; Ironshore, 952-2019

Central Rent-A-Car, Sunset Blvd., 952-1984; 25 Gloucester Ave., 952-3662

CJ's Rent-A-Car, Ironshore, 952-1099

Dud's Car Rental, 29 Gloucester Ave., 952-4905

Econocar Rentals, 5 Ramparts Cl., 952-5538

Fayden Car Rental, Coral Gardens, 952-5774 or 952-5817

Hertz, Sangster International Airport, 952-4471/2

Island Car Rentals, Sangster International Airport, 952-5771 or 952-7225

Leo's Car Rentals, 10 Sunset Blvd., 952-5662

Pleasure Tours, The Queen's Dr., 952-1441 or 952-5383

Prospective Car Rentals, 28 Union St., 952-0112 or 952-3524

Sunbird Car Rentals, 19 Gloucester Ave., 952-3015 or 952-5536

Sunshine Car Rentals, 12 Sunset Blvd., 952-4218

Thrifty Car Rentals, Sangster International Airport, 952-5989; 27 St. James St., 952-4585

Tropical Rent-A-Car, Gloucester Ave., 952-1110 or 952-0400

United Car Rentals, Sangster International Airport, 952-1081; 49 Gloucester Ave., 952-3077 or 952-1781

Vision Rentals, Gloucester Ave., 952-0323

Disco (tel. 952-4874) at the Seawind Hotel is one of the most popular in town. **Sir Winston Reggae Club** (tel. 952-2084), near the corner of Gloucester and Kent, features a likeness of the famous Sir Winston with his equally famous cigar replaced by the still-famous Jamaican equivalent. Sir Winston's opens nightly, and there is a cover charge. Cultural shows are presented on Thursday and Saturday. The **Thriller Disco** (tel. 953-2485) is located at the Holiday Inn east of town, and features nightly Top 40, calypso, and reggae.

Doctor's Cave Beach Hotel (tel. 952-4355) has a nice piano bar for a quieter time.

For a slower pace, investigate the **Strand Theatre** (tel. 952-5391), 8 Strand St. downtown; or the **Coral Theatre** on St. James St., across from the **St. James Parish Library** (tel. 952-4185).

GETTING AROUND

Public Transportation

Downtown Montego Bay is walkable. However, a quick taxi ride will get you down to Freeport for shopping or the Cave Disco, and buses are available for the hop to the east. A convenient taxi stand is located on Gloucester Ave. across from the tourist board and Cornwall Beach, and another at Doctor's Cave Beach. Taxis (remember to look for the red license plate and to negotiate before getting in) move constantly up and down Sunset Blvd. and Gloucester Ave. and are easy to catch. From your hotel, call **Doctor's Cave Taxi Stand** (tel. 952-0521) or **JUTA** (tel. 952-0813). Buses to all points can be found at the busy depot on Harbour St., downtown.

The train station, which serves the Appleton Express and Governor's Coach tours, is located on Railway Ln. off Barnett Street. The Montego Bay-to-Kingston line has been open sporadically over the last several years; when it is open, this is the place to catch it.

Rentals

Since Montego Bay is a major point of entry to Jamaica, car-rental companies abound. You'll find most at the airport or along the Sunset Blvd. strip toward Gloucester Avenue. The cost for the cheapest cars ranges US$40-60 p/d based on a week's rental, with up to 500 miles free per week or, in cases, unlimited mileage. For motorcycle rentals, try **Relax Bike Rental** (26 Hobbs Ave., tel. 952-7218). Small 80cc scooters average US$30 p/d, less for weekly rentals, and Honda 125s rent for US$40 p/d.

BOB RACE

NEGRIL AND VICINITY
INTRODUCTION

Imagine a town in the shape of a giant boomerang, the ocean nuzzled in the crook of its elbow—that's Negril. It's an extended town spread along Norman Manley Blvd., which parallels the beach, and West End Rd. (sometimes called Lighthouse Rd.), which parallels the cliff side and ends at the Negril Point Lighthouse. Most Negril businesses, banks, hotels, cottages, and restaurants are located along these two roads. A few smaller, side roads branch up into the hills near the central traffic rotary and along West End Rd., where private residences and cottages are found. In most ways, Negril has small-town intimacy—walking and biking are easy, and you really can't get lost unless you try. In other ways, Negril is loopy and gangly, like a giant centipede taking a turn.

The residents of Negril live in the hills and side roads east of town. Most locals are employed in the tourism industry, or in secondary tourist industries. Many of Negril's employed come from as far away as Lucea and Savanna-la-mar.

Early Tourism Years
For a generation of visitors to Negril, the small town will always be associated with the turn-on, drop-out counterculture that first uncovered it for foreigners in the late '60s and early '70s. It was, in the words of some Negril residents, a "hippie town," full of America's and Europe's beflowered and often cash-short bohemians, out to escape the ennui of the Vietnam years for a true Jamaican experience. The reasons were clear. Negril's white-sand beach extends for over seven miles, the longest and one of the more pristine on the island. The western end of Negril sits on a slightly elevated rock, creating caves and limpid swimming and diving pools with long views of the sunset.

In the early days, the town had few hotels, and those few were wary of the long-haired, ganja-inspired dropouts who were, some thought, less than a good influence on the town. The hippies turned to willing locals who offered room and board for next to nothing, and the tradition

> *One half of the world cannot understand the pleasures of the other.*
> —*Jane Austen, British novelist*

of small cottages and cheap accommodation was born. The question of relaxed morality became as simple as the chicken and the egg—which came first, the fun-seekers or the fun? With the youthful influx this point became moot, and the concept of living with Jamaican families became a Negril tradition. The byword was hedonism: sun, sand, reggae, rum, and a good time on a great beach.

Well, some things change and some things don't. The hippies came into some money during the '80s and the international set discovered the relaxed atmosphere of the town, thereby creating the need for a new set of hotels, some of which are not small cottages at all. Many of the private homes turned into small guesthouses. Yet the town is still unpretentious and unruffled; zoning laws prohibit any building higher than the tallest palm tree in town. There's really no bustle, just a strip of activity lining the beach and the rock cliffs, a market, a few office buildings, and motor scooters sputtering down the road.

History

Negril, the westernmost town on the island, lies only 50 miles southwest of Montego Bay, the main point of entry to Jamaica. Even on a bad day, the trip is just over an hour's drive. Negril is, today, a place to be, not just to pass through. Until 1959, however, it wasn't even a place to pass through. The small fishing village of Negril was surrounded by hills and the famous **Great Morass,** a swamp that reached close to the sea, enveloping the long sand beach (and reportedly providing good cover for drug-smuggling operations). The border between Hanover and Westmoreland parishes passes through the Great Morass.

In 1959, Norman Manley, then prime minister and PNP leader, cut a road from the town of Green Island in the north, through the morass to the small village, and tourism was born. At first, and to a great extent today, Negril was popular with Jamaicans as a holiday and weekend getaway. It suits the style and budget of middle-class Jamaicans who can't afford the money and stress of the faster-paced Montego Bay or Ocho Rios.

Yet Negril had always held some importance for early settlers. Negril Harbour, or **Bloody Bay,** takes its name from the whale industry, when the animals, caught and processed for oil, were butchered, turning the quiet bay waters red with blood. Bloody Bay was a gathering place for pirates, and it was here that the dandy Calico Jack Rackham and his two mates, Captains Mary Read and Anne Bonney, were captured in 1720 during a rum party. Calico Jack, whose name was derived from his penchant for calico underwear, was later hanged and his body displayed on the Kingston islet that's named after him, Rackham's Cay.

A British fleet of 50 warships and 6,000 men assembled in Bloody Bay in 1814 for an attack on the U.S. territory of Louisiana—an attack later known as the Battle of New Orleans. The British were defeated by U.S. Comdr. Andrew

Mary Read and Anne Bonney—pirates

Jackson and his ally Jean Laffite, a privateer and enemy of Britain.

After years of repose as a small fishing port, the Punta Negrilla ("Dark Point") of the Spanish developed into a town which is now beginning to rival some of the north coast tourist centers. It is still not the largest town in Westmoreland—that honor belongs to the parish capital of Savanna-la-mar, just 19 miles to the southeast.

SIGHTS

Most people don't come to Negril for packaged attractions and historical tours—which works out nicely because there aren't any. Negril is open and free, and the beach and cliffs are attractions in themselves. People come here to indulge in swimming, sunning, eating, and, if it's your choice, almost Herculean nighttime bacchanalia.

Driving To Negril
The drive along the coast from Montego Bay to Negril is packed with small villages and good beaches for a stop, photo, or swim. West of the Great River are the Round Hill and Tryall luxury hotels. At Tryall, an old plantation ground, you can see a 200-year-old waterwheel, still turning. Here, you'll pass through **Hopewell,** a small but energetic village with a Methodist church built in 1874. Moving on, you'll come to **Sandy Bay,** founded as a village for freed slaves who were led by the Baptist minister Rev. Thomas Burchell. Further west is **Miskito Cove,** a small inlet ringed by the road.

The town of **Lucea,** pronounced "Lucy," is the capital of the tiny parish of Hanover. The population of Lucea, 5,700, shows how small the parish is. One of the better and deeper natural harbors on the north coast, the town once bustled under its harbor's trade. Lucea is largely inactive now, except for a few manufacturing businesses, including a Jockey underwear plant. **Fort Charlotte,** built for defense from pirates and named after King George III's queen, still overlooks the harbor from its position behind the public works building. **Rusea's School** was originally part of a barracks of the fort. In the late 18th century, the barracks was created as a school at the behest of Martin Rusea, a French refugee who had lived in Hanover and left a large estate there. The clock tower over the court building has an interesting, if not wholly believable history. Rumor has it that the clock was originally destined for the Caribbean island

of St. Lucia as a gift from a German kaiser, but someone confused the names and the town of Lucea won out. Residents, who began to like the thing, refused to give it back, and eventually paid for it by taking a collection. Also in town, you'll see the **Hanover Parish Church,** which dates back as early as 1725.

Along the coast through **Cousin's Cove, Davis Cove,** and **Negro Bay,** you'll approach

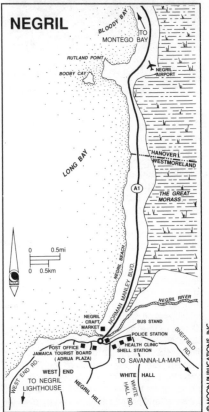

PHYLLIS LUNTTA

the view from Rick's Café

Green Island, another small coastal town. While there, stop at **Mandela Green** (tel. 956-2607), a reggae and entertainment center. **Winnie's,** the restaurant there, serves fresh fruit juices and I-tal vegetarian food, as well as snacks and pastries.

Blenheim, inland from Davis Cove, is the birthplace of Sir Alexander Bustamante, founder of the JLP and Jamaica's first prime minister after independence. A memorial service is held each year at the small, restored, thatched farmhouse where he was born.

Panorama

At the far end of **West End Road** stands the **Negril Point Lighthouse,** one of six working lighthouses on the island. The structure, 66 feet tall and 100 feet above sea level, flashes a solar-powered automatic light every two seconds throughout the night. It's located at the extreme western point of Jamaica. Don't expect organized tours, but you can climb the 103 steps to the top of the building for a panoramic view of the shore and Negril environs. Ask permission

to climb from lighthouse supervisor Leaford Barnett.

The **West End** rock cliffs, some as high as 80 feet, spell ancient dangers to sailors and navigators, but apparently none, to the droves of visitors and locals who dive from them as Negril's famous sunset approaches. It's almost a ritual for Negril visitors to congregate at one of the many rockside cafés to have a sundowner and watch divers. The cliffs have been featured in film sequences from *20,000 Leagues Under the Sea,* and *Dr. No,* and in the famous escape scene from *Papillon.*

The two bays along **Norman Manley Blvd.** are, of course, beautiful—the beaches are like white sandpaper strips floating in sapphire paint. The beach stays the same basic width all day, due to negligible tides, and you can walk most of its length. Negril beaches, with the exception of those operated by all-inclusives, are free and open to the public. Jerk shacks and beach bars can be found along the beach.

The beach stretch at **Long Bay** is the most popular and—imagine your surprise—the longest. At the north end of the beach, approaching Bloody Bay, you'll be stopped from walking on the private beaches of the all-inclusive hotels. Bloody Bay, where some clothes-optional bathing is allowed, has a quiet, intimate, beach situated behind a thick forest. You'll usually find someone selling beer and soft drinks there. **Booby Cay,** a tiny islet just offshore from Bloody Bay, also has beaches frequented by hotel groups and individuals. The cay takes its name from the booby bird, a seagoing tern that spends most of its life on the ocean and returns to small islands to lay eggs.

Various developers have been promising to open the **Royal Palm Park,** a 500-acre nature preserve that will feature areas carved into the swamp, harboring over 25 species of birds, turtles, and fish. The plan is to have a water taxi transport visitors through the park and stop at a 30-foot observation tower where you'll be able to have an unobstructed view of the entire facility. This has been planned for several years now, and it is not clear when the park will open.

Also on the drawing board is a tourist facility at **Roaring River,** near the Shrewsbury Estate at the inland town of Frome. You can swim in the river, which seems to pop out from nowhere as it emerges from a series of underground meanderings and caves.

Tours
If it's organized tours you want, Montego Bay has its share and is just over an hour's drive from Negril. Tour buses will take you to most Montego Bay attractions, including the Appleton Express, and as far as Dunn's River Falls and Ocho Rios on the north coast. Tours are also available to take you southeast to Black River and Mandeville for sightseeing and shopping. All buses pick you up at your hotel. Prices are

US$30-70 pp, and some tours start as early as 0645. Contact **Sunholiday Travel & Tour,** tel. 957-4209. **Caribic Vacations Ltd.,** tel. 957-4760, is a full-service tourism outfit, and they do everything from making hotel bookings to diving tours. They're expensive. For cruising the beach and cliffs, contact *Checkmate,* tel. 957-4218, which offers a sunset cruise (daily 1600-1900).

PRACTICALITIES

ACCOMMODATIONS

Negril is growing rapidly but, thankfully, with some forethought. Advertising posters that used to say "Negril, Jamaica's Best Kept Secret," now say "Negril, The Secret Is Out." Gimmicks aside, it is true that the hotel boom that started in the mid-'70s and continued through the '80s created over 100 hotels, bungalows, campgrounds, or guesthouses. Growth has continued into the '90s, and Negril has over 2,500 rooms today. In fact, Negril doubled its available rooms in the years 1988-90. Yet it still doesn't look crowded, and since high-rise hotels and apartments are prohibited, it may never look crowded.

Off-season rates, as usual, can be considerably cheaper than on-season rates, and are *often negotiable.* Again, off-season is roughly a Northern Hemisphere summer, or mid-April or May through mid-Nov. or December. Room taxes are required by law in most hotels and some guesthouses. Some hotels add a 10% service charge in lieu of gratuities, and the 10% GCT is applicable to most hotels. Always check with hotels first to confirm current rates and room-tax schedules.

Inexpensive
Addis Kokeb Guesthouse (P.O. Box 78, Negril, Jamaica, W.I.; tel. 957-4485, fax 957-4485), on the east side of West End Rd., is small but comfortable. The name means "New Star" in Amharic, an Ethiopian language. The complex sleeps 21, some in the six rooms of the main guesthouse and the rest in cottages on the grounds. It's a great little compound, full of fruit

trees and plants. You can use the pool at the Summerset Resort next door, and walk across the street to the cliffs. Cooking facilities are in a shared kitchen, where Deborah Luers, the manager, sells Red Stripe and soft drinks as well. Winter rates are US$40, s or d, per guesthouse room, or you can rent the whole place, with six bedrooms, for about US$240 per night. The one-bedroom cottage with a kitchen is US$50. For summer rates, deduct 20% from winter rates. Longer stays are negotiable.
Country Resort Cottages (P.O. Box 39, Negril, Jamaica, W.I.; tel. 957-4273) is situated directly on the beach next to Tree House Cottages. Designed for the "I am one with the sea" person, the cottages are rustic and on the ocean. No kitchens, but a small restaurant in the compound serves Jamaican and vegetarian.
Hilltop Villas and Apartments (Hermitage Rd., Negril, Jamaica, W.I.; tel. 957-4253, Canada tel. 514-683-3798) is small but growing. Not a particularly pretty place, but if you're traveling with friends, the price is right. It has three one-bedroom apartment units (three people each) at US$80 per unit, and 14 studio doubles at US$70 per unit. They also rent one two-bedroom unit (four people) for US$120 per night. All have kitchenettes, TVs, and fans or a/c. Call Michelle Brady for details.
Jamiana Hotel (P.O. Box 80, Negril, Jamaica, W.I.; tel. 957-4005, fax 957-4078, U.S.A. tel. 800-423-4095) is a small, eight-room inn on West End Rd., near the town center. It's a quaint place, clean, and all rooms have a/c and private bath. Try lunch or dinner at the **La Rasta Pasta** restaurant. Rates are US$40 s or d in summer, US$75 s or d in winter.

Lighthouse Park (P.O. Box 3, Negril, Jamaica, W.I.; tel. 957-4490) is located on some magnificent cliffs at the far end of West End Rd., the type of place for people who prefer to get away from even the mild hubbub of town. The site has a variety of accommodations, from cottages to cabañas, some with shared baths, to campsites with ablution blocks for campers. Water is cold, but showers are equipped with solar bags. The rooms are rustic and clean. The privacy here is a major attraction. Because of the cliff dangers, no children under 12 are accommodated. Rates are complicated because of the variety of accommodations, but count on US$40-50 d in the winter, and US$25 d during off-season. Campsites range US$15-20 per night.

LTU Resort (P.O. Box 116, Negril, Jamaica, W.I.; tel. 957-4778) is a cottage, formerly called the Olympic Resort, located at the far end of West End Rd. near the lighthouse. They've got eight rooms at US$75-90 d in the winter, US$35 d in the summer for rooms with fans. Add a few more dollars for rooms with a/c. The **LTU Pub** (under the same ownership) is across the street on the cliffs, and has one of the nicest diving pools in the area. You don't have to dive—it's about 60 feet to the water—you can take the steps down to the pool. The pub is one of the town's more lively, and people have been known to dance on the bar in the wee hours. Write to director Lucy Martens.

Roots Bamboo (Norman Manley Blvd., Negril, Jamaica, W.I.; tel. 957-4479) is one of the best deals on the beach side of Negril. On the beach, the 32 rooms are basic and designed for people who won't be spending their days inside. No maid service, although the sheets are changed, and most rooms use a shower block located on the complex. Nonshower rooms, most with two twin beds, are US$20 in the winter, cheaper in the summer. Rooms with showers are US$50 in winter and US$25-40 in summer. Camping is also available at about US$5 a space, more for a space with a hotel tent. A small restaurant/bar is located on the beach. This is a great place for those who want to roll out of bed, blink twice, and be on the beach.

Moderate
Cotton Tree Villas (West End Rd., Negril, Jamaica, W.I.; tel. 957-4450, fax 957-4473) is a new complex near the central traffic rotary of town. All 20 rooms are self-contained studios, and the location *isn't* great for swimming or beach action. The attraction is the access you'll have to goings-on in town. In summer, studios are US$60 s or d. In winter, prices start at US$85 s, US$95 d, up to US$120 d. Add 10% service charge and 10% GCT.

Jamaica Tamboo (Norman Manley Blvd., Negril, Jamaica, W.I.; tel. 957-4282) has bungalows and rooms, pizza, and a busy beach bar. One of the older hotels on the beach strip, over 15 years in operation, the hotel has managed to grow a thick, junglelike foliage throughout the grounds. The resident manager says, "It makes you feel like you're in Jamaica." Interesting concept, and the same could be said for the beach at your front door. Rates are about US$46 s and US$90 d—some a/c, some fans— in summer, and US$60-90 in winter. Add 10% GCT. Summer rates are negotiable.

Mirage Resort (P.O. Box 33, Negril, Jamaica, W.I.; tel. 957-4471, fax 957-4414, U.S.A. tel. 800-74-CHARMS) is a cliff-side set of six cottages built into a hill. The cheaper rooms have ceiling fans only and the rest have a/c and fan. The sunsets are spectacular. Rates are US$45-55 s and US$55-66 d in the summer, and US$88-98 s or US$95-110 d in the winter. Add 10% service charge and 5% GCT.

Negril Tree House Resort (P.O. Box 29, Negril, Jamaica, W.I.; tel. 957-4287/8, fax. 957-4386, U.S.A. tel. 800-423-4095) is in another great beach-side location, with a fine restaurant, bar, and room amenities, but is a bit overpriced compared to its neighbors. The gimmick here—and it's a fun one—is that the restaurant and bar are elevated and built around a tree. Winter room rates are US$105-120 s or d. Summer rates are US$65 and up, s or d. Add 10% service charge on all rates and 5% GCT.

Rock Cliff Hotel (West End Rd., Negril, Jamaica, W.I.; tel. 957-4331, U.S.A. tel. 800-JA-MAICA) is one of the nicest properties on the cliff side of Negril. In operation since 1981, the hotel has suites and rooms with balconies, all uniquely designed to face the sunset. They feature a reggae band and an all-you-can-eat Sunday barbecue for about US$25. The diving from Rock Cliff is excellent as well, and **Sundivers Jamaica,** a five-star PADI diving outfit (see p. 119) operates from the hotel. For unique additions, they've got a basketball court. Rooms are called superior and deluxe, and are US$70 s to US$90 d in summer, and from US$100 in winter. Suites (sleep six) are US$190 in summer and US$290 in winter. Add 10% GCT and 10% service charge. Contact Assistant General Manager Gloria Allen.

Hotel Sam Sara (P.O. Box 23 Negril, Jamaica, W.I.; tel. 957-4395, fax 957-4073) is another cliff-side hotel and features some of the best live reggae in Negril. On Monday the hotel brings in Jamaica's big names, such as Ziggy Marley and the Melody Makers, for a reggae party from about 2130 until early morning. The hotel draws diners with a daily 1600-1900 happy hour and a new Italian restaurant. As with any hotel on the cliff side, the snorkeling is tremendous. They've got the only tennis court on the west end. The 50 rooms are US$70-110 s or d in winter, and US$45-85 during the off-season. Add 10% service charge and 10% GCT.

Singles Negril is one of the newest resorts in town (P.O. Box 87, Negril, Jamaica, W.I.; tel. 957-4125/8, fax 957-4124, U.S.A. and Canada tel. 800-654-1337, U.K. tel. 081-908-1516, fax 081-908-5778). The 32 rooms are all modern triple suites with kitchenettes, refrigerators, a/c, TV, and the works. A swimming pool and whirlpool are available for guests, and there are several restaurants nearby. Café Laguna stands out among them. Interestingly—and one can imagine it wouldn't work for the hotel—the hotel is located in the Sunshine Village complex, a quasi-mall near the central traffic rotary. Guests are given passes to the sports facilities of nearby Swept Away Resort, possibly the best sports facility on the island. Guests are also transported to the beach. In an ironic twist, the name of the resort has nothing to do with its clientele. Couples are allowed, even encouraged. Summer rates are US$80 s, US$90 d, and US$25 per extra person. In winter, rates are US$100 s, US$120 d, and US$50 for the third person. Taxes and service charge are included.

Summerset Village is located near Drumville Cove on West End Rd., about 300 yards from the cliffs (P.O. Box 4, Negril, Jamaica, W.I.; tel. 957-4409; U.S.A. tel. 800-423-4095, Canada and Illinois tel. 312-883-1020). It's a sort of homely place, but the grounds are nice, and they do a good job at getting their guests around Negril to the various beaches and cliff-diving

spots. The restaurant serves standard but good Jamaican fare. Winter rates are US$70-80 s or d and US$120 for a cottage with a kitchen (sleeps four). Summer rates are US$50-60 d and US$100 for the cottages. Add a 10% service charge and 10% tax.

Thrills (Negril P.O., Jamaica, W.I.; tel. 957-4390, fax 957-4153) is a 20-room inn located a few hundred yards from the cliffs on West End Road. It's a very pleasant, relaxed place, with a pool, lighted tennis courts, restaurant, and bar. The standard rooms have fans but no a/c. In winter US$65 s or d, in summer US$40-45 s or d. Add 10% GCT.

T-Water Beach Hotel (P.O. Box 11, Negril, Jamaica, W.I.; tel. 957-4270/1, fax 957-4334, U.S.A. tel. 800-654-1592), on the beach side, has been in operation for over 25 years and is one of the oldest hotels in Negril. It's a family-operated hotel, and attracts families as well. The name is said to have originated with a young relative of the owner who couldn't pronounce "seawater." Though the hotel is tarnished and showing its age, it still has a certain tropical allure and, inevitably, a great beach. The rooms have a/c and prices quoted are for double rooms. Buffet breakfast and lunch are included in the price. Winter rates US$120-150, summer US$90-125. Extra charges are 10% GCT, 10% service charge, and the strange US$2 per room p/d "energy charge," which has something to do with the a/c.

Luxury

The **Grand Lido** is no doubt the most elegant resort in Negril, possibly in the country (P.O. Box 88, Negril, Jamaica, W.I.; tel. 957-4010, fax 957-4317, U.S.A. tel. 800-858-8009, Canada tel. 800-553-4320). An all-inclusive and one of the SuperClubs chain hotels, the complex sits isolated on a Bloody Bay beach north of town. The design is Caribbean/Mediterranean sleek, light marble and stucco; you expect to find the ghost of Graham Greene sitting at one of the complex's nine bars. Inclusive in the price are all meals, drinks, laundry, water sports, tennis, use of the fitness center and two beaches (one clothing-optional) with hot tubs, and—a pleasant surprise—use of a large library. Eat at any one of three very good restaurants, particularly **Piacere,** the French restaurant, which features a dessert of chocolate molded to resemble a small grand piano filled with chocolate mousse. You can cruise Long Bay on the M/Y *Zein*, a 147-foot luxury yacht once owned by Aristotle Onassis. The hotel has six rate seasons rather than the usual two, but the bottom line is that you pay for what you get, and you get it in abundance. Summer rates are basically US$215-40 pp per night, based on double occupancy. Adults over 18 only. Three-day minimum stay.

Hedonism II (P.O. Box 25, Negril, Jamaica, W.I.; tel. 957-4201, fax 957-4289, U.S.A. and Canada tel. 800-858-8009) wins the award for having the most honestly descriptive name in town. It's a pretty fleshy place, another of the all-inclusive SuperClubs. The emphasis here is on the body, generally young and single bodies, though hedonists apparently come in all ages and marital statuses. Recreation includes tennis (six lighted courts), horseback riding, body-building, sports clinics with professionals, water sports, dancing, a house band, and the requisite nude beach. And they have a hot tub that could drown a hippo. Meals are buffet style. The resort has five rate seasons, but basically you'll pay up to US$566 off-season pp based on three nights, and up to US$690 in winter pp for three nights. Singles will have to share with another person of the same sex, unless an additional daily charge of US$75 is paid. Minimum age is 16 and minimum stay is three nights.

Sandals Negril (P.O. Box 12, Negril, Jamaica, W.I.; tel. 957-4216, fax 957-4338, U.S.A. tel. 800-327-1991) is an all-inclusive for couples only, set on a nice piece of the Negril seven-mile beach. The standard here is the same as at all Sandals resorts: good food, plenty of activities in and out of the water, and the opportunity to eat and drink all you want. Accommodations vary from standard rooms to beachfront suites. The setting is serene, as is Negril in general. Although it's not in the literature, they emphasize heterosexual couples only. Sandals has three rate seasons, ranging US$335-440 per couple per night 28 March-28 June, or US$358-473 per couple per night 21 Dec.-28 March, based on six nights. Summer is cheaper. Minimum stay is three nights.

Swept Away (P.O. Box 77, Negril, Jamaica, W.I.; tel. 957-4061/6, fax 957-4060, U.S.A. and Canada tel. 800-545-7937) is a unique facility for Negril, and is an all-inclusive. It bills itself as a health and fitness resort, meaning they offer water sports (including an Olympic-sized pool), eight tennis courts, two squash courts, two racquetball courts, gyms, aerobics, yoga, hot tubs, saunas, and steam rooms. The rooms are villa type. It's all very nice on a pretty beach, but there seems to be a bit of pretense about it, possibly a personal aversion to a load of preening, flushed people munching on carrot sticks. Couples only. Rates range US$360-485 per couple per night, based on a stay of seven nights.

Rondel Village (P.O. Box 96, Negril, Jamaica, W.I.; tel. 957-4413, fax 957-4915, U.S.A. tel. 800-544-5979) is one of the least expensive luxury hotels in Negril, and one of the most quaint. It's small, only eight villas, but it seems like the right size. And it's on the beach. The villas have kitchens, upstairs lofts with bedrooms, and TVs; a small restaurant is on the grounds. Villas are US$150-175 d and US$200 for a "quad" (sleeps four) in winter; US$90-100 d, US$130 for quad in the off-season. Add 10% service charge. Meal plans are available.

Vicinity Of Negril

At Green Island, stay at **JJ's Guest House** (Green Island P.O., Hanover, Jamaica, W.I.; U.S.A. tel. 718-968-7469). The guesthouse is 12 miles from Negril, and if quiet and out-of-the-mainstream is what you want, this is a good place to start. The eight rooms are clean, with fans and two twin beds in each. JJ's has a pool, bar, and eating area, and plenty of space to explore Green Island. Winter rates are US$30 d and US$20 s; off-season rates drop to US$22 and US$15, no taxes applied.

Four miles north of Negril is **Rhodes Hall Plantation** (Green Island P.O., Hanover, Jamaica, W.I.; tel. 957-4232), a 550-acre plantation with moderately priced accommodations, tours, horseback riding, and fishing. It's a nice place to visit, but the attraction of nearby Negril seems to make it just that—a nice place to visit.

EATING AND DRINKING

A fun way to eat in Negril is to simply walk along any stretch of Negril Beach and take advantage of the many beach side snack shacks, restaurants, and bars that sit in the sand. Many are attached to hotels and generally very good, and many are independents that serve fish, jerk chicken, Rasta I-tal, and always a cold Red Stripe or rum punch. Some beach bars close with the setting sun, when the hotels and other restaurants take over the night business, but others stay open as long as the party continues, and it often does until the sun rises. Independent restaurants often change their hours with the season—open all day in winter, and for lunch and dinner or just dinner during off-season.

Along the cliff side you'll find most are independent restaurants, with quite a few good ones attached to hotels.

Negril is a big town for seafood, but remember, please don't eat or buy lobster during its reproduction season, 1 May-31 July.

Beach-side Restaurants

The following restaurants are located on the beach along Norman Manley Blvd., the main road entering Negril from Montego Bay.

De Buss is one of the best for outside dining and drinking into the wee hours. De Buss is also home of some of Negril's more contemporary reggae music, and there *is* something nice about dancing in the sand. **Fisherman's Club Restaurant** is located across from Negril Gardens, at a public entrance to the beach. Like most Negril restaurants, they specialize in seafood, and they do it well and inexpensively. Next to Fisherman's Club, and all along the beach, are dozens of small shacks offering jerk pork, chicken, and fish, other fast food, and drinks. This is the best and cheapest way to eat on the beach.

Alfred's Ocean Palace is mostly a bar, but they have volleyball on the beach and seafood. **Mark's Hurricane Bar** is also great for drinks and bar food, conveniently located next to a string of similar beach bars. You can roll through the lot if you've got the stamina. **Cosmo's** (tel. 957-4330) is more of a proper restaurant than beach bar, open nightly until 2200.

Jamaica Tamboo has a great little beach bar and a good reputation among pizza lovers. **Sober's**, incredibly, sells beer and other drinks. **Country Restaurant** serves medium-priced vegetarian.

Try **Cheap Bite** (north of the crafts park) for just that.

Farther down the road, stop at **Runaway's**

Beach Bar (tel. 957-9180), a larger hut that specializes in burgers and Jamaican fare; it offers music late at night.

If you take a left at the central rotary, heading out on the Savanna-la-mar road, you'll see **Mrs. Brown's Fine Food** on the left. Mrs. Brown's specializes in mushroom-laden omelettes and Jamaican dishes.

Cliff-side Restaurants

For fast food try **Adrija Fast Food & Pastries** at the **Adrija Plaza** just past the traffic rotary. They have drinks, carrot juice, soursop juice, goat belly, cow foot, and tripe and beans. At press time, this restaurant was remodeling and may reopen under a different name. Hopefully, the food will remain the same. Try chicken or pepper steak at **Chicken Whirl**. The chef, Rambo, says his poached snapper in hollandaise is the best in town. **Spinning Wheel** serves basic jerk chicken and pork, and beers. Further down the road try **Jenny's Favorite Cakes** for conch soup and homemade thick french toast. Some may appreciate her signature "special" cakes. They serve breakfast through dinner; open 0800-2200.

The **Silver Star Café** (tel. 957-4345) is known for their breakfasts, served all day.

For Chinese, try **Chopsticks** upstairs at **King's Plaza** next to Adrija Plaza, or **Peking House** down toward the lighthouse for seafood specials or takeout. Peking is open for breakfast and lunch only, 1000-1400.

Hurricane Café, on the low end of the cliff side, has tables on a front porch for traffic watching and in back overlooking a somewhat fetid part of the bay. But the food is good and they're open around the clock as the need presents itself. Hurricane serves steamed fish, chicken

plantain

chop suey, and spicy pork and beans. **Chicken Lavish** (you've got to love the name) is just down the street from the Hurricane, and specializes in chicken, served in a sparse room, no frills, and cheap.

Café Laguna (tel. 957-9167) is new, located at the Sunshine Village complex, and serves breakfast, lunch, and dinner—don't miss the pasta dishes here. The **Negril Jerk Center** (tel. 957-4847) is one of the best spots for pork, fish, chicken, yam, *festival,* and other Jamaican specialties. **Chef's Bar and Grill,** next to Drumville Cove, serves Jamaican as well.

Fair Flakes Pastry (tel. 957-4436) serves pastries, meat pies, and assorted Jamaican-style fast food. Try **Pastries** (tel. 957-4837) for, guess what?

Jah Beer Garden, across the street from the Hotel Sam Sara, serves bar food, beers, and music, and is a cool place to hang out for an hour away from the hot afternoon sun. The **Archway Cafe** (tel. 957-4399) on West End Rd. serves spaghetti, subs, and burgers. A plus—they deliver.

The **LTU Pub,** at the lighthouse end of West End Rd., is a personal favorite for watching the often spectacular Negril sunsets. Even when they're not spectacular, they're pretty impressive. LTU is perched on a high cliff—only the experienced, and never the even slightly inebriated, should try the dive. Food at LTU is Jamaican and German, and the fillet of beef tenderloin is a specialty.

For vegetarian I-tal, the best bet is **Hungry Lion Café.** The setting is Rasta, with paintings of Bob Marley, Marcus Garvey, and Peter Tosh on the walls. The shepherds pie with potatoes and lentils is a specialty, as is the lasagna with *callaloo* and garlic. This is yummy stuff. Does chocolate-and-butter cake sound rich? It is. Open daily 1730-2200.

Erica's Café (tel. 957-4322) serves simple Jamaican fare, and is as unpretentious as they get. Try the lobster chop suey or curried goat. They're open for breakfast, lunch, and dinner during the winter, and 1600-midnight during off-season.

Café Au Lait (tel. 957-4471), at the Mirage Hotel is one of the more romantic restaurants in town, serving very good French and Jamaican cuisine, either indoors or on the large veranda. This is a medium- to expensively priced restaurant. The chicken in lime sauce is a specialty, as is seafood. The wine list is plentiful.

Rick's Café (tel. 957-4335) is the spot where everyone goes to watch the sunset. It gets a bit crazed, with people standing three deep and the sound of cameras clicking and videos whirring—you'd think that no one ever saw an act of nature before. The medium-priced food is reputed to be good, however, and this is possibly the one place in Negril where you need to make a reservation. The sundown scene is fine if you're the type of person who likes to share intimate moments with other people's electronic equipment. Buck the trend and go to the LTU Pub or Rock Cliff for a quiet daiquiri and a relaxed collapse of the sun.

Every hotel has a restaurant, and most are good, though more expensive than the small cafés. A quick fruit or coconut juice snack can be found at the Negril Craft Market (see below). Jerk chicken and pork vendors line the street in front of the Adrija Plaza and at the east side of the rotary, near the bus stand. In fact, you can hardly walk more than 100 feet anywhere in Negril without coming across something to eat.

For food shopping, try the **Hi-Lo** supermarket at **Sunshine Village** on West End Road. It's got the most complete line in town. Upstairs you'll find a fast-food plaza, featuring the Jamaican chain **King Burger** and the U.S chain **Shakey's Pizza.** The **Save-A-Dollar** market in Negril Plaza also has basic food items.

SHOPPING AND ENTERTAINMENT

Shopping

While Negril is not exactly a shopping mecca, it's got enough, especially in the way of local crafts, to max your credit card if that's your desire.

For duty-free items and clothes, try the three main plazas downtown, west of the central rotary. **Omni Duty-Free Shop** and **Krisroan Fashions** at Adrija Plaza sell beachwear and duty-free items. Negril Plaza and King's Plaza also have clothing shops, pharmacies, and small general stores that sell everything from newspapers to stationery to soft drinks.

Crafts shopping in Negril is as easy as stepping out your front door. Starting from the outskirts of town on the approach from Green Island, you'll see carving and crafts stalls, as well

Faces of Jamaica (all photos by Phyllis Luntta)

Buff Bay River, Portland (Phyllis Luntta)

as young men holding out green baggies if they recognize you as a tourist. As you enter town, you'll see the **Rutland Point Craft Park,** near Hedonism II, a fair-sized market with the carving, T-shirt, and basket basics. It's not as big, however, as the **Negril Craft Market,** in the center of town near the traffic rotary. This is your best bet for a variety of crafts, including carvings, baskets, T-shirts, hammocks, and shell crafts. You can also eat at the fruit stalls, or at the fast-food and beer joints. See Sister Love for clothes and woven crafts, and Brother John for carvings—their sell is soft, the quality good. Fuzzy, located "somewhere in the back," also has a wide selection of carvings and shell crafts.

Plaza de Negril, which houses Save-A-Dollar supermarket, also has crafts and gallerylike shops. Try **Gallery Hoffstead** for work by artist Lloyd Hoffstead. Other galleries include **Geraldine Robins Gallery** on West End Rd., and **Patrick Weise Studio Gallery** (tel. 957-4456), also on West End Road.

One of the newer markets in town is at **Sunshine Village,** formerly the National Commercial Bank (NCB) Plaza, near the West End rotary. The whole business is indoors, behind the Hi-Lo supermarket, and features several dozen shops with much of the same crafts fare, as well as fast-food patties, burgers, beer, and more. The disadvantage is that the stalls are little more than 50% occupied, possibly due to its newness. Also in the plaza are several tourist-type crafts stores, as well as **Top Spot** (tel. 957-4542), the best place in town for magazines, local and international newspapers, and stationery. Café Laguna is located here, as is Singles Resort and several fast-food outlets on the top floor.

Along Norman Manley Blvd. and West End Rd., as well as on the beach itself, numerous crafts stalls and small markets sell T-shirts and the basics. Many of these are good, and the haggling will be ferocious. At the south end of Norman Manley Blvd. you'll see a number of stalls with T-shirts and other beachwear flapping in the wind. Buy things here, but understand that taking "no" for an answer is apparently unethical for these vendors. Browsing is tantamount to taking your money out. It's that kind of sell, so don't lose control.

In addition, most of the larger hotels have boutiques that sell nice (but overpriced) clothes and beachwear, as well as suntan lotion, postcards, and tourist items.

Nightlife

Negril gets its share of great reggae, by both local bands and Kingston imports. The action starts at about 2200 and lasts until after 0100. Cost for live reggae can be J$50 and up, depending on the band. Monday, the best bet is **Hotel Sam Sara.** On Tuesday, bands play at **De Buss** and **Summerset Hotel.** Wednesday, go to **Kaiser's Café** (tel. 957-4450) on the west end. Note the wall mural on the street side. Fine sunsets, too. Thursday, try the **Tree House Resort** on Norman Manley Boulevard. Friday is Kaiser's again, and Saturday at De Buss there's an early evening show, 1800-2200. On Sunday, De Buss has a late-night show. The **Jamiana Hotel** features reggae bands on Tuesday. **MXII** (tel. 957-4818), a bar and nightclub on West End Rd., offers live reggae bands on Thursday and Saturday.

For canned disco music, try **Compulsion** at Negril Plaza and **Close Encounters** at King's Plaza for almost nightly dancing. These are popular night spots because of their low cover charges and because the music lasts until well into the morning (for compulsively close encounters).

Just north of Negril in Green Island, check out **Mandela Green** (tel. 956-2607), a reggae and entertainment center. It also has a restaurant.

RECREATION

Water Sports

Water sports can be arranged through hotels, whether you're staying at one or not. Most of Negril's dive centers and water-sports outfits are attached to hotels but run independent operations.

Dive-center rates vary with the amount of equipment and instruction provided to begin or refresh your diving skills. **Sundivers Jamaica** (tel. 973-4069), based at Rock Cliff Hotel, is a PADI five-star dive center certified to qualify diving instructors. A four-day PADI certification course costs about US$300; an open-water referral (two days/four dives) is US$200. Other dive rates range from US$30 for a single dive to US$100 for a five-dive package. Night dives are US$35, and an unlimited day-diving package, based on one week, starts at US$225. Equipment, including wetsuits and underwater cameras and videos, are available for US$5-75 per dive.

Aqua Nova Water Sports (tel. 957-4323), located at the Negril Beach Club, offers boat tours, sailing, fishing, snorkeling, and party excursions to Booby Cay. They've probably got the widest array of water-sports equipment available, and their prices are reasonable. Snorkel equipment rents for US$5 per hour, sailboarding is about US$10 per hour. The three-hour sailing cruise costs US$30, which includes drinks and snorkel gear. Fishing is US$250 per half-day. The party cruise to Booby Cay departs Tues., Fri., and Sun. 1030-1500, and includes lunch, drinks, and snorkelgear. Cost is US$30. They also rent jet skis and parasailing equipment; contact owners Vincent and Jean Gaynair.

Negril Scuba Centre (tel. 957-4425), also at Negril Beach Club, offers dives starting at US$30. A three-dive package runs US$75, and a six-dive package costs US$125. Night dives start at US$40 (minimum of three people). Custom dives are available for small groups at US$85 pp. Their open-water certification costs US$350, while the open-water referral is US$200. Prices are subject to change.

Other smaller dive centers include **Blue Whale Divers Limited** (tel. 957-4438) on Norman Manley Blvd., and **Mariner's Diving Resort** (tel. 957-4348) on the West End Rd. cliffs.

Irie Water Sports (tel. 957-4670) organizes water-skiing, snorkel trips, banana-boat rides, and the usual suspects. **Ocean Tour Water**

Sports (tel. 957-4693), on the beach next to Fisherman's Club, offers sunset cruises, reef tours, snorkeling, parasailing, and island picnics. Also on the beach, **Pringle Water Sports** (tel. 957-4893) offers all of that plus deep-sea fishing. **Ray's Parasailing** (tel. 957-4349) is big on—here's a surprise—parasailing. They also offer sunfish sailing, jet skis, and snorkeling.

When diving or snorkeling, please remember that breaking or even touching coral can seriously upset the reef, and can have a long-range, destructive effect on reef and wildlife conservation as well as on fishing, a lifeline for many Jamaicans.

Note: Parasailing (parachute sailing) is an activity in which you're towed by a power boat, as you hang from a chute above the water. Some schools of thought consider this dangerous, say, if the tow rope malfunctions and you gently descend to the water only to have the parachute land on top of you. Otherwise, it's fun.

Other Recreation

Horseback riding is popular in Negril, and a number of places offer guided rides. Try **Babo's** on Red Ground Rd. behind Adrija Plaza. They're open daily 0800-1600 for two-hour rides (no phone). **Country Western Horseback Riding** (no phone) has rides along the coast and into the hills behind Negril. They're located on the Savanna-la-mar road, past the only gas station in Negril. **Rhodes Hall Plantation** (tel. 957-4258 and 957-4232) is located in Hanover, about four miles north of Negril. Cost is about US$30 per two-hour ride.

For a few quiet minutes of regulated meditation, try the **Negril Yoga Centre** (P.O. Box 48, Negril, Jamaica, W.I.; tel. 957-4397) on Norman Manley Boulevard. They conduct yoga and meditation classes, and provide natural meals and massages.

GETTING AROUND

Public Transportation

The normal route to Negril is from Sangster International Airport in Montego Bay. A bus or minibus is the cheapest way to go, and the most revealing. Private taxis run as much as US$50, according to approved JTB rates. An internal

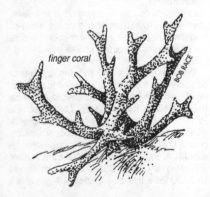

finger coral

BOB RACE

USEFUL PHONE NUMBERS IN NEGRIL AND VICINITY

Area Code 809

Air Jamaica, 957-4300 or 957-4210

American Airlines, 952-5950

Century National Bank (CNB), 957-4001/2

Fire Emergency, 957-4242

International Baby Sitting Service, 957-4287

Jamaica Tourist Board, 957-4243 or 957-4597

Key West Pharmacy, 957-4081

National Commercial Bank, 957-4117

Negril Chamber of Commerce, 957-4067

Negril Child Care Service, 957-4288

Police, 957-4268

Savanna-la-mar Hospital, 955-2523

Scotiabank, 957-4236/7

Seven Mile Medical Clinic, 957-4888

Trans Jamaican Airlines, 957-4251

flight takes about 20 minutes, US$50 OW; double that for a return flight.

Since Negril is basically two streets, it's neither difficult to find your way around, nor dificult to get there. Walking will suffice in many instances, but the midday sun can be debilitating. Minibuses cruise Norman Manley Blvd. and West End Rd., and can be flagged down for a local ride for under J$5-8. Private taxis can be flagged or called, and the cost should be no more than US$5 for any point in Negril. Discuss that with the driver. Out-of-town buses congregate east of the central rotary, on the Savanna-la-mar road (Sheffield Road). Catch a taxi either at your hotel, at the taxi stand in front of Adrija Plaza, or at the Negril Craft Market.

For pickup at your hotel, call Benjie Ricketts (tel. 957-4427) or Jervis Robertson (tel. 957-4277).

Rentals

To travel, try renting a bike, scooter, or motorcycle (see chart). They're cheaper than cars, and you won't need a car if it's only Negril you want to see. Again, Jamaica doesn't require helmets, though they're a good idea. Check the

motorcycle to see that all lights, horns, etc., work.

Find motorcycle and bike rentals along Norman Manley Blvd., on the morass side of the road, or along West End Road. Prices range from about US$20-30 p/d for a 50cc bike to US$40 p/d for a 125cc dirt bike or street motorcycle. A 500cc bike rents for about US$50 p/d. Regular mountain bicycles and others can be rented for as little as US$5 per day. In the summer, these prices are very negotiable. Many bike-rental shacks don't have phones, but don't worry about them running out of wheels. They all seem to have an unlimited supply.

Rental cars in Negril are more expensive than in Montego Bay, where competition has driven prices down. A standard, compact car without a/c will run an amazing US$70 or more p/d, tax and insurance included. Automatic and a/c cars can run as much as US$90 per day. These quoted rates, of course, are ridiculous, and you should try and negotiate. Many companies will readily negotiate either for weekly rates, or in the off-season.

In the past, it's been a temptation for motorcyclists to go for a tear on the long Negril Beach. Consider what this does to the beach, not to mention sunbathers and strollers. When sand is compacted, more is lost through wave action, and beach erosion is accelerated. And riding on the beach is against the law.

INFORMATION

Banks can be found along Norman Manley Blvd. and at Negril Plaza downtown. Remember that banking hours are Mon.-Thurs. 0900-1400, and Fri. 0900-1500.

There are doctor's offices at Adrija Plaza and Negril Plaza, and at the small health clinic on the Savanna-la-mar road. Negril does not have a large hospital. Residents use Savanna-la-mar Hospital, 19 miles southeast, or Lucea Hospital, 24 miles north. The police and fire stations are located on the Savanna-la-mar road, just beyond the Shell station.

The **Jamaica Tourist Board** (open Mon.-Fri. 0830-1630, and Sat. 0900-1400) has offices on the second floor of Adrija Plaza. See Volney Williams for information and free brochures. The JTB maintains three information kiosks for easy access: one at the Negril

NEGRIL CAR AND MOTORCYCLE RENTAL AGENCIES

Area Code 809

Motorcycles and Bicycles:

Bikini Bike Rental, Norman Manley Blvd.

B.T.'s Bike Rentals, Norman Manley Blvd., 957-4333

Gas Bike Rental, West End Rd.

I-Won, Norman Manley Blvd., 957-5941

Jah B's, Norman Manley Blvd.

Kool Brown's Rentals, West End Rd., 957-4853

Mass Bike Rental, West End Rd., 957-4859

Pedro Rent-A-Bike, Norman Manley Blvd., 957-4757

Salmon's Bike Rental, Norman Manley Blvd., 957-4671

Tanka Bike Rental, Plaza de Negril, 957-4488

Tykes Bike Rental, West End Rd., 957-4836

West End Rental, West End Rd.

Wright's Bike Rental, Norman Manley Blvd., 957-4908

Cars:

Rite Rate Rent-A-Car, Plaza de Negril, 957-4267

Vernon's Car Rental, Plaza de Negril, 957-4354 or 957-4698

Craft Market, another on West End Rd., and the third on the beach near Cosmo's Restaurant.

The **Negril Chamber of Commerce** (open Mon.-Fri. 0900-1600) is next to the JTB at Adrija Plaza. They produce an annual guide to Negril, helpful in negotiating your way around town. Jean Jackson, the director, says that they'll also type, photocopy, and fax for a small fee.

Key West Pharmacy, at King's Plaza, is the largest full-line pharmacy in Negril. Hours are Mon.-Fri. 0900-1900, and Sat. 1100-1700.

Negril's tiny post office is on West End Rd., next to King's Plaza. This is a good example of a rural postal agency—expect a long, if not interesting, wait for stamps and packages.

THE SOUTHWEST COAST AND INLAND

INTRODUCTION

The only paradise is paradise lost.
—Marcel Proust (1871-1922),
French novelist

A veritable time warp!
—from a Treasure Beach
promotional brochure

Jamaica's southwest coast generally has been untouched by the type of development that has rendered parts of the north coast tourist-dense and, in some places, as sensitively presented as your Uncle Fred's whoopee cushion. It is, for the most part, a relaxed and un-hyped place— the pace of life a notch slower than in the hurried urban centers of Montego Bay and Kingston. However, like many pockets of paradise, the southwest coast is slowly changing as developers and visitors discover the area. Plans are afoot for a large, all-inclusive resort to be built near Bluefields, an unheard-of development for

the southwest coast. New hotels have opened in the Black River and Treasure Beach areas, and several formerly unaffected and inexpensive tourist attractions have expanded. New tour companies have formed. It seems that the juggernaut of tourism is advancing toward the southwest coast, and one can only hope that it all takes place with some forethought and sensitivity to the needs of that land and the Jamaicans who live on it.

Nevertheless, today the southwest coast is still your best bet for an unrefined and charmed part of Jamaica. Your advantage will be a scenic environment, and a population that seems closer to its bedrock, less in a frenzy to make a tourist dollar.

Southern Sugar

The southwest coast and much of the interior, from Negril to Portland Point south of May Pen, is sugarcane country. The flattened plains and rolling hills of the region are not only pretty, but are an advantage in growing the tall, sweet grass. The region's weather, which is drier and more arid than that of the north coast, is also advantageous for sugarcane production.

Jamaica's weather is created by the prevailing trade winds blowing off the Caribbean from the northeast. The high mountain ranges that sit like a backbone through the center of the country force the warm and wet trade winds to rise, creating condensation and prolific rain in the windward parishes. Southern Jamaica, on the leeward side, is in a large rain shadow and gets, at times, less than half the north's rainfall.

The sugar belt is evident as you drive east from Negril to Savanna-la-mar. The drive is short, only 19 miles, but it very quickly becomes an excursion into a different world. As you drive through the waving cane fields and the small towns that grew from the sugar industry, you get a sense of the old and still-present economy of the island. Sugarcane was the basis of the slave industry in Jamaica, and the reason the English held on tenaciously in the face of bloody and destructive slave uprisings.

Pass through **Sheffield,** a small village outside of Negril, to **Little London,** a small town incorporated to provide workers and cane farmers for the giant sugar factory at **Frome** to the north.

Frome Sugar Factory, incorporated in 1939, was built as a central sugar-processing unit intended to replace several smaller and less efficient ones in the area. Local farmers and workers, wary that the central plant would eliminate jobs on the many local sugar estates, agitated for more pay and job security. Cane-field fires were set and rioting ensued, eventually leaving four dead. Local labor leader Alexander Bustamante rushed to the scene to mediate the dispute, and his efforts resulted in the formation of an inquiry commission to look into the sugar industry islandwide. In fact, bedlam spread throughout the country in the late '30s as the working class rose in the face of poor conditions and a not-so-subtle color bar that kept blacks at the bottom of the economic and social scale. Political parties, Bustamante's Jamaica Labor Party (JLP) and Norman Manley's People's National Party (PNP), were formed as almost direct results of those troubled times.

Little London is heavily populated by East Indians, brought over as indentured workers to bolster the labor-intensive sugar industry after the 1834 emancipation of slaves. The town has the basics—a church (most Jamaican East Indians are now Christian), gas station, food shops, and tailors.

SAVANNA-LA-MAR AND VICINITY

INTRODUCTION

Just before you reach town, you'll see a large market on the north side of the road. This is a traditional Jamaican market—as noisy as long-tailed cats in a roomful of rocking chairs. Piles of vegetables, coconuts, fruits, and the inevitable sugarcane crowd the open space, along with jerk meat, ice cream, and peanut vendors. The market is busier on Saturday than any other day of the week.

Savanna-la-mar, from the Spanish *sabana de la mar* for "plain by the sea," is the parish capital of Westmoreland, population 14,900. Locals reduce the cumbersome name to "Sav-la-mar," or sometimes just "Sav." The town was founded circa 1730, and has endured a number of natural disasters in its history. A 1748 hurricane is reputed to have been so severe that it

picked ships up from the harbor and dropped them on dry land. A tidal wave in 1780 and hurricane in 1912 further battered the town.

Savanna-la-mar is a busy primary shopping center for Westmoreland. The main street, **Great George,** the longest city street in Jamaica, is broad and stretches for about a mile from the tip of town to the waterfront. Note the **Savanna-la-mar Parish Church,** built at the turn of this century on the foundation of an old church built circa 1800. The **Courthouse** was built in 1925. The **Westmoreland Parish Library** (open Mon.-Fri. 0900-1800, Sat. 0900-1300) is large for the area and worth a stop. Banks, bookstores, and grocery and hardware stores line the street; if you're looking for something in particular, chances are you'll find it on Great George Street. If you're looking for duty-free or other tourist-type shopping, chances are you won't.

At the waterfront, a small market and pier are

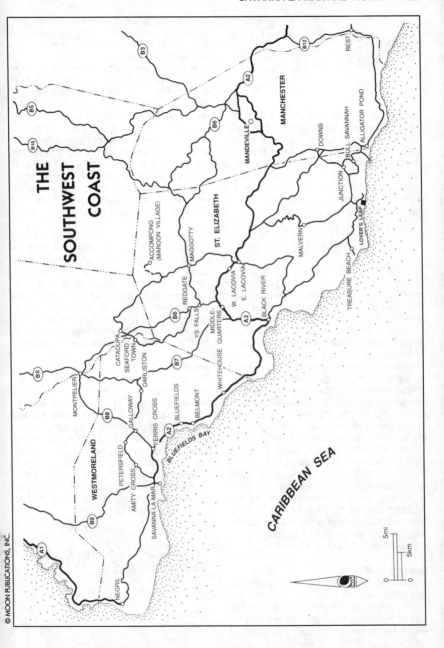

THE
SOUTHWEST
COAST

MANCHESTER

ST. ELIZABETH

WESTMORELAND

CARIBBEAN SEA

© MOON PUBLICATIONS, INC.

B3
B5
B10
B6
B12
REST.
A2
MANDEVILLE
DOWNS
BULL SAVANNAH
ALLIGATOR POND
JUNCTION
LOVER'S LEAP
MALVERN
TREASURE BEACH
ACCOMPONG (MAROON VILLAGE)
MAGGOTTY
REDGATE
W. LACOVIA
E. LACOVIA
BLACK RIVER
YS FALLS
MIDDLE-QUARTERS
WHITEHOUSE
A2
B6
CATADUPA
SEAFORD TOWN
DARLISTON
B7
B8
MONTPELIER
B8
GALLOWAY
FERRIS CROSS
BLUEFIELDS
BELMONT
BLUEFIELDS BAY
A2
PETERSFIELD
AMITY CROSS
SAVANNA-LA-MAR
B9
A1
NEGRIL

5mi
5km
0

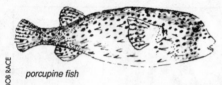

porcupine fish

BOB RACE

used for transporting sugar from the Frome estate to large bulk carriers anchored offshore. The pier is busiest during crop season, Jan.-June. The ruins of old **Savanna-la-mar Fort,** started in 1755 but never finished, crumble into the sea as they did, apparently, from the moment the fort was begun. It's not clear what went wrong with the fort's construction, but the ruins create a popular swimming area for local kids.

SIGHTS

Heading North

Savanna-la-mar is a great jumping-off point for an excursion into the mountains or along the coast. Hwy. B9 ("B" denotes a good secondary road) takes you through the hills on a 21-mile drive to Lucea, in Hanover, where you'll pass Frome and its sugar factory. At **Roaring River** (see "Negril," p. 112) you'll see signs for camping and cottages.

Also from Savanna-la-mar, take the road toward **Petersfield** through **Amity Cross,** the beginning of a lush, hilly stretch of small towns and villages. The road is winding and steep in places—definitely not the place to drive one-handed, but here is some of the west side's most breathtaking scenery. The mountains here are a third of the height of Blue Mountain Peak, Jamaica's highest point at 7,402 feet. At **Galloway,** turn north on Hwy. B8 for a 15-mile drive to Montego Bay, or head to **Darliston** and on to Seaford Town, home of one of Jamaica's German communities (see "Montego Bay," p. 98). From Seaford Town the drive north to **Catadupa,** where the Appleton Express drops its passengers for shopping and Jamaican-tailored clothing, is short and easy.

Heading Southeast

The coastal drive southeast from Savanna-la-mar along Hwy. A2 goes through more cane country and some of the prettiest bays on that side of the island. You can't help but note the **Grace Foods** processing plant just outside of town. Grace is one of Jamaica's largest food-processing companies, turning out everything from ketchup to canned *ackee,* and employs thousands nationwide.

At **Ferris Cross,** a picturesque village four miles east of Savanna-la-mar, you can catch Hwy. B8 to Montego Bay. Stop at the **Blue Nymph** restaurant before reaching the beach at **Bluefields Bay,** a popular spot with Jamaicans for picnics and swimming. It's a free beach right on the road, and faces the town of **Belmont.** Eat at **Kenny's Meals On Wheels,** a bus converted to a rolling restaurant. As well, **KD's Keg and Fish Joint** is good for a quick snack and a beer. **Judge's Beer Place** is another watering hole and quick food joint. All along the usually crowded swimming stretch you'll find jerk meat, fruit, and coconut vendors.

Belmont

Belmont is a small fishing village that has remnants of sugar glory days poking through its now rusty exterior. Some of the older homes are large with gingerbread exteriors, a popular style of the 19th century. It's a wonderfully secluded, untouched town on the edge of the bay—a real charmer with views of the hills to the north. You can get a room at **Sunset Cottages** on the water or at Pleasant View across the street (no phones).

Whitehouse

Farther down the road is Whitehouse, another largely untouched fishing town far from the tourist mainstream. The attraction is another calm and pretty beach-in-a-bay, and one of the largest fishing beaches in the country. Local fishermen take fish from as far away as **Pedro Bank,** some 80 miles offshore. You're welcome to stop, buy, and barter, and even arrange a trip with one of the boats, either for fishing or a coastal tour. Many fishermen will be happy to take you out for a fee; they charge at least what a day's catch would bring.

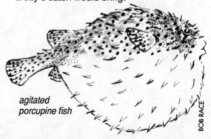

agitated porcupine fish

BOB RACE

Numerous guesthouses and cottages line the road; one of the nicest is **Natania's Guest House** (Little Culloden, Whitehouse P.O., Westmoreland, Jamaica, W.I.; tel. 969-5213), an eight-room charmer set in a garden with a swimming pool, all on its own private beach. You can hire their small boat to take you to a nearby reef for excellent snorkeling. They serve meals and specialize in seafood, as do most Jamaican restaurants worth going to. Rooms have overhead fans and either king-size or double beds. Tariff is US$50 d per night. Contact owner Peter Probst or his wife Veronica.

South Sea View Guesthouse (Whitehouse P.O., Westmoreland, Jamaica, W.I.; tel. 963-5069, fax 963-5000) is an eight-room guesthouse a bit farther down the road from Natania's. Each room has a private bath and a/c or overhead fan, and the place has a swimming pool. The guest-house is on the water. The **Red Snapper Bar** is a local favorite for Chinese and Jamaican dishes. Rooms are US$40 s and US$50 d in winter, and US$40 s and US$45 d in summer. Add US$25 for an extra person, 10% GCT, and 10% service charge.

At **Scott's Cove,** the small kiosks sell fresh fish, lobster, and other seafood cooked immediately as it's brought from the catch by local fishermen. Vendors also mix a nice batch of *bammy,* (the cassava pancake remnant of the Arawak diet), a local staple with fish. You can't get fish fresher, or, in the opinion of many, tastier than this. The sell can be brisk here, so be prepared to move quickly and barter.

At Scott's Cove you'll cross into the parish of St. Elizabeth, just minutes from the parish capital, **Black River.**

SAVANNA-LA-MAR PRACTICALITIES

Savanna-la-mar is an average Jamaican town important as an administrative center and sugar port. It is not, however, built for any kind of visitor influx. That might make it perfect for some travelers—no crowds or aggressive T-shirt salespeople, and increased opportunities to get to know Jamaicans in an ordinary environment. The town does have a few guesthouses and hotels, but you'll have to travel to get to a beach or the mountains. If you've got a car, traveling in and around Savanna-la-mar isn't a problem—just be wary of the one-lane bridges which cross small streams on the approaches to town.

Where To Stay
Orchard Great House (Strathbogie Rd., Savanna-la-mar, Jamaica, W.I.; tel. 955-2737) is a guesthouse three miles outside of town, on an old plantation grounds. The guesthouse is small and inexpensive, has a pool and bar, and is *out there.* Perfect for people who want to get right out of the tourist mainstream. Rooms start at J$150 (US$7).

Food
For Chinese food, try **Dragon Fly II** (tel. 955-2125) at Farm Pen on the outskirts of town. Their prices are reasonable, and they serve Jamaican dishes as well. Stop at the **Talk of the Town** restaurant and bar for a drink and light snack. The **Hole In the Wall** restaurant and bar on Great George St. has a questionable name, but it's a fine place to drop in for a cold drink and Jamaican fast food. **Johnnie's Pastries** serves up quick meat patties and other pastries. The **D & Y Supermarket,** near the fort, is the best bet for groceries. In fact the best bet for snack food and meals is, again, a walk down Great George Street.

BLACK RIVER

INTRODUCTION

The town of Black River (pop. 3,600) takes its name from the **Black River,** Jamaica's longest waterway at 44 miles. The river actually starts as **Hector's River** on the boundary of Trelawny and Manchester parishes, then meanders through the Cockpit Country, disappearing and resurfacing often under different names. Tributaries add to its bulk as the river moves toward the sea, and by the time it reaches town and the port, it's as much as 40 feet deep in places. The water is generally clear, but takes its name from the dark bottom soil that forms its bed. The town was originally called Rio Caobana, or "Mahogany River," by early Spanish settlers.

The town of Black River used its namesake river to become a 19th-century giant in the Jamaican economy. The product was logwood, which was floated downriver in small barges. It was highly prized in Europe for the dark dye produced from its bark. So needed was logwood for European clothes manufacturing that in the years 1893-94 the export value of logwood surpassed that of sugar and coffee. Black River was a major economic center until the production of synthetic dyes made logwood exportation an unprofitable business.

Today remnants of the logwood heyday can be seen in the architecture of large mansions and gingerbread houses on the main streets and outskirts of town. The look is of slightly tarnished English countryside gentry, colonial but crumbling.

SIGHTS

Black River is a sizeable town that today derives its income from a minor trade in logwood and the nascent tourist industry of the south coast. Yet it has a small-town feeling, mostly warm and unhurried, and the views and smell of the ocean define its ambience.

The area's main attraction is a tour of the Black River, today operated by two tour companies.

South Coast Safaris, Ltd. (P.O. Box 129, Mandeville, Jamaica, W.I.; tel. 965-2513) is the older and more experienced of the two. Located on the east end of town by the Black River Bridge, and operated by partners Charles Swaby and Shirley Chung, it may be one of the best tours on the south coast. Swaby and Chung are ardent conservationists as well as tour directors, evident on the 1.5-hour, 10-mile ride on the Black River. They'll explain in detail the flora and fauna of the waterway, pointing out some of the 2,000 snowy and cattle egrets that use the river and its surrounding swamp as a base. Another 100 species of bird, including seven types of heron, make their home here. You'll see water hyacinth and the eerie mangrove swamp trees, which drop their roots into the water from mid-trunk, creating a rope or prison-bar effect in the water. If left unchecked, mangrove trees would swallow and completely dominate the river. Note the large termite colonies, called duckant nests, lodged in the crotch of tree branches. Some are as big as a car's air safety bag. Above the mangroves, the 80-foot thatched palm, called sabal or bullhead thatch palms, act as beacons in the swamp.

Charles is also a dedicated amateur herpetologist—and crocodile enthusiast. He raises crocs on a ranch at his home in Mandeville with the hope of learning more about their growth patterns. He'll point out some of the crocs, which are American crocodiles, not alligators as some places around Jamaica would indicate. He's named a few, and he'll tell you how harmless they are and how they were ruthlessly hunted for skin and sport in the past. The crocodile is now a protected species in Jamaica—today only about 300 are left in the Black River Morass, or swamp. Harmless they may be, but this isn't the time to dangle your arm over the side of the boat and entreat old 10-foot-long Herman with snacks.

You might meet shrimp fishermen in the swamp reeds. Shrimp fishing is an area tradition more than 300 years old; many of the fishermen use a trap-basket method of fishing that originated in and is still used in Africa, passed down from slaves to the present generation.

The tour is relaxing and informative, and costs US$15 pp. Departures are at Sun.-Fri. 0900, 1100, 1400, and 1600. Monday has no 0900 departure.

The newer tour company is **St. Elizabeth Safari** (St. Bess Attractions, tel. 965-2229 or 997-6055), located across the river from South Coast Safari, behind an old rum warehouse. The tour is 1.75 hours, 12 miles roundtrip, and is much like the other tour—after all, it's not like they're using a different river. Cost is slightly cheaper at US$14.50 pp, which includes a complimentary (meaning the cost is hidden in your US$14.50) drink. Departures are at 0900, 1100, 1400, and 1530 daily. The company also operates a tour to nearby Y.S. Falls (see "Y.S. Falls," p. 130).

ACCOMMODATIONS AND FOOD

On the beach road east of town, most small bars and jerk restaurants have set up shop. You won't find any large hotels in Black River, though there is talk of developing the **Font Hill Beach** area west of town for luxury accommodation. The hotels and guesthouses in town are unpretentious and basic. Remember, rooms are often negotiable in the off-season.

Bridge House Inn (14 Crane Rd., Black River, Jamaica, W.I.; tel. 965-2631) is right on the beach, just over the Black River Bridge. It features excellent Jamaican cooking in the restaurant and 14 comfortable rooms with hot and cold water and fans—no pool. Rates are US$30 s, US$40 d year-round.

Hotel Pontio (49 High St., Black River, Jamaica, W.I.; tel. 965-2255) is a 12-room hotel on the ocean, on the east side of town. They serve three meals per day in the small restaurant, but you'll need to confirm this during the slow season—if you're the only guest (not an unreasonable assumption in summer) they may have trouble keeping the kitchen open. Rooms are US$30 s no a/c, US$45 s with a/c; and US$50 d no a/c, US$62 d with a/c. Room tax is included, but add a 10% service charge.

Port O' Call (136 Crane Rd., Black River, Jamaica, W.I.; tel. 965-2360 or 965-2410) is another oceanside guesthouse, small at 18 rooms, with a bar and restaurant. All rooms have hot and cold water and private baths. Rooms upstairs with a/c are US$30 s or d, and downstairs with fans are US$25 s or d, all taxes included. Rates are year-round.

South Shore Guest House (33 Crane Rd., Black River, Jamaica, W.I.; tel. 965-2172) is located on the beach, near the Bridge House Inn just outside of town. The guesthouse is small (12 rooms) with private baths and a bar and restaurant. Rates are US$25 s or d in summer, and US$30 s or d in winter, all taxes included.

Waterloo Guest House (44 High St., Black River, Jamaica, W.I.; tel. 965-2278) is a good example of the type of building that flourished in Black River before the economic bite of logwood became a bark, so to speak. It's reputed to have been the first building in Jamaica to function on electricity—an original owner named Leyden wanted to air-condition the stables of his racehorses. It's also reputed to have had the island's first telephone installed in 1900. (Who had the other phone? Unimportant, we're talking legends here.) Another local legend claims that the first motor car in Jamaica was imported to Black River. Whatever, Waterloo is the stuff of Black River myth. The bar and restaurant is a popular gathering place for residents. The 22 rooms vary in amenities. Rooms with a/c and hot water are J$585 s, d, or t. Without a/c and hot water the rooms are J$445, s, d, or t year-round.

Invercaud Great House and Hotel (P.O. Box 12, High St., Black River, Jamaica, W.I.; tel. 965-2750, fax 965-2751) is the newest and possibly most impressive of Black River's hotels. Built in 1889 during the heyday of sugar or logwood exporting, it has been restored by its owners. White and towering, with gingerbread trim, the hotel has 20 rooms furnished with antique reproductions. They have a pool, restaurant, and a resident reggae band. Tariffs vary with packages, but count on US$50-85 d in season.

ST. ELIZABETH INTERIOR

Highway A2 to Mandeville proceeds north from Black River into the interior, circumventing the large morass created by the river and its tributaries. The best way to travel this area is by rental car, though buses run regularly from Black River to all points in the interior and along the coast.

MIDDLE QUARTERS

At Middle Quarters you'll see roadside higglers holding up bags of shrimp, cooked over open fires by their stands. This is a real adventure in eating, but take the bright red color of the salty shrimp as a warning—they've been cooked in hot pepper sauce. If you like that type of spice, you'll love these shrimp. If you don't, eat some bread along with them to soften the blow.

LACOVIA

At Middle Quarters the road branches east toward Mandeville. Drive along **Bamboo Ave.,** a three-mile scenic road through a shaded archway of living bamboo, lined with orange groves and sugarcane fields. You'll reach Lacovia, which has the distinction of being the longest town in Jamaica. The name Lacovia may come from the Spanish *la caoba,* the word for ma-

hogany, so named in tandem with the old Spanish descriptive name for the Black River, Rio Caobana.

Note the tombstone in front of the Texaco Station. Legend has it that two young British soldiers, circa 1738, dueled and lost—they both died. They're buried here and one of the tombstones bears the name Thomas Jordan Spencer. The coat of arms indicates that he may have been related to the family that later gave us Sir Winston Spencer Churchill and Princess Diana (Spencer), wife of Prince Charles.

Y.S. FALLS

About seven miles south of Maggotty you'll find Y.S. Falls on the Y.S. River, one of the tributaries of the Black River. This is one example of encroaching tourism that has taken some of the "nature" out of a natural experience. It used to be that one would pay a small fee and hike up to the falls, perhaps spend the day there, swimming and relaxing for all one is worth. Now, you can go up by arrangement only, with a tour company. To be fair, the falls are on private land and the land is a working cattle farm, so the owners have reason to protect their farm from candy-wrapper-tossing tourists and others. Tours to the falls are operated by the afore-

Jamaica's southern interior

PHYLIS LUNTA

mentioned St. Elizabeth Safari company (see p. 129), through an arrangement with the landowners, and you can arrange a visit through the office in Black River. Cost is US$8 pp.

On old maps the name Y.S. is spelled Wyess, originating, some say, from an old Gaelic word meaning "winding," referring to the action of the river. Others say it originates from the old estate logo used to mark barrels of sugar. Land of a nearby estate was managed by Yates and Scott, who marked their barrels "Y.S."

The falls themselves are in a descending series, each emptying into a swirling swimming pool. The water is generally clear and fine for swimming, except after heavy rains when it becomes murky and rapid. The falls are wide open—no restraining rails, no guide ropes, just you, the water, and the foam.

MAGGOTTY

Highway A2 branches into B6 headed north toward Maggotty, a largish town set in the center of the Appleton Estates sugar plantations. Local legend has the name Maggotty originating from an incident on a Jamaica Railways train, which passes through town. When a stowaway youngster was asked by the conductor to produce his ticket, the youth fumbled through his pockets, then pointed to a nonexistent woman in the back of the car. "Ma got it," he said. This, of course, is a more attractive explanation than the alternative involving insect larvae.

Maggotty is a typical inland town, set amid the hills of the **Coker District** and sugarcane plains. It's not exactly a tourist town, save for the Appleton Express tours out of Montego Bay that visit the Appleton Estates sugar factory and rum distillery. You can visit the distillery if you can find a group to join, as tours for individuals are not allowed. Contact 963-2210 for details.

Maggotty is a great location to use as a base for hikes into the hills and guided hikes along the Black River Gorge and its 27 waterfalls. One of the sources of the Black River, a small "blue hole" reportedly 150 feet deep, sits in the middle of a sugarcane field just outside of town. The water source is now surrounded by a fence under construction by the National Water Commission; it may not be accessible in the near future.

The main street of the town is lined with shops, school children in uniforms, and minibus traffic. Farther down the road is the sugar works, which emits a pungent and sticky effluvium from the grounds—a by-product of molasses production and cane wash. There isn't much to master in Maggotty, and that's part of its appeal. For shopping or a cold drink stop at **Dickson's** or **Shakespeare's** across from the bus stand. They're your basic small general stores and Jamaican fast-food restaurants.

Apple Valley Park (tel. 997-6000) is one of the town's newer attractions, nominally called an eco-tourism facility. Located in the center of town, the park has a fishing pond, paddleboats, hiking trails, and camping facilities. You can arrange trips to local waterfalls by tractor, or hike to the Black River Gorge.

Accommodations

The best place to stay in Maggotty is **Apple Valley Guesthouse** (tel. 997-6000), which may be the best in the St. Elizabeth interior. The guesthouse is owned and operated by Patrick and Lucille Lee, who also operate Apple Valley Park and **Sweet Bakery,** the area supplier of bread and pastries.

The guesthouse is a 225-year-old great house on a 500-acre estate. Much of the land was previously owned by the Revere Aluminum Company, which mined it for bauxite in the late '60s. It's a small hike up from the main road, passing behind the police station and the old railroad station. The house is a small great house—five bedrooms, a sitting room, and a kitchen. Mrs. Lee caters Jamaican meals (another of her businesses), or you can use the kitchen for cooking. The housekeeper will help in the cooking if you request it. The Lees will provide a guide who will take you on the half-day Black River Gorge hike (you can tip him for it) and show you the sights in and around the center of St. Elizabeth.

Rooms at the guesthouse are US$25 s and US$40 d per night. As well, you can stay at the cabin facilities at Apple Valley Park for US$12 s and US$15 d per night. If you're at the guesthouse, make sure you wake up early to catch the sunrise over the misty mountains to the east. It's a sight unlike most in Jamaica, and utterly quiet.

Shakespeare's also runs a guesthouse, but you may be taking some chances there. It's clean enough and cheap enough, but the security is questionable.

Accompong

About eight miles north of Maggotty, at the base of the Cockpit Country near the **District of Look Behind,** is Accompong, legendary home of the western Maroons.

The Maroon settlement was established in 1739 when land was delivered to the western Maroons under terms of the treaty signed between their leader Cudjoe and the British authorities. The treaty ended years of conflict between the Maroons and British, and effectively enlisted the Maroons as allies in the British endeavor to put down threatening rebellions and recapture runaway slaves. The town is named after Cudjoe's brother and lieutenant, Accompong, probably originally named Acheampong (of the Akan language, spoken in present-day Ghana).

The drive to Accompong is through hills and small villages. You'll begin to see why the Maroons hid up here for so many years—the terrain is forbidding and tough, and it would be easy to get lost or lose someone among the crags and valleys that quickly become the Cockpit Country.

The village-state ("nation within a nation" is the way Maroons think of it) is barred by a gate on the road. This is perhaps symbolic—the gate,

they say, is usually open. It's best to send word ahead of time if you want to go to Accompong, but unannounced arrivals are treated with the same deference as expected visitors. It's also best to go with someone who can vouch for you, a Jamaican friend or guide who is known by the Maroons. You'll go first to visit the colonel, their elected leader and chief, who will have you sign the visitor's book and talk with you about Maroon life.

The colonel, currently Martin Luther Wright, is not always there, but someone will show you all the places non-Maroons are allowed to see. These include a few monuments to Cudjoe, the Peace Cave where the 1738 treaty was signed, the Kindah or family area where festivals are held, and Old Town, home of a past generation of Maroons.

Colonel Wright and the Maroons have begun to encourage cultural festivals and events, a way to attract interest and a little tourist cash flow to the town. The biggest to date is the traditional 6 Jan. celebration of the Maroon victory over the British, which led to the treaty of freedom. People from all over Jamaica and abroad attend the festival, which culminates in the reenactment of war and treaty dances. Outsiders are not allowed to participate in some secret Maroon ceremonies.

During the rest of the year, Accompong is open for visits, and you'll be asked to make a

Trelawny Maroons in ambush

NATIONAL LIBRARY OF JAMAICA

small donation to a village fund for the tour. Sadly, the village is becoming accustomed to the ways of tourism; requests for tips from a few of the young men are inevitable. Entrance fees to the village may be requested.

Ask to see the *abeng,* the original 300-year-old horn used to warn Cudjoe's people of impending British attacks. Don't be surprised if you're offered some oranges or a drink of 200-root herbal tonic before you leave. You can buy a few local crafts at the new crafts hut built near the community/health center, including an *akete,* the Maroon four-cornered drum.

An example of the capitalization on the tourism industry is the emergence of a company called **The Maroon Tourist Attraction Co.** (32 Church St., Montego Bay, Jamaica, W.I.; tel. 952-4546, fax 952-6203). Representing themselves as the only legitimate tour operating in Accompong, the visit includes a drive from Montego Bay with several sightseeing stops, continental breakfast, lunch, and a tour of Accompong. Cost is a weighty US$50 pp.

Otherwise, to get to Accompong take a taxi from Maggotty (they make regular runs) or drive up in a rental car.

TREASURE BEACH

INTRODUCTION

The flora changes during the drive south from Black River along the coast. It's a subtle change to drier soil, low scrub grass, cacti, and acacia and other thorn bushes. The area lies in the rain shadow of the Santa Cruz Mountains, which seem to stand guard over the area. The mountains move right into the sea at **Southfield** and **Yardley Chase,** creating sheer cliffs of up to 1,700 feet. This is cattle country, and you'll see small herds of Jamaica's famous red poll beef cattle grazing under the palms or squeezed around drinking cisterns scattered in the fields.

The attraction of Treasure Beach is the lack of tourism hype, even though the beaches at **Great Pedro Bay** are some of the nicest in the area. To say Treasure Beach is laid back is to understate it. To say it's dormant is to overstate it. But the emphasis is on natural, or ecotourism—no radical changes to the environment, no upsetting of local cultural norms.

Treasure Beach is a village with a postal agency, a few bars and a disco, some small general stores, churches, two hotels, and a number of guesthouses. That's about it. Use it as a base for exploring the area, and maybe to get a grip after a hectic flight or a few days in other parts of the island.

SIGHTS

Take a drive to **Lover's Leap,** about eight miles east at Southfield, where mountain cliffs reach the sea. You'll pull up to the alliteratively labelled **Lover's Leap Lighthouse.** The area, which is to include a small bar and restaurant, is under development as a sightseeing facility (tel. 965-2651 for details) yet is still natural and, in every sense of the word, breathtaking.

Legend has it that two lovers who were slaves, owned by different plantations, were forbidden by their masters to see each other. They did anyway, and when eventually cornered, ran to this cliff and plunged to their deaths rather than be separated again. They certainly picked the right spot to do the job—the drop is 1,750 feet straight down to the ocean edge and a vast expanse of Caribbean. Standing at the edge of this cliff is not for the faint of heart.

You may note a large number of blue-eyed, light-haired Jamaicans in and around Southfield—descendants, according to legend, of shipwrecked Scottish sailors.

Farther east you'll find the small, dusty town of **Alligator Pond,** which features one of the longest fishing beaches in Jamaica. You can buy fresh fish off the boats, or go for a swim on the free beach. Fish-*bammy*-beer joints abound. Take a left at the beach and you'll be on your way along a nice coastal road to **Milk River Bath** (see "Vicinity of Mandeville," p. 137).

Black River is only 18 miles away, so the sights and tours are readily accessible from Treasure Beach.

ACCOMMODATIONS AND FOOD

Cottages And Camping

Along the road that sweeps circularly through

Treasure Beach, you'll find numerous guest-houses offering rooms and camping. Remember that credit cards are rarely accepted at small cottages, and some charge the 10% GCT, while others do not. Among them:

4M's Cottage (Mountainside, St. Elizabeth, Jamaica, W.I.; tel. 965-2651, fax 965-2697) is a small guesthouse with an outdoor circular bar, just a few hundred yards from the beach. Mrs. Effie Campbell has six rooms with cold-water private baths and fans, and she can accommodate up to 13 guests. Guests can use the kitchen facilities, which include a refrigerator, stove, and table. Space for camping is also available at US$10 per tent. Rates are US$30 s or d and US$40 t, plus 10% GCT. The dirt road that leads to the beach, called Salt Boiler Rd., is as old as anyone can remember and was reputedly used by slaves to haul ocean water, which was then boiled for salt.

Golden Sands (Frenchman District, Calabash Bay P.O., St. Elizabeth, Jamaica, W.I.; no phone) is a very basic guesthouse on the beach, run by Mr. and Mrs. Lewis; but the prices are right. The six rooms have two beds each and private baths with cold water. They are clean, if not fancy. Guests can use the kitchen. Cost is J$250 (about US$11) per room, worth every penny.

I-tal Cottages and Campground (Jeanne and Frank Genus, Great Bay District, Calabash Bay P.O., St. Elizabeth, Jamaica, W.I.; no phone) is a small facility that has cottages with private baths (shared kitchen), and campgrounds with cooking facilities and an outdoor shower and toilet. Winter rates are US$25 per night for a room at a cottage, or US$40 for the whole cottage. Weekly rates are cheaper. In summer, rooms are US$20 per night and the cottage is US$35. Campsites are rented at US$7 per night, or US$10 if you need a tent and foam mattress.

In addition, **Shakespeare Cottage** (J$200-250), and **Waikiki** (three bedrooms, J$300 for the cottage) are on the main road through Treasure Beach. **"Stefan and Dirk's Camping Site"** is so named because Stefan and Dirk haven't yet been able to come up with another name. These two young Germans own a bit of property right on the beach, equipped with an outdoor toilet and cold shower, and a sort of teepee.

They let people camp there and even cook meals for campers over an open fire. Cost is US$10 or so, they think.

Hotels

Treasure Beach Hotel (P.O. Box 5, Black River, Jamaica, W.I.; tel. 965-2305, fax 965-2544, U.S.A. tel. 800-451-4398) was built in the mid-'30s, and for a while was one of the country's few hotels outside of Kingston and Montego Bay. Its current owner, Dr. John Brown, has refurbished the place and has added four rooms to make a total of 20. The hotel is on the beach and features a pool and small snack bar. The **Yabba Restaurant** is recommended (and is one of the few restaurants in Treasure Beach). The hotel offers the European plan (no meals); the continental plan (breakfast only); modified American plan (breakfast and one other meal); and the American plan (all three meals). Basic winter rack rates are US$80-130 d; summer rates are 25% less. Ask for seaview rooms. Add 10% service charge and 10% GCT.

Olde Wharf Resort (Calabash Bay P.O., St. Elizabeth, Jamaica, W.I.; tel. 962-3126, fax 962-2858) has a pool and a small beach by the old wharf. The 30 rooms and 12 suites are occasionally under lease to the Jamaica Defense Force, which uses the hotel as a base for anti-drug smuggling operations. When they aren't there, it's a secluded, relaxed place. Call for rates.

Villas

Contact Fern Spencer at **South Coast Rentals** (17 High St., Black River, Jamaica, W.I.; tel. 965-2651) for a wide range of villas and other rentals in the southwest coast area, as well as current information regarding attractions.

One of the nicer villas in Treasure Beach is **Hikaru Villa** (Mr. and Mrs. D. Noel, 141 Ridgefield St., Hartford, CT 06112-1837; tel. 203-247-0759). On the beach, with four bedrooms, two baths, a tennis court, and cook/housekeeper service, it's a good deal, particularly when sharing. In winter, rates are US$775 per week for up to four people, US$975 for five or six people, and US$1175 for up to eight. In summer, rates range US$625-925. This is not a walk-in sort of place, so call ahead for current rates and arrangements.

MANDEVILLE

INTRODUCTION

It would be a pity for anyone, even confirmed sun and beach zealots, to miss a visit to Mandeville. Here you'll find an old country town with a penchant for flower shows, golf, and afternoon teas "More English than England," while still very Jamaican, set in the lean air 2,000 feet above sea level. The elevation and mountain breezes create a temperate tropical climate—warm days and cooled nights—that is popular among Jamaican retirees and vacationers as an escape from the moist heat of the coast. Here, the tourist din is a mere whimper, and street hustling is almost unheard of. It's a finely tuned, elegant place, with village greens and private gardens full of bougainvillea, hibiscus, orchids, scarlet begonias, and a touch of the blues.

First, the facts: Mandeville (pop. 34,500) is the fifth-largest urban center in Jamaica, smaller than Kingston, Montego Bay, Spanish Town, and May Pen. It's located in central Manchester, Middlesex County, and is the parish capital. The town is almost equidistant from Montego Bay and Kingston, about 65 miles each way, and about an hour's drive from the coast.

Mandeville took its name from the Earl of Mandeville, son of the Duke of Manchester, who was governor of Jamaica in the early 1800s. The town, established in 1816, was a center of local commerce and grew into a retreat for wealthy Jamaicans who had made their money in sugar, coffee, and pimento cultivation. In the 1940s, when the red, clayey soil of the mountains was discovered to contain bauxite, alumina companies moved in, and Mandeville's economic future was built. Today, expatriates and Jamaican executives of the **Alcan Jamaica Company** (one of the few which has remained in continuous operation) live in the big homes on the outskirts of town.

Alcan, a branch operation of the Canadian Aluminum Corporation, together with the three American companies Alcoa, Kaiser, and Reynolds (Reynolds has since closed its operations) were once responsible for mining more than 10 million tons of bauxite annually in Jamaica (see "Economy," p. 35).

SIGHTS

Much can be seen in Mandeville by walking, though the town is spaced enough to consider transportation. The in-town bus system is scattered—a shared taxi or rental car is your best bet.

In **Mandeville Square,** on the east side of town off **Main St.,** the **Mandeville Courthouse** is a good example of a blend of Georgian architecture with Jamaican refinements. The building, one of the few original Mandeville structures, was finished about 1820, built from limestone cut by slave labor. **The Rectory,** also an original building, has been a pub and guesthouse and is now a private residence. The **Parish Church** was completed about 1820. The nearby police station was once the **Mandeville Jail and Workhouse,** also an original structure. Close to the square is the local market, a hubbub of vegetable and fruit trading—this area of the island is well known for its citrus groves. The *ortanique,* a hybrid of the orange and tangerine, was developed here by Charles Jackson in the 1920s. Check the **Manchester Parish Library** (34 Hargreaves Ave., tel. 962-2972) off Main St. for a wide selection of Caribbean and Jamaican history books.

Marshall's Pen Great House (tel. 962-2260) is a 300-acre property off **Winston Jones Hwy.** with a 200-year-old great house, a private residence open for tours by appointment only. The cost for a private tour of the grounds and great house is a rather hefty US$80 for up to six persons. The property will also allow experienced birdwatchers access, again by appointment only. Many local varieties of birds aren't found elsewhere in Jamaica. You'll be able to view the extensive gardens, where you'll see anthuriums, geraniums, orchids, and a great many ferns and indigenous trees.

If you're a golfer, stop at the **Manchester Club** (tel. 962-2403), established in 1868, the oldest nine-hole course on the island and one of

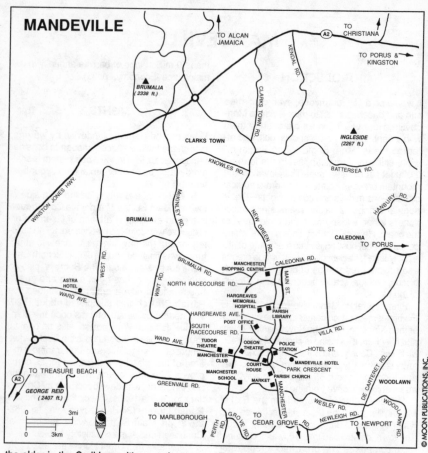

the older in the Caribbean. It's near the town center on **Caledonia Road**. Guests of hotels in Mandeville are allowed to use the facilities. For a fee you can play tennis as well. The annual **Golf Week,** Jamaica's oldest tournament, has been held there for over 55 years. Greens fees are J$100, and a caddy is J$50.

One of the town's more anomalous sights is the home of politician Cecil Charlton, former Mandeville mayor and millionaire owner of a chain of off-track betting shops. It's an octagonal, pagodalike structure at the top of **Huntington Summit,** and has gardens and a pool connected to the house by a tunnel. The ornate furniture inside is the result of years of antique hunting.

Tours can be arranged by phoning 962-2274.

The Manchester Horticultural Society (tel. 962-2328; ask for Mrs. Stephenson) was established in 1865 and is one of the oldest horticultural organizations in the world. Its annual flower show and demonstration in May is considered to be one of the country's better organized.

While you're at it, ask about **Mrs. Stephenson's Garden** (tel. 962-2328; or Manchester Information Centre, tel. 962-3265), an ornate, award-winning private garden at Mrs. Stephenson's home. She conducts the tours herself. You'll see *ortaniques,* orchids, anthuriums, and many other local plants. Cost is about US$2.

You can tour the **High Mountain Coffee**

COMMUNITY TOURISM

For some time now, Mandeville has pioneered a concept called "Community Tourism," which in some ways resembles the "Meet The People" program sponsored by the Jamaica Tourist Board. It is a program that has grown out of the not-unfounded worry that tourism often develops without concern for the needs of the local community. In order to involve the community, Mandeville and neighboring towns along the south coast have formed a Central and South Tourism Committee with the aim of attracting tourism, but not on the mass and impactful scale that has affected communities on the north coast.

The idea is to get travelers into the community for visits with local families for lunches, dinners, outings, and even overnight stays. Some homes in the community have been formed as small "bed and breakfasts," and owners are also involved as cultural contacts, guides, and even taxi drivers. Plans are on board to develop small, community-owned hotels up and down the south coast and to work out arrangements with all-inclusive hotels for guest exchanges. Even the Astra Hotel has undergone changes and is now known as the Astra Country Inn. Diana McIntyre-Pike, the energetic committee chairperson, owner of the Astra, and possibly also the hub of south and central tourism (as chairperson of the Central and South Tourism Organization), is the driving force behind the program—the person to contact if you're interested.

The program is still young and no doubt has bugs and logistics to work out. But the concept is good and the price is no more than hotel stays (even less in many cases). Input from the growing numbers of travelers who participate can only improve its effectiveness. Contact Diana at 962-3265 or 962-3377.

Factory (tel. 962-4211) and watch the process that produces some of Jamaica's finest export coffee. High mountain coffee is not the same grade as the famous Blue Mountain Coffee, but then again, not much is.

Horseback riding is available through **DalKeith Riding School** (Manchester Information Centre, tel. 962-3265).

Drive to the **Kirkvine Works** on the outskirts of town, where the Alcan Company operates its large plant. Tours can be arranged by appointment with a day's notice.

You can tour the local **Pickapeppa Company** plant (tel. 962-2928) at **Shooter's Hill** northeast of town. Pickapeppa is a spicy, Jamaican version of Worcestershire sauce.

Vicinity Of Mandeville

Milk River Bath, (tel. 924-9544) about 30 miles south of town, is the most radioactive spa in the world. It's close to the sea, about two miles from **Farquhar's Beach,** located on the banks of the **Milk River.** The water, however, doesn't come from the river, but from a small mineral spring nearby. The relative radioactivity of the spa is 50 times greater than at Vichy, France, and nine times greater than at Bath, England. The water is warm, a constant 92° F (33° C). Bathers are limited to two 15-minute baths per day due to the water's heat and the high radioactivity. No evidence suggests that the radioactivity is harmful in small doses, but part of the "cure," not uncommon in other mineral baths in Jamaica, is to take a healthy, that is to say large, swig of the water. Some swear by its curative powers, especially those afflicted with arthritis, rheumatism, and other joint conditions. They say they emerge all aglow. Who knows? It could increase your half-life by several thousand years. Cost for 15 minutes is US$1 adults and US$.50 children. The spa operates a small guesthouse; some rooms with private showers, some without. Rates are US$40 s and US$60 d per room, including breakfast and dinner.

Drive to **Christiana,** about 12 miles out of town on Hwy. B5, in the northeast corner of Manchester. You'll pass through **Walderston,** originally a free village founded by a Moravian missionary. Christiana is a small agricultural trading town high in the hills, probably as dead-center as you can get in Jamaica. The main local crop, for which a grower's cooperative has been established, is Irish potatoes. Stay at the **Hotel Villa Bella** (P.O. Box 473, Christiana, Manchester, Jamaica, W.I.; tel. 964-2243, fax 962-2762), a small country inn that serves Jamaican food and high teas on Sunday. The simple tariff: US$50 pp per night, s or d, year-round, including breakfast.

Heading east from Mandeville on Hwy. A2, you'll pass through **Porus,** a small farming town most likely named after the Spanish brothers Porras, who were marooned with and later mutinied Christopher Columbus (see "History," p. 18). Porus is interesting for its main street often lined with citrus fruit vendors in shacks hung with bags of green oranges, which they thrust out at passersby. A note to visitors: Ripe oranges are a light shade of spotty green, not the dyed orange that you often find in supermarkets at home.

Farther east, you'll pass through plains and semi-savanna on your way to **May Pen,** capital of Clarendon and one of the country's larger inland towns (pop. 41,000). May Pen was named after the estate on which it was established. Today, it's a central exchange in the road and railway systems of Jamaica.

PRACTICALITIES

Eating And Drinking

Mandeville's Main St. area and Caledonia Rd. host a slew of fast-food restaurants. **Tweetie's Fried Chicken** and **King Burger** ("Home Of The Whamperer") can be found at **Brumalia Towne Centre** on Main, and **Kentucky Fried Chicken** is on Caledonia across from the **Manchester Shopping Centre.** But don't go out of your way to find it unless you've got a special need for finger lickin'—you'll find plenty of fine Jamaican patty and fast-food restaurants around town.

At the Villa Plaza on Main St., try **Hungry Jack's** for burgers and pastries. **Little Mac's Chicken Joint** (9 Ward Ave.) serves Little Mac's chicken. **Juci Beef Patties** (3 Manchester Rd.;

USEFUL PHONE NUMBERS IN MANDEVILLE

Area Code 809
General:

Jamaica Tourist Board, 11 Ward Ave., tel. 962-1072

Manchester Information Centre, Astra Country Inn, tel. 962-3265 or 962-3377

Police Emergency, tel. 119 or 962-2106

Post Office, South Racecourse, tel. 962-3229

Medical:

Hargreaves Memorial Hospital, 32 Hargreaves Ave., tel. 962-2040 or 962-2070

Mandeville Hospital, tel. 962-2967 or 962-2744

Caledonia Medicare Centre, tel. 962-3939

Transportation and Travel Services:

Candi Car Rental, Caledonia Rd., tel. 962-3153

Delojay Car Rental, Brumalia Town Centre, tel. 962-3460

Global Travel Sevice, Manchester Shopping Centre, tel. 962-1183 or 962-2366

Hemisphere Car Rental, 51 Manchester Rd., tel. 962-1921

Hertz, Midway Mall, tel. 962-1279

Hewitt's Car Rental, 5 Wesley Rd., tel. 962-1718

Manchester Taxi, tel. 962-2021

Moon Glow Car Tours and Car Rental, Caledonia Mall, tel. 962-9000

Sterling Travel, Caledonia Plaza, tel. 962-2203

Superior Omnibus Service, Caledonia Plaza, tel. 962-2421

tel. 962-1023) serves that famous Jamaican fast food, beef patties. **Flakey Crust** (11A Manchester Rd.; tel. 962-3995) also serves pastries and patties.

Bamboo Village Restaurant (35 Ward Ave., Ward Plaza; tel. 962-4515/6) serves the best Chinese food in town, with prices ranging from J$150-380. **Options Restaurant and Lounge** (21 Main St.; tel. 962-0645) serves reasonably priced local dishes.

For barbecue and medium-priced Jamaican try **The Den** (35 Caledonia Rd., tel. 962-3603). They also have a daily happy hour 1730-1830, and music. **Pot Pourri** (Caledonia Mall; tel. 962-0397) serves breakfast, lunch, and dinner.

Bill Laurie's Steak House (Bloomfield Gardens; tel. 962-3116) sells thick steaks and has a sort of Roaring '20s ambience. The collection of vintage cars spread out over the place includes a 1929 Model A Ford truck. The view of Mandeville from the southern exposure is expansive. Tours are conducted here as well. Call for an appointment.

The **International Restaurant** (117 Manchester Rd.; tel. 962-0527) is fine for medium-priced Chinese and Jamaican cuisine. The town's two hotels, the **Astra Country Inn** and **Mandeville Hotel,** both have good restaurants serving three meals daily.

If you are cooking for yourself, you'll have enough supermarkets and grocery stores to keep you busy. Try **Cash N' Carry** (Midway Mall, Caledonia Rd.; tel. 962-2068), **Hyland Food Mart** (18 Manchester Rd.; tel. 962-0368), **Queen's Supermarket** (39 Manchester Rd.; tel. 962-1786), or **Hi-Lo** supermarket (Manchester Shopping Centre; tel. 962-2254). **Top Loaf Bakery** (23 Manchester Rd., tel. 962-1611) is a good bet for fresh bread and pastries. Also visit the **Mandeville Market,** the bustling, open-air produce market at the center of town.

Planet Disco (Mandeville Plaza; tel. 962-0360) has nightly dancing, canned music, and movies starting at 2000. **Capri** (4 Caledonia Rd.; tel. 962-1806) is a hot spot featuring live bands on the weekends.

Shopping

It's hard to count the number of malls and shopping plazas in and around Mandeville. A dozen or more sounds accurate. You won't find much in the way of duty-free and other tourist-oriented shopping, but there's plenty to satisfy your needs. The largest is the **Manchester Shopping Centre** on Caledonia Road. Fontana's Variety has department-store items, including small coffee mugs that say "Mandeville" and other souvenirs. **Bookland** has a good selection of magazines and books about Jamaican culture. **NC's Jewellery Store** (tel. 962-0741) sells just that. The venerable **Woolworth's** is there for your basic variety-store items. The center also has an ice-cream shop, clothing stores, and branches of the National Commercial Bank and Scotiabank.

Other bookstores include **Books and Things** (1 Buena Vista Cir.; tel. 962-0049) and **The Book Shop** (Villa Plaza, Main St., tel. 962-9204), which carries a large supply of school textbooks.

SWA Craft Centre (tel. 962-2138) is a workshop for unemployed school-leavers who have some basic skills. Crafts include toys, clothing, crochet work, pastries, and cakes. You can visit the complex to watch the women at work, and buy something if you like. Contact Ceceline McIntyre.

For pharmacies, the best and one of the older is **Haughton's Pharmacy Ltd.** (18 West Park Cres.; tel. 962-2246 or 962-3220). They're open daily.

Accommodations

Astra Country Inn (62 Ward Ave., Mandeville, Jamaica, W.I.; tel. 962-3265 or 962-3377) is one of Mandeville's two hotels and home of the Manchester Information Centre, which, in conjunction with the Mandeville office of the JTB, has the latest information on upcoming events, tours, and town or south coast practicalities. The hotel itself is comfortable, clean, and lived-in. But it's a warm lived-in, and the staff takes a genuine interest in making your Mandeville stay smooth. Sauna, pool, restaurants, and a bar are part of the package. Rooms rates vary, and run US$55-75 per room p/d, year-round, which includes complimentary tea or coffee daily. Suites with kitchenettes are US$85-110. Meal plans are available. Children under 12 are free in the room with parents.

The **Mandeville Hotel** (4 Hotel St., Mandeville, Jamaica, W.I.; tel. 962-2138) is the oldest hotel in town, originally a barracks when Mandeville was a garrison town. It's a great old building in a central location. Room rates are US$55-65 per room per night. A suite is available. Add 10% service charge.

About 30 miles south of town, a small guesthouse is available at **Milk River Bath** spa. Rates are US$40 s, US$60 d per room, including breakfast and dinner. Some rooms have private showers (see "Vicinity of Mandeville," p. 137).

BOB RACE

KINGSTON AND VICINITY
INTRODUCTION

Oh, I'm sad to say, farewell today,
I'll be back to Kingston town bay,
My heart is down, my thoughts are spinning around,
Because the girl I love is here in Kingston town
—lyrics from the traditional calypso song
"Jamaica Farewell,"
later adapted by Harry Belafonte

Kingston is a surprise, not because it's large (pop. approximately 700,000-plus, including St. Andrew, roughly one third of Jamaica's total population) or because it's a dynamic and sophisticated city. It's a surprise because it's generally hassle free, not the impression you get from rural Jamaicans who, when told that you're going to the city, remind you to be careful, to watch out for "da tiefs," and to stay in at night. Understandable though, the reaction many people have regarding any large city. What isn't known is often feared.

·It is true that Kingston had a reputation for

violence during elections in the troubled '70s. And, when a few hundred thousand people are squeezed together in any small space (the population density in Kingston is roughly 12,500 per square mile and growing), things tend to get a little close—hustlers hustle, crimes occur, and a visitor has to be aware of the nuances of city life. Be what you would be in any large city—on your toes—and you'll be fine. Kingston is worth it.

Kingston is not only Jamaica's government and administrative center, it's also a Caribbean center of art, music, theater, commerce, and sports. The Conference Centre, downtown, is alleged to be the largest in the Caribbean and hosts hundreds of yearly international meetings. Kingston's theaters, art galleries, museums, and events are numerous, large, and often inexpensive. Kingston's restaurants are among the better on the island—eat anything from traditional Jamaican to Syrian to Korean to fast-food patties and jerk chicken. Shopping, of course, is what large sections of Kingston are all about. Visitor activities are plentiful, including a riotous nightlife, beaches, plantation great hous-

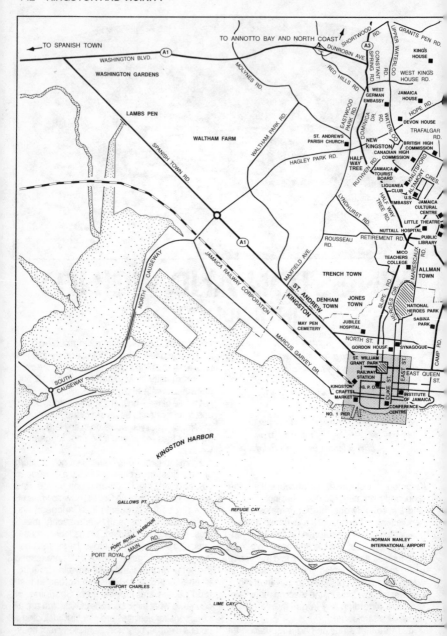

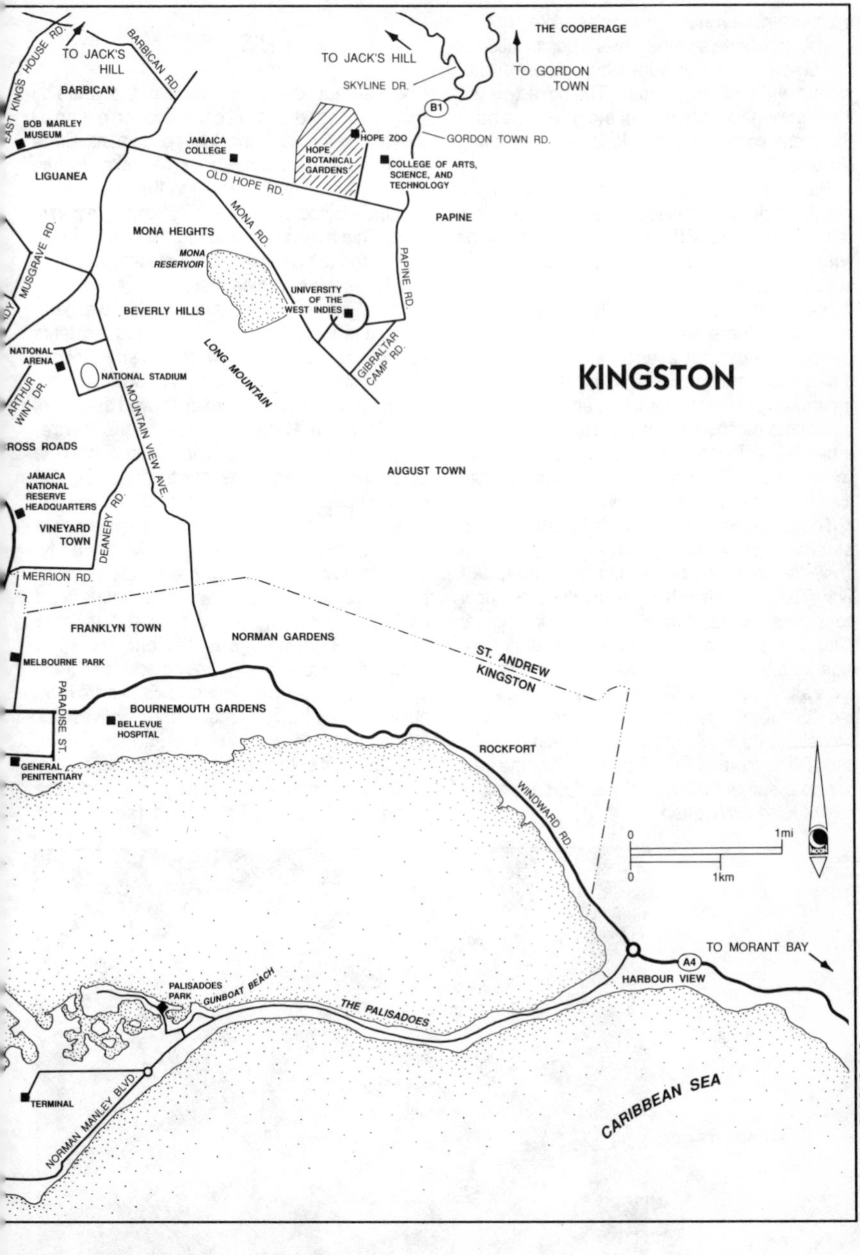

KINGSTON

THE COOPERAGE

TO GORDON TOWN

TO JACK'S HILL

SKYLINE DR.

B1

GORDON TOWN RD.

BARBICAN RD.

EAST KINGS HOUSE RD.

TO JACK'S HILL

BARBICAN

BOB MARLEY MUSEUM

JAMAICA COLLEGE

HOPE ZOO

HOPE BOTANICAL GARDENS

COLLEGE OF ARTS, SCIENCE, AND TECHNOLOGY

LIGUANEA

OLD HOPE RD.

PAPINE

MONA RD.

MONA HEIGHTS

MONA RESERVOIR

UNIVERSITY OF THE WEST INDIES

PAPINE RD.

MUSGRAVE RD.

BEVERLY HILLS

LONG MOUNTAIN

GIBRALTAR CAMP RD.

NATIONAL ARENA

ARTHUR WINT DR.

NATIONAL STADIUM

MOUNTAIN VIEW AVE.

AUGUST TOWN

CROSS ROADS

JAMAICA NATIONAL RESERVE HEADQUARTERS

DEANERY RD.

VINEYARD TOWN

MERRION RD.

FRANKLYN TOWN

NORMAN GARDENS

ST. ANDREW
KINGSTON

MELBOURNE PARK

PARADISE ST.

BOURNEMOUTH GARDENS

BELLEVUE HOSPITAL

ROCKFORT

GENERAL PENITENTIARY

WINDWARD RD.

TO MORANT BAY

A4

HARBOUR VIEW

0   1mi
0   1km

PALISADOES PARK

GUNBOAT BEACH

THE PALISADOES

NORMAN MANLEY BLVD.

TERMINAL

CARIBBEAN SEA

© MOON PUBLICATIONS, INC.

es, gardens, even a Coney Island-like park.

The architecture of the city is a combination of old Georgian and modern high rise—and of wealth and extreme poverty. The poverty is evident throughout the city, in the ghettos, and in the small camps of homeless who live along Victoria Pier.

Part of Kingston's core is in that culture. It's not the culture of theater and fine foods, but rather the culture of the hundreds of thousands who are trying to make a life on the coarse streets of ghettos and dwelling-stacked slums. In these areas—Trench Town, Coronation Gardens, and others—is the unique energy of indigence, energy that exudes a distrust for authority and a need to keep moving. Here, politics are most vehemently partisan, and when crime occurs it is particularly destructive. The culture of a place like Trench Town is one of whispers, some eruptions, and above all, the need to make a living or the resolution to live without.

The Kingston metro area can be confusing to a visitor. Uptown, which is really lower St. Andrew, includes centers like **Cross Roads, Half Way Tree,** and **New Kingston,** which are now considered suburbs of Kingston. The original Kingston is downtown. Kingston itself is considered a parish, and the two parishes, St. Andrew and Kingston, are commonly referred to as the "corporate area," administered by the Kingston and St. Andrew Corporation (KSAC) board. The town of **Port Royal,** across the harbor on a spit of land called the **Palisadoes,** is part of Kingston Parish.

HISTORY

The Palisadoes was formed over the years by the drift of sand and silt carried to the ocean by rivers, plus the additional labor of humans. Small cays that formed a natural breakwater for the harbor, the seventh largest in the world, were gradually joined by the silt drifts, forming a peninsula. This eventually housed the town of Port Royal, the extravagant home of Henry Morgan and his reckless buccaneers.

When a 1692 earthquake and tidal wave destroyed most of Port Royal, surviving residents fled across the harbor to what was then Colonel Barry's Hog Crawle, a piggery that eventually became Kingston. A large fire destroyed the rest of Port Royal in 1703, and most of the few remaining stalwarts packed it in and moved to the burgeoning settlement across the harbor, giving it more numbers and political clout.

Jamaica was without a resident governor at the time, and the Council, an advisory body, voted to buy up some of the land adjoining the piggery to found a new town. The streets were laid out in a pattern bound by **Harbour St.** to the south, **North St., East St.,** and **West St.,** which still exist. The town grew quickly and soon spilled over into the parish of St. Andrew as businessmen bought local "pens," or livestock farms, which they partitioned into residential lots and then sold to the growing number of arrivals. Some areas of St. Andrew still retain the name "pen," such as Tinson Pen. But the word

Devon House

PHYLLIS LUNITTA

soon took on a derisive tone and some pens were renamed "gardens," giving us today's Norman Gardens or Tivoli Gardens.

Kingston's importance as a harbor was evident, and it eventually did more business than all other harbors of Jamaica combined. In the mid-1700s, Gov. Adm. Charles Knowles proposed to relocate the growing nation's capital from Spanish Town to Kingston, a move that was met with understandable opposition from the St. Catherine Parish Council, but had some initial success with the King in England. Knowles's successor, Henry Moore, rescinded the proposal in 1758, and the move died an early death.

But by 1802, Kingston had grown and was given status as a corporation with a mayor and ruling council. In 1865, then-governor Sir John Grant was given the authority to reorganize the island's civil and legislative bodies in the wake of the devastating Morant Bay Rebellion (see "History," p. 29). The move was again made to relocate Jamaica's capital to Kingston—this time with success. In 1872, Spanish Town relinquished its historical seat to the adolescent Kingston. In 1923, the parishes of Kingston and St. Andrew were commingled and the KSAC was formed to administrate the corporate area.

In 1907, a major earthquake and fire destroyed much of the downtown area, which was later rebuilt after new land was acquired along **King Street.**

SIGHTS

UPTOWN

New Kingston

New Kingston is one of the best areas to base yourself for city exploration. It's central for hotels, guesthouses, and inns, as well as for office buildings, embassies, shopping malls, and dozens of restaurants. The area was once the site of the Knutsford Park Race Track, which closed down and lay dormant until development of the grounds began after independence in 1962. The only pre-independence building in New Kingston today is the **Liguanea Club,** a tennis and sports complex.

Half Way Tree

To the west is Half Way Tree, the capital of St. Andrew and an important crossroad in the corporate area. You'll know you're there by the large clock tower at the crossroads. **St. Andrews Parish Church** was built in the late 1600s, and the parish registers date back to 1666, making them the oldest in Jamaica. Half Way Tree was so named, legend has it, because of the resting area under a large cotton tree where a pub was erected for travelers. It's hard to say what places the tree was halfway between, but one rumor states that it lies between military barracks at Port Henderson and Newcastle. Another states that it was an arbitrary measure for travelers from the western parishes, heading east. The tree died in the late 19th century.

Constant Spring Rd. heads north from Half Way Tree into the large suburb of **Constant Spring,** once the site of an old sugar plantation and a series of nearly constant springs flowing from the hills nearby. **Immaculate Conception High School** was originally housed in one of Kingston's first hotels, Constant Spring Hotel, built in 1888. The hotel no longer exists.

Along Hope Road

North of New Kingston at 26 Hope Rd., **Devon House** (tel. 929-6602) is the old great house that was once the home of the island's first black millionaire. The flamboyant George Stiebel made his fortune dealing gold in Venezuela in the 1800s. The home is a fine example of period architecture, and was once home of the country's National Gallery. It's now a complex of shops and restaurants, and the house is open to the public for tours. Hours are Tues.-Sat. 0930-1700, and Sun. 1100-1600. Admission to the great house is J$44 (US$2) for adults, J$22 for children.

Farther down Hope Rd. you'll see **Jamaica House,** originally built as the prime minister's residence, but now part of the office complex of the prime minister and other government officials. Behind the offices is **King's House,** the official residence of the British Crown's representative in Jamaica, the governor general. King's House is open to visitors on weekdays 1000-1700. **Vale Royal,** an ornate complex on Montrose Rd., is the prime minister's official residence and is not open to visitors.

The **Bob Marley Museum** (56 Hope Rd.; tel. 927-9152), the old home of the reggae star, is one of Kingston's more authentic sites, and you get the impression that the staff is treating this as hallowed grounds. There's a hushed reverence about their demeanor, and no photos are allowed inside the house. The reason for the almost secular deification is the Marley legend—it remains deservedly strong in both Rastafarian and reggae circles. You'll see the Wailers' gold and platinum records and the scrapbook wall, with over 200 articles written about Marley and the Wailers. You'll even see bullet holes in a kitchen wall from a 1976 assassination attempt on Marley. Wailers tunes are piped throughout the house during the tour. A large gift shop, operated by the Marley children, features African and Rastafarian items. The **Queen of Sheba** restaurant (open Mon.-Sat. 0800-2100) serves Rasta I-tal and juices. Museum hours are Mon., Tues., Thurs., and Fri. 0930-1630; Wed. and Sat. 1230-1730. Admission is J$35 for adults, and J$5 for children under 12. The one-hour tour starts with a short video of an interview with Bob Marley.

The town suburb where the Marley home is located is called **Liguanea,** the original name of St. Andrew Parish and one of the few remaining Arawak words. It's unclear what the word actually meant, although one theory has it referring to iguanas once found in the area.

Farther east along Old Hope Rd. you'll see **Jamaica College** (high school) set against the backdrop of the Blue Mountains. Some afternoons you'll find the boys playing soccer matches with rival schools, and you're welcome to stop in and have a look.

Just beyond the college are **Hope Botanical Gardens** and **Hope Zoo** (tel. 927-1085). The 200-acre gardens, formally called the **Royal Botanic Gardens** commemorating a 1953 visit by Queen Elizabeth, are a favorite with Jamaican families on weekends and holidays. The land was originally part of the Hope family estate and is now owned by the government. The gardens are part of the national public gardens network. Hours are daily 0800-1800; no admission charge. The small zoo (17 acres) is located at one end of the garden complex and hosts a variety of Caribbean wildlife as well as animals endemic to Jamaica, including the yellow snake and the island coney. The zoo is open daily 1000-1700; admission is under US$1.

The University

At **Papine,** one of Kingston's eastern suburbs, turn south to **Mona** and the **University of the West Indies.** The giant **Mona Reservoir** supplies Kingston with its water. The school is a regional center, with campuses located in Barbados, Trinidad, and Jamaica, and smaller centers located throughout the Caribbean. Today the school, established in 1948 as an appendage of London University, is independent and grants degrees in medicine, law and social sciences, to name a few. The old aqueducts scattered around the campus were once used to carry water to Mona Sugar Estate, the site on which the university is built. Note the striking wall murals on the **Caribbean Mass Communication Building** and the **Assembly Hall.**

Also located on the campus is the **University Hospital,** one of Kingston's largest medical facilities.

National Stadium

South of New Kingston, the traffic becomes thicker and downtown becomes closer. The National Stadium on Mountain View Rd. was opened at independence in 1962, and the stadium's first event was the raising of the Jamaican national flag. Today the 20,000-seat stadium is the scene of international sporting events, and was host to the 1966 Commonwealth Games. Political rallies and large-scale entertainment events are also hosted at the stadium. Across from the stadium is **Celebrity Park,** featuring a statue of Bob Marley. The **National Arena** was built in 1966 and hosts indoor sports and other events.

Cross Roads

Downtown begins in earnest at Cross Roads. Here, at the intersection of five major up- and downtown roads, are direct veins to major parts of Kingston and the corporate area. **Nuttall Hospital** sits in the middle of it. Just south of Cross Roads you'll see **Mico Teacher's College,** reputedly one of the oldest teacher-training schools in the world. It was originally established in 1834 after emancipation to help with the education of former slaves.

DOWNTOWN

National Heroes Park

At National Heroes Park along **Marescaux Rd.,** the parish of Kingston begins. The park is a 74-acre monument to Jamaica's national heroes, some of whom are buried there, including Alexander Bustamante, labor leader and founder of the JLP; Norman Manley, founder of the PNP; and black nationalist leader Marcus Garvey, who was originally buried in London before his remains were moved to Jamaica in 1964. You'll find monuments to honor the Morant Bay Rebellion as well as its two principals, Paul Bogle

and George William Gordon. See the War Memorial, a monument erected to honor the dead of both world wars. The road encircling the park is **National Heroes Circle.** Note the statue at the south end honoring **Simon Bolivar,** the Venezuelan soldier, statesman, and ultimately failed liberator of South America. Bolivar came to Jamaica in 1818 to seek British aid in his struggle to liberate South American countries from Spanish rule, and consolidate them in a union of states.

The area surrounding the park is filled with government ministry buildings. Nearby is **Sabina Park,** home of Jamaica's international cricket grounds.

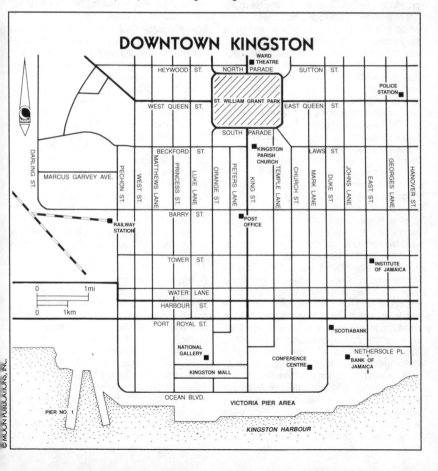

© MOON PUBLICATIONS, INC.

St. William Grant Park And The Parade

Downtown is laid out in grids, and it's easy enough to get around by foot. The center of town is St. William Grant Park, named after a labor leader and follower of Marcus Garvey. (The "saint" reference in his name is nonreligious.) Grant was an early ally of Alexander Bustamante during the labor unrest of the 1930s, but later broke with the leader and died poor and obscure. He was awarded an Order of Distinction in 1974, and the park, formerly named Victoria Park, was given his name in 1977. The park has always been a gathering place for Kingstonians, for anything from public meetings to public hangings, and was once a drilling ground for soldiers based in a nearby barracks.

The area around the park, including the roads which encircle it, has always been known as the **Parade**. The **Kingston Parish Church,** on one end of the Parade, sits on a foundation dating back to 1699. It was reconstructed after its destruction in the 1907 earthquake, which also leveled great parts of Kingston. The **Ward Theatre** (tel. 922-7071) building on **North Parade** has been in continuous use as a theater since the 18th century. Today, it's the sponsor of Jamaica's Pantomimes, held each year from Boxing Day (26 Dec.) until early April (see "Festivals and Events," p. 61). The original Kingston theater, located elsewhere in town, was the site at which American naval hero John Paul Jones made an acting debut. He later gave up his acting career for one in the navy, where he distinguished himself in the American War for Independence.

At the corner of **Duke** and **Beeston** streets you'll find **Gordon House,** named after national hero George William Gordon. It's currently the home of Jamaica's House of Representatives. The building was constructed in 1960 and has housed the legislative body ever since. The previous seat of the representatives was at **Headquarters House,** on the next block of Beeston. Jamaica's only synagogue, the United Congregation of the Israelites, is located on Duke Street. The building dates back to 1912.

On **North St.** you can see the offices of *The Daily Gleaner,* Jamaica's oldest continuously operating newspaper. The daily began as a weekly in 1834 and has the largest distribution and readership in Jamaica. The Gleaner Company, publishers of the paper, also publishes *The Sunday Gleaner* and *The Star* afternoon tabloid.

The **Institute of Jamaica** (tel. 922-0620) on East St. houses the **National Library of Jamaica,** one of the region's most extensive collections of West Indies and Jamaican reference materials. The library inherited its collection from the West Indies Reference Library, established in 1894. The Institute also houses a Natural History Division that includes a museum and reference library. The Institute is open to the public Mon.-Thurs. 0900-1700, Fri. 0900-1600, and Sat. 0900-1300.

Craft Market

Harbour St., Port Royal St., and **Ocean Blvd.** run parallel to the oceanfront at Kingston Harbour. **Kingston Craft Market,** formerly known as Victoria Market, was once located at the base of **King St.,** next to **Victoria Pier.** The old market was a gathering place for thousands on Sundays, when slaves were free from labor and allowed to congregate and sell or trade goods. Today's crafts market has been relocated to a large, hangarlike building off Port Royal St., north of Victoria Pier, near the railway station. It's a busy spot where the sell is not hard at all, and worth an hour or two of browsing through T-shirts, baskets, hats, and carvings found throughout Jamaica. The crafts stalls are open daily (see also "Shopping," p. 74).

The pier was, before the days of airplane travel, the busiest arrival spot in Kingston for overseas visitors.

The **Jamaica Conference Centre,** reputed to be the largest in the West Indies, is on Ocean Boulevard.

Downtown Museums

Nearby on Orange St., across from the Kingston Mall, is Jamaica's **National Gallery** (tel. 922-1561), home of the island's largest collection of contemporary and historical Jamaican art. Currently, much of the first floor is dominated by the work of Edna Manley, one of Jamaica's leading living sculptors until her death at 86 in 1987. Note her sculpture "Ghetto Mother" in the main lobby of the museum. Manley was the wife of Norman and mother of Michael Manley, two of Jamaica's most enduring political figures. Other exhibits in the gallery feature "Jamaican Art, 1922-present," which includes the surrealistic work of Colin Garland and Namba Roy. The sculptures of John Dunkley and other artists of the early "intuitive" school are highlighted. Note the participatory work by Dawn Scott, understatedly called "A Cultural Object." It features a walk through a graffiti- and garbage-strewn Kingston yard, with a surprise ending. The statue of Bob Marley, on the first floor, was done by Christopher Gonzales. Gallery hours are Mon.-Sat. 1000-1700; admission is J$20 adults, J$5 for children.

The **Coin and Note Museum** is in the Bank of Jamaica on Nethersole Pl. at the base of East St., an interesting visit for coin and note buffs.

SIGHTS THAT TAKE SOME EFFORT

They may not take much effort to get to, but some sights off the tourist mainstream are not as easy to be a part of without feeling out of place. A good feeling? Not always, but a feeling of being closer to a Jamaica that is living the harsh reality—the truth, in other words—rather than that which is presented with a "No problem, mon," and "Irie, mon" face for tourists. Here, the Jamaicans you encounter might be a little more suspicious of your presence and not at all adept in dealing with tourism issues.

Coronation Market
Take a drive down Coronation Market on the west side of Kingston, just a short distance from the Parade. It's a truly local market, with piles of yams, potatoes, fruit, and cane dumped on the ground, lining both sides of the litter-strewn street. Market buses, trucks, and cars park haphazardly about, making an obstacle course out of the half-mile or so selling ground. Chaff and piles of rotting fruit are piled among the produce to deteriorate in the sun or rain, drawing flies and seabirds. It may be the smell you remember about Coronation Market, or it may be the stares.

West Kingston
Trench Town and **Denham Town** in the lower corporate area's west side are Kingston's proof that there is indeed trouble in paradise. The government yards are a sea of zinc, faded sideboard, and political slogans splashed on the

walls of fortresslike enclave barriers. "PNP Town," says one, and "JLP Only Enter Here," says another. You'll drive through with your windows rolled down to allay suspicion, but you'll encounter it nonetheless, sometimes in the form of hissing. If you are foreign-faced, all the more so. The people of Trench Town spend a great deal of time on the street, watching their world amble by. As a visitor, you are generally not part of that world. Therefore, it is not recommended that a visitor casually amble alone through Trench Town, picking up conversations here and there, or snapping photos.

Yet this is the stultifying poverty and severely partisaned political environment that has produced Jamaica's most vibrant and enduring cultural commodities to date—Rasta and reggae.

The government has taken on the task of cleaning up the ghettos, but the process is long and the human toll large—it is hard to move people who have nowhere to go, and difficult to beautify a place from the outside in. However, West Kingston's **Tivoli Gardens** is a recent example of urban transformation, and an apparent success story. The impetus came from then-Finance Minister Edward Seaga in the '60s, when the ghetto was known as **Back o' Wall**, one of Kingston's most fierce. It was razed and transformed into a large planned community, complete with community centers, a comprehensive high school, and decorative gardens on its perimeter. Tivoli Gardens dwellings are stacked and urban of course, but they're clean, and seem to hold a promise.

Jubilee Market spills out into the street along the west side of the Parade. This market, originally called Solas Market, was named in honor of the jubilee of Queen Victoria's reign, circa 1887. Here, you can buy everything from shoes to combs to ceramic Lassie heads, food, fruits, and candy. The market is one of Kingston's most hectic, and the higglers are impressively in command.

Along Spanish Town Rd., you'll find the **Kingston Industrial Garage**—a visit for a true individualist. The garage is believed to be the longest continuously operating Ford dealership in the world, and was Ford Company's first overseas dealership, established in 1907. Other than that, it's just a garage, but a great garage.

Victoria Pier was damaged considerably by 1988's Hurricane Gilbert, and has yet to undergo substantial repairs. Today, young boys who wash cars along Ocean Blvd. use the broken docks to swim and play in, and the waterfront has become residence for many of Kingston's homeless. The scene is all too sad and familiar—men in soiled rags and tattered shoes pulling sacks of rubbish in aimless directions, muttering private litanies to keep their demons at bay.

PRACTICALITIES

ACCOMMODATIONS

New Kingston, as well as being central, is the area where quite a few of the town's hotels are established. Summer, roughly mid-April through mid-Nov., is the slow season when rates are sometimes cheaper or more negotiable. Reduced rates, however, are less applicable in Kingston than in tourist centers due to the year-round nature of business travel to the city. Some hotels include a service charge and 10% GCT in their rates, while others tag it on at the end. Since rates are subject to change, it is best in all cases to call, write, or fax for details.

Inexpensive

Altamont Court Hotel (1 Altamont Cres., Kingston 5, Jamaica, W.I.; tel. 929-4497/8 or 929-0189, fax 929-2118) has 18 rooms consisting of studios and flats with cooking facilities. Some rooms have fans, some have a/c. Cost is US$45 for the small studio apartment to US$52 for the one-bedroom, tax and service charge included.

Chelsea Hotel (5 Chelsea Ave., Kingston 10, Jamaica, W.I.; tel. 926-5803) is a New Kingston flophouse, and, without appearing to take a gratuitous potshot, resembles a whorehouse on a bad day. It's that rough. The rooms have a bed and TV, a/c, and hot and cold water. The security is dubious. But, at J$300-350 (about US$14-16) per room, it may be just what you are looking for.

Holborn Guest House (3 Holborn Rd., Kingston, Jamaica, W.I.; tel. 926-0296) is a small, no-frills, New Kingston guesthouse. Rooms are clean and basic, no hot water, no a/c. Tariff is US$20 pp per night, breakfast (make that a small breakfast; but for US$20, who's complaining?) included.

The **Indies Hotel** (5 Holborn Rd., Kingston, Jamaica, W.I.; tel. 926-2952 or 926-0989) is small (14 rooms) and has a/c in all rooms. The restaurant serves all meals. Tariff is US$46 s and US$54 d year-round, including tax and service charge.

Sandhurst (70 Sandhurst Cres., Kingston 6, Jamaica, W.I.; tel. 927-7239 or 927-8244) has rooms US$36-40 s and US$42-46 d year-round. Rooms with a/c are slightly more expensive, and single rooms are slightly cheaper. Add 10% GCT. They have a small pool and restaurant.

Scorpio Inn (Gordon Town Square, St. Andrew, Jamaica, W.I.; tel. 927-1602) is out of town at the base of the Blue Mountains. Take a bus from Papine near the university. The town is almost rural Jamaica, and close enough to enjoy both Kingston and the cool of the Blue Mountains. The inn has six basic rooms with shared baths, a restaurant, and a disco. Tariff is about US$20 per room, tax and service charge included. The meals are also basic and inexpensive at under US$10. This place has had a rocky history, so contact Carolyn Jackson to confirm that it is still open.

Sunset Inn Apartment Hotel (1A Altamont Cres., Kingston 5, Jamaica, W.I.; tel. 929-7283) is a 16-room hotel in New Kingston, and has very basic studio apartments, and one- and two-bedroom flats. The two-bedroom business is nominal in some cases, as the "other" bedroom is in a small alcove. The water is hot and cold, and some rooms have stoves and refrigerators. Rates are J$550-700 (about US$25-32), all taxes inclusive.

Moderate

The Courtleigh (31 Trafalgar Rd., Kingston 10, Jamaica, W.I.; tel. 926-8174/8 or 929-5320/4, fax 926-7801) is a well-situated apartment hotel in New Kingston, just a short walk from Devon House and the King's House complex. Tariff is US$96-175 s and US$99-188 d in the summer, room tax and service charge included. They also have suite apartments for US$97 s and US$99 d during the winter. Rates increase in the winter.

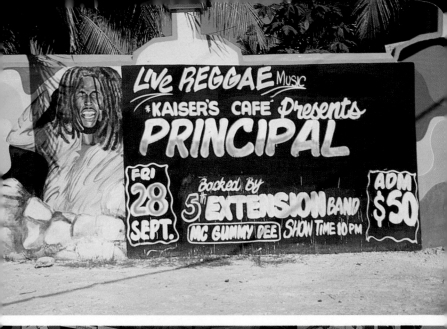

top: Negril hosts a multitude of reggae shows (Phyllis Luntta)
bottom: Mento, ska, and reggae album covers adorn the walls of this Negril music shop (Phyllis Luntta)

top: Bamboo-bedecked home on the road to Mandeville (Phyllis Luntta)
bottom: policemen, Negril (Phyllis Luntta)

Four Seasons (18 Ruthven Rd., Box 190, Kingston 10, Jamaica, W.I.; tel. 929-7655/7, fax 929-5964) is an old, European-style great house on Half Way Tree Rd. in New Kingston, a great location for exploring the city. You'll get passes for tennis and the pool at the Jamaica Pegasus Hotel. The dining room, serving German fare (thanks to Helga Stockert, a transplanted German and the hotel's owner for 30 years) and Jamaican specialties, is elegant. The 39 rooms are standard to superior, and all are comfortable. All rooms have a/c and television. Rates are US$62-70 per room per night, s or d, year-round. Add US$15 per extra person and 10% service charge.

Ivor Guest House (Jack's Hill, Kingston 6, Jamaica, W.I.; tel. 977-0033, fax 926-7061) is an old pastor's home with three guest rooms and a great view of Kingston. Even if you don't stay here, drive up for dinner one night and stay for the night lights. The guesthouse is on Jack's Hill, one of Kingston's pricey suburbs and home of the Marley family estate. The place is antique, elegant, quiet, and worth the ride. The guesthouse provides daily trips to Kingston and back, and a taxi from Kingston is J$100-120. Rooms are US$60 s and US$80 d, including continental breakfast. Add a 12% service charge.

Mayfair Hotel (4 West King's House Rd., Box 163, Kingston 10, Jamaica, W.I.; tel. 926-1610/2, fax 926-7741) has 30 rooms in eight old buildings, each in its own garden. The governor general's residence is right next door, adding a dignified ambience. The restaurant is basic and moderately priced, but has that old whitewash magic. Rooms are US$40-86 s, US$50-110 d year-round. Suites are available. Add 10% GCT and 10% service charge.

Medallion Hall Hotel (53 Hope Rd., Kingston 6, Jamaica, W.I.; tel. 927-5721 or 927-5866, fax 927-0048) is located across from the gate to King's House. It's a regal old great house with space and charm. No pool but a good location. The rooms are US$76 s and US$80 d, year-round. Suites are available. Add 10% service charge and 10% GCT.

Terra Nova Hotel (17 Waterloo Rd., Kingston 10, Jamaica, W.I.; tel. 926-9334/9, fax 929-4933) is down the street from the King's House and Jamaica House complex, in a central location. The restaurant has a good reputation, and the hotel is just this side of elegant. Room rates are a basic US$88-99 s or d and don't change radically with the seasons. Add 10% service charge and 10% GCT.

Luxury
Jamaica Pegasus Hotel (81 Knutsford Blvd., Box 333, Kingston 5, Jamaica, W.I.; tel. 926-3691/9, fax 929-5855) is a prime gathering place for Kingstonians in government and in the money. Businesspeople rendezvous, princesses stay, and political meetings take place here. It's an imposing, high-rise hotel with all the usual amenities, including a formal restaurant, an executive floor, and a lunch terrace by the pool. Rooms average US$172 s or d. Suites are available for much, much more—up to US$500 per night. Rates remain the same year-round.

Wyndham Hotel (77 Knutsford Blvd., Box 112, Kingston 10, Jamaica, W.I.; tel. 926-5430/9, fax 929-4933) is just down the street from Pegasus, and is the same type of hotel, but in a different place. The food at the Palm Court restaurant is very good, and the hotel is centrally located. Tariff is US$125-170 s and US$135-180 d, year-round. Add 10% service charge and 10% GCT.

Oceana Hotel and Conference Centre (2 King St., Box 986, Kingston, Jamaica, W.I.; tel. 922-0920/9, fax 922-3928) is considered one of the largest conference centers in the Caribbean. It sits on Kingston Harbour and looks like a large box, but it does the job, which is to accommodate Kingston's large business and conference population. Rooms are about US$100 s or d per night, plus 10% GCT.

EATING AND DRINKING

Kingston restaurants are among the best in the country, and the most diverse. You can eat anything from restaurant patties cooked in a mobile kitchen to jerk chicken to fast food, Mexican, Korean, or a wide variety of international foods.

Fast Food
Downtown and the malls of New Kingston have the handle on fast-food chain shops in the city. Try **Tastee** for quick meat patties, about J$3.50; or **Mother's,** which has shops all over the city. Mother's has a decent ice-cream line as well. **King Burger, Burger King, Shakey's Pizza,**

and **Kentucky Fried Chicken** are available for the less adventuresome, though they're popular with Jamaicans as well. **Munch Wagon** also has stores around town, serving the usual suspects. **Patty King** on Barry St. downtown is popular with the local business lunch crowd and serves coconut cakes and pastries as well. **Swanks Pizza** (tel. 924-0707, 925-3353) promises 30-minute delivery around the city.

Fish Pot at Manor Park Plaza serves fried fish and dumplings.

International Eats

Kohinoor (11 Holborn Rd.; tel. 926-3675) serves East Indian fare at moderate prices. **Fee Fee** on South Ave. sells East Indian *rotis* with meat or vegetable filling. **Chico's** (2 Dumfries Rd.; tel. 929-1222) serves scalding Mexican food. You can get a huge slab of meat at **Herb's Steak House** (5 Belmont Rd.; tel. 926-7361).

For Chinese food, try **Lychee Garden,** (New Kingston Shopping Centre, Dominica Dr.; tel. 929-8619) or **Mee Mee Restaurant** (15 Northside Dr.; tel. 927-0150) for dining or takeout. **The Mandarin Restaurant** (14 Northside Dr.; tel. 927-0237) serves Cantonese dishes. **Gordon's Restaurant** (36 Trafalgar Rd.; tel. 929-1390) serves Korean dishes, among others.

Jamaican And Vegetarian

Jamaican is the fare at **Hot Pot** (2 Altamont Ter.; tel. 929-3906). **Chelsea Jerk Centre** on Chelsea Ave. serves reasonable jerk chicken and pork, and is a local favorite. **Peppers** (31 Upper Waterloo Rd.; tel. 925-2215) is a popular gathering place for Kingston's young professionals, and serves a mean jerk chicken. Good vegetarian can be had at **Lyn's Vegetarian Restaurant** (7 Tangerine Pl.; tel. 929-3852). Great vegetarian can be had at **Minnie's Ethiopian Herbal Healthfood Restaurant** (176 Old Hope Rd.; tel. 927-9207), but only if you can remember the name, which is a mouthful in itself. Try Minnie's homemade ginger beer for colds and the flu. **Uptown Restaurant** at Hagley Park Plaza on Half Way Tree Rd. is a good example of a Jamaican working-class restaurant. Lunch hours are crowded with workers from the city. The fare is basic but tasty pork, chicken, and rice dishes for US$2-5.

Seafood

Seafood is the specialty at **Seawitch** (69 Knutsford Blvd.; tel. 929-4386), but the fare can be pricey. **Victoria Pier** (Ocean Blvd.; tel. 922-3129) down by the waterfront is less expensive. In Port Royal, try **Sir Henry's** at Morgan's Harbour Hotel (tel. 924-8464) for excellent seafood and local dishes. One plus is that they will pick you up and drop you back at your hotel for free. The **Fort Charles Restaurant** at the Oceana Conference Centre and Hotel (2 King St.; tel. 922-0920) also has good seafood at reasonable prices.

Hotel And Other Restaurants

New Kingston's hotels have very good restaurants, but they'll tax your resources if you're on a budget. For a splurge, however, try **Palm Court** at the Wyndham, which serves mostly Italian food and one of the better bottles of Chianti in the neighborhood. **Le Pavillion** at the Pegasus should be suspect because of the affected French name, but the food is actually very good and down-to-earth. **The Devonshire** at Devon House on Hope Rd. serves seafood and elegance. **Norma's** (8 Belmont Rd.; 929-4966) does lunch and dinner and the food is exotic and tasty, though the place seems pretentious. **Hotel Four Seasons** (18 Ruthven Rd.; tel. 926-8805) serves wonderful German dishes, including homemade sausages. **Ivor Guesthouse** (Jack's Hill; tel. 927-1460) is great for fine dinners served while gazing at Kingston's lights below. **Blue Mountain Inn** (Gordon Town Rd.; tel. 927-1700), on the way to the Blue Mountains, is reputed to be worth the short drive for its continental cuisine.

ENTERTAINMENT

Special note: **Rockfort Mineral Baths** (tel. 938-5055) on the eastbound road to Norman Manley Airport and Port Royal has been an on-again, off-again restoration project for several years, and is now open for business. The mineral baths, which are situated in what used to be Rock Fort, first fortified in 1694, are a monument under the Jamaica National Heritage Trust. Legend has it that the mineral water first appeared after an earthquake in 1907, though some contend it had been there for years. Nevertheless, Kingstonians have traveled to the slightly saline baths for years, and now you can do it as well. Cost is J$25 (about US$2) for adults and half that for children. The baths are open Tues., Wed., and Fri. 0630-1800; Sat. and Sun. 0800-1800.

Shopping

For local crafts, the best bet is the Kingston Craft Market down by Victoria Pier (see p. 149). Local shopping experiences are strongest at Jubilee Market near the Parade.

Otherwise, Kingston has a plethora of malls and shopping plazas for anything from clothes to books and gifts. They start on Constant Spring Rd. north of Half Way Tree Rd. and are scattered throughout the city. One of the latest is the **New Kingston Shopping Centre** on Dominica Dr. in New Kingston. The mall features a food court as well for quick eating. The **North-side Plaza** in Liguanea has restaurants and shops. Try the Mall Plaza on Constant Spring Rd., apparently so-named to cover all bases, for duty-free items, jewelry, and gifts. For an interesting twist, try the Sunday flea market at the **New Kingston Drive-In Theatre** on Dominica Dr. in New Kingston.

For books, the best bet is **Sangster's Book Stores** (tel. 922-3640) which has branches on Water Ln., King St., Harbor St., Old Hope Rd., and the Mall Plaza. Also, try **Bookland** (53 Knutsford Blvd.; tel. 926-4035) for books and local and international newspapers.

Crafts can also be found at **Things Jamaican** (Devon House; tel. 923-8928), a branch store that features Jamaican carvings, crafts, T-shirts, and the usual suspects.

Kingston is not only the best, but probably the most fascinating place in Jamaica to buy reggae music. After all, this is where it started. Start at **High Times** at the **Kingston Mall** near the National Gallery. They have possibly the best selection in town. **Bunny Wailer's Cash and Carry** on Orange St. is worth a stop for its association with one of the few surviving original Wailers. **Tuff Gong** studios (220 Marcus Garvey Dr.), a Marley legacy, is where up-and-coming reggae musicians record. They also operate a record shop on Orange St., and the selection is Marley-oriented.

Art

Kingston's art galleries, including the National Gallery and the Institute of Jamaica, hold some of the country's best art. In the tourist shops, art can be overpriced and spuriously executed, though great finds happen in the best and worst of places. **The Frame Gallery Centre** (10 Tangerine Pl.; tel. 926-4644) has contemporary Jamaican painting and sculpture, including that of Ken Abendana Spencer, a Long Bay artist and one of Jamaica's better known (see "Port Antonio and the East Coast," p. 182).

Other local galleries include: **Chelsea Galleries** (12 Chelsea Ave., no listed phone); **Patoo** (Manor Park Plaza on Constant Spring Rd., tel. 924-1552); **Babylon Jamaica** (10A West King's House Rd., tel. 926-0416), which features secular as well as Rastafarian art; **The Artisan** (14 Dominica Dr., tel. 929-4214); **Frame Art** (7 Belmont Rd., tel. 926-5014); **Frame Centre Gallery** (10 Tangerine Pl., tel. 926-4644); **Bolivar Book Shop and Gallery** (1D Grove Rd., tel. 926-8799), which has the added attraction of a bookstore; and **Gallery Pegasus,** located on the bottom floor of the Jamaica Pegasus Hotel.

Theaters

Jamaica's theater tradition is strong in Kingston, perhaps stronger than anywhere in the country. Certainly it is oldest in Kingston, and **Ward Theatre** is proof. Located on the North Parade (tel. 922-5415 or 922-0318), the Ward occupies a site that's been in continuous operation as a theater since the 1770s. The Ward is most often associated with Jamaican traditional theater, such as the Pantomimes, held every year beginning on Boxing Day (26 December).

The **Little Theatre** (4 Tom Redcam Ave.; tel. 926-6129) is known as the "Likkle" Theatre to Jamaicans, and is closely associated with the Little Theatre Movement (LTM). The LTM was founded in 1941 and has since promoted Jamaican cultural events. The Little Theatre stages traditional post-Christmas Pantomimes as well as a Season of Dance performed by the National Dance Theatre Company (NDTC), usually July-August.

Other, smaller theaters include **The New Kingston Theatre** (Altamont Cres., tel. 929-2618); **The Theatre Inside** (6 Cargill Ave., tel. 926-6711); and **The Barn Theatre** (5 Oxford Rd., tel. 926-6469).

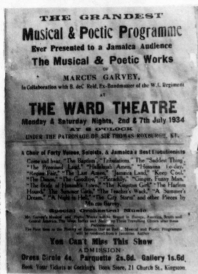

THE GRANDEST

Musical & Poetic Programme

Ever Presented to a Jamaica Audience

The Musical & Poetic Works

OF

MARCUS GARVEY,

In Collaboration with B. deC Reid, Ex-Bandmaster of the W.I. Regiment

AT

THE WARD THEATRE

Monday & Saturday Nights, 2nd & 7th July 1934

AT 8 O'CLOCK

UNDER THE PATRONAGE OF SIR THOMAS ROXBURGH, Kt.

A Choir of Forty Voices, Soloists, & Jamaica's Best Elocutionists

Come and hear, "The Baptism", "Tribulations", "The Saddest Thing", "The Promised Land", "Hallelujah Amen", "Hosanna To-day", "Regina Pacis", "The Last Amen", "Jamaica Land", "Keep Cool", "The Dunce", "The Goodbye", "Piccadilly", "Ginger, Funny Man", "The Birds of Humanity Town", "The Kingston Girl", "The Harlem Hounds", "This Summer Girls", "The Teacher's Work", "A Summer's Dream", "A Night in Hell", "The City Storm" and other Pieces by Ma cus Garvey.

Special Orchestral Music

Mr. Garvey's Musical and Poetic Works will be heard in Europe, America, South and Central America, The West Indies and Africa by Three Travelling Choirs after these Performances.

The First time in the History of Jamaica that an Bell — Musical and Poetic Programmes will be rendered from a Jamaican Author

You Can't Miss This Show

ADMISSION

Dress Circle 4s. Parquette 2s.6d. Gallery 1s.6d.

Book Your Tickets at Coxings's Book Store, 21 Church St., Kingston

Cinemas: Kingston has two drive-in theaters. **Harbour View Drive-In** in Harbour View has been around for a while and shows the standards, including incomprehensible martial arts films. **New Kingston Drive-In** doubles as a flea market on Sunday. **Carib Cinema** at Cross Roads is large, air conditioned, and a good place to enjoy cultural differences in movie-going. **Cineplex I & II** at Sovereign Centre on Hope Rd. shows two films.

Music And Nightlife

Kingston is a good place to forget the fire-eaters and limbo honchos of the resort hotel circuits. The entertainment here is trend setting, original, and often pretty raw. Since most of the country's top musicians record in Kingston, you may be able to catch them at clubs and concerts—keep an eye on posters and an ear to the radio.

Epiphany (1 St. Lucia Ave., New Kingston; tel. 929-1130) features live performances on Thursday, with a cover charge. Dancing is on weekends, featuring "oldies" on Sunday. It opens around 2100. **Mingles** at the Courtleigh Hotel has a nightly disco and Friday happy hours. They have a cover on Friday, about US$5 for men and less for women, which is possibly how they can afford that happy hour; no cover on Saturday. **Illusions** (New Lane Plaza; tel. 926-7419) has a

happy hour every evening 1730-1930, and a cover charge for dancing, starting at 2200. **Godfather's** (tel. 929-5459) on Knutsford Blvd. in New Kingston is new and popular. Try **Rock Club** (7 Chancery St.; tel. 925-8261) for loud, contemporary music.

Live reggae is often found in weekend concerts at local beaches such as **Cable Hut** on the Morant Bay road. Watch for long weekends or national holidays when the possibility of outdoor shows grows. The same goes for *soca*, a calypso hybrid, and "oldies" shows. The annual **Superjam**, featuring reggae, *soca*, and pop is held in December at the National Stadium. One of Kingston's premier reggae spots is **Skateland** at Half Way Tree, where you might catch a rising star.

A jazz combo plays poolside at the Pegasus—cool jazz featuring piano, bass, and trumpet played by three gray-haired gents who loll in it. Call for specific days and times.

GETTING AROUND

Public Transportation

Buses and taxis are no problem anywhere in Kingston. Major bus stations at the Parade, on King St. south of the Parade, at Half Way Tree, and just next to the Kingston Craft Market can take you most places in the city and country. The Parade stand is the main downtown hub to all points. The stands at Papine and Barbican take passengers northbound to the Blue Mountains.

Taxis are the standard meterless type, so discuss fees with the driver before you get in. Make sure you get into only those taxis that have red or blue license plates, designating them as approved taxis. Gypsy cabs or unmarked cars offering lifts *are not safe*. Your best bet is to call a taxi service. Call **Blue Ribbon Taxis** (tel. 928-7739), **Checker** (tel. 922-1777), **Principal** (tel. 924-4043), or **Yellow Cab** (tel. 922-6444/6) for pickups. **JUTA** (tel. 926-1537) is slightly more expensive, but reliable.

The **Jamaica Railway Corporation or JRC** (Barry St.; tel. 922-6620) is in operation again, and makes regular trips between Kingston and Montego Bay, with stops. This is one of the more fun and inexpensive ways to get to the interior, Montego Bay, and the west coast. (See "Getting Around" in the Introduction, p. 89 for a full schedule.)

2516) for internal flights. See "Getting Around" in the Introduction, p. 90 for a more complete schedule.

Rentals

Driving around Kingston is no easy task, but if you need to be independent of walking and public transportation, a number of rental companies are reliable. You must have a valid driver's license and be at least 25 years old. Listed in the chart below are some of Kingston's car rental agencies.

INFORMATION

Banks are located throughout the city, with a concentration in the downtown area. Scotiabank (tel. 922-1000) has branches at Duke and Port Royal streets, 35 King St., Knutsford Blvd., and other locations. Jamaica Citizens Bank (tel. 922-5850/6) has branches at 4 King St., 17 Dominica Dr., 15 Hope Rd., and elsewhere throughout the city. This is the way it is with banks in Kingston: Walk a block, you've passed two banks. General banking hours are Mon.-Thurs. 0900-1400, and Fri. 0900-1200, 1430-1700.

Local airlines fly from Sangster International Airport and from **Tinson Pen Aerodrome,** just outside of Kingston, to all major points in Jamaica. Typically, the most expensive flight is Port Antonio to Negril, which is US$85 OW. Contact **Trans Jamaican Airlines** (Kingston, tel. 923-8680; Montego Bay; tel. 952-5401), **Airways International** (Box 50, Kingston 11, Jamaica, W.I.; tel. 923-6614 or 923-8557); or **Timair** (Sangster International Airport; tel. 952-

KINGSTON CAR RENTAL AGENCIES

Area Code 809

Avis Rent-A-Car, 2 Haining Rd., tel. 926-1560 or 926-1568; Norman Manley Int'l Airport, tel. 924-8013

Bargain Rent-A-Car, 10 Merrimack Ave., tel. 926-8237

Budget Rent-A-Car, 1½ Upper Elletson Rd., tel. 928-4779 or 928-2833

Caribbean Car Rentals, 31 Hope Rd., tel. 926-6339

Coxe's Rent-A-Car, 94b Old Hope Rd., tel. 927-9074 or 927-4240

Compact Car Rental, 33b Hope Rd., tel. 929-6475 or 926-2668

Econocar Rentals, 11 Lady Musgrave Rd., tel. 927-0178 or 927-6761

Galaxy Car Rentals, 75 Red Hills Rd., tel. 925-4176

Hertz, Jamaica Pegasus Hotel, tel. 926-3690 or 29 Hagley Park Rd., tel. 926-0181

Island Car Rentals, 17 Antigua Ave., tel. 926-8861 or 926-5991

Jiffy Rent-A-Car, 66 Hagley Park, tel. 929-1713

National Car Rentals, 19 Carlton Cres., tel. 929-9190

Pleasure Tours Car Rentals, 153 Constant Spring Rd., tel. 924-4140

Robinson's Car Rental, 1 Brompton Rd., tel. 927-6030 or 927-9138

Travellers Rent-A-Car, 20 Lords Rd., tel. 926-6114 or 926-4924

Value Rent-A-Car, 8 Worthington Ave., tel. 926-0921

The **Jamaica Tourist Board** (Tourism Centre, 21 Dominica Dr., Box 360, Kingston 5; tel. 929-9200/19, fax 929-9375) is the main office of the JTB worldwide. Their reception desk has about every brochure and pamphlet available on the country. The **Jamaica Chamber of Commerce** (7-8 East Parade; tel. 922-0150) can be helpful with business information. The **General Post Office** (13 King St.; tel. 922-2120) is large and busy, but worth a stop. The **Philatelic Bureau** is located on South Camp Rd., tel. 922-9430, but the post office maintains at least 14 branches throughout the city, from Norman Manley International Airport to Constant Spring. For faster overseas deliveries, you can find a **Federal Express** office at 75 Knutsford Blvd. (tel. 926-1456/9).

Embassies are generally found in the New Kingston area (see "Introduction," p. 81, for addresses and telephone numbers). All major airlines are represented in Kingston (see "Introduction," p. 85, for contacts), either at the airport or New Kingston offices. Additionally, other useful numbers are: **American Express** (Stuart's Travel Services, 9 Cecilio Ave. tel. 929-2346); **Bellevue Hospital** (Windward Rd., tel. 926-1380); **Fire and Ambulance** (tel. 110); **Police Emergency** (tel. 119); and **Weather Information** (tel. 924-8055).

VICINITY OF KINGSTON

PORT HENDERSON

Port Henderson is a small but growing suburb community of Kingston, though in the past it was the main port for Spanish Town's commerce and travel trade. It then had strategic value as well—its position across the water from Port Royal virtually ensured that no enemy warships could slip into Kingston Harbour undetected or unmolested. The village was also once fashionable after a mineral spring was discovered and a health resort and spa attracted the rich and unhealthy to the area. The spring has since dried, and the village is now a secondary suburb of **Portmore**, a large industrial and shopping center of Kingston. Today, some of the older buildings in town have been restored by the National Trust, including **Rodney's Arms**, a tavern and restaurant.

Nearby Beaches

The beaches south of Port Henderson are an attraction in the area. **Fort Clarence** beach was the site of a defense fortification that remained active into the late 19th century, a time when Jamaica was threatened by both France and Spain. Today's beach is popular with Jamaicans for weekend getaways and for reggae and other concerts. It has all amenities, including changing rooms, fish and *bammy,* lifeguards, and good security.

The **Hellshire Hills** rise on a large nub of land that juts out to the sea west of Kingston Harbour. The hills are composed of porous limestone soil and the rainfall is low—fewer than 30 inches per year—which has made the accumulation of surface water a problem. This has arrested the area's human settlement, despite Urban Development Corporation schemes for large-scale growth. Conversely, the natural and relatively untouched environment has fostered the growth of wildlife unique to the Hellshire Hills. The island coney (as opposed to Coney Island), Jamaica's endangered mammal, makes its home in the hills, and the iguana, presumed extinct here, was recently sighted in the area.

Hellshire Beach, one of the Kingston vicinity's most energetic and Jamaican-flavored bathing spots, is popular on weekends and holidays. It's a panorama of fish and *bammy* huts, horses galloping, boys thumping soccer balls, and radios blasting reggae late into the night. Whiffs of ganja drift from nowhere or everywhere (depending on your awareness), often overpowered by the smell of lobster grilling on open flames. You'll pick your fish from a tub filled with ice, and they'll grill it on the spot. Try *festival,* the cornmeal, flour, and sugar cake that goes well with anything. Wash it down with coconut water. (**Note:** When choosing your fish, avoid those with cloudy eyes; they might have spoiled.) The beach is free, though parking can be a problem on crowded weekends. The best way to get there by bus is from Half Way Tree in Kingston.

Hellshire was once heavily populated by Arawaks, and the hills and caves of the area are said to contain many more artifacts than

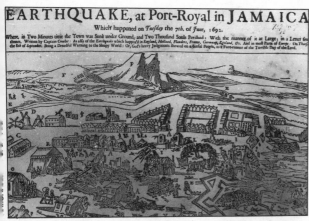

EARTHQUAKE, at Port-Royal in JAMAICA

Which happened on *Tuefday* the 7th. of *June*, 1692.

Where, in Two Minutes time the Town was Sunk under Ground, and Two Thoufand Souls Perifhed : With the manner of it at Large; in a Letter from thence. Written by Captain Crocker : As alfo of the Earthquake which happen'd in England, Holland, Flanders, France, Germany, Zeland, &c. And in moft Parts of Europe On Thurfday the 8th of September. Being a Dreadful Warning to the Sleepy World : Or, God's heavy Judgments fhewed on a Sinful People, as a Fore-runner of the Terrible Day of the Lord.

*earthquake at
Port Royal*

have already been found. **Two Sisters Cave** on the beach contains a rock carving of a human face thought to have Arawak origins.

PORT ROYAL

To say Port Royal is in the vicinity of Kingston is almost a misnomer—in fact, the small fishing village is still part of Kingston Parish, even though it lies across the harbor.

What remains of the great buccaneer fortress and city of sin is a sleepy village consisting of rows of houses, a few clubs, restaurants, and churches. The remains of one of the many forts that protected Port Royal and the rest of Jamaica for years is also here; the great 1692 earthquake and tidal wave washed most of it out to sea.

History

When the British captured Jamaica in 1655, one of their first tasks was to build a fort on the island they called Cagway, or the Point. They first named it Fort Cromwell in honor of then-leader Oliver Cromwell. When the British monarchy was reestablished after Cromwell's rule, it was renamed **Fort Charles** in honor of the king. The town that grew up around the fort was called Port Royal, and the settlers soon began the task of filling in the marshy waterways between the string of cays known as the **Palisadoes**. Nature helped by way of silt deposits from inland rivers, and the Palisadoes strip was soon joined to the mainland.

The buccaneer period of Port Royal saw five more forts added to the town's strategic layout, with a total of over 140 guns in place. At one point, over 2,500 armed soldiers were stationed at the forts.

The town under the buccaneers was one of unbridled vice—drinking, gambling, prostitution—all the incumbent debauchery associated with quick and easy money.

In the late morning of 7 June 1692, an earthquake convulsed the town. It's said that the morning's weather portended disaster. The air was thick and balmy and the harbor's waters shimmered under a windless sun. At 1140 the first shock was felt as far away as upper St. Andrew. The second followed quickly, and the third was accompanied within two minutes by a monstrous tidal wave which washed a good piece of Port Royal away forever.

More than 2,000 people perished and 90% of the town's buildings ended up at the bottom of the sea.

For years, Port Royalists labored to rebuild their town, but a 1704 fire and repeated hurricanes battered the residents, drove away the buccaneers, and convinced many an honest citizen to depart for the growing merchant city of Kingston across the harbor. Though Port Royal remained an important trading center for years, it was eventually surpassed by Kingston. It continued as a primary British naval base in the Caribbean through the 19th century.

Rumors persist that a great treasure accompanied the buildings and residents of Port Royal to the bottom of the Big Drink—not an unreasonable assumption considering the occupations of most of the dead. But apparently many survivors forewent the maxim of honor among thieves by looting the city during the disorder and confusion following the great quake, making off with whatever treasures were left. No hard evidence exists of a great treasure under the sea. Numerous dives have been conducted since the '50s, sponsored by the National Geographic Society, the Smithsonian Institute, and the Institute of Jamaica. A recent 10-year excavation uncovered a monogrammed fork, a nutmeg grinder, porcelain, silver, and some 35 plates made by Samuel Benning, a Port Royal pewterer. As well, they discovered the skeletons of two young children who were among the 2,000 assumed to have perished in the disaster.

Getting There

Port Royal is at the tip of the Palisadoes, just west of Norman Manley International Airport. The simplest and most fun way to get there is to take a ferry from No. 1 Pier at Victoria Pier. The boat departs Mon.-Fri. 0600, 0700, 1000, 1230, 1430, 1700, and 1830. On Saturday it departs at 0600, 0800, 1000, 1230, 1400, 1630, and 1830. On Sunday and on public holidays its confusing timetable is slightly simpler, with departures at 1130, 1430, 1630, and 1830. The return trip from Port Royal Harbour departs 30 minutes later, Mon.-Sat., and one hour later on Sunday and holidays. The cost is minimal, J$1 Mon.-Sat., and J$1.50 on Sunday and holidays.

The drive or bus from Half Way Tree via **Harbor View,** a southeastern suburb of Kingston, is along the Palisadoes, the scrub- and cactus-filled strip of land linking Kingston with Port Royal.

Sights

The original Port Royal church was destroyed by the earthquake and replaced in 1725 with **St. Peter's Church.** A tombstone in the small churchyard commemorates the escape from death of Lewis Glady, a church warden at the time of the earthquake. It appears that Glady was "swallowed up in the Great Earth-quake in the Year 1692 & By the Providence of God was by another Shock thrown into the Sea & Miraculously saved by swimming until a Boat took him up." A guide will show you around the church, still used by a local Anglican congregation.

Fort Charles, reputed to have the oldest foundation in Jamaica, was one of the few buildings to survive the earthquake, though it receded some feet during the shock and ground waves. The building was started in 1656, a year after the British took Jamaica from the Spanish. Lord Nelson was in charge of the fort for a few weeks in 1779, while Jamaica anxiously awaited a French invasion which never materialized. Admission to the fort is J$2, and it's open daily. The **Fort Charles Maritime Museum** in Lord Nelson's private quarters displays ship artifacts, including protractors and compasses, models of the fort, ship models, and ship chandeliers.

Giddy House is really the old Royal Artillery Store, which pitched into the ground during a 1907 earthquake. It's now at a somewhat precarious angle, and giddy is the visitor who tries to walk across its floor.

The **Old Naval Hospital** is a long, two-storied structure that looks like a hotel of old. It was built, surprisingly for the time, from prefabricated iron sections brought from England in 1819. The **Archaeological Museum and Conservation and Research Centre,** a division of the National Heritage Trust, is housed in the hospital. It features research on Jamaican peoples from Arawak times, and has detailed descriptions of digs, excavations, artifacts, and natural history of the country. The museum was damaged during Hurricane Gilbert in 1988, and is still under repair. It's gradually opening to the public. You can walk around the hospital grounds, enjoying the architecture and building style.

The old **Gaol** on Gaol Alley is thought to retain building parts from before the 1692 earthquake.

The **Naval Cemetery,** on the outskirts of town, holds the remains of sailors, many of whom died from a yellow fever epidemic in the early 1800s. Nearby was the cemetery that held Henry Morgan's remains. The cemetery disappeared during the 1692 earthquake.

Practicalities

A trip to Port Royal is great for sightseeing or the beaches in its vicinity. The town is authentically Jamaican and a striking contrast to the fast streets of Kingston. Sure there are cars, but not many. The buildings are ramshackle and the streets narrow, and locals regard visitors with the slight nonchalance of the carefree.

Lime Cay, offshore south of the Palisadoes, is great for splashing, diving, and sunning. Get there by arranging with a local tour company (expensive) or by meeting up with one of the many fishermen who use Port Royal as a base. As many as nine coral cays lie in the waters off the south coast of Port Royal, and they are possibly the best Kingston-area swimming and snorkeling spots. Fishermen can be found at many local restaurants famous for their fish and *bammy* dishes.

Port Royal restaurants are often no larger than small shacks, set up at precarious angles all over town, but the fish is fresh and the beer fresher (or at least colder) still. Try **Fisherman's Cabin** or the **Cabin Seafood Restaurant** for seafood. **Gloria's Rendezvous** is famous for lobster and as a hangout.

You can stay at **Morgan's Harbour Hotel** (Port Royal, Kingston 1, Jamaica, W.I.; tel. 924-8464/5, fax 924-8562). Substantial renovations over the last few years have added rooms and expanded the marina, and Sir Henry's restaurant has some of the best seafood in Kingston. Year-round rates for deluxe oceanview are from US$105 s or d off-season, and from US$130 s or d in winter. Add 10% GCT and 10% service charge.

SPANISH TOWN

Much of the original Spanish Town has been destroyed, but the town remains important because of its historical significance as Jamaica's first capital.

History

Spanish Town, originally called Villa de la Vega ("Town on a Plain"), was moved to its present site by the Spaniards after an unsuccessful attempt to establish a capital at Sevilla la Nueva on Jamaica's north coast. Villa de la Vega was designed by Diego Colon, Christopher Columbus's son, and became the capital of the Spanish colony in 1534. The Spanish were never deeply interested in Jamaica as a colony, treating it more as an outpost and trading station of little significance, and the town never grew to more than several hundred inhabitants. When the British took Jamaica in 1655, they sacked Spanish Town (which they called St. Jago de la Vega, referring to Christopher Columbus's name for

the island, St. Jago) and destroyed much of the original architecture. But it remained the British capital of Jamaica for over 100 years, enough time to build what remains some of the finest examples of Georgian architecture in the region, some constructed on original Spanish foundations. The capital was moved to the merchant center of Kingston in 1872.

Spanish Town (pop. 89,100) is 14 miles west of Kingston on Spanish Town Rd., and is the capital of St. Catherine Parish. It's clearly an important place to visit—for its history, and for its significance as a major town and crossroads in eastern Jamaica.

Sights

Spanish Town Square is a good place to start exploring the area. It lies along **King St.,** the main road through the town center. The **Court House** was built in 1819 and now houses the local court as well as the town hall, where public performances are held. The **Rodney Memorial** at the north end of the square was commissioned in the late 1800s as a monument to British Adm. George Rodney, who saved Jamaica and the West Indies from French domination after Britain's losses during the American War for Independence. The French, America's allies during that war, went in for the kill after the British defeat, trying to claim the sole remaining British New World territories, starting with Jamaica. They were defeated by Rodney in 1782, who sailed into Port Royal with the French flagship in tow. The monument to Rodney in an anomalous Roman toga was moved to Kingston with the transfer of the island's capital, but outraged Spanish Town residents reclaimed it, by force it's said, and the statue has remained in the old capital since 1889.

The square is also home to the local **Archives Office,** the **General Register,** government offices, and the post office. The register holds numerous historical documents, including the last will and testament of Henry Morgan, one-time buccaneer and governor of Jamaica.

The **Old House of Assembly** on the square's eastern side was the home of Jamaica's first lawmaking body. Before construction of the building around 1762, the Assembly met in available buildings in town. Across the street is the facade of **Old King's House,** the residence of

Jamaica's first governors. The building was destroyed in 1761 and rebuilt by 1802, and was the governor's residence until the capital was moved to Kingston. A 1925 fire burned the old building down, leaving only its facade. Today the **Jamaica People's Craft and Technology Museum** is housed in its stables. The small museum, open Mon.-Thurs. 1000-1700, Fri. 1000-1600, exhibits the technology of Jamaica's Arawak, African, and European settlers over the centuries. Admission is under J$5.

The **Spanish Town Baptist Church,** northeast on French St., was often called Phillippo's Church after its first pastor, Rev. J.M. Phillippo. Phillippo was an early champion of emancipation, and was instrumental in the establishment of "free villages" around the country. First built in 1827, it was damaged by a hurricane but restored in 1951.

A few blocks to the south, on **Barrett St.,** you'll see the **Cathedral of St. James,** the Anglican Parish Church of St. Catherine. The cathedral is the second-oldest foundation in Jamaica, after Fort Charles in Port Royal. Built by the Spanish in 1525 as a Catholic church, called the Chapel of the Red Cross, the church was destroyed by British conquerors, earthquakes, and hurricanes before it was last restored in 1908.

The iron bridge over the nearby **Rio Cobre** is a national monument and thought to be one of the oldest cast-iron bridges in the Caribbean. The bridge is no longer in use.

White Marl Arawak Museum is in White Marl, a small industrial suburb on the road to Kingston. The museum is small, built in the shape of an Arawak hut, and is on the seven-acre site of the largest known Arawak settlement in the country. It features displays of Arawak tools, pottery, carvings, and some skeletons. This unpretentious museum is a must for those who want to delve into Arawak history and culture. Hours and admission are the same as for the People's Museum.

The **Caymanas Park** horse-racing facility, halfway to Kingston, is open Wed., Sat., and public holidays.

Spanish Town Vicinity
The fishing towns of **Old Harbour** and **Old Harbour Bay** to the west have historic importance, though their commercial influence has dwindled. The bay was originally called Puerto de la Vaca ("Cow Bay") by Columbus, probably in honor of the manatees he discovered, though it is report-ed that he initially believed the sea cows were mermaids—causing one to wonder what sort of women Columbus associated with during his life. At any rate, the area was rife with Arawaks, who exchanged gifts with Columbus and his crew. Later, Old Harbour Bay became a chief port on the southeast coast.

The two large islands off the Old Harbor Bay coast are **Little Goat** and **Great Goat** islands. It's not clear how they got their names, but Great Goat was a U.S. Naval base during WW II. Both islands are used by fishermen as a base and fishing grounds. The beaches in and around this area are largely unexplored.

North of Spanish Town, the 40-mile road to Ocho Rios cuts through interior mountains, plains, and bauxite mines. **Bog Walk,** an English corruption of the Spanish Boca d'Agua ("Water's Mouth") is a small commercial center and crossroads. **Linstead** was once a bustling market town due to its central location. Alcan Jamaica operates a large bauxite and alumina plant in **Ewarton,** at the base of **Mt. Diablo. Sligoville** is a small village northeast of Spanish Town, important because the Reverend Phillippo bought the land in 1835 and established Jamaica's first post-emancipation "free village." The name comes from the Marquis of Sligo, a champion of early missionaries and governor of Jamaica just before emancipation.

Arawak image

THE BLUE MOUNTAINS

Walk good.

*—Jamaican colloquialism,
used between departing friends*

The standard image of Jamaica is of beaches, sun, and dreadlocked legions bumping to the beat of reggae bands. It is hard to believe there is a place where you can stand in the downright cold and see nothing but green forest and a blue haze settling into deep mountain valleys. But you can, almost anywhere you turn in the Blue Mountains.

The fact is, most tourists don't make it to the Blue Mountains. The trip requires some effort, either in renting a car, taking wild bus rides through the hills, hiking, or a combination of all three. But the effort is worth it. The mountain region may be quiet and serene, but it encompasses a great amount of activity—plantations, villages, a botanic garden, the highest point in Jamaica, staggering scenery, and, of course, mountain people far removed from the tourism hustle of the coast.

The mountains form the interiors of St. Andrew, St. Thomas, and Portland, stretching about 44 miles from the corporate area's suburbs to the coast at Port Antonio. They rise from relatively small foothills to **Blue Mountain Peak,** the country's highest at 7,402 feet. Their temperature, which drops with altitude, averages 65° F (18° C), though temperatures as low as 40° F (4° C) have been recorded.

The rocks (the oldest in Jamaica) which form the mountains are igneous and metamorphic, and are believed to have been thrust from the ocean in a series of violent volcanic surges over 25 million years ago. The mountains themselves are characterized by sharp peaks and ridges in the central sections, and by limestone formations in the east, where the smaller **John Crow Mountains** begin. Subsidiary ridges run north and south from the main ridge.

The southern part of the Blue Mountains is formed by the **Port Royal Mountains,** a series of ridges that run from **Catherine's Peak** (5,056 feet) south to the coast in St. Thomas—the view northeast from Kingston. Other peaks, included in the main east-west ridge, are **Sugar Loaf Peak** (7,000 feet), **Sir John's Peak** (6,332 feet), and **Mossman's Peak** (6,703 feet).

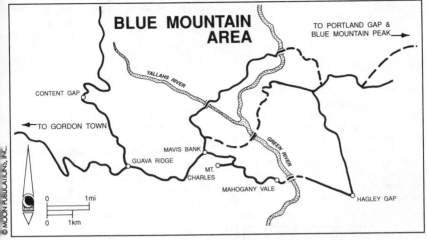

JACK'S HILL

Maya Lodge

Explore the Blue Mountains either on your own or with the services of guides and experts. If you're hiking, a guide is almost a must, and one of the best places to start making contacts is **Maya Lodge and Café** on Jack's Hill. Maya is owned by Peter Bentley, a Jamaican and pioneer of alternative tourism in Jamaica. "Alternative" here means adventure, and Peter is the president of the **Jamaica Alternative Tourism, Camping and Hiking Association (JATCHA),** as well as **Sense Adventures** tour company, located at Maya.

Maya is a small camping and lodging facility, a great place to start for a hike farther into the mountains. Peter and his guides run the place while conducting tours, cooking meals, and dispensing hiking advice. You can stay in the main building or hostels, which accommodate up to 15 people, or in one of the five cabins (six to eight people per cabin). Maya has about a dozen camping spots on the grounds. Private rooms for one person per night are US$20; US$10 for an additional person. Hostel-style rooms are US$10; US$7.50 for an additional person. If you have your own tent, one person is US$5 and additional people are US$2.50 each. They'll rent you a tent for US$2.50 per night. Ponchos, backpacks, daypacks, umbrellas, flashlights, etc. are also for rent at US$2.50.

You can use the kitchen for about US$2.50 p/d per group, or have fresh basic meals prepared for about US$5-10 pp.

Peter and his group will take you on tours, hikes, and bike rides anywhere on the island, but the Blue Mountains are a specialty. The Blue Mountains guided hike is also US$27.50 PP (cost of a guide), and an overnight at the peak will vary in cost—included are guides, bed linens, and minibus transportation to as close as you can get. As well, Sense has a two- or three-day "hut to hut" hike with Blue Mountain Peak as the premier destination. Excursions to the newly developed **John Crow National Park** are available. Sense also specializes in naturist tours of clothing-optional beaches and skinny-dipping spots all over the country. Guide service apart from tours is US$27.50 p/d; the company employs both men and women.

Sense adventures also conducts customized, all-inclusive tours of specific eco-aspects of Jamaica, for about US$50-100 pp. Expert ornithologists, botanists, and others are available for truly involved nature lovers, about US$100 p/d.

To get to Maya, take a bus or taxi from Papine to Jack's Hill and get off at Foxy's Pub. Walk about 100 yards and you'll see the sign. To contact Maya ahead of your visit, write to Sense Adventures (Box 216, Kingston 7, Jamaica, W.I.; tel. 927-2097 and ask for Peter or Toni). Or, you can contact Pauline Stuart, a partner in JATCHA, at Stuart's Travel (tel. 926-0727) in Kingston.

NEWCASTLE AND NORTH

Newcastle is now a Jamaica Defence Force camp, and was estabiished in 1841 as a defense position. The camp, just 16 miles from Kingston, was once the site of a large coffee plantation and a camp for British and Canadian soldiers during WW II. Nearby is **Hollywell National Forest,** where you can rent a small cabin by the night or by the week. The **Forestry Department** (173 Constant Spring Rd., Kingston 8, Jamaica, W.I.; tel. 924-2612) operates the cab-

ins and that's where you'll have to go to reserve one. You'll pay in advance and take a voucher up to the watchman, who opens the doors for you. The cabins rent for about J$80 s and J$100 d per night during the week, or for J$200 s and J$300 d for a weekend, the most popular time. They'll also rent the cabin by the week. Bring your own bed linens, and expect cooking items to be scarce. Cabins are supposed to have a refrigerator, stove, and beds, but in the past some items have been missing. Book well in advance for weekend visits.

East of Newcastle you can turn north at **Silver Hill Gap** to reach **Clydesdale National Park,** another Forestry Department plantation and pine nursery. They maintain one small cabin there for visitors, and the tariff and rules for rent-

THE STORY OF BLUE MOUNTAIN COFFEE

Coffee was first introduced into Jamaica in 1728 when estate owner Sir Nicholas Lawes imported seedlings from Hispaniola. The cash crop quickly caught on among planters unhappy with increasing competition for land and sales among sugarcane farmers on the coastal plains. In the 1790s, revolutions in Haiti forced refugees from that island to move to the more moderate political climes of Jamaica, and among these refugees were skilled coffee growers. Many settled in the Blue Mountains, where their expertise contributed considerably to the nascent coffee industry. The 1838 abolition of slavery allowed former slaves to set up small fields in the mountains, where it had become evident that the green coffee bean grew best.

During the Napoleonic Wars of the early 19th century, with Britain in need of funds to finance the war, heavy duties were levied on coffee importation. British subjects began to look to substitutes such as tea, and the Jamaican coffee industry suffered.

Further trouble came during the middle of the 19th century, when Jamaican coffee growers suffered under a Free Trade policy instituted by Britain, which no longer gave them protected status under advantageous duties. This enabled Colombia and Brazil to encroach on the world market, eventually flooding it with their commendable coffees, but virtually burying small Jamaican farmers. In addition, a 1951 hurricane destroyed large tracts of coffee plantations and virtually destroyed the coffee industry completely. By the 1950s, there were only three coffee processing plants, called *pulperies,* operating in the Blue Mountains: Mavis Bank, Silver Hill, and Moy Hall.

The Coffee Industry Board was established in the '50s to help revive the faltering coffee industry, and it established guidelines of quality in cultivation and processing that stand today. In the early '80s, Japanese investors purchased major parcels of prime coffee plantation land, as well as a great house near Irish Town. The investment has helped to infuse the industry with some energy and competition. More factories have grown, and the coffee industry, while never regaining its former glory, has carved a formidable niche among gourmet coffee circles of the world.

Blue Mountain Peak stands at 7,402 feet above sea level. Above the 5,000 foot mark, the land is heavily wooded and maintained by the government as a forest reserve. Just below this line is the only place where Blue Mountain Coffee is grown. In 1973, the government established guidelines regulating the name Blue Mountain Coffee, mandating that only coffee processed by the Mavis Bank, Silver Hill, Moy Hall, and Wallenford factories could use the name, and only under strict quality controls. Other coffee beans grown in Jamaica, which are often very good but inferior to Blue Mountain Coffee, go by the names High Mountain or Low Land coffee.

Over the years, coffee grown in the Blue Mountains has established a reputation as some of the best in the world. The cool mountain mists and unique soil of the area produce a hearty berry that, in turn, produces a full-bodied, earthy coffee with a unique, almost woody flavor.

ing are the same as at Hollywell.

Farther east is **Cinchona Botanic Gardens,** in existence since 1868. The gardens are high-elevation pretty, sitting on a hill over 5,000 feet above sea level with views of the Blue Mountains, parts of Kingston, and the Caribbean Sea. The gardens were once a cinchona plantation, the plant from which quinine, an anti-malarial drug, is derived. Assam tea was also once grown here, but both cash crops eventually failed due to the logistical problems of the plantation's location, and to advanced production in other places. The section of the garden that remains includes cork, ferns, pecan and peach trees, orchids, and hydrangeas.

MAVIS BANK AND
BLUE MOUNTAIN PEAK

Turn east at Gordon Town for some serious mountain scenery and driving. On the left you'll see **World's End** (tel. 926-8888), a small factory that produces the **Old Jamaica Liqueurs** line. The place looks like a bar, with a mural painted on the roadside wall. Dr. Ian Sangster, a chemist with the National Sugar Institute, reportedly got into liqueur production as a hobby and expand-

Stony Hill Road

Newcastle Looking Toward Kingston

IN THE BLUE MOUNTAINS

ed his operation to Old Jamaica Liqueurs. You can arrange a tour by calling ahead. Have a taste or two of their ginger or coffee liqueur as you sit on the outside patio and look down at Newcastle and the mountains.

About 10 miles east of Gordon Town, you'll reach **Guava Ridge.** Turn north toward **Content Gap,** and you'll know you're in the heart of coffee country. Plants grow on mountainsides in even rows of small, green bushes; you'll see farmers spraying insecticide and tending to their crops.

Nestled in the hills on a 23-acre plantation is **Pine Grove Guest House** (c/o 62 Duke St., Kingston, Jamaica. W.I.; tel. 922-8705 or 924-9848, fax 922-5895). It's 3,500 feet up with a perfect view of Kingston, especially at night when the town lights up. The rooms are suite style and comfortable, and the mist and quiet of an early morning just have to be included as one of life's finer moments—sort of like being underwater. The style of the guesthouse is also quiet. Tell Lloyd, the chef, what you want and he'll try and get it for you, or you can cook for yourself if you'd like. The rooms are US$63 d per night year-round, taxes included. The taxi ride from Kingston is about US$30-40.

From Pine Grove, you can get to Blue Mountain Peak by either 4WD or hiking. Ask Mrs. Barbara McKenley, the guesthouse manager, about trips and peak hiking. Lloyd can arrange a guide, who you'll be expected to compensate.

Farther east is **Mavis Bank,** a small town built around the **Mavis Bank Central Factory,** the area's producer of Blue Mountain Coffee. The town is typically Jamaican and rural—rolling hills with children on foot darting into small shops and schools. If you want to see the factory, get permission from Norman Grant, the manager. They don't actually give tours, but he'll be happy to show you around and let you taste their product, on display in his office. Grant is a professional coffee taster, one of the few in the country, and will be happy to explain the difference between Blue Mountain Coffee and other types grown in Jamaica. Buy a couple of bags on the spot; you won't get it cheaper anywhere in the world.

The hike to Blue Mountain Peak from Mavis Bank takes five or six hours, and the town is just about the last place to which you can drive without a 4WD vehicle.

MOUNTAIN DRIVING

Driving in the mountains may be unlike driving you've done before, so go slow and follow some simple rules.

Gas up in Kingston. One tank should get you around the mountains area, and to see it well you might want to set aside several days. Distances in the mountains from peak to peak are not great—it's the dips and valleys that take time and eat up the petrol. Gas is available in mountain towns, but don't count on being in the right place at the right time to gas up.

Unless you want to blaze a few trails of your own, you'll not need a 4WD vehicle, except near the very base of the peak. The higher the ground clearance of the vehicle, however, the better for you and the car.

During and after rains the roads get mighty testy, and passage becomes difficult. Mud and rocks slide down the mountains and can bury sections of road. Mountain streams, which sometimes cross roads, can swell and make passage impossible. Sometimes the soil under the road shifts and creates potholes that would make a New York cabbie cry. Ask a Jamaican in the area how the road ahead is, and if he says, "Bad," it's probably worse.

Sound your horn liberally as you turn hairpin corners, and hope that the driver approaching is doing the same. This warning is very important on these roads and allows one car to move over (not too far) so the other can pass.

Most people make the assault on Blue Mountain Peak in the early morning—the mist is light, and you get to spend the day literally on top of the immediate world. To do so, you'll have to stay nearby overnight at **Whitfield Hall** (owner John Allgrove, 8 Armon Jones Cres., Kingston 6, Jamaica, W.I.; tel. 927-0986). Whitfield Hall is near the village of **Penlyn Castle**—the last place any vehicle can negotiate. It's a 140-year-old house set up with hostel-style dorm beds, rustic, but the place to hang out for the early morning walk to the peak. Most hikers get up around 0200 to start the five-mile hike, arriving at sunrise. You'll have to bring your bedding and any food you want to eat, and it's best to book well in advance—although few tourists climb to the peak, those that do, sleep here. Cost is about US$10 pp. Campers are welcome to pitch their tents outside the house at one of the seven campsites, but remember to bring a sweater for the night and for the climb. Camping is US$2.50 pp. If you're not into hiking, you can arrange a mule trip to the peak by contacting Allgrove.

The walk passes through the **Elfin Woodland** at about 5,000 feet, a forest of small, twisted trees covered with green moss and lichen. Look low for dwarf orchids among the ferns. Once on the peak, the best thing to do is sit back, relax, and pat yourself on the back. The mist usually kicks in from 1000 to 1600, and on a clear morning they say you can see Cuba, some 90 miles to the north. A small rat-run hut with a toilet is on the peak, but it seems safer to stay away from it.

Trails And Hikes

Choose from dozens of hikes through the mountains and to Blue Mountain Peak, including access from **Hagley Gap,** southeast of Mavis Bank. The best source for concise hike information is *A Hiker's Guide to the Blue Mountains* by Bill Wilcox, available at Maya by contacting Peter Bentley's Sense Adventures for a full information packet.

Getting There

A number of roads weave their way in and around the Blue Mountains area, some of which are principal roads, tarred, and passable. Others are secondary roads that wind around mountainsides overlooking sheer drops of hundreds of feet.

Highway A3 runs north from Kingston to **Annotto Bay** and passes through the western end of the mountain range. The scenery is magnificent and, though the road is winding, it's paved and always in fairly good shape. On the way to Annotto, about 20 miles north of Kingston, stop in at **Castleton Botanic Garden,** a 15-acre garden established in 1862. The garden includes many indigenous and introduced plants, including over 25 varieties of palms, some of which are as old as the garden. The poinciana, which is now prolific throughout Jamaica, was first introduced here. Admission is free.

The road north from Papine, the B1 road, heads toward **Gordon Town,** and you can branch up Skyline Dr. to **Jack's Hill,** Kingston's ritzy little suburb in the hills. The road splits and the northern branch winds its way to **Newcastle,** then on to **Buff Bay** on the north coast. The east branch continues on to Gordon Town, **Guava Ridge,** and **Mavis Bank.** One place to catch the road toward Blue Mountain Peak is here, though at times it's no more than a path.

Public transportation is sporadic and hard to rely on in the hills. Buses into the mountains depart from Papine or Barbican in Kingston, and go only to major mountain villages. It's best to use one place as a base for hiking, or to rent a sturdy car to drive around the mountain sights.

BOB RACE

PORT ANTONIO
AND THE EAST COAST
PORT ANTONIO

To travel is to discover that everyone is wrong about other countries.
—Aldous Huxley (1894-1963)

The American poet Ella Wheeler Wilcox is said to have called Port Antonio "the most exquisite port on earth." Errol Flynn once said he had never met a woman as beautiful as Port Antonio. Which first proves that poets and actors can be hyperbolic at times, but that aside, Port Antonio is no doubt *one* of the prettier ports in the world, and certainly the most exquisite in Jamaica. The port is set amid twin east and west harbors and the lush, verdant foothills of the Blue Mountains, and the town has a nonchalant grace, like the person who has been given too much beauty and has grown used to it. Yet even with that, Port Antonio, the capital of windward and rainy Portland Parish, isn't Jamaica's most popular tourist destination. It is often overlooked in favor of the Big Three—Montego Bay, Ocho Rios, and Negril—which garner the majority of the

country's tourist business. Of course, that may be its finest point.

The reason is distance. The largest town in eastern Jamaica (pop. 16,000), Port Antonio lies on the north coast 60 miles northeast of Kingston, 134 miles east of Montego Bay, and 67 miles east of Ocho Rios—out of the tourist mainstream. The fact is, getting there will take a bit of time and effort on the visitor's part.

It wasn't always that way. As early as the 19th century, Port Antonio was the first and most successful of Jamaica's hot spots for foreigners due to an entirely different business, the banana trade.

HISTORY

The town's twin harbors were named Puerto de Anton (or Puerto de San Antonio) and Puerto de Francisco after the sons of a Spanish governor. But the port was a sleepy place under the

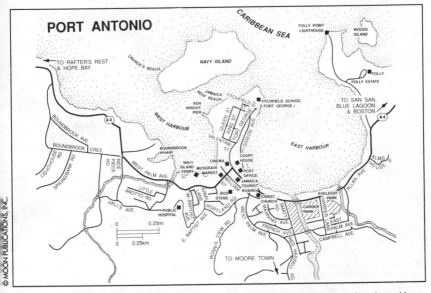

Spanish, and wasn't really developed until after the British overthrow of Jamaica in 1655. The area always lagged behind Kingston and the sugarcane districts in development, and eventually the British colonial government offered incentives to British families, in the form of land grants and tax-free inducements, to come out and settle the region.

The parish was officially formed in 1723 and named after then-governor Lord Portland. Port Antonio, as the main town was called by the British, and its natural harbor created an excellent defense position against the Spanish, French, and ever-prowling pirates. A fort was built on the Titchfield Hill, named after Lord Portland's estate, a peninsula between what is now known as East and West harbors. A naval outpost was established on Navy Island.

Going Bananas

The town and Portland Parish drifted through the years, making little impact on what was becoming a Jamaican economy based on sugar production. The Spanish, however, had left behind one important import that soon changed Port Antonio history. It was the banana, which they had brought from the Canary Islands off the northwest coast of Africa. In the early 1870s,

Capt. Lorenzo Dow Baker, an American skipper from Wellfleet, Massachusetts, took home a load of coconuts and bananas and made a staggering profit selling them to New Englanders. He returned to Jamaica with employees of his Boston Fruit Company and established banana plantations, encouraging the local population to do the same. They soon learned the rules of the business. Bananas, which are seeds of the plant, grow in clusters on the stalks of the banana tree. Each cluster, or hand, on the stalk was counted, and nine hands made one bunch. Growers were paid by the bunch, giving us the line in the folk melody, "The Banana Boat Song," later adapted by Harry Belafonte. The tallyman counts, "Six hand, seven hand, eight hand, BUNCH!"

Captain Dow Baker soon formed a major company and shipping line to handle the business. The shipping company later merged with other interests to become United Fruit, and Captain Dow Baker's banana ships began to bring visitors, the first tourists, to the island.

In 1905, the now-rich captain built the Titchfield Hotel, the island's first, on Titchfield Hill. Business boomed for 30 years while Port Antonio and its residents became very well off, and the town became the playground of North Amer-

corner of West and Harbour streets, facing the courthouse and post office

ica's rich. Then, the Panama banana blight hit. The devastating disease ravaged Port Antonio's crop, destroyed its economy, and very nearly wiped out the banana business (which has never really recovered) entirely. Eventually, new species were introduced, but buyers had turned elsewhere; improved technology made growing bananas in other climes possible. Though you can still see banana plantations today and the crop remains important in the area, Port Antonio's heyday is past.

Enter Hollywood, Or In Like Flynn
Over the years Port Antonio became a quietly elegant place for luminaries such as Randolph Hearst, Bette Davis, Ginger Rogers, and J.P. Morgan. Errol Flynn, the foreigner perhaps most closely associated with Port Antonio, sailed in on his yacht *Zacca* and stayed for the rest of his life, with occasional forays to Hollywood for moviemaking. He acquired property, starting with the old Titchfield Hotel. (Which later burned to the ground, only to be reincarnated on the same property as the Jamaica Reef Hotel, which also burned down. Bad luck, that property.) Flynn also bought Navy Island and plantation land on the outskirts of town, where he raised coconuts, bananas, pimento, and cattle. His widow, former actress Patrice Wymore, still lives there.

The quiet elegance and money of the world's elite eventually spawned Frenchman's Cove, which was one of the most impressive and expensive hotels in the world during the '60s. Guests flew private aircraft, and were driven

about the sprawling grounds in golf carts. Today the hotel's villas have sadly fallen into almost haunting disrepair, but some facilities remain open (see p. 176).

The Town Today
Today, Port Antonio is somewhere between sleepy andbustling, hoping for the tourist dollar, but looking for ways to keep the grace of the town intact.

Cruise ships used to provide a weekly shot in the arm for the town's crafts and market higglers, as well as for the local restaurants. That has changed. In the mid-'80s, cruise ships grew large, and big bulk carriers outgrew the twin harbors' natural capacity, moving on to the deeper ports of Montego Bay and Ocho Rios. Smaller cruises are infrequent these days, calling perhaps three or four times per year.

Yet, this is still a town with some commerce. Large trucks and buses pass through the center of town on Hwy. A4, a major north coast route. Banana boats still converge in the harbor to carry the crop off to faraway places. A bustling energy exists downtown, and main streets can be tarnished and grubby at times, filled with truck exhaust and the smell of hot tar.

Hollywood rediscovered Jamaica and Port Antonio in the '60s, using it as a close and cheap place to film generic island environments. *Live and Let Die, Dr. No, 20,000 Leagues Under the Sea,* and *Papillon* were all filmed in parts of Jamaica. In the '80s, Port Antonio became *the* place to film. A small cottage industry has developed for locals playing bit parts in scenes from movies such as *Clara's Heart, Club Paradise* (which starred Robin Williams and Jamaica's Jimmy Cliff), *Cocktail, The Mighty Quinn, Lord of the Flies,* and *Treasure Island.* Even television shows such as the soap opera *As The World Turns* have used Port Antonio as a location. A 1992 music video, featuring the Jamaican dancehall artist Shabba Ranks and American comedian Eddie Murphy, was shot at Folly, a famous Port Antonio sight (see below).

SIGHTS

Much of Port Antonio is within walking distance from the center of this compact and intimate town. The town includes small restaurants, guesthouses, bus stands, banks, information sources, and the main market. The attractions listed below can be reached either by a walk or a short bus or taxi ride. Remember to discuss price before jumping into a taxi.

Bonnie Views

The **Bonnie View Plantation Hotel** sits on a 25-acre hill estate overlooking the harbors and town. It is one of the oldest continuously operating hotels in the Caribbean, having started during the tail end of Port Antonio's banana boom in the '40s. Even if you're not staying or having a meal there, have a drink on the large deck and indulge in the view, the best in town. You can see not only Port Antonio's, but the entire island's banana crop being loaded at **Boundbrook Wharf** or **Ken Wright Pier. Navy Island** looms large in the harbor, and the landmark **Christ Church** dominates the town skyline. It's a steep hike up the hill and about a mile, so take a taxi if you're not feeling up to it. Try Maurice's fruit punch; it's like drinking an orchard. (See p. 176 for more Bonnie View information.)

Christ Church, Portland's Anglican parish church, was built in 1840 and features the Romanesque style popular in church architecture throughout Jamaica. Note the lectern donated by Captain Dow Baker's Boston Fruit Company. It's downtown on Bridge St. (tel. 993-2600).

Crystal Springs

This is where Jamaica was first introduced to the mongoose in 1872 by farmer William Espeut. Located about eight miles west of town, it features exotic bird displays, fish ponds, a small museum, and a restaurant. Take a bus or share a taxi. Open daily 0900-1800, J$27.50 entry; contact Stuart's Travel (23 Harbour St.; tel. 993-2609).

Folly

On a small peninsula east of East Harbour lies Folly Estate, a large monument to excess and the baroque. An American engineer named Alfred Mitchell (various tales have him originating from New York or Connecticut; some call him a jeweler) and his wealthy wife, a member of New York's Tiffany family, built the pantheonesque estate in 1905 and lived in it until his

playing a stalactite tune in Nonsuch cave

KARL LUNTTA

death in 1912. Complete with concrete pillars, stairways, and 60 rooms, it was the wildest and most ostentatious private home in Port Antonio. Mitchell apparently kept monkeys and a menagerie of wild animals on the property. It was all concrete. That was its undoing, some say. The concrete was mixed with seawater and that, combined with the deterioration of the salt-ravaged steel supports, caused the thing to slowly crumble. By the mid-'30s it was unoccupied and the government acquired Folly in 1949. Today it's a sad, gaping structure, filled with graffiti and broken bottles. No admission, just walk out to Folly Point and have a look. Scenes from the movie *The Mighty Quinn* and the Eddie Murphy/Shabba Ranks music video were shot here. Across the water is tiny **Woods Island,** and at the tip of the peninsula is the **Folly Point Lighthouse.**

Fort George

Fort George still stands, in parts, on Titchfield Hill. Built in 1729 as part of the fortification of Port Antonio's West Harbour, the fort had 10-foot-thick walls and 22 cannons mounted as its original impressive arsenal. Some of the cannons with original 18th-century dates are still intact. The fort is now owned by the government, and is part of **Titchfield School.** It's a short walk from the center of town.

Market

Musgrave Market is in the center of town and has entrances on West St. and Harbour Avenue. This large but not overbearing market is well worth the walk around. The front of the market, on West St., is the produce and jerk chicken or pork section. Here, get the best deals on fruit, vegetables, and spice in town, and the market women are a slice of life. Have a talk and buy a June (sometimes Jew) plum, and discover what the brightly colored spices are in the plastic bags. The indoor room smells earthy and ripe, as if the fruit needs to be bought or it will soon spoil.

Toward the middle is a flea marketlike set of stalls that sells everything from books to shoes to cosmetics. Take a look; the prices aren't bad. Haggle if you'd like.

In the rear is the crafts market, which had its heyday in the days of the cruise ships. Sadly, it now gets fewer customers, only the occasional

tourist or busload from Ocho Rios. The craftspeople are tenacious, though, and hang on. See Rockbottom ("You know why they call me that? Because my prices are . . .") and Mr. Charlie Brown, at the rear of the building, for carvings. Their selections are probably the best in town.

In and around the market block, you'll find plenty of small food stalls and hole-in-the-wall restaurants; good food, better prices.

Moore Town

Moore Town is the traditional home of the Windward Maroons, also called the Blue Mountain Maroons. The town, originally called New Nanny Town after a well-known heroine of the Maroon Wars, was given to the Maroons in 1739 after their leader, Quao, followed the Western Maroon leader, Cudjoe in signing a peace treaty with the British. It was later named Moore Town after a British governor.

Contact Col. C.L.G. Harris, their leader, before you go. The Windward Maroons still value their secrecy, legacy to hundreds of years of Spanish and British persecution. The colonel will have to approve your visit beforehand. If possible, go with someone from Port Antonio, someone who knows the area and customs.

In town, you'll see **Bump Grave,** a monument to Nanny, a national hero and once the leader of the Windward Maroons. Nanny, or Queen Nanny, was believed to possess magical powers and led the Windward Maroons through some of their fiercest fighting with the British. She is said to have kept a cauldron of water boiling without the aid of fire, in order to cause British soldiers to fall to their death in the soup. She was never, they say, wounded in battle. Neither was she armed, in a manner of speaking; Nanny was alleged to possess the ability to catch British bullets with a certain part of her anatomy and deliver them, straight and true, back to the enemy—powerful woman.

The ride to Moore Town is 10 miles of a rocky road ascending into the John Crow Mountains, east of the Blue Mountains and south of town on the road toward Seaman's Valley. You'll pass through winding mountains, banana plantations, and small villages.

Nonsuch Cave And Athenry Gardens

Located about four miles south of town into the hills (head south to Breastworks, then east toward Nonsuch), the caves and gardens are situated on the 185-acre estate of one Mr. Toby. In the cave's nine chambers, 55 feet underground, see limestone stalactites and stalagmites, evidence of volcanic activity, and fossils that suggest the cave and entire island were once underwater. The cave is believed to be more than 1.5 million years old. Bats fly overhead but don't worry; they're afraid of you. The cave is lit and a concrete pathway has been constructed. Athenry Gardens is a pleasant stroll among bird of paradise, red ginger, royal poinciana, and other plants and trees. Stop for a spectacular view at the pavilion. The luncheon restaurant is currently a Hurricane Gilbert casualty, but will be reopened soon. Guided tours operate daily 0830-1700, adults US$5, children US$2.50; tel. 993-3740. Ask your guide to play tunes on the natural stalactite marimba in the chambers.

River Rafting
Rafting on the **Rio Grande** is one of Port Antonio's premier attractions. The river was once used to raft bananas down from inland plantations, and it's said that Errol Flynn and his cohorts introduced river rafting as a leisure activity. Rafter's Rest, located off the road a few miles west of Port Antonio, is the end point of the journey and where it starts, in a manner. If you have a car, a driver will take you to the beginning point upriver where you board a guided bamboo raft for two (plus a small child). He'll drive back and wait for you. The trip is two to three hours of quiescent ambling through plantation land and tall, dark hills. Bring sun gear and an umbrella if it's threatening rain (or sun for that matter). Food and refreshments are sold at Rafter's Rest. Moonlight trips can be arranged. Buy tickets only from tour operators or your hotel, or at Rafter's Rest. Open daily 0830-1630 except Christmas and Good Friday; US$40 per raft for two, plus tip (tel. 993-2778).

Somerset Falls
Another poolside attraction to the west of Port Antonio, this is a nice place for a picnic and a swim. The area was settled over 400 years ago by the Spanish; it has a garden, guided tour, geese, and gushing falls from the Daniels River. One mile east of Hope Bay, it's open daily 0900-1700, about US$4 admission.

Trident Castle
This sight is not really a site, that is, it's not open to the public. On the north side of the road, just east of town in tiny Turtle Crawle Harbour, the castle is best viewed as you are approaching from the east. Described by one Port Antonian, "like it came from Disneyland," it's completely white, with monolithic pillars and wide steps leading to the sea. The castle is Bavarian in style and is truly a castle, somewhat out of place among the small houses of Port Antonio, like a sequoia in a cornfield. The castle is owned by the Trident Villas and Hotel, and is used for special functions and as a private residence by the Levy family, the Trident's owners. It is also available to rent as a vacation unit. Interesting photo opportunity.

BEACHES

Port Antonio Beaches
Jamaica Reef Beach was built on the north side of Titchfield Hill. Walk up Queen St. and the ruins of the Jamaica Reef Hotel will be at the end of the road to the left. It doesn't look inviting but walk through and follow the path to the beach below. There is usually a jerk stand and drinks for sale. This is a secluded, small beach.

Folly Beach, by the ruins of Folly Estate, is also secluded. Swim out to **Wood's Island,** only a few hundred yards away. Watch out for sea urchins.

Navy Island has beaches open to the public. Take the water taxi from the Navy Island berth on West St., where a guard will ask you to sign in at the gate. There you can securely park your car. The water taxi leaves every 30 minutes until late night, depending on demand, 24 hours if necessary. On the north side of the island is **Crusoe's Beach and Barefoot Bar,** with lounge chairs and thatched tables. Restrooms, showers, and snorkeling equipment are available. The beach gets interesting at low tide when the sandbar appears. Try one of Richard's weighty fruit punches. (See "Eating and Drinking," p. 73, for the recipe.) The beach bar closes at dusk. Another beach at Navy Island, the Cove, is clothing-optional. This beach has no facilities and, at high tide, hardly any beach at all. Nominal water-taxi fee only (tel. 993-2667).

Area Beaches

Heading east of town, stop at **Frenchman's Cove.** One of the Caribbean's premier hotels during the '60s, the hotel is now closed and crumbling. The management does maintain the small beach, however, which is one of the prettiest in the area, fed by a clear-blue mountain stream. You'll recognize it in the re-made *Lord of the Flies* film. For about J$22 you can use the beach facilities all day. The hotel runs a bar and jerk stand on the beach. Ask Nigel, the barman, about the old days of the hotel. He'll tell you how guests have returned recently and wept at its condition. Open 0900 till whenever.

Farther east is the San San District with the longest, most popular beach in the area, **San San Beach.** The beach gets crowded on weekends and holidays when Jamaicans charter buses and come up from Kingston for the day. It has crafts vendors, a snack bar, restrooms, and water-sports equipment for rent. The small private island you see from the shore is the former Pellew Island, often called Monkey or Princess Island—a honeymoon gift from U.N. diplomat Prince Sadruddin Khan to his wife. The reef here is good, as is snorkeling. At press time, this beach was closed for major renovations (though people seem to sneak in all the time), and plans are afoot to turn it into a major tourist attraction complete with all amenities and, possibly, a hotel or guesthouse.

Blue Lagoon, or Blue Hole, just around the corner from San San, also figures into the plethora of Flynn legends in the area. It's reputed that he dived the 180 feet to the bottom of the hole. Well, more hyperbole aside, this still is a pretty place for a dip. The water is an eerie blue, almost pastel. The area was hit hard by Hurricane Gilbert, and most facilities are currently closed awaiting repair or a miracle. Don't count on either, but you can still swim there. There is no admission, except to try and bypass the trinket bead and shell higglers who seem to descend instantly as you walk down the lush path to the swimming hole. It's an unfortunate scene, another example of the excessive and sad dependency some people develop on tourism.

Farther east is **Fairy Hill Beach,** or Winnifred's Beach, a secluded public beach not often visited; no admission.

The village of Boston is home to **Boston Beach,** another of the parish council's public beaches. The beach is large and the water can get rough, good for surfing some days. There is no admission. Eat lobster at the beach concession, or walk along the road and try jerk chicken or pork from one of the many stalls. Boston is reputed to be the home of Jamaican jerk cooking, and some say it is the best in the country. It may or may not be, but it certainly is competitive. The stalls along the road are stacked like votes in a Chicago election. Cooks here jerk their chicken and pork the old way, on hardwood slats over coals, covered with mahoe or zinc sheets. Chicken should be about J$90 per half a bird. Look for Boppy, who changes stalls occasionally. His special jerk sauce combines over 35 ingredients and is truly hot, but he can give you the lighter stuff. He bottles his sauce and will sell a jar for about US$5, which, unless it's declared dangerous by airport authorities, is a nice gift to carry home.

ACCOMMODATIONS

Many of Port Antonio's inexpensive and moderate hotels and guesthouses are within walking distance of town. The more expensive area hotels and villas dot the coast to the east of town. Many of the small guesthouses do not increase their rates for the winter season, nor do they all charge the 10% GCT; contact them to be sure.

Inexpensive

Camp Sunnyside Guest House (tel. 993-2127), Fort George St., Titchfield Hill, is one of the cheapest accommodations in town. It has 10 rooms on East Harbour, though there's no beach. Bathrooms and showers are shared, and the hotel provides towels, soap, and fans for the rooms. The place is cheerful though a bit flimsy, with a lot of traffic through the halls. The manager can point you to goings-on about town. The small restaurant and bar next door are basic and cheap. Rooms are upstairs and down, and start at US$5 pp, per night.

Holiday Home (P.O. Box 11, Port Antonio, Jamaica, W.I.; tel. 993-2882) is run by Shirley Silvera and has two locations: 12 French Ave. in town, and 12 King St., Titchfield Hill. They're clean, solid buildings, and she provides fans and towels. The rooms share cold-water baths and toilets; no cooking facilities, but she'll sell soft drinks and Red Stripe beer. Rooms are J$220 s and J$290 d (about US$10-13).

Hope View Guest House (26 Harbour St.; tel. 993-3040), across from the Tunnel 54 Club, is clean but has seen better days. The location is convenient but the club across the street can get rambunctious in the wee hours. The guesthouse's burglar-proof bars give the place the ominous dank of prison. You can have a cool drink at the bar upstairs. Cooking is done by request or guests can use the kitchen. Of the four rooms, some have private baths, some share. One room has a fridge. Rooms are about US$10.

Ivanhoe Guest House (tel. 993-3043) at 9 Queen St., across from the old Titchfield Hotel ruins, is one of the cleaner guesthouses in the area. It's a very nice little operation here, with a total of 22 rooms. All have private toilets and cold showers—hot will soon come. The original house was built in 1911, during the banana dollar days, and has a TV sitting room for guests. Meals can be arranged for J$40-60, but guests cannot use the kitchen. Room tariff is J$200 (US$9-10) per night, clearly one of the better deals in town.

Little Reef Guest House is as cheap as they come, but its better days were, alas, long ago. It's a cheerful place in a surrealistic sort of way. Mickey Mouse murals adorn the walls. Nine rooms, basic and small, come with a private toilet and shower, or without. Some have fans. Guests can use the kitchen for a small daily rate, or order meals. Rooms are J$120-200 (US$5-10). No phone, just find the house at 1 Queen St., Titchfield Hill, across from the Jamaica Reef Hotel ruins.

Scotia Guest House (tel. 993-2681), also a Queen St. home, has 10 rooms arranged around a central sitting room featuring a TV and spring-attack couch. The house is old, rambling, and not level, but a glass will stay upright. Some rooms have private cold-water baths. The guesthouse has neither a kitchen for guests nor meal arrangements. The bare hanging bulbs are scary, but the porch is nice. For some incomprehensible reason, the guesthouse staff is not allowed to give out room rates to travel writers. Plan on about US$10 per night.

Sista P's near Hope Bay offers a more rustic and completely different type of experience for travelers with a penchant for nature and family life. Sista P says, "I do it as a business and I don't do it as a business." Her philosophy is that she doesn't operate a hotel, she opens the door to an experience. Sista P and Brother John own a 40-acre farm with grapefruit, avocados, plantains, coconuts, and more about three miles high into the hills south of Hope Bay, 10 miles west of town. They have several comfortable, small cabins around the property that have no running water or electricity. Guests bathe in a nearby mountain stream or use water from a rain barrel. The two also run a one-room school with over 25 grade-schoolers, supported by proceeds from their farm and guesthouses. These children might not have any education if the school did not exist. Guests are invited to go over to the school and teach when they have free time. Long-term guests who might teach in exchange for room and board are invited to write and inquire.

Accommodation cost depends on which cabin you stay in and how many of you there are—set rates are not Sista P's style. Count on about US$20 per night if you cook for yourself. All food growing on the farm is open for the guests to "harvest." Sista P and Brother John, who are Rastafarian, can arrange to have meals cooked for you, but please make that arrangement well ahead of time—they are often busy at the school or farm. Cost for that arrangement can be discussed. There's a concentrated reflective quality about Sista P and Brother John, and they are more than happy to talk about the "what" and "why" of Jamaica, particularly the roots culture in which they live. If nature and temporary freedom are your desire, this is the place. Sista P's place is unmarked and not easy to find: Turn south at the Hope Bay Police Station, following the sign for Fruitful Vale. Drive for just over a mile and turn left at a small food kiosk. Then take the second gravel road to the left. This is a steep and rocky road—an ordinary saloon car will not make it to the top of the hill where the house is. Write or send a Western Union cable to: Sista Petinaud, Content District, Hope Bay P.O., Jamaica, W.I.

Way Valley Guest House (West Palm Ave.; tel. 993-2753) is cheap, J$150-300 (about US$7-14) s, d, or t. But that's about it to recommend this guesthouse on the edge of town. The rooms are at the back of a small beer hall, and they smell like it. Cheaper rooms share baths. Water is cold only, and fans can be rented for J$20 per night. This is not the kind of place you'd go on, say, a honeymoon, but the price is appealing.

In addition, the Jamaica Tourist Board office in Port Antonio recommends three bed-and-breakfast homes in the area that average US$25 per room per night. Contact them for details.

Moderate

Bonnie View Plantation Hotel has been in operation since 1945. Aside from the view, which is a must, the hotel has a pool, horseback riding in the mountains, hiking, and nice rooms. They can arrange water activities and tours. They've even constructed a small sand beach by the pool for those who miss it. The meals are good and moderately priced as well. Basic room rates are US$40-58 s and US$50-78 d in winter; and US$38-48 s and US$46-70 d in summer. Honeymoon and other packages are available. Add 10% service charge and 10% GCT. (P.O. Box 82, Port Antonio, Jamaica, W.I.; tel. 993-2752; or Unique Destinations, Ltd., P.O. Box 135, 201 N. Orange St., Morrison, IL 61270 U.S.A.; tel. 800-448-5398.)

DeMontevin Lodge (21 Fort George St., P.O. Box 85, Port Antonio, Jamaica, W.I.; tel. 993-2604) was built in 1881 as a private home and is a relic of more prosperous times, but has a lot of charm today. The outside is gingerbread and the inside is, for some reason, many shades of green and lace, sort of like your grandmother's parlor. The hotel has 13 slightly threadbare but comfortable and clean rooms, some with bath, some without. Seafood dinners are a specialty, from J$140. Winter room rates are US$30 s, shared bath, to US$48-60 d, private bath. Summer rates are US$24 s to US$36-48 d, plus 10% GCT.

Faith Cottage (P.O. Box 50, Port Antonio, Jamaica, W.I.; tel. 993-3703 or 993-3408) is in the Dolphin Bay residential area, across from the Trident Hotel, about a US$3-4 taxi ride from Port Antonio. They've got five rooms, a restaurant, and a pool. The well-appointed rooms have private baths and hot water. Summer rates are currently US$60 s and US$95 d, a little pricey for this type of guesthouse. It might, however, be just the place you're looking for—a quiet, suburban setting.

The Admiralty Club and Navy Island (P.O. Box 188, Port Antonio, Jamaica, W.I.; tel. 993-2667, fax 993-2041), a 64-acre island in West Harbour, used to be Errol Flynn's private playground. It's now a hotel and villa complex. The island is surprisingly large once you get on it, with hikes and trails encircling it (bring mosquito repellent). The pool is small but cool. Crusoe's Beach has a bar and water-sports activities. The hotel can arrange snorkeling trips aboard the *Tiki Antonio*. The Cove, on the island's north side, is clothing-optional. The half-hourly water taxi is free for hotel residents. The Errol Flynn Memorabilia Room features posters and stills from his movies, and every Tuesday features a Flynn film. Rooms range from standard to comfortable studio villas to three-bedroom villas. Winter prices range from US$90 s, US$100 d in a guest room, to US$300 for six persons in a villa, plus 10% service charge.

Triff's Inn (1 Bridge St., Port Antonio, Jamaica, W.I.; tel. 993-2162, fax 993-2062) is right smack downtown in Port Antonio. The location is convenient, and the 17 rooms have private baths with hot and cold water, a/c, and fans. The restaurant downstairs is reasonably priced and specializes in seafood. Upstairs, star-gaze from the balcony. Owners Roy Grant and Barbara Pratt-Grant built it from old family property. It's been in operation for just a few years, but it looks like a winner. It's the best place to stay if you want to be close to the action. Winter rates are US$44 s and US$60 d, in summer US$36 s and US$54 d, plus 10% GCT and US$10 for each additional person. Children under 12 are free in same room with parents.

Luxury

Dragon Bay Villas (P.O. Box 176, Port Antonio, Jamaica, W.I.; tel. 993-3281, fax 993-3284) is a 50-acre complex of villas located on the ocean east of town. Each villa comes with all the amenities, including kitchen. The restaurant and bar are outdoors (you'll recognize them from the Tom Cruise movie *Cocktail*), or you can include a cook with your villa. Villas have one, two, or three bedrooms, and are called "beach" villas or "hill" villas. Rates remain the same year-round. Beach villas are US$156-192 per night and hill villas are US$96-156 per night, all taxes included.

Fern Hill Club (Box 100, Port Antonio, Jamaica, W.I.; tel. 993-3222, fax 993-2257, North America tel. 800-263-4354, Toronto tel. 416-620-4843) is an all-inclusive resort situated on 40 acres in the hills just south of the old Frenchman's Cove. It features all the standards, including three pools and private whirlpool spas on the balconies of the villas. The hotel organizes trips to the beaches and town, as well as other tours. They'll even arrange a wedding if the mood(!) strikes. This is a great place to unwind if you've got the money and want luxury. Typical package is US$825 pp (based on double occupancy) for four nights in a standard, and US$1105 pp (double occupancy) for seven nights, winter rates. The price includes all meals, drinks, tips, room tax, and air transfers from Montego Bay.

Goblin Hill Villas at San San (reservations: 11 East Ave., Kingston, Jamaica, W.I.; tel. 925-7896 or 925-8108, fax 925-6248, U.S.A. tel. 800-472-1148) overlook the beach at San San in a family-oriented environment. The price includes maid/cook service and you can include a standard-shift car with unlimited mileage. Winter weekly rates with car, US$1830 for a one-bedroom, and US$2130 for a two-bedroom. In summer, rates drop to US$1795 for the one-bedroom, and US$2095 for the two-bedroom. Babysitting service is available at US$10 p/d, or US$2 per hour after 1800.

Jamaica Palace Hotel (P.O. Box 277, Port Antonio, Jamaica, W.I.; tel. 993-2020/1, fax 993-3459, North America tel. 800-423-4095, Illinois tel. 312-883-1020) gets points for accurately describing itself. It *is* a palace, designed with the old plantation great-house motif in mind. The hotel is certainly elegant—it's pillared and extremely white, everywhere, and the suites are very nicely decorated. The excruciating charm of it all will appeal to some. Winter rates are about US$110-350 s or d, exclusive of 10% service charge and 10% GCT. Summer rates US$95-280 per room. Packages and meal plans are available.

Trident Villas and Hotel (P.O. Box 119, Port Antonio, Jamaica, W.I.; tel. 993-2602, fax 993-2590, North America tel. 800-237-3237 or 800-235-3505, U.K. tel. 01-730-7144) sets the standard for elegance in Port Antonio. The hotel has 26 suites and villas spread out over the rocky oceanfront and private beach. You'll recognize the pool and rooms from the famous seduction scene in *The Mighty Quinn*. Dinner features white-gloved waiters and semiformal attire for guests. The wine list is extensive and the food superb. Helicopter service is available from Kingston. This is not a hotel with whistle-blowing and rah-rah activities—the emphasis is on quiet refinement. During the summer, European-plan rooms range from US$130 s in a superior room to US$450 d in an imperial suite. Winter rates range from US$250-750. All-inclusive and other meal plans are available. Add 10% service charge and 10% GCT. The Trident Castle (see p. 173) is also available for private rental.

Villas

In addition to Port Antonio's hotel and guesthouse rooms, over 40 privately owned villas are available for US$900-5200 per week in the summer, and US$1300-5400 in the winter. Your best bet is to contact JAVA in Ocho Rios at 974-2508 or Vacation Network at (800) 423-4095 (see "Information," p. 80).

EATING AND DRINKING

All the hotels mentioned above have restaurants with prices proportionate to their room rates. In particular, dinner at Trident Villas and Hotel, lunch or dinner at Bonnie View Hotel, and dinner at DeMontevin Lodge or Triff's Inn are recommended. The public restaurants around town are generally good, and if you want a quick, inexpensive meal, they're the best bet. Most restaurants open Mon.-Sat. 0800 and close anytime from 1700-2200. On Sunday it is difficult to find a restaurant, but the hotels will inevitably be open.

Restaurants

Atlantis Club and Restaurant is in a small alley across from the tourist board office on Harbour Street. The eggs and bacon are good, and the prices cheap. Some cooking is done over a wood fire in the back. The strange camouflage motif is hard to figure out. Meals are J$15 and up.

Chuck Wagon on West St. has fast food, specializing in fried chicken. Good for a quick drink.

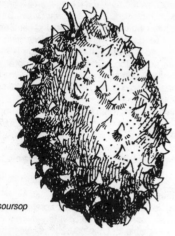

BOB RACE

soursop

Daddy Dee's on West St., a personal favorite, serves liver, beef stew, boiled bananas, or *ackee* and saltfish for breakfast; about J$15. Lunches are fish, cow's foot, curry goat, and tripe and beans, about J$20. Their bread is a real treat in the early morning. If you use milk in your coffee, get used to sweetened condensed milk, as fresh milk is hard to find in these small restaurants.

Delicious Delight in Goebel Plaza across from the police station on Harbour St. offers drinks, patties, burgers, ice cream, and desserts at takeout prices. Snacks are about J$20.

Early Bird Restaurant on West St. is a popular local diner featuring the usual suspects. It looks smudged from the outside but the food is fine and the prices are right. Try **Shadow's Restaurant**, across the street from the Princess Club, for the same.

Golden Happiness, on the corner of West and Harbour streets, serves extensive Chinese and Jamaican cuisine. The food is good and ample. Get the half-serving unless you have a need to carbo-load. The tasty, mixed fried rice has a little of everything in it—even some things you are not sure about. The restaurant has two dining areas, one with a/c and one without. The food, the same on both sides, costs more with a/c. Prices are US$3 and up.

Huntress Marine Wharf Club is a small dockside restaurant on the harbor off West Street. They serve lunch, dinner, snacks and drinks, and their specialties are lobster and fish. Prices about US$3 and up.

Lammar's Restaurant, on William St. at the bus stop square, serves vegetarian. The music next door and the buses outside make it hard to hear. (But who listens to food anyway?) Expect to spend J$20 or more.

In an alleyway next to Musgrave Market, you'll find **Round the Clock** and **Eleganza,** two small restaurants that serve the standard boiled bananas and other typical, and tasty, Jamaican fare.

Tri-Me, another personal favorite, has chicken and beef livers, plantains, tripe, and *ackee* and saltfish in half and full servings. It's located on West St. behind a swivel door. Prices are around J$20.

Stop Brap is an outdoor bar and jerk joint with some of the best jerk chicken in town, and one of the most confusing names. On Folly Rd. east of the town center, it's across from Mizpah Funeral Home—only a coincidence. Chicken is J$90 per half. Nearly across the street is the brightly colored **Caribbean Jerk Hut,** which serves good jerk chicken and meats.

Markets And Bakeries

Musgrave Market is the best place for fruit and vegetables, and market activity intensifies on Friday and Saturday. Sunday, the market shuts down.

Ekklesia Supermarket (28 Harbour St.; tel. 993-2555) is big and fairly full scale. They will deliver, free, to area hotels, villas, and guest-houses.

For fresh fish, check the fishing beach just west of Stop Brap. The catch comes in at all times of the day, so it's best to go and ask who has or will have something for sale.

Bakeries are always a good bet for fresh bread, meat patties, and sweets. Try the hard dough bread and coconut cakes. Three local bakeries serve the populace: **CC Bakery** (1 West Palm Ave.), **Coronation Bakery** (18 West St., across from Daddy Dee's), and **Three Star Lion Bakery** (27 West Street). All are good and, in fact, serve the same sort of items.

ENTERTAINMENT

Shopping
Port Antonio is not a shopping mecca. Musgrave Market has the best crafts in the area, and a few duty-free shops are found on Harbour Street. Clothing, luggage, and general stores line West and Harbour streets. Try **Pete's Record Store Centre** (West Palm Ave.) or **Limelight Music** (William St.) for reggae and other music. The prices, US$5 and more, are good but have them play the cassette before you buy it to check for recording flaws.

City Centre Plaza, located on Harbour St., has several small shops that sell crafts and tourist-type items such as suntan lotion, postcards, books, etc. As well, look to the hotel shop of the Trident for rums, coffees, postcards, books, and crafts.

Nightlife
The **Roof Club** is Port Antonio's biggest nightlife draw. If you're in the mood, you can hit most of the town's popular clubs in one night by simply walking around town. All feature canned and sometimes live reggae, cold beer, and lurching droves of sweating frolickers eating up the dance floor. From the Roof Club on West St., walk about a hundred yards west to the **Princess Club,** just past the Early Bird Restaurant. Later, try the **Tunnel 54 Club** and the **Taurus Club,** a.k.a. "Mango Tree," on Harbour St. and Somerset St., respectively. Things start to move around 2200 and don't wind down until 0300 or so. For a more intimate atmosphere, the **Centre Point Club** on Folly Rd., across from Stop Brap, is quieter and serves meals as well. **Shadows** on West Palm St. is an upscale disco. **Mullview** (tel. 993-3424), just west of town, is another nightspot. Watch posters and listen to the radio for announcements of live entertainment.

SPORTS AND RECREATION

Fishing
The annual **Port Antonio International Marlin Tournament** has been held since 1963. The week-long event happens in October, when men and women come from Jamaica and around the world to compete. The only time in recent history the contest was cancelled was in 1988, due to the devastation of Hurricane Gilbert. Contact the JTB for details on entering.

If it's pleasure fishing for marlin, barracuda, bonito, wahoo, or other game fish you want, contact **Huntress Charter and Marine Services** (tel. 993-3318) or **Port Antonio Marina** (tel. 993-33209) for charter fishing boats. Cost is usually US$250-300 half-day, and US$400-600 full day, which includes bait and tackle.

Try the *Bonita* (tel. 993-3086) for one of the least expensive charters in town. The 25-foot boat is small but equipped for the marlin tournament.

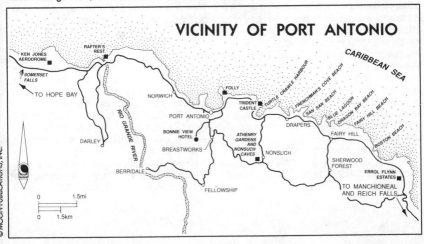

VICINITY OF PORT ANTONIO

Bicycling

Port Antonio is a natural for bicycle travel for three reasons: 1) The town itself is compact; nothing you'll need to do downtown is too far from the last place. Besides, while parking a car in town is not the worst experience you could have in this life, it certainly won't be the best; 2) Port Antonio's beaches and other attractions are a short and easy ride from the town center; 3) The area is relatively flat. That's the good news. The bad news is that renting a bike in Port Antonio is not an easy thing to do. The one place that has bikes is **Stuart's Travel** (Tunnel Plaza; tel. 993-2609). Stuart's will also rent mopeds.

Otherwise, try **Blue Mountain Tours Ltd.** (P.O. Box 84, Port Antonio, Jamaica, W.I.; tel. 993-2242), at the Old Railway Station on Palm Ave., for one of Port Antonio's newer attractions. This tour company provides guided bicycle tours and hikes of the Blue Mountains. Their "downhill" tour is a clever idea: You are transported to the Blue Mountains area, most probably Hollywell, in a van, and the bike ride is downhill, so to speak, from there. You descend through some of Jamaica's most stunning scenery. The tour, which includes transportation, bicycle, refreshments, lunch, and a guide, is US$81 pp. You will depart Port Antonio at 0730 and are on your bike by 0900, riding until the early afternoon. Guided hiking tours up to Blue Mountain Peak are also offered.

Other Activities

Horseback riding through the Janga Gully or to Shotover Mountain can be arranged through the Bonnie View Plantation Hotel. Reserve a day in advance; cost is US$30 pp. The Bonnie View, from which you can see Blue Mountain Peak on a good day, is a good place to start a hike, and they will provide guides.

Contact the Admiralty Club for snorkeling and harbor tours aboard the *Tiki Antonio*. All other water sports can be arranged through your hotel or at the beach at San San.

The **Delmar Theatre** (tel. 993-3304) on Fort George St. is the only movie game in town, aside from the weekly Flynn Film Festival on Navy Island.

TRANSPORTATION

Getting There

To get to Port Antonio, many fly into Kingston and take ground transport either north to Buff Bay and east to Port Antonio, or east from Kingston to Morant Bay via the coastal road. Both are exceptional rides, one through the Blue Mountains and the other along the shore. If you're pre-booked, find out if your hotel will pick you up. Luxury hotels inevitably do. You can fly to Ken Jones Aerodrome from Kingston in about 30 minutes, about US$100 RT. If you fly into Montego Bay, you can make the 130-mile drive to Port Antonio along the north coast, another breathtaking drive, or fly for US$140 RT. Again, the drive either by bus or by rental car is recommended.

Public Transportation

The bus and taxi stand is located on West St., between Love Ln. and William Street. Buses go to all points, and you'll have to ask and read their destination signs for your bus. You can either grab a taxi from there, or call from your hotel: **Sunshine Taxi,** tel. 993-2123; **Tyrell's Taxi,** tel. 993-3124; or **JUTA,** tel. 993-2684. A useful central contact is the **Port Antonio Cab Driver's Co-op** (tel. 993-2684).

Hitching is not uncommon and buses run along the coastal road to San San and Boston constantly. Getting into the hills, caves, or Moore Town is a problem and will require hired transport. If you ask a taxi to wait for you to return, it'll cost. Consider renting a car for a couple of days.

Rentals

Jamaica has hundreds of car rental companies; unfortunately most are in Montego Bay and Kingston. Port Antonio has five agencies, four of which are located on Harbour St.: **Avis,** tel. 993-2626; **Eastern Rent-a-Car,** tel. 993-3624, **Hopeview Car Rental,** tel. 993-3040; and **Hertz,** tel. 993-2690. On West St., try **Don's Car Rentals,** tel. 993-2241.

As well as the aforementioned Stuart's Travel, you can rent a motorcycle or scooter from **Portland Motorcycle Rental,** 17 Boundbrook

USEFUL PHONE NUMBERS IN PORT ANTONIO

Area Code 809

Bank of Commerce, 1 West St., tel. 993-2785

Scotiabank, 3 Harbour St., tel. 993-2523

City Plaza Pharmacy, Harbour St., tel. 996-3624

Customs, tel. 993-2551

Fire, tel. 993-2525

Port Antonio Hospital, Naylor's Hill, tel. 993-2646/7

Immigration, tel. 993-2527

Jamaica Tourist Board, City Center Plaza, tel. 993-3051

Ken Jones Aerodrome, St. Margaret's Bay, tel. 993-2673

Police Emergency, tel. 119

Post Office, Post Office Square, tel. 993-2526

Trans Jamaican Airlines, Ken Jones Aerodrome, tel. 993-2405

Cres., tel. 993-3653 or 993-3677. Remember to drive on the left, and watch for motorcycles at night that drive with no lights. Stuart's Travel is also a contact for the **Jamaica Alternative Tourism, Camping, and Hiking Association (JATCHA)**.

INFORMATION

If you stand on the corner of West and Harbour streets, you can see the courthouse, post office, parish library, police station, two banks, and most of the town's shops, in one sweep.

Try **City Plaza Pharmacy** (upstairs is the **Jamaica Tourist Board** office) for news and magazines. The pharmacy sells *The Sunday Gleaner* as well. The **Jamaica Information Service (JIS)**, a government mouthpiece, is across the street at Goebel Plaza. They carry interesting pamphlets dealing with government policy, women's issues, and disaster planning, as well as copies of speeches by the prime minister and historical data on Jamaica. The **Portland Parish Library** (tel. 993-2793) is a good stop for a quiet read.

Gal Gal on Harbour St. is a drop-off/pick-up laundry service.

THE EAST COAST

SIGHTS

Jamaica's east coast is well traveled, but not by tourists. The area is out of the mainstream, so much the better for an unencumbered drive along this thundering coast.

Passing through Boston, the road winds and dips with the coastline, past the **Errol Flynn Estates** at Priestman's River and Fair Prospect. The estates are still maintained by Flynn's widow, Patrice Wymore Flynn, and include over 2,500 acres of coconut and grazing land. At Priestman's River you can follow an old road along the river to the sea, where it dumps its brown silt into the surf.

Long Bay

About five miles south of Boston, the small village of Long Bay is almost on the water. The public beach is long and picturesque, but the windward nature of this side of the island produces an often churlish surf and strong undertow. Even on a calm day, watch for the undertow. Stop anywhere for a picnic and a swim. While passing through the village, visit one of Jamaica's most well known artists, Ken Abendana Spencer. Spencer, a modernist whose paintings hang in government offices, hotel lobbies, and galleries throughout the island, welcomes drop-ins to take a look at his work. You can't miss his house; it's a big, multileveled affair that looks like a fort. Turn inland at the post office.

Seven miles farther down the coast you'll reach **Manchioneal,** named after the poisonous manchineel tree that used to grow here. The village once was important as a shipping port for bananas. Now it's best known as the turnoff point to **Reich Falls,** also spelled (and pronounced) Reach Falls. Just over two miles from the main road, it is said to be the prettiest spot in the country. No admission, just the cascading foam and limpid water of Driver's River. The falls area is maintained by farmers who work the abutting land, and a guide will show you around. A small donation would be appreciated. The small public beach at **Innis Bay** is good for a rest and a splash.

The road continues through **Hector's River,** which forms the border between Portland and St. Thomas parishes. Stop at **Quaw Hill** for a good view of the **Morant Point Lighthouse,** built in 1841 at the easternmost point in Jamaica. At **Golden Grove** you can turn off for the lighthouse—a five-mile drive past **Holland Bay Beach.** The road to the lighthouse from Holland Bay, however, is gutted and passes through a morass; it may be difficult to manage in a sedan car.

Bath
Back along the main road (Hwy. A4), continue six miles to **Port Morant,** an erstwhile export center for bananas and sugar, now a largely inactive fishing town. North of town, an eight-mile drive takes you to Bath, home of the legendary **Bath Fountain.** Along the road, note signs of building damage due to Hurricane Gilbert. St. Thomas Parish was badly hurt during that storm, and many businesses and homes are still being rebuilt.

Legend has it Bath Fountain was discovered in 1609 by a slave wounded in a flight to freedom. He stumbled upon the mineral spring, and a plunge into the water healed his wounds. By 1699, the owner of the land had sold it to the government, and the village of Bath began to grow. Word spread about the alleged healing powers of the spring, and Bath became popular among the English gentry seeking relief from the common cold, arthritis, venereal disease, rheumatism, "the depraved appetite," and the day's common ailments. Some even drank the water (sort of a turbo-injection method of getting straight to the problem) and it was said to produce a slight high. By 1747, the building surrounding the fountain was erected. Not surprisingly, a hospital was built to care for the infirm during their bath treatments.

Bath flourished as a cultural center for the English elite, some of whom had country homes in the area, until political infighting among residents ruined the ambience of the town and caused people to stay away. The village plummeted from its briefly fashionable stature, and the town has never regained its former glory.

The spring itself produces both hot, up to 128° F (53° C), and "cold" water (really just cooled slightly), a trait that is uncommon in mineral springs. Analysis of the water's mineral content shows calcium, magnesium, sodium, sulfate, silica, and chloride as the main ingredients. The water has a radioactive rating in curies per liter of 4.9 x 10-10 for the hot water, and 0.09 x 10-10 for the cold, which means nothing to the casual reader or writer, nor to the staff at the bath. Apparently, it does mean slight radioactivity, but only a fraction of the amount present in some of the world's famous spas such as Baden-Baden in Germany, and Milk River Bath, the world's most radioactive spa in south-central Jamaica (see "The Southwest Coast," p. 137).

The 13 baths are private and cleaned after each use. Cost is J$25 per adult and half that per child for each 20-minute use. The spa doesn't recommend more than two sittings in a row, as your loss of body fluids could become critical after that. They're open 1000-1700 Tues.-Sun. and public holidays when, presumably, they get their best business from the Kingston area. The spa runs a small coffee shop (goat's head soup, pastries, etc.) that opens when Bath gets busy (tel. 982-2132).

The **Bath Fountain Hotel,** bruised by Hurricane Gilbert, has undergone a massive renovation, and is now open for business. One can see that the hotel, even before the hurricane, was losing its luster. It still needs work, but the rooms are clean and comfortable. Rates are J$420 s or d with shared bath, and J$525 s or d with private bath. Rooms with private bath and balcony are J$580 s or d; rates do not include meals. This works out to about US$19-26, a good deal for a different Jamaican experience.

Bath Botanic Gardens is another relic of the glory days of Bath. Established in 1799, it's the oldest botanical garden in Jamaica. It was the first home of many of Jamaica's imported plants, including the *otaheite* apple, jacaranda, and bougainvillea. Descendants of Captain Bligh's original breadfruit tree can be seen. The garden, suffering from floods and hurricane damage, is today much smaller than it was in its heyday and the heyday of Bath.

Morant Bay

Morant Bay is the parish capital of St. Thomas and is remembered as the scene of Paul Bogle's 1865 Morant Bay Rebellion (see "History," p. 29). Bogle led a contingent of freed slaves to the courthouse to protest the unfair arrest of a man the day before. The scene became ugly, shots were fired, and in the ensuing riot over 25 were killed and the courthouse burned. Riots spread throughout St. Thomas before they were quashed, summarily and barbarically, by the authorities. Bogle and George William Gordon, a popular mixed-race legislator, were tried for sedition and hung in front of the courthouse. Over 600 were executed as conspirators. Thousands were flogged and former slaves' homes were burned to the ground.

Today Bogle and Gordon are national heroes, and a monument to Paul Bogle stands in front of the reconstructed **Morant Bay Courthouse.** The statue, a work by Edna Manley, is prominent in the square. Just east of the statue is a monument to WW I heroes. The courthouse stands in front of the old **Morant Bay Fort,** which still has cannons at guard. In 1965, excavation behind the courthouse uncovered remains of some rioters killed in the 1865 rebellion's aftermath. The remains were removed to a mass grave and a small memorial stands in honor of their sacrifice.

PRACTICALITIES

Accommodations

From Boston to Morant Bay a number of small guesthouses offer rooms. However, this area has not been developed for great numbers of visitors. **Morant Villa Hotel** (1 Wharf Rd., Morant Bay, Jamaica, W.I.; tel. 982-2422) is the best bet in Morant Bay, with prices ranging from about US$25 per night for a bed and private bath, to US$50 for a bridal suite with water views. Just east of town, on the main road at **Lyssons,** find the small and inexpensive **Goldfinger Guest House.** The beach at Lyssons is worth a visit as well.

Eating And Drinking

The jerk stands in Boston offer the best eating experience on the east coast. Long Bay and Manchioneal have roadside stands and small diners. In Morant Bay try **Chef's Seaview Restaurant and Drinking Saloon** (Lyssons Rd.; tel. 982-2449) for seafood, a pleasant view, and nightly entertainment. The Morant Villa Hotel has a restaurant and is the most likely place in the area to find live entertainment and stage shows.

Useful Phone Numbers

Reach the **Morant Bay Police** at tel. 982-2233 or 982-2521, and the **Morant Bay Post Office** at tel. 982-2294.

OCHO RIOS AND VICINITY

I think it made me a better person. It reminded me that what really matters to a man is his name, his word, and his lady.

—Mr. Busta Prendergast, commenting on the complete destruction of his Galina guesthouse by Hurricane Gilbert

Few who visited Ocho Rios 20 years ago would recognize it today. The town has grown from a small, even isolated, fishing village to a full-tilt resort area, complete with high-rise hotels and tourist-dense activities. The town's growth has been planned by the Urban Development Corporation (UDC) and the St. Ann Development Company, both government bodies charged with the appropriate evolution of the area. In Jamaica, development sometimes means tourist development, and that's what has happened in Ocho Rios. The town is, basically, a one-industry town, with over 1,000 hotel rooms added in 1992 alone. The harbor has been dredged, some of the natural white-sand beach reclaimed, piers built, and the waterfront turned into a showcase. Cruise ships, which bring great amounts of foreign exchange into the town, arrive almost

daily, sometimes stacking up in the harbor. While you can still find the charm and beauty of an older Jamaica, malls and looming hotels rule in some places.

The name Ocho Rios apparently doesn't refer to the obvious "Eight Rivers"—only three major rivers are located in the area. Most believe it's a corruption of the Spanish *chorrera,* meaning "spout," or "waterfall," of which the coastline has quite a few, including the island's most well known at Dunn's River. More falls, many of which have been harnessed for hydroelectricity, dot the beaches along the north coast.

Ocho Rios (pop. 7,800), called "Ochee" by residents, has plenty to offer and is a good jumping-off point to other hot spots and inland sights along the coast. It may not be quiet, but it's a civil place, and has a natural beauty that penetrates the planned cosmetics of developers.

ST. MARY

East of Ocho Rios lies St. Mary, one of Jamaica's smaller parishes and once a bustling center of the sugar and banana trade. Highway A4 from **Buff Bay** brings you to **Annotto Bay,** a small port town with the typical look of the north side's once-busy ports—slightly run-down but with a hint of former glory days. The Baptist church on the town's main street was built in 1894. Anotto Bay was once the center of trade for 48 area sugar estates and the capital of a parish called Metcalfe. The town took its name from *anatto* or *anatta*, a small tree that was a source of dye for the Arawaks. The tree, used by Arawaks as body paint and by later cultures to darken cooking oil, probably grew prolifically in the area. Today it is rarely seen.

At Annotto Bay you can branch south on the A3 road toward **Castleton,** where you can stop at a 15-acre botanic garden on the banks of the **Wag Water River.** The gardens have been neglected over the years, but you can still see species of teak, mango, pandanus (from the Pacific), and coffee on the grounds. Admission is free and the gardens are open daily. The road south from Castleton continues on a wind through the hills following the Wag Water, toward Kingston.

PORT MARIA TO ORACABESSA

Port Maria

The west branch of the A3 from Annotto Bay brings you toward **Port Maria,** capital of St. Mary. Turn north at **Albany** toward **Sonrise Christian Retreat** (tel. 996-2351, formerly Strawberry Fields) and **Don Christopher's Point,** the site of an extraordinary series of beaches and small coves where you can camp. Don Christopher's Point is believed to be the place where the defeated Spanish, under Ysassi (see "History," p. 21) fled forever from Jamaica. Look for **Tacky's Falls** along the way.

When you reach Port Maria you can tell by the town's layout that it once was a thriving port. Now it is one of the poorest on the north coast. The Spanish considered it an important town, second only to Spanish Town as a center for commerce and trade. They dubbed it Puerta Santa Maria, and its natural port, separated into two parts by a large jetty of rocks, is one of the prettiest in the area.

The main street passes through a small market and bus stands. At the west end of town is St. Mary Parish Church, built in 1861. Next to the church is **St. Mary Parish Library** and a monument to **Tacky,** the Cormorantee slave who led one of the island's first slave uprisings (see "History," p. 27). Tacky's Rebellion originated at **Frontier Estate** on Easter in 1760, and continued for a month before the fighting was put down and Tacky was shot by a Maroon marksman.

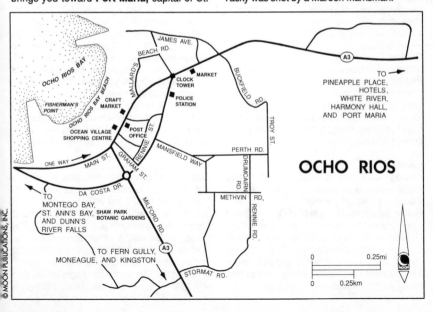

OCHO RIOS

*work by artist
Lenbert Pearlson*

Across the street from the church is the gutted police station, destroyed by fire in 1988, and the parish council offices. In the Port Maria Courthouse, the labor and political leader Alexander Bustamante was tried in a 1946 manslaughter trial.

You can turn south to **Brimmer Hall,** a working Jamaican plantation that features lunches, shopping, and an open jitney ride through the coconut and banana fields. It's a tourist thing, but can be fun and informative. The plantation is open daily and runs tours at 1100, 1330, and 1530. Cost is about US$15.

Quebec

Nearby in **Quebec** you can stop at **Quebec Plantation** (tel. 994-2532) for lunch. The plantation is a working banana, citrus, and coffee farm, and they're soon to open the great house for accommodation and tours. For now, they have horseback riding, a bar, and a moderately priced restaurant.

Galina

Back on the A3, head up to **Galina,** another small village with rows of homes lining both sides of the coastal road. At the crest of a nearby hill is **Firefly,** the estate of the late Noel Coward, British playwright and bon vivant. Coward lived the last 20 years of his life here, and left the estate to the Jamaica government through his longtime companion, Graham Payn. It's said that the two first discovered the 1,000-foot-high plot of land during a visit to **Goldeneye,** some three miles

away, then the home of Ian Fleming, author of the James Bond series and others. (Goldeneye is not open to the public.)

The home has been left pretty much as it was when Coward died on 26 March 1973. You can see his bedroom, painting studio, and living room with two pianos, even the Coppertone suntan lotion in the bedroom where he died. His composing room, the infamous "Room With a View," has a wide window with a view of the Caribbean. The view toward Port Maria includes **Galina Point and Lighthouse,** the northernmost point in Jamaica, and **Cabarita Island,** just off the coast. (You can swim at **Pagee Beach**, across from the small island, or arrange with a fisherman to take you out to Cabarita where you can pass the day swimming and walking the island.)

Coward is buried in a grave surrounded by a white cage on the slope of the estate's hill. Daily hours are 0900-1700, and the cost is about J$20 for adults and J$5 for children.

Oracabessa

Oracabessa is a small town with a series of fine beaches ensconced in resort complexes. You'll begin to see the resort syndrome get stronger here, with roadside craft shacks and small restaurants springing up all about. The name Oracabessa is either derived from the Spanish *oro,* meaning "gold," or *aura,* meaning "air" or "breeze," and *cabeza,* meaning "head" or "highland." The translation might be "Golden Highland" or it might be "Air Head," but the interpretation most give is "fanciful."

Stop at **Murdock's Beach** for a swim and a rest. At **Rio Nuevo** you can see a monument to the famous battle in which the last remaining Spanish were defeated in their bid to retake the island from their English conquerors (see "History," p. 21). From the vantage point high on the hill, you can see the river and **Fisherman's Beach** below in Rio Nuevo Bay. The small park is free, and open until sunset daily. Ask John, the caretaker, to show you around the small garden on the grounds where they grow pimento, soursop, aloe, chili peppers, and mangoes. Later, go down to the small fishing village and beach where you can talk with the fishermen and possibly arrange a coastal trip.

SIGHTS

Ocho Rios is not the kind of place that's steeped in obvious history, at least not in its present incarnation. It is, for the most part, a planned town that's growing to service tourism, and many of its sights are based on that.

The proximity of Ocho Rios to Montego Bay (67 miles) and to Kingston (54 miles) makes it easily accessible, and the airport at Oracabessa makes it even more so for those who want to get there quickly. The harbor, which has been dredged, is not only appealing but has made Ocho Rios a prime stopover spot for cruise ships. Nearly 75% of all cruise-ship calls to Jamaica stop over in Ocho Rios, which means close to 300 cruise-ship calls per year with a total of over 300,000 passengers—more than double the number of passengers going to Montego Bay, Kingston, and Port Antonio combined. Since the passengers stay only for a few hours, perhaps a day, they're interested in fast sights, fast foods, and shopping. In a sense, that's what Ocho Rios offers.

Dunn's River Falls

Dunn's River Falls (tel. 974-2857) is probably Jamaica's most well known attraction. Just a couple of miles west of town, the falls are a 600-foot climb from a white-sand beach where the river empties into the ocean. The photos you see in area hotel brochures of people holding hands while climbing over cascading water were taken here. It's a Disney World-esque scene, paradise paved, with altogether too many crafts stalls and big tour buses about. Most people like it and get a kick out of the climbing, but this is certainly not untouched Jamaica. Admission is US$3, open daily 0900-1800. Guides will take you up the falls, and most people tip them after it's over. You don't have to climb; a paved path alongside parts of the river allows you to walk and take in the view.

Prospect Plantation

Prospect Plantation (tel. 974-2058) east of town is a working plantation on which pimento,

statue of black consciousness leader Marcus Garvey, in front of the parish library, St. Ann's Bay

PHYLLIS LUNITA

cassava, pineapple, *otaheite* apple, sugarcane, and coffee are grown. You can see trees planted by visitors such as Prince Philip, Pierre Trudeau, and Sir Winston Churchill. The 11,000-acre ground is set in the hills with views of the ocean and the **White River** gorge. The tour is about 1.5 hours long. It may seem a little hokey, but this is a great way to learn about commercial crops grown in Jamaica, and the setting is spectacular. The farm also offers guided horseback rides through the White River gorge, and on trails throughout the farm. The tour is US$12 per person, Mon.-Sat. at 1030, 1400, and 1530. Sunday the tour runs at 1100, 1330, and 1500.

Fern Gully

Fern Gully is a scenic three-mile drive along Hwy. A3 south toward Spanish Town. The area is a protected reserve, and the attraction is a green-tinted passage through a forest of ferns that form an archway over the road. It's believed that the gully, which was an old watercourse, was planted in the 1880s. Prolific exhaust from traffic has killed off some species of ferns, but the majority still grow. Along the road you'll see a number of crafts stalls, some tacky but fun, where bargains can be struck for carvings and straw crafts.

White River

The White River forms the boundary between St. Mary and St. Ann parishes. It's the longest river in St. Ann, and is now somewhat subdued due to a hydroelectric station at **Cascade,** near the small town of **Upton,** which has slowed its flow.

You can take a short trip down the river in a guided raft on the **Calypso Rafting** tour. Cost is US$30 per raft. At the White River Bridge just west of Prospect Plantation, follow the sign to the **Jungle Lobster House,** a tawdry little lobster shack on the banks of the river with some of the better eats in town. The bamboo river rafts are next door.

Botanic Gardens

Shaw Park Gardens, a small botanic garden on the west side of town, has an array of exotic plants and trees common in Jamaica. It's open daily 0800-1800, and admission is J$25.

Helicopter Tours

One of the newer tours in town is operated by **Helitours Jamaica** (120 Main St.; tel. 974-2265, fax 974-2183). Big and little kids love it. The company offers three tours: a 15-minute hop of the Ocho Rios area at US$45 pp; a 30-minute run that also flies west to Oracabessa along the coast; and a 60-minute flight for US$180 that takes you over Kingston and Spanish Town and across the Blue Mountains.

Beaches

If you begin to think of Jamaica's north coast topography as one long beach, you won't be far off—you can go few miles without finding somewhere to splash and dunk. Ocho Rios is no exception. Aside from prime beachfront reserved for hotels, the two most popular beaches in town are **Fisherman's Beach** and **Ocho Rios Bay Beach.** Fisherman's is located at **Fisherman's Point,** next to the cleverly named **Fisherman's Point Resort,** and is a public beach—meaning no admission, no maintenance. But it's an available place to swim.

Ocho Rios Bay Beach is often known as Turtle Beach, in reference to a high-rise hotel and condominium complex on the beach called **Turtle Towers.** The beach is maintained by the Urban Development Corporation (UDC) and is also known as the UDC Beach. The beach is clean and free of hassles. It has facilities, including fast-food shacks and changing rooms. Admission is J$7.

Other area beaches are at the base of Dunn's River Falls and along the banks of the White River.

Vicinity Of Ocho Rios

Highway A3 past Fern Gully takes you to **Moneague,** formerly an important crossroad on the Ocho Rios-to-Spanish Town journey. The name probably comes from a corruption of the Spanish *managua,* referring to an area underground lake which surfaces on occasion. The town used to house elegant hotels, but when Spanish Town lost its glory and the advent of motorcars made the trip less time consuming, Moneague became just another inland town waiting for something to happen. South of Moneague the road climbs **Mt. Diablo,** some 1,800 feet above sea level.

Turn north and take Hwy. A1 toward **St. Ann's Bay,** birthplace of Marcus Garvey and capital of St. Ann Parish. St. Ann's Bay is also only seven miles from Ocho Rios, so the trip can be easily accomplished in a day by Hwy. A3. The town is built on a hill, with streets that run like river estuaries down to the ocean. The bay was originally called Santa Gloria by the Spanish, and nearby is the site of Sevilla la Nueva, the old Spanish capital abandoned in 1534. The site extends from the **Columbus Monument** west of town toward St. Ann's Bay.

A statue honoring Marcus Garvey stands in front of the parish library, on the main road by the **Negro River.** Garvey was born in 1887 at 32 Market St., and went on to become considered

the father of black nationalism in Jamaica and worldwide. Through his Universal Negro Improvement Association (UNIA), he aimed to "unite all the Negro peoples of the world into one great body" and to espouse the cause of black pride and nationalism through writings, rapport with world leaders, and the establishment of financial institutions that favored black enterprises. He was persecuted, even prosecuted, during his lifetime, and died in England in 1940, frustrated and stymied in many of his efforts. His remains were returned to Jamaica in 1964 and interred at National Heroes Park in Kingston.

Along the St. Ann's Bay coast, stop at **Mammee, Roxborough,** or **Alterry** beaches.

PRACTICALITIES

ACCOMMODATIONS

The Ocho Rios boom has produced a plethora of accommodations ranging from tent camps and guesthouses to super-luxury, all-inclusive hotels. Remember, accommodation is cheaper and often negotiable during the off-season, roughly spring through early fall. Some hotels charge an additional 10% service charge, or tip, on top of your bill. Some include it in the bill, and others leave tipping to your discretion. A government tax of 10% is charged for most hotels, depending on class. In all cases it is best to write or call ahead to confirm current tariffs.

Inexpensive
Hummingbird Haven (Box 95, Ocho Rios, Jamaica, W.I.; tel. 974-5188) is a camping and cabin site located east of town on the main road near White River. Operated by Audre Barned and the very informative and slightly eccentric Peter Hudson, the camp is in an excellent spot to explore the river or town that's two miles down the road. There are 20 campsites at US$5 for two per night if you have a tent, and US$7.50 if you rent one. Cabins start at US$20 for two persons, and you can pack more than two in some of them at extra cost. The cabins have hot and cold water and private bathrooms. A small restaurant serves meals on request, full breakfasts at about J$130,

sandwiches for about J$50-80. Hummingbird charges no room tax and no service charge.

Hunter's Inn (86 Main St., Ocho Rios, Jamaica, W.I.; tel. 974-5627) is a small guesthouse in a central location, just east of town. Rooms per night are J$450 s and J$550 d (US$20-25). The location makes eating out an easy adventure.

Hunter's Lodge (Tower Isle, Ocho Rios, Jamaica, W.I.; tel. 974-5627) is owned by the same family that operates the Inn, the Jonssons. It's about seven miles east of town, near Rio Nuevo Beach. They've got six rooms with double beds, cold running water, and an outdoor public bar. Breakfasts are available on request. The rooms are J$400 s and J$500 d, no tax, no service charge.

Little Shaw Park Guest House (21 Shaw Park Rd., Milford, Ocho Rios, Jamaica, W.I.; tel. 974-2177) is owned by Trevor and Deborah Mitchell and located in the hills above town on the road to Shaw Park. It's a beautiful little place with great views, and currently has five guest rooms with three more on the way. The water is hot and cold, soap and towels provided. They will cook breakfast and dinner on request. You can buy your food and bring it up to the house. It's five minutes by foot to town and a beach, and a short hike to **Milford Falls.** Doubles are US$40, no tax or service charge, and negotiable in off-season. Camping is allowed on the grounds at US$15 d, per tent.

Marine Villas (6 James Ave., Ocho Rios, Jamaica, W.I.; tel. 974-2822) is just around the corner from the Marine View Hotel, which has the same owners (see below). There's a disco upstairs and others across the street, so expect some mighty sounds at night. You can buy food at Happy Grove Grocery next door, where the proprietor, in fact, appears to be truly happy. Tariff is about US$40 s or d, year-round, negotiable in off-season, no added charges.

Seeker's Lounge and Guest House (25 James Ave., Ocho Rios, Jamaica, W.I.; tel. 974-5763) is located in the corner of a small shopping plaza. It's got 20 rooms, including some with water beds, and both private and shared baths. The location is central, and you can eat at the **Sun Glow Restaurant** in the plaza. A tennis court is available for guest use. Year-round rates are about US$20 per room, no tax and no service charge. This hotel has had some problems with security in the past.

Pentus Guest Villa (3 Shaw Park Rd., Ocho Rios, Jamaica, W.I.; tel. 974-2313) is owned by Leila Rutty, an Ocho Rios fixture and wonderfully informative woman. Her comfortable house is small and located in the hills near Shaw Park, but town is close by. This may be the best deal in town for inexpensive accommodation, though she has only four rooms. Ask her to show you her garden in the backyard, where she grows pawpaw, pimento, soursop, breadfruit, and more. Rutty's recipe for pimento liqueur is featured in "Eating and Drinking," p. 73. Rooms are US$20 s, US$30 d, and US$40 t, year-round, no added costs. If she can't fit you in, she has friends whom she'll contact to put you up.

Special mention should go to **Reynold's Brooklyn Inn** (188 Main St., Ocho Rios, Jamaica, W.I.; tel. 974-2480) only because it is on the main road and very visible. It's inexpensive in a flophouse kind of way, though no one seems to be there long enough to check guests in. Rooms have shared baths and are about US$12 s and US$15 d, year-round, certainly cheap, but you get your share of noise and exhaust from the road. No charges are added.

Moderate
Carleen's Villa (85-A Main St., Ocho Rios, Jamaica, W.I.; tel. 974-5431) is a five-room guesthouse near the center of town, with a concrete

beachfront. This is a good place if you want to be close to the busy town area. Rooms are Caribbean-cheery, and there is a restaurant. Tariff is US$50 s or d, per room, no added charges.

Falcon Crest Hotel (Box 552, Ocho Rios, Jamaica, W.I.; tel. 974-5416) has had some problems getting business. It's central, off Main St., has 24 rooms, several restaurants, bars, and discos, and is more nightclub than hotel. Main attraction: an enormous indoor theater/arena that seats 2,500, possibly one of the premier reggae and performance spots in town. Rooms are a bit expensive at US$58 per room or US$65 with breakfast in the summer, all charges included. During the busy season, add about US$30 per room.

Hermosa Resort Village (Lot 8, Hermosa Beach, Ocho Rios, Jamaica, W.I.; tel. 974-2660) has townhouse-type villas, kitchens, and a pool. Tariff is US$90 d in the winter and US$75 d in the summer, all taxes and service charges included. It may seem more expensive than moderate, but you can fit up to four in a villa (for slightly more cost) to reduce the pp rate.

Hibiscus Lodge Hotel (Box 52, Ocho Rios, Jamaica, W.I.; tel. 974-2676 or 974-2183, fax 974-1874) is the home of the famous Almond Tree Restaurant. The hotel itself is small, just 26 rooms, and sits on a beautiful perch overlooking the ocean. You access the water from a sundeck; there is no beach. Summer rates are US$77 s or d for a room with a ceiling fan, to US$101 s or d with a/c. Winter rates range US$89-110. All taxes and charges are included, as is continental breakfast.

Jeff's (10 Main St., Ocho Rios, Jamaica, W.I.; tel. 974-2664) is as downtown as downtown gets, across from the UDC Beach. Jeff's restaurant features excellent seafood. The rooms are apartments and most have a/c and private baths. Rates are US$35 in summer, US$40 in winter, s or d, all charges included.

Little Pub Complex (Box 256, Ocho Rios, Jamaica, W.I.; tel. 974-5826 or 974-2324, fax 974-5825) is another Main St. hotel and something of an Ocho Rios tradition. The complex has shops, a bar and nightclub, restaurants, and the hotel. The place is very central and very busy. Summer rates are US$55 d, and winter is about US$70 d—government taxes, service charges, and breakfast included.

Marine View Hotel (9 James Ave., Ocho Rios P.O., Jamaica, W.I.; tel. 974-5753) is central, just off Da Costa Dr. in the center of town. It's medium sized (45 rooms) and basic, with a pool and a homey atmosphere. Some rooms have a/c, some have fans. They serve breakfast and dinner in a funky restaurant. Summer rates: US$50 d a/c, US$44 non a/c. Winter is more expensive at US$53-63 d. Room tax and service charges are included.

Ocean Sands Hotel (Ocho Rios P.O., Jamaica, W.I.; tel. 974-2605) is another downtown hotel on James Ave., this one with its own private beach. There's a pool, restaurant, and gift shop but the real attraction is its walking distance to everything around. Tariff (includes breakfast) is US$65 s or d in the summer and US$85 s or d in the winter.

Parkway Inn Hotel (60 Main St., Ocho Rios, Jamaica, W.I.; tel. 974-2667) is a new addition to the popular local restaurant and hangout, the Parkway. The inn has 21 clean rooms and a honeymoon suite, all with a/c, private baths, and hot and cold water. The downtown location is convenient. Rates are US$55 s, d, or t on the first floor, and US$66 s, d, or t on the second floor, which features balconies. Rates include all taxes and service charges.

The Village Hotel (54-56 Main St., Ocho Rios, Jamaica, W.I.; tel. 974-9193/6, fax 974-5440, U.S.A tel. 800-835-9810) is another downtown hotel, right on Main St. in the shopping district center. The hotel is small at 22 rooms, is clean, and smells like a new car. Rooms have all the amenities, and there's a small and inexpensive restaurant. Rooms are standard or deluxe, US$50-75 s or d in summer, and US$70-95 s or d in winter. Two- or three-bedroom suites with kitchens are US$100-150 in summer, and US$140-210 in season. Add 10% GCT and 10% service charge.

Luxury

Ciboney Ocho Rios (P.O Box 728, Ocho Rios, Jamaica, W.I.; tel. 974-1027/36, fax 974-5838, U.S.A tel. 800-777-7800) is built from an old plantation great house, surrounded by villa suites. The hotel is all-inclusive, and that means the standard meals and drinks, plus complimentary massages and sports. Ninety, that's nine-oh, swimming pools dot the grounds, many private or semi-private, attached to suites. You're not on the beach here, but transport is arranged. Basic rates are US$290 s and US$380 d in the high season for a standard room, to US$400 s and US$530 d for a one-bedroom villa. Two- and three-bedroom villas are available.

Couples (Box 330, Ocho Rios, Jamaica, W.I.; tel. 974-4271, fax 974-4439, U.S.A. tel. 800-858-8009, Canada tel. 800-553-4320) is a SuperClubs all-inclusive hotel for, you guessed it, couples only. Recent million-dollar renovations, which include the addition of a jungle garden and several two-bedroom villas, have made it one of the nicest in Ocho Rios. The hotel has an excellent beach, including a nude beach on a small offshore islet, all water sports, five tennis courts, racquetball, squash court, golf, horseback riding, cycling, four restaurants, and entertainment, including comedy. The emphasis here is romance, and the hotel performs a staggering average of three weddings per day (included in the package—you bring the rings and the gown). The hotel is located just east of town on the old Tower Isle complex. The tariff changes four times per year, but the basic off-season rate is US$2399-2599 per couple per week, three nights minimum stay. Suites off-season are US$3059 per couple per week.

The Enchanted Garden (P.O. Box 284, Ocho Rios, Jamaica, W.I.; tel. 974-1400, fax 974-5823, North America tel. 800-323-5655, U.K. tel. 081-688-1418) is a newly refurbished resort complex on the grounds of the old Carinosa Gardens in the hills above Ocho Rios. The concept here is unique: an all-inclusive resort spa devoid of rah-rah beach resort activities, set in a 20-acre sculpted garden. The grounds are lush, with 14 waterfalls (one was apparently named "Brain Falls" by Mick Jagger) and trees and plants labelled for those interested. Five restaurants are spread across the grounds, including the gourmet L'Eau Mirage and the Seaquarium, a central gathering spot with a Middle Eastern motif and aquariums holding rare and exotic fish. Spa-type activities, such as massages, steam baths, facials, pedicures, and the like, are included in the package. Accommodation is 112 rooms, suites, or villas, scattered everywhere. All meals, drinks, entertainment, disco, sports, and taxes are included. Winter rates are US$1100-1400 pp per week (based on double occupancy) for rooms and junior suites. One- to three-bedroom garden villas are US$1300-1500 weekly pp based on double occupancy per bedroom.

Two Ocho Rios resorts have combined to form the new **Jamaica Grande** (P.O. Box 245, Ocho Rios, Jamaica, W.I.; tel. 974-2201, U.S.A. tel. 800-228-9898), a Ramada resort. The former **Americana Beach Resort** and **Mallards Beach Hotel** now make up the 720-room mega-hotel on Mallards Bay beach. The resort is all high rise and glitz, with five restaurants, several waterfall-enhanced swimming pools, water sports, fitness center, and the rest, and will appeal to many because of its central location and busy ambience. Rooms are standard, superior and deluxe, and suites are available. Standard rate is US$190-210 d per night in winter, and US$117 d in summer. Add 10% GCT.

Sandals Ocho Rios/Sandals Dunn's River are two of the Sandals all-inclusive chains in the area. The hotel at Dunn's River is relatively new. Each hotel has the standard all-inclusive packages, and rates vary up to four times per year. Remember, they're for couples only and, though not explicitly stated, for heterosexual couples. Sandals Ocho Rios runs US$2465-2960 per couple per room, seven nights, during the high season. The Dunn's River hotel is slightly more expensive, at US$2920-4195 per couple per room, for seven nights (7610 S.W. 61st Ave., Miami, FL 33143, tel. 800-SANDALS; or 161 Fulham Rd., London, SW3 6SN, tel. 01-581-9895; Jamaica tel. 974-5691/3).

Villas

Ocho Rios happens to be the headquarters of the **Jamaica Association of Villas and Apartments (JAVA),** a representative body of those types of accommodation in Jamaica. JAVA (Box 298, Ocho Rios, Jamaica, W.I.; tel. 974-2508, fax 974-2967, U.S.A. tel. 800-221-8830) lists over 75 villas and apartments along the north coast in the Ocho Rios-Falmouth area, as well as hundreds throughout the country. Villas and apartments, which hold from two to a dozen people, range from US$300 to over US$6000 per week. Villas are usually located near or on a beach, and often have colorful names such as "Fantasy" and "Xanadu." A personal favorite: "Cirrhosis." Stop in at their offices on Pineapple Place, on the main road east of downtown, and ask for Carmen McKnight.

Port Maria-Oracabessa Area

Accommodation in the Port Maria-Oracabessa area isn't a problem. **Mannings Hotel** in Port Maria has rooms with shared baths for US$10 and up.

Blue Harbour (P.O. Box 50, Port Maria, Jamaica, W.I.; tel. 994-2262), is a group of three villas on a seven-acre estate once owned by Noel Coward, near his Firefly estate. The estate overlooks the ocean, and the villas are decorated with some of Coward's original furniture. Meals are available. Rates range from US$25-60 pp, depending on the accommodation and time of year.

Casa Maria Hotel (P.O. Box 10, Port Maria, Jamaica, W.I.; tel. 994-2323, fax 994-2324, U.S.A. tel. 800-222-6927) has 20 rooms plus suites and is comfortable in a '60s sort of way. It sits on a hill outside of town overlooking its own beach and bar, the **Kokomo,** and has views of Port Maria and the coast. It's an easy 18-mile ride to Ocho Rios for shopping or whatever. All the rooms are different (get number 27 for the best ocean view and a breezy corner balcony) and run US$50-70 s and US$60-80 d in the summer, US$70-90 s and US$80-100 d in the winter. Triples and quads are also avaliable for as much as US$110. Add 5% tax, plus a 10% service charge year-round. Slide onto the comfortable deco barstools in the hotel bar and wonder if life gets any better.

Blue Rock Estate (Galina District, P.O. Box 151, Port Maria, Jamaica, W.I.; no telephone) is run by the aforementioned Busta Prendergast, a former soldier in the British army and repatriated Jamaican. If nothing else, go down to the guesthouse and have a drink and chat with him. His perspectives on Jamaica are refreshingly incorrigible, formed from years of living around the world. Yet he's been pulled home by a fierce patriotism and a love for the country.

The guesthouse sign is on the north side of the main road in Galina. Prendergast has 10 rooms called anything from the Blue Room to the Sunny Room to the Gym. Summer rates run J$150-450, and one room even has a water bed. The rooms have private baths but the water is cold. Get the Sunny Room, which has an ocean view and private patio. Prendergast will cook what he calls Jamaican/Canadian cuisine—seafood moose perhaps? The room rates include laundry. Swimming from the small rock cliffs is excellent.

Boscobel Beach Resort (P.O. Box 63, Ocho Rios, Jamaica, W.I.; tel. 974-3331/8, fax 974-3270, U.S.A. tel. 800-858-8009) is one of the SuperClubs chain of all-inclusive hotels. The concept of this hotel, which makes sense today, is that it's geared toward families—one child under 14 per parent stays free if sharing the parent's room. They offer activities and baby-sitting services for children (or is it for the parents?) and the whole place is squeaky clean. The grounds are huge and the beaches, which feature special children's activities, are among the best in the area. There are six rate schedules throughout the year. Rooms have either lanais or mountain views, starting at US$725 per parent (based on double occupancy) for three nights, to one-bedroom suites at US$949 per parent (double occupancy) for three nights, in the highest season. Rates are less p/d for longer stays, and less in the summer. All meals, drinks, transfers, and activities are included.

EATING AND DRINKING

Downtown Ocho Rios consists of two main roads: Main St. is a one- way road heading east when downtown, but becomes a regular two-way road east of the clock tower; Da Costa Dr., often confusingly referred to as the Main Rd., is the A3 bypass. The two roads are parallel, and much of the shopping, eating, dancing, swimming, and fooling around happens on or between these roads. Certainly Main St. is a place to start exploring Ocho Rios, and it's also a place to eat.

ackee

BOB RACE

Fast Foods

The standard fast-food restaurants are all represented on Main St.—**Burger King, Shakey's Pizza, Kentucky Fried Chicken,** and the ubiquitous Jamaican chain, **Mother's.** All are good quality, in their own fast-food way.

For pastries, bread, and meat pies, try **Tropical Oven** or **Honey Bee's,** both on Main Street. The **Leaf of Life Lounge** on Main St. has patties, boiled eggs, and bar food mostly, but it's a nice place to sit and watch Ocho Rios pass by.

More fast and reasonable food can be found at **Double Happiness** (14 Newlin St.; tel. 974-2984), with Chinese and Jamaican; and **Won Ton Foods** (75 Main St.; tel. 974-2418), the same. **China Town Restaurant** (Island Plaza, Main St.; tel. 974-5667) is open for lunch and breakfast only. **Hong Kong International** on Main St. is another Asian-cuisine restaurant.

Park-Way Restaurant and Lounge (Da Costa Dr.; tel. 974-2667) is a very popular local hangout, moderately priced, and is noted for its seafood. **Beach Bowl** (Ocho Rios Bay Beach; tel. 974-5008) has beach food—burgers, fries, jerk meat, *ackee,* drinks, some seafood. **Ocho Rios Jerk Centre** (Main St.; tel. 974-2549) is, no, not a place where used-car salesmen congregate to exchange apparel secrets, but one of the better-known jerk-meat centers in Ocho Rios. Open until the late hours, it's a popular hangout as well. Try **Jungle Lobster House** below the bridge on the White River—a very Jamaican atmosphere with a "Heart of Darkness" ambience, complete with Rastas and fishermen hanging around— and excellent lobster at about US$20 for a 1.5-pound beast. **Lobster Pot,** next to Jeff's on Main St., is good for inexpensive seafood.

Try **Mom's Restaurant** (7 Evelyn Ave.; tel. 974-2811) for inexpensive Jamaican, but make sure you wash your hands before sitting down to dinner. **The Forever Café** (50 Main St.; tel. 974-9287) serves good Jamaican and American-style breakfasts, as well as lunch and dinner. **Double V Bunny Hutch** (109 Main St.; tel. 974-0174) serves jerk pork and barbecue chicken and has, strangely, a small garden and zoo on the grounds. The zoo holds guinea pigs, rabbits, mongooses, donkeys, and other local animals.

Mexican

You'll note some confusing business with the two **Blue Cantina** Mexican restaurants in town. One is east of town on the A3, and is billed as the "Original Blue Cantina." The other, called "Blue Cantina #1," is at the corner of James Ave. and Main Street. The owner of the latter is the original owner of the Blue Cantina, and an ex-partner now owns the original. Clearly, a name dispute is going on here. Nevertheless, they're both fine and moderately priced, and serve the best—meaning only—Mexican food in town.

Gourmet

On a more elegant note, try **Harmony Hall** (on Hwy. A3, four miles east of town; tel. 974-4478), an 1886 "great house" with a lunch-dinner restaurant and bar, as well as one of the most popular art galleries on the north coast. Restaurant owner Pam Chong and Chef Egbert Gibbs's recipe for *ackee* and saltfish sandwiches is featured in the general "Eating and Drinking" section, p. 71.

Almond Tree (Hibiscus Lodge, Main St.; tel. 974-2676) is one of the town's finest gourmet restaurants, with a nice setting on the water. **Evita's** (tel. 974-2333) is located in the hills west of downtown. The food is authentic Italian, as is Eva, the owner, and prices are reasonable (more so when you opt for the ample half-servings, offered at lunch and dinner). The view of town and the ocean is worth the trip, and members of The Rolling Stones, who own houses in the area, are reportedly frequent diners. The **Carib Inn Restaurant** (Main St.; tel. 974-2445) serves solid seafood.

The Ruins (Da Costa Dr.; tel. 974-2442) is a Chinese-and-continental cuisine, lunch-and-dinner restaurant, set next to a 40-foot waterfall. Impressive stuff. Take a drive east on the A3 toward Boscobel, and you'll find **Piccolo Mondo** (tel. 974-3234), formerly Moxon's, which serves Italian. Their advertisement honestly states "Reputedly the Best."

In addition, all hotels have good to excellent restaurants and most are open seven days a week.

Markets

For food shopping, the first place to start is the farmer's market on Main St., east of the clock tower. An authentic Jamaican market, it has fruit, vegetables, jerk vendors, and hustle and bustle all day long. On Main St. downtown, across from the post office, you'll find **General Food Supermarket,** a complete-line store that has the added bonus of air-conditioning. General has a large selection of Jamaican products as well, including rums, liqueurs, spices, and Blue Mountain Coffee. Go next door to **The Healthy Way** for vegetarian food. They also serve take-out breakfast and lunch, including steamed fish or veggie burgers with soursop or carrot juice.

SHOPPING

Because of its popularity with cruise ships, Ocho Rios is something of a frenzied shopping mecca. In addition to the dozens of duty-free shops, you'll find a half-dozen shopping complexes, another half-dozen crafts markets, and an equal number of art galleries. Many are very good; many just offer the same old stuff. For some people, though, that's what shopping is all about.

Ocean Village Shopping Centre is the largest in town, with over 50 shops. Half are curio and tourist shops, but try **Everybody's Bookshop** (tel. 974-2932) for magazines, newspapers, and books. **Vibes Music Shack** (tel. 975-5145) has a good selection of reggae and contemporary Jamaican music, plus T-shirts, posters, and Rasta crafts. The Jamaica Tourist Board (JTB) has its offices on the second floor of Ocean Village, above General Food Supermarket.

Other shopping complexes include **Pineapple**

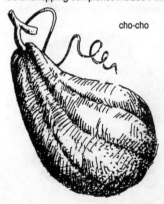

cho-cho

BOB RACE

Place Shopping Centre in which the JAVA offices are located (on Hwy. A3). To the east is **Coconut Grove Shopping Centre,** another string of duty-free shops and crafts stores. **Little Pub Shopping Complex,** at the west end of Main St., has more of the usual suspects, with a bar for the weary of foot. **Taj Mahal** on Main St. is another crafts and trinket center. **Island Plaza** behind Burger King on Main St. has clothes shops, restaurants, and an art gallery.

For photography equipment, go to **Frank Bailey Photographic Studio** (2 Rennie Rd.; tel. 974-2711).

Crafts Markets

Next to Ocean Village is the **Ocho Rios Craft Park,** a large, stall-filled, outdoor market where the sell is hard but the crafts are fairly priced. Across the street is the **Olde Market Craft Shoppes,** more of the same, but suspect because of the "olde" and "shoppe" business. Behind Pineapple Place is the **Pineapple Craft Circle,** which has carving and curio stalls. Best bet for Ocho Rios shopping: Take a long walk down Main St., end to end, and if you can't find it there, you can't find it. There's also a crafts market at Coconut Grove.

Perhaps the better deals, especially in woodcarvings, can be found along Fern Gully, where there are numerous stalls and one complex called the **Fern Gully Craft Centre.** Here the sell can be hard, nothing new, but the prices are better than in town at the outset.

Art Galleries

Art galleries are all about, and the best are not necessarily downtown. **Lloyd's Ceramics** (Tower Isle; tel. 974-4416) is out of town, near Couple's resort, but worth the drive. You can go in and see potters at work, at wheels or paint stations. The ceramics are known throughout the country, and the prices are reasonable. They're open Mon.-Sat. until 1600, Sunday until 1300.

Harmony Hall Gallery (tel. 974-4222) is in the same building as the restaurant. It has a wide selection of work by well-known artists, including Rita Genet and George Rodney, plus displays of jewelry, crafts, and books.

Frame Centre Gallery (Island Plaza; tel. 974-2374) is located behind Burger King on Main Street. The gallery is small but carries art from some of Jamaica's finest contemporary artists. **The Art Mart** (Ocean Village Shopping Centre; tel. 974-2243) is a small crafts shop that sells art as well.

SPORTS AND RECREATION

Water Sports

As you'd expect, water sports dominate activity in and around Ocho Rios Bay. The bay and area beaches range from good to excellent for diving, though at river mouths visibility is reduced by sediment. **Fantasea Divers** (tel. 974-5344, U.S.A. tel. 800-522-DIVE) is located at both the **Sans Souci** resort hotel on the main road part of Main St., and at **Boscobel Beach Club** in Oracabessa. They're a PADI facility and offer dive packages that include accommodation at those hotels, starting at about US$550 pp per week.

Garfield Dive Station (tel. 974-5749) is located at Ocho Rios Bay Beach. They offer a full line of diving, snorkeling, and water sports equipment, including glass-bottom boat rides, parasails, jet skis, and sailboarding. **Water Sports Enterprises** (tel. 974-2185) is located at the Jamaica Grande, with much of the same.

Princess of the Sea (tel. 974-1480) water sports is located at the UDC Beach, and provides a wide range of diving and snorkeling services. Basic rates are US$40 for a one-tank dive with equipment, US$70 for a two-tank dive, and US$50 for a night dive. US$15 will get you a snorkel safari, and US$25 is the cost of a sunset cruise. Half-day fishing charters from US$200 are also arranged.

Rafting down the White River, called calypso rafting, is a 45-minute drift down the largest river in Ocho Rios. It's a relaxing way to spend some time—relaxing, that is, after running the gamut of "helpers" who will try to steer you in the right direction. The cost is about US$30 per raft for two, including the services of a guide. Turn off at the White River bridge, three miles from town. They're open daily 0900-1700 (tel. 974-2527).

Cruises and chartered fishing boats are most often found at the public dock on The Ocho Rios Bay Beach. The *Triple B* (tel. 974-3312), a 37-foot boat, is available for fishing charters. The *Red Stripe* (tel. 924-5762) is a cruise ship,

Dunn's River Falls

and takes groups out for sunset or day cruises. The *Heave-Ho* (tel. 974-5367) does the same. Prices for fishing charters range from US$1200 per half-day and up.

Ocho Rios is the host of the annual **Ocho Rios International Marlin Tournament,** held in late September or early October. The tournament involves prize money, trophies, really big fish, bigger boats, and a flurry of local activity; if you're interested in participating, plan to register early. Call 922-7160 for details.

Horseback Riding

Horseback riders will find easy trails at **Prospect Plantation** (tel. 974-2058), sometimes along the same trails used by the guided tours. You'll go along White River Gorge and through parts of the 900-acre working plantation. **Chukka Cove Farm** (tel. 972-2506) is an equestrian farm located west of St. Ann's Bay. They specialize in polo instruction, jumping, and overnight trail rides (see "Runaway Bay and the North Coast," p. 206).

Golf

Golfers can play at **Upton Golf and Country Club** (tel. 974-2528). Set 700 feet in the hills above town, the course is worth it just for the view. Greens fees vary from summer to winter, but range about US$20-30. Caddy and carts fees are about US$15 and US$25 respectively.

NIGHTLIFE

Ocho Rios rocks and reggaes at night. Since this is a tourist town, weekends are nothing special to the going-out crowd, so you'll find discos and music venues filled from Monday on.

The Acropolis (70 Main St.; tel. 974-2633) is on the top floor of the Mutual Security Centre. The disco has DJ nights, reggae nights, singles nights, and happy hours on Friday. The real action starts at about 2100, and the cover charge varies. **Silk's Disco** (Shaw Park Hotel; tel. 974-2552) is busy every night except Tuesday, playing canned reggae accompanied by strobe lights. The cover charge varies nightly. **The Little Pub Complex** (tel. 974-5826) has live music and shows, some tending toward the "you'll-be-happy-if-you-limbo" tourist fare, but it's a fun place; some cover charges.

The **Reggae Lobster Party** at the Coconut Grove Great House, near the White River Bridge, is a blow-out affair so exhausting that the organizers can apparently only do it once per week. On Thursday, it's a barbecue plus all-you-can-but-shouldn't drink, a live "native" show, and partying with lobsters. From 1900 to 2300, the cost is about US$35. Call 974-2619.

The **Marine Disco,** the **Roof Club,** and the **Spinning Wheel** on James Ave. are, incredibly, neighbors, and create the wall of sound you might expect. The music is generally DJ mix.

The ominously named **Jack Ruby's Lounge** on Main St. is a quieter, well, lounge. **Bill's Place** is a bar located on Main St., across from Shakey's. It's got a great jukebox, '70s redux lounge-lizard atmosphere, and Bill. Have a drink at the **Ease Tension** bar and watch that tension slip onto the floor.

For a quieter evening, see what's playing at the **Cove Theatre** on Main St., near the post office.

TRANSPORTATION

Getting There

Ocho Rios is accessible by public transportation from all points in Jamaica, though the common access is from Montego Bay or Kingston. The airstrip at Oracabessa services Ocho Rios from Montego Bay, the most frequent route; or from Port Antonio, Kingston, or Negril. The airfare on **Trans Jamaican Airlines** (Ocho Rios tel. 974-3254, U.S.A. tel. 305-665-8109) is US$60 OW from Montego Bay.

Buses arrive from all points in the country, and the main drop-off point is at the farmer's market east of the clock tower.

Getting Around

Taxis and minibuses run throughout town. The cost from White River to downtown can be as lit-

tle as J$5, or as much as J$30, depending on the type of taxi you take. Minibuses and taxis that take more than one passenger charge less. Check with the driver before you get in.

Downtown, however, from busy Main St. to the beaches, is walkable. If you don't want to walk, and don't want to spring for a rental car or taxi, alternatives are available.

Motor scooters, motorcycles, and bicycles are all available, year-round. The scooters, automatic-transmission mopeds, start at US$27-30 p/d; the price decreases the longer the rental period. The most popular motorcycles are the 125cc and 200cc sizes, though larger engines are available. Smaller bikes start at US$40 p/d, which decreases with length of rental period. You can opt to pay a collision damage waiver that usually runs US$5 p/d, or try and convince the clerk that your automobile insurance covers such damage. It should if you are licensed to drive a motorcycle.

Motor Trails (Carib Arcade, Main St.; tel. 974-5058), **Manhattan Bike Rental** (60 Main St.; tel. 974-2126), and **Cycle World** (8 Main St.; tel. 974-5916) rent scooters and motorcycles. Manhattan and Cycle World also rent bicycles, with prices starting at US$10 p/d for a 10-speed, and US$12 for a mountain bike. **Abe Rentals** (73 Main St.; tel. 974-1008) rents motorcycles starting at US$40-50 p/d, and will pick

OCHO RIOS CAR RENTAL AGENCIES

Area Code 809
Alpha Rent-A-Car, 1 Evelyn St., tel. 974-2178
Budget/Bluebird Rent-A-Car, Pineapple Place, tel. 974-5617
Caribbean Car Rentals, 99A Main St., tel. 974-2513
Coxe's Rent-A-Car, 86 Main St., tel. 974-2376
Galaxy Car Rentals, Village Hotel, 54-56 Main St., tel. 974-2645
Gemini Car Rentals, Double V Plaza, tel. 974-2068
Happy Holiday, Main St., tel. 974-2396
National Car Rental, Carib Arcade, Main St., tel. 974-2266
Sunshine Car Rentals, Pineapple Place, tel. 974-2980 or 974-5025
Thrifty Car Rentals, Main St., tel. 974-2834
Triple-A Car Rental, 180 Main St., tel. 974-2859

USEFUL PHONE NUMBERS IN OCHO RIOS

Area Code 809

Air Jamaica, tel. 974-2566

American Express, Stuart's Travel, 12 Main St., tel. 974-5369

Century National Bank, Ocean Village Shopping Centre, tel. 974-5865/6

Chamber of Commerce, tel. 974-2629

Fire and Ambulance, tel. 110

General Post Office, Main St., tel. 974-2526

Jamaica Citizen's Bank, Newlin St., tel. 974-5953/7

Jamaica Tourist Board, Ocean Village Shopping Centre, tel. 974-2570 or 974-2582

Police Emergency, tel. 119

St. Ann's Bay Hospital, tel. 972-0150

Trans Jamaican Airlines, Boscobel Aerodrome, tel. 974-3254

up in Ocho Rios. Deposits up to US$200, usually secured by a major credit card, are necessary for most bike and motorcycle rentals.

Car rentals are plentiful and competitive. The trick is to arrange pickups from Montego Bay, if that's where your arrival is, or pickups from your area hotel. In off-season, some of the smaller companies are willing to negotiate packages, but the cheapest cars run US$50-70 p/d, based on a week's rental. Daily rentals start at about US$65. The killers are a 10% government tax and the hassle over the insurance charge, but you can negotiate unlimited mileage.

Taxis can be hailed or found at the bus stand under the clock tower at Main St. and Da Costa. If you need to call a cab, try **Ocho Rios Cab Operators** (1 Newlin St.; tel. 974-5929), **Maxi Taxi** (Pineapple Plaza; tel. 974-2971), or **JUTA** (Coconut Grove Shopping Centre; tel. 974-2292).

INFORMATION

Banks and bureaux de change are found along Main St., downtown. The post office is on Main St., across from the Ocean Village complex, and has a philatelic bureau. The Jamaica Tourist Board (tel. 974-2582) offices are located on the second floor of the Ocean Village complex. The JTB maintains information kiosks in various places around town, including Pineapple Place and at the Mallard's Beach road, off Main Street. The St. Ann's Chamber of Commerce, Ocho Rios branch, has offices at Pineapple Place, where they offer duplication, typing, telephone, and fax services.

The major parish hospital is in St. Ann's Bay, seven miles away.

RUNAWAY BAY AND THE NORTH COAST
INTRODUCTION

*If Jamaica's businessmen would only
awaken to their opportunity and organize for 20th-century progress in the
building of suitable, if small, hotels
throughout the island, it would become
one of the world's finest and most populous midwinter playgrounds, where the
charm of the tropics and the health-giv-
ing coolness of the mountains meet and
join hands in a successful effort to please.*
—National Geographic, *Jan. 1927*

The area from Runaway Bay to Falmouth is a
quiet, mostly unhurried slice of Jamaican coastline, secreting small harbors, beaches, and a
few discreet settlements. It's a place tourism
hasn't truly discovered, though resorts and
restaurants are the main industries along the
coast. The reason is simple—no large towns
between Ocho Rios and Montego Bay can lo-

gistically support large-scale tourism. Therefore, the coast remains pristine, and although the
larger resorts have claimed some of the nicer
beaches, a number of them are still open to the
public.

HISTORY

In the '60s, bauxite mining operations and related industries contributed to the quiet wealth of
the area. In the hills of **Mammee Bay, Runaway Bay,** and **Rio Bueno** you'll see the large
villas and townhouses of wealthy Jamaican and
expatriate executives. Kaiser Jamaica operates
a large plant and port west of **Discovery Bay,**
servicing mines in the bauxite-rich hills of the
southern interior.

Runaway Bay has its name for a reason,
though some historians disagree on that reason. Most today think the area is the spot from

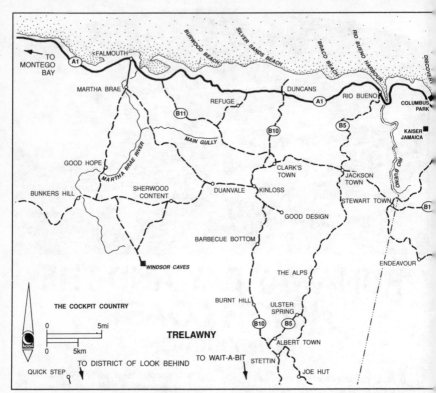

which runaway slaves regularly fled to Cuba. In the days of the slave trade, Cuba, some 90 miles away, was a major trading partner with Jamaica's north coast settlements. Slaves who were able to steal away generally found safe harbor in Cuba, more often if they converted to Catholicism. The Cuban authorities were reluctant to return Catholics to the hands of nonbelievers.

Others erroneously believe that Runaway Bay was the spot from which the Spanish commander Cristobal Ysassi finally fled after successfully harassing the British conquerors for five years. Ysassi was finally defeated by British Gov. Edward D'Oyley at the Battle of Rio Nuevo, and probably fled from the area now known as Don Christopher's Point, south of Port Maria.

Discovery Bay, five miles west of Runaway Bay, takes its name from an older historical event, the discovery of Jamaica by Columbus. Some believe that he actually set foot in Rio Bueno, some six miles west, and that the confusion stems from Columbus's description of the harbor in which he landed—both are relatively close and similar in shape. The Rio Bueno argument is stronger, however, because of the freshwater river Columbus claimed to have used to bolster his water supplies during his three-day layover. Discovery Bay has no such large river.

The Arawaks were known to have thickly settled Jamaica's north coast and, as Columbus wrote in his diary during his first encounters with Jamaica: "The earth was covered with them." Upon encountering the indigenous people, the Spanish reacted with a typical show of force and sent bowmen and dogs to shore where they routed the Arawaks, even killing a few. Days later, when Arawak elders returned bearing fruits and offers of capitulation, the capture of Jamaica began and the hapless Arawaks' fate

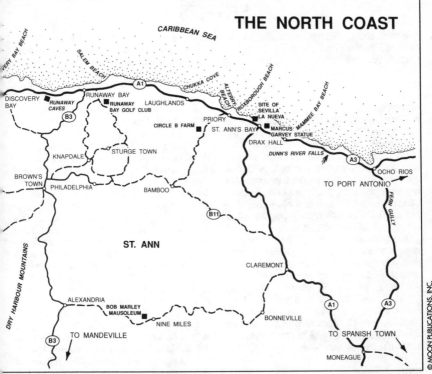

THE NORTH COAST

was sealed—they would all die within a few generations.

Various groups continue to conduct historical excavations at Sevilla la Nueva, site of the first Spanish settlement in the New World. When the Spanish abandoned Sevilla la Nueva in 1534, some 25 years after its inception, they left behind a city which all but disappeared from years of British domination and modern development. Today, the highway crosses the original site, east of St. Ann's Bay, and most of the original town is underground. At least three Arawak villages are thought to have been in the area, as well as the first sugar mill constructed in Jamaica. Excavation also continues for evidence of two caravels, the *Santiago de Palos* and the *Capitana,* which were scuttled, worm-eaten and sinking, by Columbus in 1503 on his last voyage to Jamaica. They are believed to be underwater about four miles off the Sevilla la Nueva shore. The 500th anniversary of Columbus's first voyage to the New World occurred in 1992, and historians had hoped to discover something for the important celebrations throughout the Caribbean. They were, however, unsuccessful.

SIGHTS

The north coast's laid-back ambience and superb beaches are its enticement. Tourist attractions here are limited and, at any rate, exist by the dozen in nearby Ocho Rios and Montego Bay.

Richmond Hill

At **Priory,** west of Ocho Rios, follow the signs north toward Richmond Hill where you can find the **Circle B Farm** and **Sleepy Hollow Park.** Circle B (tel. 972-2988) is an award-winning farm (11 parish titles, two national titles) that offers tours of its banana, coconut, avocado, and vegetable plantation. You'll sample the produce. Daily tours start at 1000 until whenever. The tour is US$20 pp with a traditional Jamaican buffet lunch, US$10 without.

Sleepy Hollow (no phone) is a small park that features a nice view of the bay at Priory, and a chance to look at common Jamaican plants and herbs such as coolie mint, pepper elder, and dog blood. It's a new attraction, actually in the making, and all the kinks haven't been worked out yet. But the setting is pleasant, as is Millicent, your tour guide. Daily hours are 1000-1800. Admission for adults is about US$2 (children are free) and includes a complimentary drink.

Inland

From Runaway Bay, take the road south from **Taylor's Supermarket** toward **Brown's Town.**

Brown's Town is a large inland town in St. Ann, named after Hamilton Brown, an Irishman and local land baron who died in 1843. The town is an important trading center for farmers who live in the hills of the surrounding **Dry Harbour Mountains.**

Follow the road south to **Alexandria,** then east to **Nine Miles,** the birthplace of reggae legend Bob Marley.

Marley's humble beginnings are evident in this small farming village, no larger than a Brooklyn block. Look for the **Bob Marley Foundation & Gift Shop** sign at the base of the hill where the Marley family's original kitchen stands. Next to the kitchen is a mausoleum where Marley is interred with his guitar. Rastas in various altered states—some who work for the Marley foundation, some who were friends, and some who are just there—will offer to show you around the compound. They'll point out Marley's rock, where he used to sit for inspiration, and the stained-glass windows (imported from Africa) of the mausoleum building. Some of these men had been on concert tours with Marley and will be able to regale you with stories of Bob on the road. A large stage off to the side holds reggae concerts every year on 6 Feb., Marley's birthday and a national holiday, and on significant Ethiopian Church holidays. Rita Marley, Bob's widow, as well as his children, including Ziggy, often perform at these functions.

Bob Marley mausoleum at Nine Miles

PHYLIS LUNITA

Ziggy Marley

Tours are led outside the mausoleum, but recent legal entanglements concerning the Marley estate have disallowed the possibility of viewing the casket and memorabilia that adorn the walls. Find Bongo Joe, who runs the place and collects admission. The admission shouldn't be more than the equivalent of about US$4-5, though there is no apparent hard-and-fast rule about it. Ganja grows in the garden surrounding the mausoleum. After walking through the compound, you can buy T-shirts, cassettes, and Marley memorabilia. The tours are open daily, no set hours.

The 1981 funeral procession to this small village in St. Ann is said to have stretched 50 miles along the road from Kingston.

Discovery Bay

In Discovery Bay, stop at **Green Grotto,** where you can tour limestone caves thought to have been a last hiding place for the Spanish before they escaped to the sea via an underground passage. The half-hour tours start daily from 0900, US$3.50 adults and US$2 children 5-12.

Columbus Park, built in 1968 and operated in Discovery Bay by Kaiser Jamaica, is a free, open-air museum and crafts park with old waterwheels and other farm implements on display. The view of Discovery Bay alone is worth the stop here. You can do some crafts shopping in the stalls toward the back, and you probably won't get better prices elsewhere in the area.

You can't miss the monstrous Kaiser Jamaica plant on the south side of the road across from the park. **Puerto Seco Beach** is also operated by Kaiser, and has tennis courts. Puerto Seco ("Dry Harbor") was the original Spanish name for Discovery Bay. The **Kaiser Sports Club** is the venue every August for the **Push Cart Derby,** an interparish competition featuring young boys racing the ubiquitous market pushcarts for prizes. The whole thing has a lively carnival atmosphere, and Derby Day is complete with bands and cultural shows. Stop at **Quadrant Wharf,** the ruins of a small cannon emplacement and the spot believed by some to be where Columbus first set foot on the island.

Near Columbus Park, you'll see the **University of the West Indies Marine Research Laboratory,** a regional branch that attracts scientists and students from the world over. It features the island's only **decompression chamber,** a must for a country where diving is both sport and occupation.

Rio Bueno And Duncans

Crossing into Trelawny Parish, you'll encounter **Rio Bueno,** probably the true site of Columbus's first landing in Jamaica in 1494. The town contains historic remnants of the early British occupation, including **Fort Dundas,** visible behind the government school. The Anglican and Baptist churches date back to 1832 and 1834, respectively.

BOB RACE

Duncans is another small and clean coastal Trelawny town, said to have been established and named after property-owner Patrick Duncans, circa 1784.

Cockpit Country

Trelawny is the home of the Cockpit Country, Jamaica's own version of a sci-fi moonscape: impenetrable, and once home to thousands of warrior Maroons during their years of evading and battling with Spanish and British authorities. The deep limestone pits and crevices were perfect cover for the escaped Africans—on foot. Today, a car won't take you far, and a 4WD is not much better. You can visit towns surrounding the Cockpit Country, to which roads give relatively easy access. **Maroon Town,** west of the Cockpit Country, was once actually home to the eponymous Maroons, but is now settled by others. East of Maroon Town is **Flagstaff,** once called Trelawny Town, which was also once a

Maroon settlement but was destroyed by British militia during the Maroon Wars (see the general "Introduction" section, p. 26).

Windsor Caves are about as deep into the Cockpit as you can go. These caves are thought to be a source of the Martha Brae River, which eventually flows north to Falmouth. Access is via **Sherwood Content** or **Bunkers Hill** north of the Cockpit Country. The caves' first few sections, or chambers, are navigable, but beyond that only experienced spelunkers should venture. In all cases a guide is necessary. Jamaican bats, "rat bats," have formed the inevitable colonies here, and their manure is collected and used as fertilizer.

Many of the towns surrounding the Cockpit Country have names that mirror the eeriness of the land's formations, as well as their function as hideouts of strangers in a strange land: **Quick Step** in the **District of Look Behind** in the **Land of Yu No Call Mi No Come** to the south; **Wait-A-Bit, Burnt Hill, Barbecue Bottom,** and **Kinloss** to the east; and **Good Hope** to the north.

BEACHES

The north coast's beaches are among the best in the country, only because there are so many. Finding them is as easy as driving along Hwy. A1, the coastal road. From Ocho Rios in the east to Falmouth in the west, try any of the several "public" beaches, meaning no fee. As well, numerous small coves and inlets are great for a splash. Many of the hotels, of course, have privatized their beaches.

Roxborough Beach and **Alterry Beach** are just east of Priory. **Salem Beach** is the first you encounter in Runaway Bay, and has changing rooms, snack shacks, and some crafts vendors. In Discovery Bay, you'll find **Discovery Bay Beach** as well as **Puerto Seco Beach.** Both have facilities. **Braco, Silver Sands,** and **Burwood** beaches are spread along the road from Rio Bueno to Falmouth. For food, the road is peppered, so to speak, with jerk shacks, fruit and fast-food vendors, and roadside bars.

PRACTICALITIES

RUNAWAY BAY ACCOMMODATIONS

North coast accommodations are lined along the beach strip from Runaway Bay to Falmouth, and beyond to Montego Bay. They're lined, but not crowded. Part of this area's attraction is the gentle dispersion of its businesses, and the hotels and guesthouses manage to maintain a unobtrusive presence.

Remember that tariffs are often cheaper in the summer, and hotels that charge nightly government room tax adjust the tax with the season. Most guesthouses, unless indicated otherwise, use the same rates year-round. Some hotels include a 10% service charge, in lieu of tipping, in the tariff. Some add it on at the end, and others leave tipping to the discretion of guests.

Inexpensive

Cliff's Apartments (tel. 973-2601) are located on Hampton Rd. on the south side of the main road through Runaway Bay. Mrs. Scott operates the apartments, which are in a number of houses, some of which are hers, some not, in the neighborhood. If she can't put you up, she'll find someone who will. This is a truly Jamaican experience, and one of the least expensive in town. Accommodation is sometimes just a room, sometimes a room with a bath. Some showers are cold water only; some have hot. Some have a/c; some have only fans. You get the picture. Tariff starts at US$20 per room per night, no tax, no service charge.

Cozy Alcove (tel. 973-2023) has three furnished apartments that haven't been used in a while, but Eulah Christie will open them up for her guests. Across from the Club Caribbean, the flats have bedrooms, small kitchens, and basic furniture. Rates are negotiable, but figure about US$40 per flat per night.

Eagle's Paradise (tel. 973-2508) is another Hampton Rd. guesthouse, higher up on a hill overlooking the ocean. Some rooms share baths, and the water is both hot and cold. Rates vary with the number of persons in a room. One person per night is under US$20; two, US$25; three, US$30 and up. No tax or service charge.

Hampton View Villa (Runaway Bay P.O., St. Ann, Jamaica, W.I.; tel. 973-4337) is operated by Lloyd Brown in his home. The guesthouse is relatively new. Some baths are shared, some rooms have ceiling fans, and guests are allowed to use the kitchen. Brown has fixed tariffs starting at US$25 or US$150 per week, and negotiation is the way to go.

Salem Guesthouse (Runaway Bay P.O., St. Ann, Jamaica, W.I.; tel. 973-4256) is across from Salem Beach in Runaway Bay, an excellent location. The guesthouse has a seafood restaurant attached, where meals can be had for moderate prices. Lobster is a specialty. The hotel has eight rooms, all with private baths. Some include, incredibly, bidets. A swimming pool and outdoor sports bar on the grounds complete the picture. Rooms are US$45 s and up to US$75 d, per night. Add 10% service charge.

Whilby Resort Cottages (Box 11, Runaway Bay, Jamaica, W.I.; tel. 944-2701) is a warm and inviting guesthouse on Hampton Rd., and has a nice view of the ocean from a hilltop location. Operated by Sista Pat Cassier, the guesthouse is a small breath of her Zion in a Babylonian world. The rooms are eclectic, and start at about US$50 d per night, all charges inclusive. Rooms have hot and cold water, a/c, and kitchen facilities. If you've got a tent, you can set it up on Sista Pat's property for about US$7. You can buy passes to use the beach at the nearby Jamaica Jamaica resort, and Salem Beach is close by. If it's communication with a genuine and heartfelt Jamaica you're seeking, this is the place in Runaway Bay.

Moderate

Alamanda Inn (P.O. Box 65, Runaway Bay, Jamaica, W.I.; tel. 973-4030, fax 973-3509, U.S.A. tel. 800-223-9815) is a small apartment complex set in a garden near the center of things. The complex has a pool, and the beach is a short walk away. All apartments are self contained. In summer, a one-bedroom is US$55, two-bedroom is US$90; extra person US$15. In winter, a one-bedroom is US$80, two-bedroom US$110; extra person US$20. If you want a/c, it's US$10 p/d extra. These apartments are good deals if you are traveling with a small group. Up to two children under 12 are free when staying with parents. Meal plans are available. Add 10% GCT and 10% service charge.

Caribbean Isle (Box 119, Runaway Bay, Jamaica, W.I.; tel. 973-2364, fax 974-1706) is west of the road to Brown's Town, on the beach. It's a small and quaint place in the center of things, it has a pool, and you're right on the beach. Summer rates are US$54 s and US$66 d. Winter rates are US$66 s and US$84 d. All rates are inclusive of taxes and breakfast.

H.E.A.R.T. Country Club (Box 98, Runaway Bay, Jamaica, W.I.; tel. 973-2671/4, fax 973-2693, U.S.A., tel. 800-526-2422) is a training facility for hotel and tourist resort personnel. Consequently, the service is excellent—you may be someone's final exam—and the prices are just right. The meals are very good and reasonable, and you can get hot dogs. Winter rates are US$60 s and US$100 d, plus 10% GCT and 10% service charge. Summer rates are cheaper. H.E.A.R.T. (Human Employment and Resource Training) has packages with many different options, including meals, airport transfers, bicycles, golf fees, and more. A typical winter package: four nights for two, US$816, which includes all meals and sports.

Silver Creek Cottages (Box 227, Runaway Bay, Jamaica, W.I.) are a set of bungalows that can be rented by the room, apartment, or villa. Go south at the Shell station across from Salem Beach. The villas can accommodate up to 17 people, the cottage can accommodate four, and the apartments can accommodate from one to five. Basic charges are US$50 in the summer and US$60 in the winter, tax and maid service included. Book through Ms. Chung at H.E.A.R.T.

Silver Spray Resort (P.O. Box 16, Runaway Bay, Jamaica, W.I.; tel. 973-3413, fax 973-3473. U.S.A. tel. 800-241-7795) is another beach resort north of the main road. It's small, eight acres and 13 rooms in all, and cozy. The hotel has a pool and open-air dining area, all directly on the beach. **Bananas** nightclub is one of the hotter nightspots in town. Hotel rates start at US$40-50 d for standard and superior rooms in the summer. Winter rates increase the tariff to US$60-70. M.A.P. (breakfast and dinner) is available for US$22 pp. Private villas are also available. Add 10% GCT and 10% service charge.

Tamarind Tree Hotel (Box 235, Runaway Bay, Jamaica, W.I.; tel. 973-2678) does in fact have a tamarind tree on the grounds. The hotel is another small one, 16 rooms with a pool, set on the south side of the main road. The restaurant is reputed to be excellent, and the **Stinger Disco** is Runaway Bay's most well known club. Basic rates are US$43 s and US$58-80 d in the summer. Winter rates are US$50 s and US$62 d. All taxes and service charges are included.

Luxury
Ambiance/Jamaica (Box 20, Runaway Bay, Jamaica, W.I.; tel. 973-2066 or 973-4705, fax 973-2067) is a large beach resort in the center of town. All the amenities are available, including pools, bars, and restaurants. Standard rooms in winter are US$98 s and US$107 d, suites from US$134. In summer, figure on US$96 s and US$114 d, all taxes included. Standard rooms include breakfast for two. Some suites have private whirlpool baths.

Chukka Cove Farm (Box 160, Ocho Rios; tel. 972-2506, 972-2804, or 974-2593) is at **Laughlands,** about five miles east of Runaway Bay. The farm is geared to equestrian activities, yet is a beautiful setting in its own right. Rides range from two-hour excursions to two-day overnights roaming the Jamaican interior. Guided horseback tours range US$20-160 along some of the best trails in the country. Accommodation is in one of five villas. Each villa accommodates four people in two bedrooms, and the rate is the same for any number less than four. In the winter, the tariff is US$1725 per villa for seven nights. In the summer, the rate is US$1380 per villa for seven nights, and includes a rental car. All rates include a full villa staff and room taxes.

Club Caribbean (Box 965, Runaway Bay, Jamaica, W.I.; tel. 973-3507/8, fax 973-3509) is a nicely situated resort on the beach, near the public Salem Beach. A variety of plans are available, but the basic winter rates are US$128-148 s and US$228-248 d, which includes breakfast, dinner, water sports, and tax and service charges. Off-season, rates are US$184 d and less.

Franklyn D. Resort (Box 201, Runaway Bay, Jamaica, W.I.; tel. 973-4591, fax 973-3071, U.S.A. tel. 800-654-1FDR) is an all-inclusive hotel geared toward families. Accommodation is in self-contained apartment suites. The standard all-inclusive packages include transfers, meals and drinks, sports, and entertainment. Specials include free stays for children under 14 accompanied by a parent, baby-sitting, and occasional free grandmother specials. A "Girl Friday" comes with each suite to help out with the kids or with cooking, should you choose not to eat in one of the resort's two restaurants. Basic summer rates are US$1590 pp for seven nights based on double occupancy, and US$1690 pp for seven nights in winter, all charges included.

Jamaica Jamaica (Box 58, Runaway Bay, Jamaica, W.I.; tel. 973-2436/8, fax 973-2352, U.S.A. tel. 800-858-8009, Canada tel. 800-553-4320) is a SuperClubs resort, all-inclusive, and the largest resort in Runaway Bay. The emphasis here is on sports, particularly golf and water sports. All sports, including greens fees for the Runaway Bay Golf Club across the street, horseback riding, tennis, and water sports, plus meals, transfers, and the lot, are included in the tariff. The beach is one of the longest private beaches in the area, and includes a clothing-optional section. Scattered about the resort are three hot tubs, four bars, and two restaurants—it's the kind of place you can easily never leave, if that's your plan. Summer rates start at US$577-754 pp for three nights based on a shared twin—if you are alone and want to stay that way, add a US$75 guaranteed single occupancy rate per night. Winter rates start at US$1400 pp for seven nights based on shared twin. All taxes and service charges are included. Children under 16 are not accommodated, and the minimum stay is three nights.

Villas

For villas in the Mammee Bay area, contact **Sunshine Villas** (Philadelphia tel. 215-790-1190, fax 215-790-0064). In Runaway Bay, one of the better villa complexes is **Caribbean Village Beach Resort** (P.O. Box 140, Runaway Bay, Jamaica, W.I.; tel. 973-3453). The resort is a series of privately owned and rental units that have, in some instances, seen better days. The pool and restaurant on the grounds were damaged by hurricanes, but the beach is fine, and what you'd probably be there for anyway. A three-bedroom, three-bath self-contained villa is US$100 per night. Since this accommodates up to six persons, the price can be attractive. **Sunflower Beach Resort Villas** (P.O. Box 150,

Runaway Bay, Jamaica, W.I.; tel. 973-2171, fax 973-2381, U.S.A. tel. 800-223-9815) operates over 45 one- and three-bedroom villas at Club Caribbean. All have a pool, cook, and house-keeper, with commensurate rates.

DISCOVERY BAY AREA ACCOMMODATIONS

On the road to Falmouth, you'll find numerous villas (see "Villas and Apartments" in the general "Accommodations" section, p. 65) for rent, as well as a few hotels and small guesthouses.

The Accommodationer (Main St., Discovery Bay, Jamaica, W.I.; tel. 973-2559, fax 973-3020) is a six-room guesthouse on the main drag in Discovery Bay. The rooms are clean and tag-sale basic, which should mean that they are inexpensive. At US$40-50 s or d, including breakfast, you can draw your own conclusions about that. Nevertheless, they say they are flexible about rates. A kitchen is available for use by guests.

Portside Villas and Apartments (P.O. Box 42, Discovery Bay, Jamaica, W.I.; tel. 973-2007 or 973-3135, fax 973-2720) is one of the nicer places to stay in Discovery Bay. Located on Discovery Bay harbor, they have tennis courts, a pool, and one of the better seafood restaurants in the area. Some villas are located on the south side of the main road, but all are within walking distance to the water. All accommodations are in self-contained units. Winter rates are US$105-115 d per night in studios, to US$275 for six persons in a three-bedroom unit. Weekly rates are cheaper. Annoying extra cost: a/c is US$35 extra pp per week. In off-season, expect US$90-100 d, and up to US$225 for the three-bedroom units. Children under 12 sharing bedroom with parents are free.

In Duncans, **Silver Sands Beach Club** (Duncans P.O., Trelawny, Jamaica, W.I.; tel. 954-2001) has self-contained villas that accommodate 2-12 people. A basic villa for two goes for about US$1000 per week (seven nights) in the summer, and US$1400 in the winter. The tariff includes airport transfers and villa staff, but food is left up to you. All taxes are included in the rate.

Trelawny Beach Hotel (Box 54, Falmouth P.O., Jamaica, W.I.; tel. 954-2450/8, fax 954-2173) is a large high rise on a great beach just outside of Falmouth. Its tariffs include breakfast and dinner, transfers, sports, taxes, and service charge, making it a semi-inclusive. Drinks, lunch, and incidentals are left up to the guests. Basic summer rates are US$142-154 s, US$192-216 d. In the winter, rates are US$160-190 s and US$246-290 d.

Bodmint Resort (Rock District, Falmouth P.O., Jamaica, W.I.; tel. 954-3551, U.S.A. tel. 908-370-8159 and ask for Mr. Taylor) is a small set of guesthouse-type cottages, very basic but clean, on a phosphorescent lagoon just outside of Falmouth. The lagoon is an attraction, and glows at night due to light-absorbing properties of microscopic sea creatures. The three-acre property includes fruit trees, available for guest consumption. Taylor will transport you to a white-sand beach on a private island across the lagoon. He also offers fishing trips at about US$10 pp, a third of the amount that local operations charge. His summer rates, based on a seven-night stay, are US$375 per two persons in a one-bedroom villa, US$700 for four persons in a two-bedroom villa, and US$1500 for eight in a four-bedroom villa. Add 20% for winter rates. Longer stays are negotiable. Add 10% service charge.

EATING AND DRINKING

The larger hotels have elegant restaurants, but you'll find plenty to eat along the main road in clean taverns and small jerk huts. In Runaway

Bay, try **Charlie's** for basic chicken and seafood. The **Northern Jerk Center** has very good barbecued meat Jamaican-style. **Runaway's Pizza and Spirits** (tel. 997-7053) serves, you guessed it, pizza and drinks. **Seafood Giant** is a large, circular bar, a popular Jamaican hangout, that serves some of the best grilled lobster around. (See recipe in "Introduction," p. 71)

Try the **Almond Grove Restaurant** (tel. 973-4652) for slightly more upscale ambience. The **Island Queen Restaurant,** on the north side of the road, serves Jamaican takeout and other solid fare.

The Bird Watching Beer Joint, just west of town, is at a small fishing beach visited each evening by literally hundreds of white egrets, who come from their foraging trips in the hills to roost in the trees of the small lagoon. It's a clamorous scene, worth a drink or two of white rum poured from a plastic gas can while you watch the birds assemble. Hang out with the fishermen and play dominoes, the Jamaican national pastime, or *ludo,* a board game that's a cross between backgammon and anarchy. Here, arrange fishing or coastal sightseeing trips.

Next door is a small crafts hut. In fact, this section of road is peppered with crafts and jerk huts.

Aunt May's Blue Bird Restaurant on the main road in Runaway Bay specializes in seafood, and it's not expensive. **Greg's Hot Spot Bar** is a nice place to cool off with a beer. The **Patty Place** near the corner of the main road and the Brown's Town turnoff serves quick,

PHYLIS LUNTA

takeout patties and pastries. **Taylor's Supermarket,** at the same corner, is the best bet in town for food shopping. Markets are sparse, and most people go to St. Ann's Bay or Ocho Rios for heavy marketing. West of the Pear Tree River is **Pam's Patty Hut,** for meat patties and pastries.

West of Runaway Bay, restaurants and jerk stands dot the coastal road. Try **El Africano,** across the street from the tourism-developed Green Grotto Caves. Columbus Park has numerous small restaurants in and around it. The **Mickey Mouse Fun Club** has interesting possibilities. **Arawak Sunset Joint** is in Rio Bueno. Also near Rio Bueno, stop at the incredible **Aeroplane Jerk Stop,** a small restaurant marked by a gutted, single-engine airplane near the road.

In the Duncans-Falmouth area, stop at **Time 'N Place Restaurant** or **Glistening Waters Restaurant** on the phosphorescent lagoon for a relaxing meal. The **Fisherman's Inn** (tel. 954-3427), one of the oldest in the area, serves excellent lunches and dinners inside or out by the pool. The inn, which has diving facilities, also arranges sailboat charters, diving, and cruises on the phosphorescent lagoon.

ENTERTAINMENT

Shopping
The shopping you'll do in Runaway Bay and the north coast will probably be for small crafts and some art. The road to Falmouth is interspersed with small crafts stalls, particularly those selling hammock and wicker furniture. The wicker is well constructed and inexpensive, though the practicality of shipping or carrying furniture home is something you'll have to weigh.

In Runaway Bay, stop at Cozy Alcove and find **Trevor Fairclough,** an award-winning woodcarver who maintains an ascetic lifestyle on the north coast. He's got his carvings hung all around the closed restaurant, not a gallery per se. These carvings, in a dimly lit and cluttered room, are some of the finest in the country.

At Rio Bueno, stop at **Gallery Joe James,** a combination gallery, seafood restaurant, and hotel. Joe James is a celebrated Jamaican impressionist and expressionist artist whose work is exhibited throughout the country.

Just east of Falmouth is **Caribatik,** a design house under the direction of artist Muriel Chandler. The gallery is large, and features framed batik designs as well as clothes. It's open from mid-Nov. to mid-May, Tues.-Sat. 1000-1500.

For music, try **Soul Sensation Record Centre** or **Future Shock Records,** both on Main St., Runaway Bay.

Sports And Recreation
The **Runaway Bay Golf Club** (tel. 973-2561) is across the street from Jamaica Jamaica. It's apparently a challenging course, and purists admire it for its sand traps.

For water sports, go to **Ambiance/Jamaica** where SunDivers Jamaica (tel. 973-2346, U.S.A. tel. 800-522-DIVE) runs a diving and water sports package in conjunction with the hotel. **Reef Divers** (tel. 973-3413) at the Silver Spray Resort offer diving, snorkeling, and some water sports. Basic one-tank dives start at US$30 with rented equipment, and US$25 if you have your own. Five- and ten-dive packages are available, as is night diving (US$50). Snorkeling trips are US$15. Numerous smaller rental companies operate at Salem Beach.

GETTING AROUND

Runaway Bay lies almost midway between Ocho Rios and Montego Bay. Buses and minivans operate along the main road, Hwy. A1, between the towns, and transportation is regular and accessible.

Runaway Bay is stretched out, and if you want to do a lot of exploring, a rental car is the best bet. Bicycles are not available here, but can be rented in Ocho Rios. For cars, try **Econocar Rentals** (Caribbean Village Beach Resort, Box 140, Runaway Bay, Jamaica, W.I.; tel. 973-3453) or **Caribbean Car Rentals** (Salem Cres., Runaway Bay, Jamaica, W.I.; tel. 973-3539). Cars usually come with free mileage, and rates are negotiable in off-season.

For motorcycles, call **Jake's Rent-A-Bike** (Main St., Runaway Bay, Jamaica, W.I.; tel. 973-4406). Rates are US$35-50 p/d, cheaper by the week. Add 10% GCT.

Taxicabs can be flagged down almost anytime along the road.

INFORMATION

For police emergencies call 119. For fire and ambulance service dial 110.

The nearest hospital is St. Ann's Bay Hospital (tel. 972-2272). Money can be changed at most hotels, but a branch office of the National Commercial Bank (tel. 973-2261) can be found in Discovery Bay. The Runaway Bay Post Office (tel. 973-2477) is a small rural branch on the main road. Main libraries, banks, JTB offices, and airline representatives can be found in Ocho Rios, St. Ann's Bay, and Montego Bay.

BOOKLIST

This booklist is by no means complete, and is intended simply to highlight a handful of the many books available on Jamaican and Caribbean culture, history, language, literature, art, science, and religion.

CARIBBEAN ISSUES

Abrahams, Roger D. *After Africa*. New Haven: Yale University Press, 1983. Chronicle of Africans as slaves in the West Indies.

Bourne, Edward G. *Spain in America (1450-1580)*. New York and London: Harper & Bros., 1904. The Spanish were major influences in North, South, and Central America, as well as the Caribbean. The Spanish in Jamaica left their mark on name places and popular culture.

Cripps, L.L. *The Spanish Caribbean from Columbus to Castro*. Cambridge, MA: Schenkman, 1979.

Davison, Robert Barry. *Black British: Immigrants to England*. Boca Raton, FL: Florida Atlantic University Press, 1972. Explores the impact of large numbers of West Indian arrivals to the U.K.

Hamshire, Cyril. *The British in the Caribbean*. Cambridge, MA: Harvard University Press, 1972. Historical analysis of the British presence in the Caribbean, to modern times.

Knight, Franklin W. *The Caribbean*. London: Oxford University Press, 1978.

Lewis, Gordon K. *Main Currents in Caribbean Thought: The Historical Evolution of Caribbean Society in Its Ideological Aspects*. Baltimore: Johns Hopkins University Press, 1983.

Parry, J.H., and P.M. Sherlock. *A Short History of the West Indies*. London: Macmillan, 1956.

Patterson, Orlando. *Sociology of Slavery*. London, 1967.

Vallette, Jim, and Heather Spalding, eds. *The International Trade in Wastes; A Greenpeace Inventory*. 5th edition. Washington, D.C.: Greenpeace, 1990. An alarming exposé on the trade of waste, some of it toxic, among countries worldwide.

Van Sertima, Ivan. *They Came Before Columbus: The African Presence in Ancient America*. New York: Random House, 1976.

Wright, Irene A. *Early History of Cuba—1492-1586*. New York: Macmillan, 1916.

CULTURE AND PEOPLE

Alleyne, Mervyn. *Roots of Jamaican Culture*. London: Karia Press, 1988.

Ammar, Nellie. "They Came from the Middle East." *Jamaica Journal* (March 1970): Vol. 4, No. 1. A discussion of the Middle East influence in Jamaican culture.

Andrade, Jacob A. *A Record of the Jews in Jamaica*. Kingston, 1941.

Barrett, Leonard E. *The Rastafarians: The Dreadlocks of Jamaica*. London: Heinemann Educational Books, 1977.

Barrett, Leonard E. *The Rastafarians: The Sounds of Cultural Dissonance*. Boston: Beacon Press, 1977.

Beckwith, Martha. *Black Roadways—a Study of Jamaican Folklife*. Chapel Hill, NC, 1925.

Beckwith, Martha. *Jamaican Proverbs*. New York: Negro University Press, 1970. The richness of Jamaican folklore and language in a concise collection.

Boot, Adrian, and Michael Thomas. *Jamaica: Babylon on a Thin Wire.* New York: Schocken Books, 1977. Photographic essay of Jamaica during the turbulent '70s.

Brathwaite, Edward. *The Development of Creole Society in Jamaica 1770-1820.* Oxford: Clarendon Press, 1971. Studies the emergence of a racially regulated society, where Creole refers to generations of Europeans born in Jamaica.

Brown, Aggrey. *Colour, Class, and Politics in Jamaica.* New Brunswick, NJ: Transaction Books, 1979.

Clarke, Edith. *My Mother Who Fathered Me.* London: Allen and Unwin, 1966.

Cumper, George E. *The Social Structure of Jamaica.* Kingston: University College of the West Indies, 1949. Over 40 years old, but contains a thorough discussion of postemancipation and early 20th-century Jamaica.

Garvey, Amy Jacques. *Garvey and Garveyism.* New York: Collier Books, 1970. Marcus Garvey's widow discusses his history and thought.

Hart, Richard. *The Origin and Development of the People of Jamaica.* Montreal: International Caribbean Service Bureau, 1974.

Heuman, Gad. *Between Black and White.* Westport, CT: Greenwood Press, 1981.

Kuper, Adam. *Changing Jamaica.* Kingston: Kingston Publishers, 1976. Since the book was written, quite a bit more has changed, but the issues still ring true.

Mansingh, Lakshmi. "Indian Heritage in Jamaica." *Jamaica Journal:* Vol. 10, Nos. 2,3, and 4.

Nettleford, Rex. *Caribbean Cultural Identity: The Case of Jamaica.* Kingston: Institute of Jamaica, 1979. Written by one of Jamaica's foremost social commentators. Nettleford is also a University of the West Indies lecturer and National Dance Theatre choreographer.

Nettleford, Rex. *Identity, Race and Protest in Jamaica.* New York: William Morrow & Co., 1972.

Nicholas, Tracy. *Rastafari: A Way of Life.* Garden City, NY: Anchor Books, 1979.

Waters, Anita M. *Race, Class, and Political Symbols; Rastafari and Reggae in Jamaican Politics.* New Brunswick, NJ: Transaction Books, 1985. Fascinating look at the rise of Rastafarianism as a political symbol—eventually necessitating the capitulation of traditional Jamaican politics.

Waters, Anita M. *The Ras Tafari Movement.* New Brunswick, NJ: Transaction Books, 1985. Concise treatment of Rastafarian thought in a historical and religious context.

DESCRIPTION AND TRAVEL

Beckford, William. *A Descriptive Account of the Island of Jamaica.* 2 vols. London, 1790.

Benghiat, Norma. *Traditional Jamaican Cookery.* London: Penguin Books, 1985. Lively text, obscure and delicious recipes punctuated with Jamaican proverbs.

Cave, Hugh B. *Four Paths to Paradise—A Book about Jamaica.* Garden City, NY: Doubleday, 1961. Dated, but an excellent look at pre-independence Jamaica.

Chen, Ray. *Jamaica.* Montreal: Ray Chen, 1985. Photography and text in a coffeetable book by one of Jamaica's finest photographers.

Cohen, Steve. *The Adventure Guide to Jamaica.* Edison, NJ: Hunter Publishing, Inc., 1988. Contains relevant insights, good advice for this specialized form of travel.

Floyd, Barry. *Jamaica: An Island Microcosm.* New York: St. Martin's Press, 1979. Dated, but worth a look if you can find it in a discount bin.

Graves, Charles. *Fourteen Islands in the Sun.* New York: Hart Publishing, 1968. Includes Trinidad and Tobago, Grenada, St. Lucia, and St. Vincent as well as Jamaica.

Hawkes, Alex. *Rum Cookbook.* Kingston: Collins-Sangster, 1976. A splash here, a dash there, a spot for the chef—cooking with rum can be heady stuff.

Jeffrey, Nan. *Best Places to Go, Vol. I.* San Francisco: Foghorn Press, 1993. Highlights of popular vacation spots, with an emphasis on culturally sensitive family travel.

Martin, L. Emile, ed. *Dining Out in Jamaica.* Montego Bay: Unlimited Exposures, 1989. Best restaurants in Jamaica, complete with maps and menus.

Nugent, Lady. *Lady Nugent's Journal of her Residence in Jamaica from 1801-1805.* Philip Wright, ed. Kingston: Institute of Jamaica, 1966.

Senior, Olive. *A to Z of Jamaican Heritage.* 2nd edition. Kingston: Heinemann Educational Books, 1987. Concise and thoroughly researched Jamaican backgrounder.

Sherlock, Philip, and Barbara Preston. *Jamaica, The Fairest Isle.* London: Macmillan Education Ltd., 1992. Written by two prominent Jamaicans, this is an insider's guide to the country.

Sibley, Inez Knibb. *Dictionary of Place Names in Jamaica.* Kingston: Institute of Jamaica, 1978. Considering the Arawak, Spanish, British, African, and other ethnic naming of places in Jamaica, the task must have been a formidable one. Interesting and amusing at times.

Zach, Paul, ed. *Insight Guide: Jamaica.* Singapore: APA Publications Ltd., 1989. This fifth edition of the well-known series is chock-full of photography and writings from Jamaican authorities.

HISTORY

Black, Clinton. *History of Jamaica.* 4th edition. London: Collins-Sangster, 1983. Comprehensive work by one of Jamaica's most prominent historians.

Black, Clinton. *Port Royal.* 2nd edition. Kingston: Institute of Jamaica, 1988. History of the famous buccaneer stronghold, from hangout to washout.

Burney, James. *Buccaneers of America.* London: Allen & Unwin, 1949 (reprinted from an 1816 edition).

Campbell, Horace. *Rasta and Resistance: From Marcus Garvey to Walter Rodney.* Trenton: Africa World Press, Inc., 1987. In-depth treatment of the roots of Rastafari. The rhetoric is sometimes inundated with righteous socialist overtones, but the facts are indisputable.

Dallas, R.C. *The History of the Maroons.* 2 vols. London, 1803. The Maroon presence, formidable today, was even more so at the turn of the 19th century.

Dunn, Richard S. *Sugar and Slavery—the Rise of the Planter Class in the English West Indies (1624-1738).* Chapel Hill, N.C.: University of North Carolina Press, 1972.

Graham, Tom. *Kingston 100: 1872-1972.* Kingston: Tom Graham, 1972.

Hall, Douglas. *Free Jamaica, 1838-1865: An Economic History.* New Haven: Yale University Press, 1951. History of Jamaica from emancipation to the Morant Bay Rebellion.

Hill, Richard. *Light and Shadows of Jamaica History.* Kingston: Ford and Gall, 1859.

Hurwitz, Samuel J., and Edith F. Hurwitz. *Jamaica: A Historical Portrait.* London: Praeger Publishers, 1971.

Long, Edward. *The History of Jamaica.* 3 vols. London: Frank Cass, 1774.

Ragarz, Lowell Joseph. *The Fall of the Planter Class in the British Caribbean, 1763-1833.* New York: Octagon Books, 1971. Interesting, if somewhat esoteric, investigation of the crash of the wealthy British landowner class. Good companion to Mr. Dunn's book, above.

Wynter, Sylvia. *Jamaica National Heroes.* Kingston: Jamaica National Press Commission, 1971.

LANGUAGE

Adams, L. Emilie. *Understanding Jamaican Patois.* Kingston: Kingston Publishers Ltd., 1991. Excellent introduction to, as the author calls it, Afro-Jamaican grammar, sentence structure, and vocabulary. Written well and written for the nouveau linguist, the slim book includes a childhood tale told in Patois. Best bet for beginners.

Cassidy, Frederic G., and Robert LePage. *A Dictionary of Jamaican English.* 2nd edition, London: Cambridge University Press, 1980. The granddaddy of all Jamaican Patois vocabulary compendiums.

Cassidy, Frederic G. *Jamaica Talk: 300 Years of the English Language in Jamaica.* London: Macmillan 1961. The brother to the granddaddy of all Jamaican Patois vocabulary compendiums.

Loftman, Beryl. *A Language Guide to Jamaica.* New York: Research Institute for the Study of Man, 1962.

Maxwell, Ken, and Livingston McLaren. *How To Speak Jamaican?* Kingston: Christopher Issa, 1981. A humorous look at Jamaican Patois, sold mainly as a tourist item.

Rosen, Brian, and Peter Shepard. *Speak Jamaican.* Kingston: Newmarket Investment, 1977. Another humorous look at Jamaican Patois, sold mainly as a tourist item.

LITERATURE AND FICTION

Banks, Russell. *The Book of Jamaica.* Boston: Houghton Mifflin, 1980. An American writer searches for the truth about Errol Flynn, the Maroons, and magic.

Bennett, Louise. *Anancy Stories and Dialect Verse.* Kingston: Pioneer Press, 1950. Ms. Bennett's written interpretation of these traditional tales is fascinating, and listening to her recordings is even better.

Bennett, Louise. *Jamaica Labrish.* Kingston: Collins Sangster, 1966. Tales told in Patois.

Delisser, Herberts G. *The White Witch of Rose Hall.* London: Ernert Benn, 1929. The legend, largely fictional to begin with, lives through this work.

Duffus, Lee R. *The Cuban Jamaican Connection.* Kingston: Kingston Publishers, 1983.

Fisher, Leonard. *Sweeney's Ghost.* Garden City, NY: Doubleday, 1975. Duppy tales—a vacationing family discovers that their rented villa is haunted by a pirate's ghost.

Hughes, Richard Arthur. *A High Wind In Jamaica (The Innocent Voyage).* 2nd edition. New York: Harper & Row, 1957. British children in Jamaica, kidnapped by buccaneers, live an adventurous life on the high seas. The plot focuses less on Jamaica than on the children and their capricious, yet sometimes difficult, existence among the buccaneers. The writing is exceptional.

Kerr-Coombs, Stennett. *I Am No Slave and other poems.* Kingston: The Jamaica Times, 1956.

Manley, Edna, ed. *Focus: An Anthology of Contemporary Jamaican Writing.* Kingston: University College of the West Indies, 1956.

Patterson, H.O. *Children of Sisyphus.* London: Hutchinson, 1964.

Pomerantz, Charlotte. *The Chalk Doll.* New York: Lippincott, 1989.

Reid, Victor Stafford. *The Leopard.* New York: Viking Press, 1958.

Rolbine, Seth. *Sting of the Bee.* New York: St. Martin's Press, 1987. A Jamaican emigrant returns home to rediscover his father and his heritage.

Thewell, Michael. *The Harder They Come.* New York: Grove, 1980. The movie, starring one of Jamaica's first bona fide reggae kings, Jimmy Cliff, is the story of a country boy's rise through the "rude boy" gangs of mean Kingston to music stardom. The movie preceded the book.

Winkler, Anthony C. *The Great Yacht Race.* Kingston: Kingston Publishers Ltd., 1991. Satirical exposition of pre-independence Montego Bay society, set against the traditional Easter yacht race.

Winkler, Anthony C. *The Lunatic.* Secaucus, NJ: Carol Publishing Group, 1987. A village lunatic falls in love with a sexually voracious German tourist amid hilarious, trenchant commentary on Jamaican small-town life. The writing is extraordinary. The book was made into a movie of the same name, screenplay penned by the author.

Winkler, Anthony C. *The Painted Canoe.* Chicago: University of Chicago Press, 1989. An obstinate, honorable, "unspeakably ugly" fisherman is lost at sea and struggles for survival.

MUSIC AND THE ARTS

Baxter, Ivy. *The Arts of an Island.* Metuchen, NJ: Scarecrow Press, 1970.

Bergman, Billy. *Hot Sauces: Latin and Caribbean Pop.* New York: Quill, 1984.

Clerk, Asley. *Music and Musical Instruments of Jamaica.* Kingston, 1916. Before the electric guitar, before the synthesized dub beat, there were drums, symphonies, and more.

Davis, Steven, and Peter Simon. *Reggae Bloodlines; In Search of the Music and Culture of Jamaica.* 2nd edition. London: Heinemann Educational Books, 1981. First published in 1977, this book is a classic photographic essay.

Davis, Steven, and Peter Simon. *Reggae International.* New York: Alfred A. Knopf, 1982.

Dalrymple, Henderson. *Bob Marley: Music, Myth, and the Rastas.* London: Carib-Arawak, 1976.

Ekwene, Laz E.N. *African Sources in New World Black Music.* Toronto, 1972.

Green, Jonathan. *Bob Marley and The Wailers.* London: Wise Publications, 1977.

Lewin, Olive. *Brown Gal in de Ring: 12 Folk Songs from Jamaica.* London: Oxford University Press, 1974. For those who thought Brown Gal in de Ring was merely a '70s hit by the pop group Boney M, this book sets the record straight.

Murray, Tom. *Folk Songs of Jamaica: 32 Songs with Words and Music.* London: University Press, 1952.

Tucker, Jimmy. *Sing, Jamaica!* Kingston: Reliance Jamaica Productions (Box 244, Kingston 19, Jamaica, W.I.), 1990. Mr. Tucker, a well-known Jamaican singer and patriot, is the executive producer of Reliance Jamaica, an organization that seeks to promote nationalism. This book is part words and music (includes the national anthem), and part historical notes.

Walton, Oritz M. *Music: Black, White and Blue.* New York: William Morrow, 1972.

White, Timothy. *Catch a Fire: The Life of Bob Marley.* London: Corgi Books, reprinted 1989. Powerful analysis of the early Jamaican music scene and the rise of Marley as the country's first, possibly only, international reggae superstar. Fairly complete discography.

NATURAL SCIENCE

Adams, C. Dennis. *Flowering Plants in Jamaica.* Kingston: University College of the West Indies, 1972.

Bond, James. *Birds of the West Indies.* London: Collins, 1960 edition. Author Ian Fleming took the name of this famous naturalist for his super-agent, 007.

Bourne, M.J., G.W Lennox, and S.A. Seddon. *Fruits and Vegetables of the Caribbean.* London: Macmillan, 1988. Pamphlet describing major Caribbean species.

Gosse, Philip Henry. *Illustrations of the Birds of Jamaica.* London: Van Voorst, 1849. The times have changed but the birds haven't.

Greenberg, Idaz, and Jerry Greenberg. *Guide to Corals & Fishes of Florida, the Bahamas and the Caribbean.* Miami: Seahawk Press, 1977. Waterproof book with excellent illustrations of warm-water coral and sealife.

Greenberg, Idaz, and Jerry Greenberg. *Sharks and Other Dangerous Sea Creatures.* Miami: Seahawk Press, 1981. The authors have photographed sharks for the National Geographic Society, and many startling photos appear here. Excellent illustrations and knowledgeable text.

Hawkes, Alex, and Brenda Sutton. *Wildflowers of Jamaica.* Kingston: Collins-Sangster, 1974.

Hargreaves, Dorothy, and Bob Hargreaves. *Tropical Trees.* Lahaina, HI: Ross-Hargreaves, 1965. Picture guide to tropical trees from Hawaii to the Caribbean.

Kaplan, Eugene. *A Field Guide to the Coral Reefs of the Caribbean and Florida.* Princeton, NJ: Peterson's Guides, 1984.

Kaye, W.J. *Butterflies of Jamaica.* London: The Entomological Society of London, 1926.

MacFayden, James. *The Flora of Jamaica.* London: Longman, 1837. Early account of Jamaican plantlife.

Robertson, Diane. *Jamaican Herbs: Nutritional and Medicinal Values.* 2nd edition. Kingston: self-published (Box 978, Kingston 8, Jamaica, W.I.), 1988. Good, concise description of accepted, proven, and mythological folk remedies.

Romashko, Sandra. *The Shell Book of Jamaica.* Miami: Windward, 1984.

Storer, Dorothy. *Familiar Trees and Cultivated Plants of Jamaica.* London: Macmillan and the Institute of Jamaica, 1958.

PERIODICALS

The Affordable Caribbean. 8403 Colesville Rd., Suite 830, Silver Spring, MD 20910. Published as an adjunct of *Caribbean Travel and Life* magazine, this newsletter lists value-oriented travel destinations throughout the region.

Caribbean Newsletter. Friends of Democracy, Box 8838, Kingston C.S.O., Jamaica, W.I. A 12-page newsletter covering current and controversial Caribbean issues.

Caribbean Travel and Life. Box 6229, Syracuse, NY 13217-7921. A bimonthly glossy magazine devoted solely to travel in the Caribbean.

Caribbean Week. Lefferts Place, River Rd., St. Michael, Barbados, W.I. Newspaper covering Caribbean issues in an often tough and incisive way.

Condé Nast Traveler. Box 57018, Boulder, CO 80322. Another glossy monthly which features fairly candid reporting.

Consumer Reports Travel Letter. Box 53629, Boulder, CO 80322-3629. Unbiased travel reportage, covering the world. The report is not inexpensive (over US$35/year/monthly), but is highly regarded.

Jamaica Naturalist. Natural History Society of Jamaica, Department of Zoology, UWI, Mona, Kingston 7, Jamaica, W.I. (see p. 146).

Specialty Travel Index. 305 San Anselmo Ave., San Anselmo, CA 94960. Biannual listing of hundreds of tours, tour companies, and other groups involved in unique and specialized travel.

RELIGION

Beckwith, Martha. *Jamaica Folklore*. New York: American Folklore Society, 1928.

Cumper, George E. *The Potential of Rastafarianism as a Modern National Religion*. New Delhi: Recorder Press, 1979.

Hurston, Zora Neale. *Voodoo Gods—an Inquiry into Native Myths and Magic in Jamaica and Haiti*. London: J.M. Dent & Son, 1939.

Mbiti, John S. *African Religions and Philosophy*. London: Heinemann Educational Books, 1969.

Mullings, Bing. *The 1860 Spiritual Awakenings in Jamaica*. Kingston: Jamaica Theological Seminary, 1972.

Seaga, Edward. *Revival Cults in Jamaica*. Kingston: Institute of Jamaica, 1982. Written by a former prime minister and leader of the JLP.

GLOSSARY

abeng—cow's horn used as a musical instrument and for communication, especially among Maroons

ackee—fruit imported from West Africa which, when boiled and combined with saltfish, forms the "national dish"

akete—drums used by Rastafarians in ceremony and prayer

Anansi—also "anancy," "ananci"; chief character, usually a spider, of Jamaican folk tales, thought to have originated in West African traditional stories

Arawak—refers to Amerindian group, Jamaica's first inhabitants

Armageddon—as predicted in the Bible, the final showdown between the forces of good and evil

archipelago—group of islands

asiento—"contract" in Spanish; at the end of the War of Spanish Succession in 1713, England was awarded France's Asiento for supplying slaves to Spain's Caribbean possessions

Babylon—in Rastafarian creed, nonbelievers and institutions which obstruct or simply are not of the faith

balm—from the English balm, also from the Twi *abam,* or name of a fetish, refers to natural folk-medicine treatments by herbs, administered by balmists

bamboo—A member of the grass family originating in the Far East, the fast-growing plant is resilient and prolific, and has had myriad uses in Jamaican life.

bammy—dense cassava bread, once the staple of Arawak and Carib Indians, now popularly served with fried fish

barbecue—rectangular platform, formerly made of sticks and wood, now of cement or stone, on which coffee beans, pimento, and other produce are spread to dry in the sun

bauxite—naturally occurring aluminum oxide from which commercial aluminum is produced

bongo—spirits invoked in ceremonies, as well as devotees, of the Convince cult

breadfruit—Imported to the West Indies from Polynesia in 1793 by Capt. William Bligh, the starchy fruit helped overcome food shortages among slave populations, and today is a popular food source.

bulla—small, hard, flat sweetcake made with molasses and ginger

burru—an arrangement of "talking" drums, used by slaves in celebration, now utilized by Rastafarians in ceremonies

calabash—tree native to South and Central America that produces a gourd used for food storage and as an eating utensil

callaloo—also "calulu," "calalou," etc.; green, spinachlike vegetable used in, among other foods, the Caribbean's famous pepperpot soup

calypso—lilting, West Indian music, popular in Jamaica, originating in Trinidad

Carib—refers to the peripatetic and bellicose Amerindian group that conquered and inhabited many of the West Indian islands (hence, the Caribbean) before Columbus's arrival. So fierce were Carib warriors that today's English term "cannibal" is probably derived from the Spanish word for them, *caribe,* which meant "savage."

cassava—starchy tropical root crop of the manioc family used, in Jamaica, to make the popular fried bammy cake, among other foods

cay—bank, reef of sand, or small island, from the Spanish *cayo,* or "shoal" (pronounced "kay" or "kie")

cho-cho—pear-shaped fruit, also called "christophene," very popular as a vegetable dish when cooked or eaten raw *cimarron*—"wild" or "untamed" in Spanish; thought to be the origin of the word Maroon

cocoa—the tree from which the cocoa bean is cultivated (Jamaicans refer to the hot drink produced from the bean as "chocolate")

coolie—denigrating reference to a person of East Indian ancestry

coney—small, brown land rodent indigenous to the Caribbean, threatened with extinction in Jamaica

coral—calcified skeletons of tiny marine animals called "polyps," which often grow as colonies into larger structures along ocean reefs

Creole—a person of European blood born in the West Indies. The term also refers to mixed-race persons, languages spoken, cooking, or, in general, blending of cultures in certain areas, particularly Spanish America, Louisiana, and the U.S. Gulf of Mexico states.

crocodile—Mistakenly called alligator (hence place-names such as Alligator Pond), the large reptile is found only on the south coast. It was threatened with extinction after years of being hunted for skins and sport, until preservation laws were enacted.

doctor bird—member of the hummingbird family endemic to Jamaica, once revered by the Arawaks as the reincarnation of dead souls and known as "God bird"; Jamaica's national bird

dread—shortened from the term "dreadlocks," referring to a Rastafarian or person with hair in the Rastafarian style

duppy—spirit of the dead, believed to be on earth to influence lives of the living, therefore figuring prominently in folk tales and obeah or other ritualistic practices

duppy **conqueror**—popular expression and the name of a Bob Marley song, it means "belligerent, fighting person"

endemic—in referring to species of animals or plants, those found in one place and nowhere else

escoveitch—Spanish method of cooking fish with vinegar and other spices

Ethiopian Orthodox Church—religious denomination established in Jamaica in 1970, attracting mainly members of the Rastafarian sect

ferns—Over 550 indigenous species are found in Jamaica.

festival—cornmeal sweet cake commonly served with fried fish or seafood

fig banana—species of small, sweet banana

flag—Jamaica's national flag has two yellow diagonal lines which cross to form two black and two green triangles in juxtaposition. Black symbolizes hardships overcome and to be faced; green, hope and agricultural success; and gold, the wealth and beauty of the sun.

galliwasp—harmless lizard that nevertheless carries many superstitions and is often included in Jamaican folktales

ganja—East Indian word for marijuana, which was imported to Jamaica during the influx of indentured laborers after the abolition of slavery

goombay—also "gombay," "gombah," etc.; drum made from wood and covered with animal skin, often used in Revivalist ceremonies and by Maroons

guava—small tropical tree which produces a gritty, succulent fruit eaten fresh or used to make guava jelly or nectar

guinep—small green fruit that grows in clusters on the guinep tree, thought to be a native of Surinam

gungo **peas**—popular pea found in traditional Jamaican dishes such as rice and peas; also known as "congo" or "pigeon peas"

higgler—traditional peddlers or vendors who, in the past, traded exclusively in Jamaica's markets, and who are found today in all walks of street commerce

hurricane—a large, swirling, high-pressure storm that revolves around a placid, low-pressure center, or eye. Caribbean hurricanes, known as cyclones or typhoons in other parts of the world, often originate off the west coast of Africa and travel west, generating destructive winds of 100 or more miles per hour. Word derivation is thought to be from the language of the Taino, ancestors of the Arawaks and Caribs.

iguana—large, herbivorous, tropical lizard, extinct in Jamaica due to hunting for its prized flesh and to the introduction of the mongoose. The name derivation is Spanish, from the Carib language.

indigenous—originating in the locality; not imported

Irish moss—gelatinous drink prepared from edible seaweed, considered to be health food

jackfruit—a relative of breadfruit, originating in India, which produces a yellowish, edible fruit and seeds that resemble chestnuts

janga—small freshwater crayfish

JATCHA—Jamaica Alternative Tourism, Camping, and Hiking Association

JAVA—Jamaica Association of Villas and Apartments

JBC—Jamaica Broadcasting Corporation

jerk meat—meat (usually chicken, pork, or fish) seasoned with a multi-spice mixture heavy on pimento and roasted slowly over a woody fire. The method originated with the eastern Maroons of Portland, when cooking and seasoning pork to preserve it was a method of survival.

JHTA—Jamaica Hotel and Tourist Association

JIS—Jamaica Information Service

John Crow—large scavenger bird, resembling the American turkey buzzard, found throughout Jamaica

Jonkanoo—also Jonkonnu, John Canoe, etc.; post-Christmas festival originating from slavery days. Groups of masqueraders dressed as animals, kings, and other mythical and comical figures parade through the streets of towns and villages.

JRC—Jamaica Railway Corporation

JTB—Jamaica Tourist Board

June plum—also called "jew plum." The large plum, introduced from the South Pacific, is eaten raw or stewed in desserts.

JUTA—Jamaica Union of Travellers Association

kling-kling—small black bird, prolific throughout the island; resembles a mockingbird

Kumina—popular ancestor-worship cult steeped heavily in African tradition. Singing, dancing, spirit possession, and drumming play important roles in the ceremony.

leeward—the direction of the sheltered side, opposite that against which the wind blows, called the "windward" side

lignum vitae—"tree of life," which bears the blue national flower of Jamaica. The tree's wood is so heavy and strong it sinks in water and has been used as ship's propeller shaft bearings.

ludo—popular Jamaican board game similar to backgammon

mahoe—The national tree of Jamaica, the blue mahoe is found naturally in only one other country, Cuba.

manatee—large, herbivorous marine mammal, also called sea cow or dugong, threatened with extinction. Columbus's crew is rumored to have seen the animals and mistaken them for mermaids.

mangrove—genus of tropical trees and shrubs growing in swamps and marshland which, when left unchecked, will create new land masses by trapping soil between its roots, eventually building it above the water line

manteca—"lard" in Spanish; thought to be the origin of the place name Montego Bay

Maroons—slaves that first broke away from their Spanish, then British overseers to escape and live in small but effective guerilla bands throughout the country, eventually conducting wars with the British crown government

mento—previously popular folk and dance music, antecedent to ska and reggae, nowadays performed by specialists at cultural events

mongoose—small, brown, carnivorous mammal first introduced to Jamaica in 1872 to help control rat damage in sugarcane fields; later became a troublesome nuisance and contributed to the near-extinction of the coney and iguana *myal*—old magic cult, with basis in religion, that practiced "white," or good, magic and herbalism; now largely incorporated in the Kumina cult

naseberry—Known as sapodilla elsewhere, the sweet, pulpy fruit grows on a low bush and is popular throughout the country.

obeah—Also called "black magic" and "blackheart," the cult is based on the manipulation of herbs, duppies, and religious practices. Though it enjoys widespread acceptance, it is practiced illegally in Jamaica.

opia—in Arawak culture, a spirit of the dead

ortanique—citrus fruit hybrid created from the orange and the tangerine (the word "unique" also factors into the moniker); first developed in Jamaica

otaheite **apple**—Brought over by Captain Bligh in the same cargo in which the breadfruit arrived, the otaheite apple tree produces both striking blooms and succulent fruit.

PADI—Professional Association of Dive Instructors

Pantomime—annual musical show featuring stock characters (not a pantomime in the traditional, lack-of-dialogue sense). Sponsored by Kingston's Little Theatre Movement.

patu, patoos—owl

pear—avocado, also called "avocado pear"

pepperpot—traditional soup made with callaloo and other greens, beef or pork, and spices

pimento—spice indigenous to Jamaica, combining the flavors of pepper, nutmeg, clove, and cinnamon, marketed as allspice in other parts of the world

pineapple—Introduced from South America, the fruit became so successful it was exported to Hawaii, now the world's leading producer, and is featured on the Jamaican coat of arms.

plantain—looks like, but is not simply, a large banana, and must be cooked for consumption

Pocomania—also called Poco, Pukumina; a Revivalist religious cult

quadrille—European dance with African influences widely seen today at cultural festivals

Rastafarianism—religio-cultural group with members called Rastas or Rastafarians, whose tenets are based on the belief that Ethiopian Emperor Haile Selassie was the reborn savior, and who believe that redemption will occur through repatriation to Africa. The movement originated in the 1930s, partly springing from the teachings of black nationalist Marcus Garvey, and enjoys great influence in Jamaican culture today.

rat-bat—nocturnal flying mammal, commonly called "bat" in standard English

reggae—widely appreciated Jamaican music form characterized by choppy rhythms, lilting melody, and somewhat politicized lyrics; often associated with Rastafarianism, and popularized by Bob Marley and The Wailers

Revivalism—compendium of syncretic religious cults, blending large doses of African, European, and Jamaican influences

rhumba box—also "rumba"; a musical instrument constructed with metal strips over a hollowed core, which provides bass rhythm primarily for mento bands

rock-steady—musical form considered the precursor of reggae, and credited with originating reggae's bass beat

roti—East Indian flat bread, popularly served with curry dishes

rum—liquor derived from sugarcane, originally developed on a wide scale in Barbados and called "rumbullion" for its propensity to inspire reckless behavior in imbibers. Rum is used socially and ceremonially in, for example, Kumina services.

ska—onomatopoeic name of music popular in the '50s and '60s, a hybrid of U.S. R&B and lush, jazz-oriented horn arrangements, named after the scratch sound of the rhythm guitar

soca—form of calypso music, popular in Jamaica

sugarcane—Jamaica and the West Indies' most widely successful cash crop, a grass; responsible for the colonization of the islands and introduction of slave labor to work large plantations

syncretic—syncretistic; conciliation of several often disparate concepts, particularly in religion, to form an amalgamated belief

tamarind—tropical tree which bears the pod from which acidic, sour fruit is eaten and a relishlike syrup is made

tea—in Jamaica, refers to most hot drinks

tody—endemic Jamaican bird that digs tunnels in which to lay its eggs

ugli—self-descriptive name of a hybrid citrus fruit, a cross between the grapefruit and the tangerine, discovered and developed in Jamaica in the early 1900s

UWI—University of the West Indies, regional institution established in 1948 and headquartered at Mona, Kingston

windward—the side facing the prevailing winds, as opposed to "leeward" side

Xaymaca—Arawak name for the country, thought to have meant "Land of Wood and Water" or "Island of Springs"

yabba—large earthenware bowl of African origin, still used in Jamaica to carry water and food

yard—reference to slum dwelling; tenement

yuca—cassava; the starchy tropical root crop that was the staple of the Arawaks and remains popular today

zemi—Arawak stone idol in which the personal spirit of the owner was believed to dwell

Zion—the homeland, usually in reference to Africa; Ethiopia; heaven, utopia

INDEX

Page numbers in **boldface** indicate the primary reference. *Italicized* page numbers indicate information in captions, special topics, charts, illustrations, or maps.

ABOUT THE AUTHOR

Karl Luntta went to Botswana in 1977 as a teacher with the U.S. Peace Corps, and remained in Africa for six years as a training consultant with the Peace Corps and various volunteer organizations. He then lived and worked in the Solomon Islands, Kiribati, Fiji, Western Samoa, Cook Islands, Barbados, and Grenada, returning to the U.S. in 1989. He now lives with his wife Phyllis and son Kaarlo in Massachusetts, and has decided that even though answers to life's great questions are revealed infrequently, life itself is *raison d'être*, which is a gratuitously dropped French phrase that he thinks means "dirty raisins." He has published fiction and non-fiction in literary and national magazines, and writes a column for his local newspaper, *The Cape Cod Times*.

Phyllis Luntta, who is the primary photographer for *Jamaica Handbook,* spent years in television and video production as a director, producer, and operations manager in Denver, Phoenix, New York, and Boston before settling in Cape Cod.

MOON HANDBOOKS—THE IDEAL TRAVELING COMPANIONS

Open a Moon Handbook and you're opening your eyes and heart to the world. Thoughtful, sensitive, and provocative, Moon Handbooks encourage an intimate understanding of a region, from its culture and history to essential practicalities. Fun to read and packed with valuable information on accommodations, dining, recreation, plus indispensable travel tips, detailed maps, charts, illustrations, photos, glossaries, and indexes, Moon Handbooks are ideal traveling companions: informative, entertaining, and highly practical.

To locate the bookstore nearest you that carries Moon Travel Handbooks or to order directly from Moon Publications, call: (800) 345-5473, Monday-Friday, 9 a.m.-5 p.m. PST.

THE PACIFIC/ASIA SERIES

BALI HANDBOOK   by Bill Dalton
Detailed travel information on the most famous island in the world. 428 pages.   **$12.95**

BANGKOK HANDBOOK   by Michael Buckley
Your tour guide through this exotic and dynamic city reveals the affordable and accessible possibilities. Thai phrasebook. 214 pages.   **$10.95**

BLUEPRINT FOR PARADISE: How to Live on a Tropic Island   by Ross Norgrove
This one-of-a-kind guide has everything you need to know about moving to and living comfortably on a tropical island. 212 pages.   **$14.95**

FIJI ISLANDS HANDBOOK   by David Stanley
The first and still the best source of information on travel around this 322-island archipelago. Fijian glossary. 198 pages.   **$11.95**

INDONESIA HANDBOOK   by Bill Dalton
This one-volume encyclopedia explores island by island the many facets of this sprawling, kaleidoscopic island nation. Extensive Indonesian vocabulary. 1,000 pages.   **$19.95**

JAPAN HANDBOOK   by J.D. Bisignani
In this comprehensive new edition, award-winning travel writer J.D. Bisignani offers to inveterate travelers, newcomers, and businesspeople alike a thoroughgoing presentation of Japan's many facets. 960 pages.   **$22.50**

MICRONESIA HANDBOOK: Guide to the Caroline, Gilbert, Mariana, and Marshall Islands
by David Stanley
Micronesia Handbook guides you on a real Pacific adventure all your own. 345 pages.   **$11.95**

NEW ZEALAND HANDBOOK   by Jane King
Introduces you to the people, places, history, and culture of this extraordinary land. 571 pages.
$18.95

OUTBACK AUSTRALIA HANDBOOK   by Marael Johnson
Australia is an endlessly fascinating, vast land, and *Outback Australia Handbook* explores the cities and towns, sheep stations, and wilderness areas of the Northern Territory, Western Australia, and South Australia. Full of travel tips and cultural information for adventuring, relaxing, or just getting away from it all. 355 pages.   **$15.95**

PHILIPPINES HANDBOOK   by Peter Harper and Evelyn Peplow
Crammed with detailed information, *Philippines Handbook* equips the escapist, hedonist, or business traveler with thorough coverage of the Philippines's colorful history, landscapes, and culture. 587 pages.   **$12.95**

SOUTHEAST ASIA HANDBOOK   by Carl Parkes
Helps the enlightened traveler discover the real Southeast Asia. 873 pages.   **$16.95**

SOUTH KOREA HANDBOOK   by Robert Nilsen
Whether you're visiting on business or searching for adventure, *South Korea Handbook* is an invaluable companion. Korean glossary with useful notes on speaking and reading the language. 548 pages.   **$14.95**

SOUTH PACIFIC HANDBOOK   by David Stanley
The original comprehensive guide to the 16 territories in the South Pacific. 740 pages.   **$19.95**

TAHITI-POLYNESIA HANDBOOK   by David Stanley
All five French-Polynesian archipelagoes are covered in this comprehensive guide by Oceania's best-known travel writer. 235 pages.   **$11.95**

THAILAND HANDBOOK   by Carl Parkes
Presents the richest source of information on travel in Thailand. 568 pages.   **$16.95**

THE HAWAIIAN SERIES

BIG ISLAND OF HAWAII HANDBOOK   by J.D. Bisignani
An entertaining yet informative text packed with insider tips on accommodations, dining, sports and outdoor activities, natural attractions, and must-see sights. 347 pages.   **$11.95**

HAWAII HANDBOOK   by J.D. Bisignani
Winner of the 1989 Hawaii Visitors Bureau's Best Guide Award and the Grand Award for Excellence in Travel Journalism, this guide takes you beyond the glitz and high-priced hype and leads you to a genuine Hawaiian experience. Covers all 8 Hawaiian Islands. 879 pages.   **$15.95**

KAUAI HANDBOOK   by J.D. Bisignani
Kauai Handbook is the perfect antidote to the workaday world. Hawaiian and pidgin glossaries. 236 pages.   **$9.95**

MAUI HANDBOOK   by J.D. Bisignani
"No fool-'round" advice on accommodations, eateries, and recreation, plus a comprehensive introduction to island ways, geography, and history. Hawaiian and pidgin glossaries. 350 pages. **$11.95**

OAHU HANDBOOK   by J.D. Bisignani
A handy guide to Honolulu, renowned surfing beaches, and Oahu's countless other diversions. Hawaiian and pidgin glossaries. 354 pages.   **$11.95**

THE AMERICAS SERIES

ALASKA-YUKON HANDBOOK   by Deke Castleman and Don Pitcher
Get the inside story, with plenty of well-seasoned advice to help you cover more miles on less money. 384 pages.   **$13.95**

ARIZONA TRAVELER'S HANDBOOK   by Bill Weir
This meticulously researched guide contains everything necessary to make Arizona accessible and enjoyable. 505 pages.   **$14.95**

BAJA HANDBOOK   by Joe Cummings
A comprehensive guide with all the travel information and background on the land, history, and culture of this untamed thousand-mile-long peninsula. 356 pages.   **$13.95**

BELIZE HANDBOOK   by Chicki Mallan
Complete with detailed maps, practical information, and an overview of the area's flamboyant history, culture, and geographical features, *Belize Handbook* is the only comprehensive guide of its kind to this spectacular region. 263 pages.   **$14.95**

BRITISH COLUMBIA HANDBOOK   by Jane King
With an emphasis on outdoor adventures, this guide covers mainland British Columbia, Vancouver Island, the Queen Charlotte Islands, and the Canadian Rockies. 381 pages.
$13.95

CANCUN HANDBOOK   by Chicki Mallan
Covers the city's luxury scene as well as more modest attractions, plus many side trips to unspoiled beaches and Mayan ruins. Spanish glossary. 257 pages.   **$12.95**

CATALINA ISLAND HANDBOOK: A Guide to California's Channel Islands
by Chicki Mallan
A complete guide to these remarkable islands, from the windy solitude of the Channel Islands National Marine Sanctuary to bustling Avalon. 245 pages.   **$10.95**

COLORADO HANDBOOK   by Stephen Metzger
Essential details to the all-season possibilities in Colorado fill this guide. Practical travel tips combine with recreation—skiing, nightlife, and wilderness exploration—plus entertaining essays. 422 pages.   **$15.95**

COSTA RICA HANDBOOK   by Christopher P. Baker
Experience the many wonders of the natural world as you explore this remarkable land. Spanish-English glossary. 600 pages. $17.95

IDAHO HANDBOOK   by Bill Loftus
A year-round guide to everything in this outdoor wonderland, from whitewater adventures to rural hideaways. 275 pages.   **$12.95**

JAMAICA HANDBOOK   by Karl Luntta
From the sun and surf of Montego Bay and Ocho Rios to the cool slopes of the Blue Mountains, author Karl Luntta offers island-seekers a perceptive, personal view of Jamaica. 230 pages. **$14.95**

MONTANA HANDBOOK   by W.C. McRae and Judy Jewell
The wild West is yours with this extensive guide to the Treasure State, complete with travel practicalities, history, and lively essays on Montana life. 393 pages.   **$13.95**

NEVADA HANDBOOK   by Deke Castleman
Nevada Handbook puts the Silver State into perspective and makes it manageable and affordable. 400 pages.   **$14.95**

NEW MEXICO HANDBOOK   by Stephen Metzger
A close-up and complete look at every aspect of this wondrous state. 375 pages.   **$13.95**

NORTHERN CALIFORNIA HANDBOOK   by Kim Weir
An outstanding companion for imaginative travel in the territory north of the Tehachapis. 850 pages.   **$19.95**

OREGON HANDBOOK   by Stuart Warren and Ted Long Ishikawa
Brimming with travel practicalities and insiders' views on Oregon's history, culture, arts, and activities. 461 pages.   **$15.95**

PACIFIC MEXICO HANDBOOK   by Bruce Whipperman
Explore 2,000 miles of gorgeous beaches, quiet resort towns, and famous archaeological sites along Mexico's Pacific coast. Spanish-English glossary. 450 pages.   **$15.95**

TEXAS HANDBOOK   by Joe Cummings
Seasoned travel writer Joe Cummings brings an insider's perspective to his home state. 483 pages.   **$13.95**

UTAH HANDBOOK   by Bill Weir
Weir gives you all the carefully researched facts and background to make your visit a success. 445 pages.   **$14.95**

WASHINGTON HANDBOOK   by Dianne J. Boulerice Lyons and Archie Satterfield
Covers sights, shopping, services, transportation, and outdoor recreation, with complete listings for restaurants and accommodations. 433 pages.   **$13.95**

WYOMING HANDBOOK   by Don Pitcher
All you need to know to open the doors to this wide and wild state. 495 pages.   **$14.95**

YUCATAN HANDBOOK by Chicki Mallan
All the information you'll need to guide you into every corner of this exotic land. Mayan and Spanish glossaries. 391 pages. **$14.95**

E INTERNATIONAL SERIES

EGYPT HANDBOOK by Kathy Hansen
An invaluable resource for intelligent travel in Egypt. Arabic glossary. 522 pages. **$18.95**

MOSCOW-ST. PETERSBURG HANDBOOK by Masha Nordbye
Provides the visitor with an extensive introduction to the history, culture, and people of these two great cities, as well as practical information on where to stay, eat, and shop. 260 pages. **$13.95**

NEPAL HANDBOOK by Kerry Moran
Whether you're planning a week in Kathmandu or months out on the trail, *Nepal Handbook* will take you into the heart of this Himalayan jewel. 378 pages. **$12.95**

NEPALI AAMA by Broughton Coburn
A delightful photo-journey into the life of a Gurung tribeswoman of Central Nepal. Having lived with Aama (translated, "mother") for two years, first as an outsider and later as an adopted member of the family, Coburn presents an intimate glimpse into a culture alive with humor, folklore, religion, and ancient rituals. 165 pages. **$13.95**

PAKISTAN HANDBOOK by Isobel Shaw
For armchair travelers and trekkers alike, the most detailed and authoritative guide to Pakistan ever published. Urdu glossary. 478 pages. **$15.95**

STAYING HEALTHY IN ASIA, AFRICA, AND LATIN AMERICA
by Dirk G. Schroeder, Sc D, MPH
Don't leave home without it! Besides providing a complete overview of the health problems that exist in these areas, this book will help you determine which immunizations you'll need beforehand, what medications to take with you, and how to recognize and treat infections and diseases. Includes extensively illustrated first-aid information and precautions for heat, cold, and high altitude. 200 pages. **$10.95**

> **New travel handbooks may be available that are not on this list.**
> **To find out more about current or upcoming titles,**
> **call us toll-free at (800) 345-5473.**

MOONBELTS

Made of heavy-duty Cordura nylon, the Moonbelt offers maximum protection for your money and important papers. This all-weather pouch slips under your shirt or waistband, rendering it virtually undetectable and inaccessible to pickpockets. One-inch-wide nylon webbing, heavy-duty zipper, one-inch quick-release buckle. Accommodates traveler's checks, passport, cash, photos. Size 5 x 9 inches. Black. **$8.95**

IMPORTANT ORDERING INFORMATION

FOR FASTER SERVICE: Call to locate the bookstore nearest you that carries Moon Travel Handbooks or order directly from Moon Publications:

(800) 345-5473 • **Monday-Friday** • **9 a.m.-5 p.m. PST** • **fax (916) 345-6751**

PRICES: All prices are subject to change. We always ship the most current edition. We will let you know if there is a price increase on the book you ordered.

SHIPPING & HANDLING OPTIONS: 1) Domestic UPS or USPS first class (allow 10 working days for delivery): $3.50 for the first item, 50 cents for each additional item.

Exceptions:
- **Moonbelt** shipping is $1.50 for one, 50 cents for each additional belt.
- Add $2.00 for same-day handling.
- UPS 2nd Day Air or Printed Airmail requires a special quote.
- International Surface Bookrate (8-12 weeks delivery):
  $3.00 for the first item, $1.00 for each additional item. Note: Moon Publications cannot guarantee international surface bookrate shipping.

FOREIGN ORDERS: All orders that originate outside the U.S.A. must be paid for with either an International Money Order or a check in U.S. currency drawn on a major U.S. bank based in the U.S.A.

TELEPHONE ORDERS: We accept Visa or MasterCard payments. Minimum order is US$15.00. Call in your order: (800) 345-5473, 9 a.m.-5 p.m. Pacific Standard Time.

ORDER FORM

Be sure to call (800) 345-5473 for current prices and editions or for the name of the bookstore nearest you that carries Moon Travel Handbooks • 9 a.m.–5 p.m. PST
(See important ordering information on preceding page)

Name: _____ Date: _____

Street: _____

City: _____ Daytime Phone: _____

State or Country: _____ Zip Code: _____

QUANTITY	TITLE	PRICE

Taxable Total_____

Sales Tax (7.25%) for California Residents_____

Shipping & Handling_____

TOTAL_____

Ship: ☐ UPS (no PO Boxes)   ☐ 1st class   ☐ International surface mail

Ship to: ☐ address above   ☐ other _____

Make checks payable to: **MOON PUBLICATIONS, INC.** P.O. Box 3040, Chico, CA 95927-3040 U.S.A. We accept Visa and MasterCard. **To Order**: Call in your Visa or MasterCard number, or send a written order with your Visa or MasterCard number and expiration date clearly written.

Card Number: ☐ **Visa**   ☐ **MasterCard**

☐☐☐☐ ☐☐☐☐ ☐☐☐☐ ☐☐☐☐

Exact Name on Card: _____

expiration date:_____

signature_____

THE METRIC SYSTEM

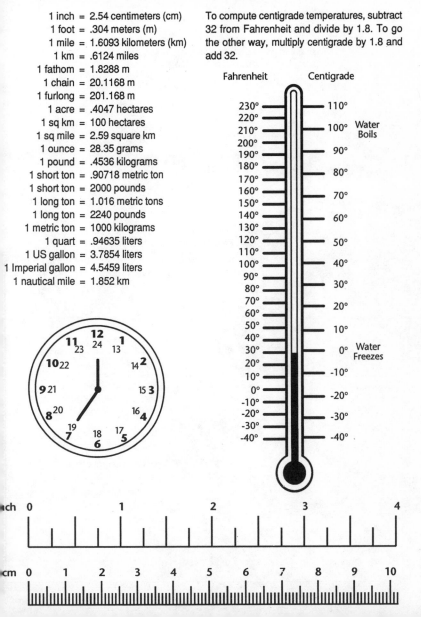

1 inch = 2.54 centimeters (cm)
1 foot = .304 meters (m)
1 mile = 1.6093 kilometers (km)
1 km = .6124 miles
1 fathom = 1.8288 m
1 chain = 20.1168 m
1 furlong = 201.168 m
1 acre = .4047 hectares
1 sq km = 100 hectares
1 sq mile = 2.59 square km
1 ounce = 28.35 grams
1 pound = .4536 kilograms
1 short ton = .90718 metric ton
1 short ton = 2000 pounds
1 long ton = 1.016 metric tons
1 long ton = 2240 pounds
1 metric ton = 1000 kilograms
1 quart = .94635 liters
1 US gallon = 3.7854 liters
1 Imperial gallon = 4.5459 liters
1 nautical mile = 1.852 km

To compute centigrade temperatures, subtract 32 from Fahrenheit and divide by 1.8. To go the other way, multiply centigrade by 1.8 and add 32.

Fahrenheit | Centigrade

230° — 110°
220°
210° — 100° Water Boils
200°
190° — 90°
180°
170° — 80°
160° — 70°
150°
140° — 60°
130°
120° — 50°
110°
100° — 40°
90°
80° — 30°
70° — 20°
60°
50° — 10°
40°
30° — 0° Water Freezes
20°
10° — -10°
0° — -20°
-10°
-20° — -30°
-30°
-40° — -40°